D1230780

THE WEB OF EMPIRE

The Web of Empire

English Cosmopolitans in an
Age of Expansion
1560–1660

ALISON GAMES

OXFORD
UNIVERSITY PRESS

OXFORD
UNIVERSITY PRESS

Oxford University Press, Inc., publishes works that further
Oxford University's objective of excellence
in research, scholarship, and education.

Oxford   New York
Auckland   Cape Town   Dar es Salaam   Hong Kong   Karachi
Kuala Lumpur   Madrid   Melbourne   Mexico City   Nairobi
New Delhi   Shanghai   Taipei   Toronto

With offices in
Argentina   Austria   Brazil   Chile   Czech Republic   France   Greece
Guatemala   Hungary   Italy   Japan   Poland   Portugal   Singapore
South Korea   Switzerland   Thailand   Turkey   Ukraine   Vietnam

Copyright © 2008 by Alison Games

Published by Oxford University Press, Inc.
198 Madison Avenue, New York, New York 10016

www.oup.com

First issued as an Oxford University Press paperback, 2009

Oxford is a registered trademark of Oxford University Press

All rights reserved. No part of this publication may be reproduced,
stored in a retrieval system, or transmitted, in any form or by any means,
electronic, mechanical, photocopying, recording, or otherwise,
without the prior permission of Oxford University Press.

Library of Congress Cataloging-in-Publication Data
Games, Alison, 1963–
The web of empire : English cosmopolitans in an age of expansion, 1560–1660 / Alison Games.
    p.   cm.
Includes bibliographical references and index.
ISBN 978-0-19-973338-5
1. Great Britain—Colonies—History.   2. Great Britain—Commerce—History—16th century.
3. Great Britain—Commerce—History—17th century.   4. Great Britain—Foreign relations—1558–1603.
5. Great Britain—Foreign relations—1603–1688.   6. Imperialism—History.   7. Great Britain—Civilization—
16th century.   8. Great Britain—Civilization—17th century.   I. Title.
DA16.G36 2008
909'.0977124206—dc22   2007041087

Printed in the United States of America
on acid-free paper

For Doug

ACKNOWLEDGMENTS

I think every author must anticipate impatiently not only the completion of a project but also the opportunity to thank the many people and institutions who have helped out along the way. My research was consistently facilitated by welcoming staff at numerous libraries, including the Huntington Library, the John Carter Brown Library, the Massachusetts Historical Society, the Folger Shakespeare Library, the Library of Congress, the National Archives of Scotland, the Edinburgh University Library, the National Library of Scotland, the National Archives of the United Kingdom, the British Library, and the Bodleian Library. The interlibrary loan office at Georgetown University's Lauinger Library is a marvel of efficiency and sleuthing. Stephen Tabor of the Huntington Library, Bettina Smith of the Folger Shakespeare Library, and Sara Rodger of Arundel Castle helped me obtain images, and I thank them for their assistance and their efficiency.

My ability to do research in repositories on both sides of the Atlantic was facilitated by the many public and private foundations that support scholarly research. I am grateful to the National Endowment for the Humanities, to the Mellon Foundation (which supported research fellowships at the John Carter Brown Library, the Massachusetts Historical Society, and the Huntington Library), and to the American Philosophical Society for a Franklin Research Grant that supported research trips to the United Kingdom. Georgetown University's Graduate School of Arts and Sciences provided various research grants over the years. Jane Dammen McAuliffe, Dean of Georgetown College, is a great facilitator of faculty research, and I thank her and three successive department chairs, Jo Ann Moran Cruz, Jim Collins, and John Tutino, for helping make many semesters of research leave possible.

Stints in research libraries are always enhanced by the presence of colleagues. I was fortunate during a blissful year at the Huntington Library to enjoy the company of Hal Barron, Lisa Bitel, Heidi Brayman Hackel, Steve Hackel, Jean Howard, and Peter Mancall. Roy and Louise Ritchie were generous hosts beyond the Huntington's grounds. Julie Hardwick and Bob Olwell were splendid companions during a semester at the John Carter Brown Library, and I am also grateful to the JCB staff for their gracious welcome during my time in Providence. I have presented portions of this research at many different conferences and seminars, and I thank those colleagues who commented on aspects of my work for their time, assistance, and helpful feedback, especially members of the Forum on European Expansion and Global Interaction. I would also like to thank Dan Green for his advice and expertise, Susan Ferber for her careful and helpful editing, Gwen Colvin for her assistance in the book's production, Bill Nelson for the maps, and two anonymous readers for Oxford University Press for their thoughtful advice.

This book took me to parts of the world far beyond my area of expertise, and time and again colleagues have shared their knowledge and research with me. One of the delights of my work on this project has been the constant reminder of what a pleasure it is to work within such a generous scholarly community. I am especially grateful in this regard to David Armitage, David Hancock, Wim Klooster, Henriette de Bruyn Kops, Pier Larson, and Philip J. Stern. I found similarly generous assistance in the cramped corridors of my department. Georgetown's History Department justly prides itself on its collegiality and on its international orientation. I have benefited greatly from both. Several colleagues read all or part of the manuscript at an especially busy time of year: for their reckless generosity, careful reading, constructive feedback, and willingness to be pestered by my questions on all sorts of topics, I would like to thank Osama Abi-Mershed, Tommaso Astarita (polyglot friend and patient translator of Italian and Latin items), Henriette de Bruyn Kops, Chandra Manning, Bryan McCann, Meredith McKittrick, John McNeill, Jo Ann Moran Cruz, Adam Rothman, Jordan Sand, Judith Tucker, and Aparna Vaidik. I would also like to thank Carol Benedict, David Collins, Amy Leonard, Joe McCartin, Jim Millward, and Aviel Roshwald. These attentive colleagues caught numerous mistakes and misstatements; sadly, convention dictates that I must take responsibility for those that remain. They have also provided good company over the years and I feel fortunate indeed to work with such a fun and interesting collection of people.

Extended research trips in the United Kingdom were facilitated by the generous hospitality of Robin Lumsdaine, Julie Hardwick, Julie Edwards and Stefano, Caterina, Carlo, and Angiolina Quadrio Curzio in London; Jonathan and Katherine Clark in Oxford and at Callaly Castle in Northumberland; and Simon Newman and Marina Moskowitz in Glasgow. Simon introduced me to the Wissahickon Wanderers, and I thank Simon, Tom

Humphrey, Susan Branson, and Dan and Sally Gordon for many miles of camaraderie and some unusual runs featuring pumpkins, bagels, snow-capped mountains, cows, a wedding, and a tiara. Jim Williams and Karin Wulf have been my good friends since we met in Philadelphia many years ago and it continues to be a joy to share with them both new projects and new chapters in our lives. My family has always supported my academic pursuits. My delightful nieces Emily, Margaux, and Lillian appeared on the scene during the years I have been working on this project, and my world is richer for their presence. Finally, I thank Doug Egerton for his steadfast support, his copy-editing, his good humor, and for all of the delectable Cosmopolitans that he has concocted for my consumption as I have labored to make sense of the other cosmopolitans I wrote about in this book.

CONTENTS

THE WEB OF EMPIRE

INTRODUCTION

The voyage from England to Asia was never an easy one, and Patrick Copland's trip was about as bad as one could be. A chaplain on his second East India Company tour, Copland knew well the rigors of long-distance ocean travel. It took several months to reach Japan from London, at least ten if one sailed directly, which no one ever did. Departures were dictated and delayed by winds, currents, and tempests, and by the ability of merchants to fill a ship's holds with commodities. More than a year might lapse before the fleet reached the English trading post in Japan, and a roundtrip could take as long as two or three years. English ships stopped regularly along the way to replenish their stores so that men too weak and malnourished from the ordeal of the passage even to walk ashore could recuperate with fresh provisions. Once in the Indian Ocean, the fleet visited the Company's scattered trading posts in Surat and Masulipatam in India, Acheh (on Sumatra), Bantam (on Java), and elsewhere before making the final leg to the small English post at Hirado. On this last jaunt from Bantam to Japan, Copland's fleet encountered a terrible storm, which Copland described later as "five or six dayes of perpetuall horror," and one of the ships sank off Macao. Copland and the other shaken survivors limped ashore, delivered by God "safely to Firando," in December of 1620.[1]

There was much that was memorable about this trip. The storm so impressed Copland that he invoked it in a subsequent sermon once safely home in London. But it was during this voyage, Copland later recalled, that he spoke with Sir Thomas Dale, an English soldier hired to protect East India Company trade from Dutch rivals. This conversation transformed Copland's life.[2]

Like many of his English and Scottish contemporaries, Thomas Dale had launched his military career fighting alongside the Dutch in their protracted revolt against the Spanish. In 1611, however, he left his Dutch company to serve as a governor of the new colony of Virginia. Dale completed his job in the struggling American settlement in 1616, when he traveled home and finally returned to the Low Countries, resuming his military service. But in 1618 Dale set out again, this time for the East Indies. On the other side of the world from his Chesapeake posting, the English soldier regaled the Scottish chaplain with stories of Virginia. In turn, Copland educated Dale, a newcomer to the Indies, about the region (see figure I.1).

Dale's curiosity about his new post competed with a continued engagement with Virginia. He still had financial interests in the precarious enterprise, and in one letter to his employers in London, he longed to know how the colony fared. In the wake of the recent loss of all his goods "to [his] shurt" when an East India Company ship sank, Dale was likely preoccupied by bolstering his fortunes through whichever investments remained. Perhaps he was even homesick for his earlier post, although this citizen of the world had known many places he might call home. To the curious Copland, Dale praised the soil in Virginia, saying that it eclipsed the best ground in Europe. As a result of these conversations, Copland resolved to go to Virginia himself after his return from India. His enthusiasm for the venture was so great that on the long and tedious journey home, he raised money for a new school in Virginia. Understandably deterred by news of the Powhatan leader Opechancanough's deadly attack on the English settlements in 1622, Copland did not ultimately go to the Chesapeake. Instead he chose the safer climes of Bermuda. There he made his home until religious conflicts in the 1640s prodded him to relocate to the Bahamas. He died by 1655, well over eighty years old.[3]

Dale and Copland would have found much to talk about. Both men had befriended—in their own way, and on their own terms—the foreigners they encountered. Copland took in an East Indian boy, a slave given him by a mariner, taught him English and Latin and the ways of Christianity, renamed him Peter Pope, and baptized him in London in a public relations coup for the East India Company in 1615. Dale's friend John Rolfe married the American Indian convert Rebecca, formerly known as Pocahontas, during Dale's tenure in Virginia. Dale himself improbably proposed marriage to Pocahontas's sister, although her father politely declined on her behalf, since like Dale she was already married to another. When he journeyed home, Dale was accompanied by the Rolfe family and other Powhatan emissaries on a mission to London, in another spectacle of public entertainment and edification only a year after Peter Pope's public baptism.

We know of their encounter because Copland reported it later to the Virginia Company to explain his new zeal for their settlement. It was, however,

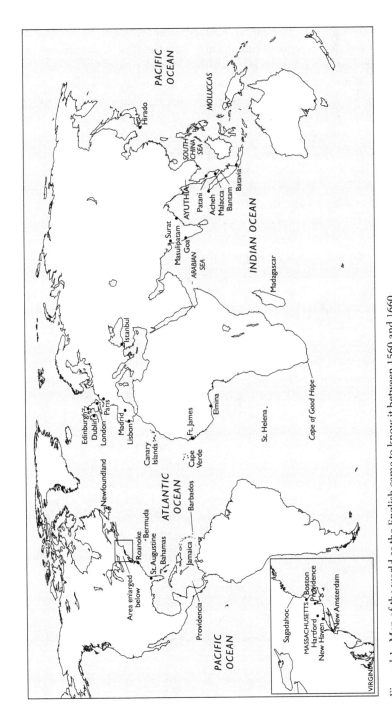

Figure I.1. Map of the world as the English came to know it between 1560 and 1660.

only one of countless conversations men had during their long ocean voyages or during quiet periods in settlements and trading posts. Sometimes these exchanges were more than ways to pass the time: they could be transforming. Copland's and Dale's paths intersected thousands of miles from home, and their meeting set Copland off in two new directions. One was geographic, literally a new direction, as he left the Indian and Pacific Oceans for adventures on one of the Atlantic's smallest islands. The other was occupational, a metaphorical departure, as he sought to pursue the evangelical activity that the East India Company almost always had to renounce if it hoped to trade. So he hoped, as a result of talking to Dale, to embark on a new way of interacting with foreign worlds and their inhabitants, no longer content to minister among the English.

These two men met at different stages of their careers. Dale was almost at the end of a long and varied military career that had taken him from western Europe across the Atlantic and into the Indian Ocean. He had fought Spanish forces; he had taken on the indigenous people of the Chesapeake, engaging in a notable assault in 1614; and in 1618 as commander of the English fleet he challenged the Dutch, the people with whom he had launched his career. Copland had journeyed to the Indies at least twice, serving as a ship's chaplain and ministering to the men in the East India Company's trading posts, but after this voyage, he had a change of heart, and decided to try firm ground over his floating chaplaincies. One was Scottish and a man of the cloth, the other English and a man of the sword, yet by the time they met in the East Indies they were participants in a common enterprise: England's struggle for power and wealth through overseas expansion.

Copland and Dale offer us a fortuitous entrée into a remarkable period of English transformation. Global processes knit the early modern world together, enabling people to perceive in its entirety a world once experienced only in fragments. Maritime and navigational advances accelerated the pace of connection and the rate of communication among distant continents. Places long familiar became more quickly reached, their goods more readily and cheaply exchanged, their oddities more rapidly assimilated. In their sea voyages, Europeans also came upon entirely unknown lands in the western hemisphere, places populated by such a bewildering array of unfamiliar people, languages, cultures, plants, animals, and commodities that old intellectual frameworks were irrevocably challenged.

At first England remained on the sidelines of these major global trends. Perched on the western fringes of Europe, a remote sovereign kingdom in an old trading world centered around the Mediterranean, England was a nation characterized in the middle of the sixteenth century by the state's fiscal constraints that hindered its ability to maneuver in Europe or to impose itself in the Americas or Asia. Annual fleets carrying silver and other treasures from the Americas enabled Spain to achieve unprecedented power in Europe and the Mediterranean while the English and other rivals watched in frustration. But by 1660, England had transformed itself from a kingdom on the European margins to one well-positioned to take advantage of new opportunities all around the world. In this remarkable period the English dislodged the Spanish from some of their holdings in the Americas, challenged Spanish dominion over the American continents, and established new long-distance trade routes to the eastern Mediterranean and the East Indies. England emerged in the seventeenth century as a kingdom on the rise.

The English pursued overseas opportunities in a distinctive way that was a product of royal strategies, fiscal constraints, and military weakness. Although the English state was unusually centralized in this period, with an effective system of taxation, a national church, a single language, and a uniform legal system, all functioning (with some exceptions) throughout England, the state could not impose its power beyond its borders. In 1558, England had even lost Calais, its last remaining territory in France. England's inability to play a significant role in Europe or beyond was largely connected to finances. How, then, did this constrained state manage to project itself outside of Europe, emerging in the 1660s as a real power in the Atlantic and with strong trade in the East Indies? How did this weak state become an empire? This book engages these questions by looking at the people like Copland or Dale who were at the heart of the decentralized strategy the English pursued. I argue that these globetrotters and their many adventures offer one important way to understand how a state too weak to intrude effectively on European affairs in 1560 grew to become a powerful kingdom with global reach by 1660. My goal is to provide a vantage point on English expansion in these crucial years before an empire emerged by focusing on the overlapping and intersecting worlds of commercial and colonial enterprises and the transoceanic global perspectives that men derived through their travels from one ocean basin to another. These men reveal the cosmopolitanism and adaptability central to English success overseas in the first decades of English expansion beyond western Europe. A vantage point is not a comprehensive analysis of all English activity in this period, however, and readers seeking such an overview should supplement this book with other sources.[4]

The English crown organized its global enterprises through joint-stock companies, composed of private investors with royal monopolies. This strategy of financing expensive and risky overseas ventures from India to America not only had financial implications but also introduced a different method of empire-building, one lacking the centralizing power of a single crown or council that characterized Spanish endeavors. Apart from essential royal charters, English investment companies were free to create their own worlds overseas. They hired and equipped their own armies; they fortified their settlements; they placed guns on their merchant ships. With the latitude permitted by their charters these companies established an astonishing range of colonial and commercial experiments. The Dutch, like the English, pursued their ventures through private enterprise, and the similarities between these two nations in their strategies for geopolitical advantage were pronounced. The Dutch often showed the English how to adapt to new circumstances, whether cultivating sugar cane in Barbados or dining Japanese style in Hirado.

There were multiple incentives for England to pursue overseas enterprises. Most urgent was the struggle for political power in Europe, but England's fiscal weakness dictated that the quest for dominion would be fought overseas in parasitic settlements to threaten Spanish shipping and in trading posts to undermine the commercial interests of Portuguese, Spanish, Dutch, and French rivals. Economic and political theory intimately linked a nation's trade with its political strength, and thus English military action against European rivals and commercial expansion around the globe were part of the same larger struggle for advantage. Those who invested in trading ventures may have hoped to fill their purses, but they also attached themselves to national goals; their profit was inextricable from English prestige and power. English expansion was a multipronged enterprise, and it required all sorts of people, including soldiers and diplomats, merchants and mariners, ministers and colonists. In this period of transition, a soldier like Thomas Dale and a minister like Patrick Copland were equally and intimately involved in national and commercial strategies for global power and dominion, all carried out by London investors.

As Patrick Copland's presence in the East India Company and Somers Island Company suggests, moreover, the men who traveled among English ventures were occasionally Scots. Although their two kingdoms were united under a single sovereign after James VI of Scotland became James I of England in 1603, the Scots were not allowed to form their own long-distance trading companies in territory claimed by England. Within this constraint, Scots seeking opportunities overseas found them with the Spanish, Dutch, French, Portuguese—and especially with the English.[5] Loyal to a single king yet inhabitants of separate kingdoms, the Scots and the English sometimes shared common interests and at other times were enemies. Their proximity overseas casts light on their shifting national attachments in a period when the relationship among the three kingdoms of Ireland, England, and Scotland was volatile. What emerged over this century was an empire governed by an English crown and Parliament, yet Scots were part of this process of expansion. Their presence in colonies, trading posts, fisheries, and armies made foreign settlements precociously British before the two kingdoms joined in a formal union in 1707.

At the center of England's vigorous global expansion were people, individuals like Dale and Copland who circulated the globe in multiple ventures. Some fled economic uncertainty and outright despair at home, while others were lured overseas by the desire for adventure and opportunity. A minister referred to his "inbred curiosity," and one Scottish soldier explained to his parents as he headed to Indonesia, "I was borne to travell."[6] And so he did, joined by thousands of others who found their way to India, the Americas, Madagascar, Japan, Istanbul, and countless other destinations.

These men—merchants, proprietors, promoters, adventurers, soldiers, governors, travelers, ministers, and diplomats—supported risky overseas ventures. They probed the very limits of the world known to the English; they directed and protected colonies; they fought to establish English supremacy; they secured commercial alliances and solidified trade routes and networks. Mostly they traveled without wives and children, although they were often part of enterprises that involved sons, fathers, uncles, cousins, and nephews, so family ties endured as often as they were ruptured by foreign ventures. Those who journeyed abroad merely acted more enthusiastically on impulses that led their counterparts at home to invest in overseas companies, or to pounce avidly on new commodities in the marketplace, or to read about foreign ventures in the steady stream of travel accounts, promotional literature, and histories that English printers produced for an interested market.

Their interest in the world beyond England's shores turned many travelers into cosmopolitans, men who were often able to encounter those unlike themselves with enthusiasm and curiosity. Cosmopolitans in this new era of global interaction were made, not born, and so they approached the world not only from the specific religious, political, and cultural context of the British Isles but also from their own immediate circumstances, shaped by gender, class, ethnicity, religion, occupation, education, and temperament. There was no monolithic response to foreign worlds and people, nor was there a coherent cosmopolitanism in this period. It encompassed a range of behaviors across a wide spectrum.

Some men detached themselves altogether from any national affiliation. More common, however, were those individuals who came to develop a distance from and an ability to critique their own nation and customs. Travelers, for example, sometimes deployed their observations of foreign practices to criticize English mores. Merchants often flung themselves into trading worlds far from home, eager to learn the tastes and fashions that would dictate commercial success. Colonial governors and trade ambassadors balanced their obligation to serve as symbols of English authority with the need and inclination to adapt to new circumstances. Some ministers found their way to ecumenism, the clerical variation on the merchant's cosmopolitanism. Although colonists, who emerged by the middle of the seventeenth century as an important population of English overseas, tended to have little interest in appreciating the customs of indigenous people, they happily pursued new economic opportunities, learned how to cultivate new crops, lived with and governed African and Indian laborers, and devised innovative social forms to sustain their colonial ventures. Their willingness to adapt and to learn from the examples of rivals and predecessors was the colonists' expression of cosmopolitanism. All of these men were diverse and complex people, torn as all individuals are by multiple loyalties, attachments, interests, and affections, and always challenged and stimulated by their lives outside of England. They responded to their new homes with all the personal idiosyncrasy and human variety we might expect, whether scowling in disapproval at unfamiliar practices or immersing themselves into alien ways.

Cosmopolitanism facilitated survival and success overseas, and thus emerged in part as a series of learned behaviors. It was often a posture derived from weakness, and central to English expansion when the kingdom itself was weak. In that respect, cosmopolitanism defined English expansion in this century of transition and transformation. But it came to define people, too. Far from home, dispersed around the world wherever opportunity might lurk, the English learned foreign languages, visited synagogues and mosques, befriended Asian and European traders, pursued sexual and romantic relations with indigenous women, fathered children and sometimes shipped them home to England, and sought to understand the cultural mores of an alien land. They pursued avocations as amateur botanists, hosted foreign neighbors for English holiday meals, attended plays, studied foreign music, and fought and sickened and died thousands of miles from home. These cosmopolitans collected manuscripts, books, ancient ruins, artifacts, tacky souvenirs, plants, animals, paintings, furniture, captives, friends, and experiences. With their trips home and new voyages out, they fabricated connections over thousands of miles, linking ties of knowledge and custom and practice. Cumulatively, they wove a web of empire.[7]

London was the geographic and financial center of this web, as travels took men through the metropolis on their repeated voyages. Patrick Copland had journeyed from Scotland to London to sail to the Indies, and back to London in order to get to Bermuda. The logistics of sea travel made this hub and spoke system essential for those who wished to move legally on English ships and within company ventures. But the position of London as a transportation and financial entrepot rivaled the cultural significance of places scattered around the globe. My approach deliberately inverts the trajectory of an older style of imperial history in which Britons were capable of imposing their will on subject people and places, by casting light instead on how places and people far from Europe defined how the English experienced the world and the empire that emerged in their wake.[8] This empire was not driven and shaped solely by events and actions from a single center, but rather continuously redefined by men who circulated around the globe. They established and reinforced in their migrations an interlaced and ever-expanding network stretching among America, Europe, and Asia, on top of which commercial regulations and state efforts to direct the movement of people ultimately developed. This was an empire built on the ground, in the peripheries, in colonies and trading posts, on islands and in port towns, on board ship and within fortifications. Models devised in different colonial and commercial settings were subsequently adapted and transported around the globe by men like Dale or Copland, whose travels tangibly linked one enterprise to another. New undertakings were conceptualized in light of prior experiences.

When Bermuda's governor Nathaniel Butler wrote in the 1620s that "as geography without historye seemeth a carkasse without motion, so history without geography wandreth as a vagrant without certaine habitation," he used this logic to embark on a long description of the climate and features of Bermuda.[9] But history and geography are inseparable for many reasons. England's geographic expansion was shaped by a precise chronology: when the English went where, and where they went next, affected each subsequent experiment. The knowledge, expertise, and expectations of people are thus inseparable from the places they visited and settled. The chapters that follow by necessity link these perspectives on people and on places. Four chapters analyze the experiences of different types of men who traveled outside of England (travelers, merchants, governors and ambassadors, and ministers), and four chapters investigate important regions of exchange (in the Mediterranean) or colonial undertakings (in Virginia, in Madagascar, and in Ireland) in order to look at how regional cultures were defined and how new overseas enterprises were constrained by the accumulation of prior knowledge and experience. English precedent was not the only guide. The English were also inspired by the successes of Spain (the English sought mines to rival Potosí everywhere, including Tangier) and also of the Dutch and the Portuguese in Asia. Case studies of colonization attempts in Virginia, Madagagascar, and Ireland illustrate this process of emulation and improvisation.

I interweave these chapters, alternating analyses of globetrotters with case studies in order to illustrate the emergence and impact of key groups of people involved in supporting overseas expansion, the cumulative knowledge men transported, and how they sought to implement it. My story begins in the interlaced worlds of trade and travel. Chapter 1, on travelers, argues that the English and Scots who traveled first to Europe and then farther afield introduced the two kingdoms to a wider world, making the foreign familiar to a domestic audience: this was a critical precursor and accompaniment to global networks of trade and settlement. One consequence of looking at individuals who traveled outside of England is that it orients the initial English experience with the world solidly in Europe and especially in the Mediterranean, the first region (beyond northern Europe) where the English acquired experience with long-distance trade. Chapter 2 introduces the Mediterranean as the origins of the British empire. There, the English were weak and vulnerable, and they learned a model of cultural interaction defined by dissimulation and accommodation. This new geographic starting point for English ventures around the globe places English adaptability at the center of the story.

Chapter 3 pursues this theme of accommodation by analyzing merchants and the worlds they created overseas, focusing especially on the period from 1590–1660 and examining trading worlds in the Ottoman Empire, Lisbon, and Japan. The comparison brings out the special challenges Protestant English traders faced in those places closest to home, such as Lisbon, while the worlds of the east that later came to be seen as alien and exotic often offered more security and comfort. In this world of uncertain foreign opportunities, the English who sought prosperity at one new venture, Jamestown, brought a jumble of expectations and experiences with them, many embedded in the world of trade, with colonization the unexpected result of local opportunities and constraints. Chapter 4 explores this North American settlement, setting what became a new style of English overseas venture—the plantation colony—in the context of the trading world that produced it. Because of the heightened interest some English investors showed in colonies in the wake of Virginia's successful establishment, by the 1610s and 1620s a new population of experienced colonial governors emerged, men who ventured from one post to another. I pair these men with their commercial counterparts, trade consuls and ambassadors, in chapter 5. Charged with representing the crown overseas and governing English communities, these political leaders acquired valuable experiences that defined successive ventures, both through the tangible presence of leaders who participated in multiple overseas ventures and through the many accounts they published of their exploits around the world. Their presence, moreover, helped a weak state use private companies to project itself abroad through these informal civil authorities.

Chapters 6, 7, and 8 focus on the period of political and religious upheaval surrounding the Civil War and Commonwealth, from roughly 1640 to 1660. Chapter 6 examines two English colonization efforts on Madagascar, imagined in the 1630s and enacted in the 1640s. Madagascar might have succeeded as a colonial settlement in the 1640s had not its English organizers sought so assiduously to emulate recent colonial successes in the Atlantic and Caribbean. These prior English experiences overrode two equally relevant models, those of the Dutch at Batavia and the Portuguese at Goa. The accumulation of colonial experiences, evident by the 1640s, constrained subsequent commercial or colonial efforts.

The religious and political instability of this period produced a population that was central to English overseas ventures, the clergy, and chapter 7 focuses on these wandering clerics. Working as chaplains on ships and in trading posts and in colonies in the Atlantic, English ministers of all religious dispositions sometimes found their time overseas a respite and occasionally an opportunity for religious experimentation that in turn shaped the religious settlement in England during these tumultuous years. The war years were a time of realignment in England, not only in terms of politics and religion, but also in the state's desire and ability to intrude in overseas ventures. By the 1650s, England devised a vigorous policy concerned not only with the commercial regulation of English ventures but also with the physical regulation of the English bodies who made these enterprises possible. A final chapter on Ireland in the 1650s illustrates England's new commitment to brute force (expressed through a new standing army and expanded navy) and to forced migration around the Atlantic as a strategy for colonial success and national power. This imperial reshuffling of people linked Britain, Ireland, the Caribbean, and North America, and exposed the government's new vision of a more centralized empire devised in the wake of several decades of private enterprise.

As these studies of colonial ventures and cosmopolitans illustrate, the worlds of commerce and colonization intersected in important ways. Colonies inspired trade, and trade inspired colonies. Investors risked their money in a variety of overseas enterprises, and people imperiled their lives as well, trying their fortunes in a succession of endeavors. Numerous examples point to the optimism early adventurers expressed that endeavors that ultimately turned out to be dead ends might bring profits to investors and honor to England. Did fortune and fame lurk in Bermuda or the Amazon, Madagascar or Tangier? Juan Pedro, back from the West Indies and the Wiapoco River in 1615, reported to the Dutch on English activities in South America. He predicted that their profits would exceed those from the East Indies.[10] Nathaniel Butler, who was in some position to know as a former governor of the islands, maintained in the 1620s that Bermuda—with its safe harbor, advantageous location, and healthful climate—was the most valuable place the English crown held.[11] By the 1640s, the English merchant Richard Boothby believed that *Madagascar* was the route to prosperity in India, likely to be a boon for the English as Batavia had been for the Dutch. And in 1661, an English proponent of settlement in Tangier named James Wilson was certain that English colonization on Africa's northern coast would eclipse *both* the East and West Indies.[12]

The map of the first British Empire, had it followed these nodes of activity in Bermuda, South America, Madagascar, and Tangier, would have looked very different from the centers of commerce, plantation production, and strategic power the English ultimately established in the Caribbean, the North American mainland, the Mediterranean, and the East Indies. These unrealized visions of English success bring into focus the great uncertainty that accompanied overseas expansion. This was a period of experimentation. Only with much loss of life and great difficulty did the English learn what kinds of exploitative or extractive activities might succeed in different parts of the world and in different ocean basins, each with their own distinctive existing and emerging commercial networks, rivalries, and indigenous populations. A global perspective illustrates this complex process, one riddled with trial and error, success and failure, triumph and despair.

Participants understood the many opportunities and adventures that awaited them in different ports, to further their ambitions, to gain honor, to save souls, to seek profit. But historians have approached English expansion as a story largely understood within the context of separate ocean basins. The historian H. V. Bowen has memorably called this legacy an "atomized inheritance," with the Indian Ocean containing a world of trade and the Atlantic a world of colonial endeavors.[13] To early American historians, Dale is a familiar name for his famously harsh reign in Virginia, but his continental and Asian military service is unknown. Historians of the early East India Company might encounter Copland in the Company records, but would never notice his Bermuda career. And yet it is precisely their global vision, their casual conversation that set Copland off in a new direction, which helps us see a world of English expansion as its participants experienced it, and that helps us understand why the English empire developed as it did in the seventeenth century. Individuals' migratory choices might seem arbitrary, the intervention of fate and new opportunity unpredictable at best, but these contingencies could be transforming. A global perspective brings out this process, helping us to see how new ventures were shaped by prior experience and the cumulative effect of this painfully acquired wisdom. It also shows us a world spanned by private enterprise and defined by cosmopolitanism before the sensibility waned and was replaced and eclipsed by the state's commitment to centralized authority and to coercive strategies.

Nation, region, and the world were all intertwined in this period, as European states and kingdoms struggled for dominance in Europe and turned to overseas holdings to finance or reinforce that power. The power of a state within Europe was necessarily connected to that state's ability to project itself beyond the region. The English accomplished their own transition from a marginal European kingdom to a key player around the world by relying on men who served simultaneously their sovereign, their pocketbook, their employer, and whatever personal satisfaction they derived in their global ventures. The repeated migration of the people at the heart of English expansion reveals the webs of connection that first linked England to a wider world and then, through multiple voyages, tightened the web, and embedded England firmly in a world of uncertain and tantalizing opportunity.

1

Before the Grand Tour

The Domestication of Travel

"It is pleset god yt I was borne to travell." So wrote the Scot James Spens from somewhere on the western coast of Africa to his parents in Edinburgh in 1632.[1] Spens was a soldier, employed since 1628 as a drum major with the king of Sweden's regiment in Riga during Gustavus Adolphus's successful push for domination of the eastern Baltic. Like thousands of other young Scottish men, Spens could not find employment at home, so he joined those who traveled to the continent in search of work as soldiers, peddlers, and merchants.[2] His military career forced his separation not only from his parents, but also from his wife. The distance placed an enormous strain on their marriage, although only the economic opportunity afforded by distant employment enabled Spens to marry at all. "I marvell mikell at yor unkyndnes towards me," he rebuked his wife in one epistle for her failure to write him as faithfully as he wrote her.[3] James implored her to join him in Riga. Finally she did, but no sooner had she reached the city than she died, a blow Spens described to his parents as "a great greiff to [his] heart." But Spens did not take this occasion to return to the solace offered by his family and friends in Scotland. Instead, he ventured even further away, planning never to return.[4] He received a pass from the commanders of his regiment, left the army, and traveled south to Holland. Once Spens reached the vibrant port of Amsterdam, he found work with the Dutch East India Company, which was always in need of soldiers to defend its trading posts in Asia. In this capacity, Spens commenced his travels again, bound for Batavia for at least seven years as a soldier, anticipating, he wrote his mother, that this would be the best journey he ever took. He welcomed the long voyage, repeating his refrain: "I have bein borne to Travill."[5]

Spens's self-identification as a traveler placed his life in perspective. Likely in his early thirties when he wrote these final letters to his parents, Spens transformed what was once financial exigency into divine destiny. Like any good Calvinist who embraced the doctrine of predestination, he sought God's will in the most mundane aspects of his life. When he lost his clothes on his journey from Gotenburg to Stockholm and was left with nothing, he prayed that his "worst day is past and my best day is coming."[6] With his optimism and his faith, Spens integrated the terrible vicissitudes of life into a temporal vision in which his peregrinations and his ordeals together followed God's special plan for him. The inconveniences and dangers of travel described in earlier letters emerged as the features that defined who he was: a soldier, a Scot, a widower, a son, a friend, a Christian, a traveler. If the act of travel is most literally a movement through geographic space, for Spens it offered a larger metaphor for his passage through life.

Spens's self-definition would have required no explanation for his contemporaries, for whom travel encompassed a wide range of enterprises. It was both a serious business and an art with its own special codes. It was undertaken not (ostensibly) for personal pleasure but in service of a larger purpose, and it therefore included people whom modern readers might describe otherwise. Thomas Palmer provided a typology of travel in 1606 in *An Essay of the Meanes how to make our Travailes, into forraine Countries, the more profitable and honourable*. In an elaborate chart, he divided travelers into three sorts: involuntary (those voyaging on missions of church, state, or law), nonvoluntary (those such as exiles or refugees who traveled for reasons of religion), and voluntary (merchants, mechanics, artisans, or tradesmen). Palmer specifically included soldiers in his book within the category of special travelers and delineated the constraints that should guide men's decisions to serve in foreign armies. Anyone who ventured out of England or Scotland for any purpose was a traveler in the parlance of the time. Thus when the East India Company pondered the application of one potential employee in 1607, Company members praised the trader's skills, for he "hath beene a Traveller."[7]

Although most occupational groups were composed of travelers, this chapter examines people whose recreational and educational travels might initially seem most akin to our own. It artificially separates them from other people whom they would also have identified as travelers, and it similarly segregates one portion of their traveling lives from other stages of the life cycle in which these people would have characterized themselves as still traveling when they worked as merchants or consuls, ministers or governors. As educational travel became more common, it domesticated a world beyond England's shores. Travelers brought foreign experiences (and souvenirs) home, and as travel became normative they also conquered fears of the foreign. Travelers first knit England and Scotland into Europe through their adventures, and then took their experiences farther afield, connecting England to Asia and America literally in their voyages and also in the many manuscript and published accounts they generated about these new and unfamiliar worlds. These texts shaped perceptions of the sedentary public and by the middle of the seventeenth century circumscribed subsequent tours of future travelers. The increased enthusiasm for travel, moreover, proved indispensable as the English and Scots took their language skills and the traveler's necessary practice of accommodation with them around the world in these decades of new global enterprises launched by the English.

Although travel may have improved and entertained the traveler, published advice manuals insisted that it must also improve the commonwealth. Palmer's book guided travelers in making their tours "profitable and honourable" for both themselves and the state. The subtitle of James Howell's *Instructions for Forreine Travell* (first published in 1642 and revised with an added section on Turkey in 1650) likewise conveys the importance of the task. The full subtitle reads: *Shewing by what cours, and in what compasse of time, one may take an exact survey of the kingdomes and states of Christendome, and arrive to the practicall knowledge of the languages, to good purpose.* The emphasis rests on the utility, the "good purpose," the "practicall knowledge," of travel, as well as the precise mechanisms to make this travel possible: *how* to understand and analyze the new places to be seen, *how* to travel conveniently within a given time constraint. These manuals agreed that travel abroad, although a dangerous endeavor for any number of reasons, hazardous both to a traveler's safety and to his conscience, benefited the state and was intimately connected to the successful growth of commerce and the smooth functioning of diplomacy.

Emphasis on public utility countered the vigorous attacks of critics, both those who had ventured abroad and those who regarded travelers with apprehension and disdain. The scholar Sara Warneke has timed the emergence of critical images of the traveler to the second half of the sixteenth century, particularly around 1570, with the publication of Roger Ascham's attack on the Italianate traveler in *The Scholemaster*.[8] These critiques emerged precisely and of course not coincidentally with the rising popularity of continental travel. Images of the traveler as corrupt, degenerate, and foppish recur in popular literature. Authors associated particular destinations with corruption: first Italy (popular in the sixteenth century), and subsequently France, the main destination for young men in the first decades of the seventeenth century.[9]

The popularity of travel agitated its critics. In *Quo Vadis: A Just Censure of Travell* (London, 1617), the cleric Joseph Hall deplored casual travel. Hall had himself traveled abroad twice. Despite his enjoyment of France and its inhabitants, he found himself "searching into the proofe of that ordinary Travell," and "the more I saw, the lesse I liked." Hall was not troubled by the dangers to one's personal safety, or even by the many temptations travelers confronted, but rather by the peril to one's soul. Those who traveled for personal refinement, Hall worried, returned "as empty of grace and other vertues, as full of words, vanitie, mis-dispositions." Hall understood the necessity of travel. While England's geographic isolation might indicate that God had intended to "shut us up," God's invention of navigation suggested that the opposite was the case. Yet he believed travel should be undertaken only for state or trade, not for "the Travell of curiosity," or educational travel, which prudent parents should forbid for their young and immature sons. He worried that too many men pursued travel to acquire better "table-talke." Of those skills young men sought in France, such as dancing or fencing or music, all that, Hall complained, was only "varnish." Hall's greatest concern, however, was not with the superficiality of recreational and educational travel, but rather with the risk of conversion to Catholicism. The bulk of his book focused on this hazard, and particularly on the "sorcery" of the Jesuits. Far better, Hall advised, to travel "into learned and credible Authors" than to venture off England's shores. His final recommendations were first to the gentry, to be happy at home, and, second, to the king, to enforce existing restrictions on travel. And for those who had to travel for commerce or state, Hall ominously exhorted them to "stand fast, for yee shall be shaken."[10]

Rejecting Hall's advice to travel only into the world of books, Howell, both a traveler and a travel writer, emphasized the importance of active travel. It was not sufficient, he wrote, to "traverse the world by Hearesay," or to be a "Sedentary Traveller." One must be an "Eye-witnesse."[11] English and Scottish men responded enthusiastically to this call for active travel, despite both those who attacked the enterprise and their own concerns about the perils of travel. It was an age when the English (along with the Germans) were known as great travelers.[12] Travel, of course, was neither a novel activity nor in any way unique to the English or to Europeans. When the English and Scots left their homes, they joined a tradition that reached from the ancient tale of Odysseus to the holy trek of the pilgrim. And these sixteenth- and seventeenth-century English-speaking travelers enjoyed access to these stories. Tales of travel circulated in various forms. Manuscript accounts, including at least 300 versions in multiple languages (from Irish to Czech) of the English traveler Sir John Mandeville's imaginative journey in the fourteenth century, joined published accounts of famous voyagers such as Marco Polo, Vasco da Gama, Jean Ribault, or Francisco de Coronado to entertain and sometimes to educate Europeans, whether at home or abroad. Thanks to the global commercial and maritime ventures of Spain and Portugal, southern Europeans were among the most prolific producers of such accounts, and one of the most important compilations in this period was the multivolume work of Giovanni Battista Ramusio, *Navigationi et Viaggi* (Venice, 1554–1556), which heavily influenced his English counterpart, Richard Hakluyt, in his own massive collection of voyages.[13]

Most of the trips young Englishmen pursued took place in Europe, yet men also ventured farther afield. The period between 1580 and 1660 witnessed the domestication of first European, and then global travel. The adventures recorded in Richard Hakluyt's and Samuel Purchas's compendiums were replicated by the recreational and educational traveler and by those who ventured abroad with more serious commercial and diplomatic purposes.[14] Published travel accounts brought the world into the hands of readers, but travelers could also take these accounts as models and manuals for their own ventures: trading companies provided copies of Hakluyt and Purchas to overseas merchants. Travelers in turn recorded and published their experiences, and later used the skills they had acquired for professional advantage. By the middle of the seventeenth century, travel became so perfunctory that diarists tried to avoid writing about places easily read about in published books.

Young men who traveled on the continent in their late teens or early twenties often ventured abroad later in diplomatic and commercial capacities. Their privileged birth predicted and frequently guaranteed public and political careers. The early Tudor monarchs had aggressively supported the circulation of scholars and courtiers between England and the continent, particularly to Italy, to study statecraft.[15] Elizabeth herself sponsored some continental travelers.[16] Their experiences with foreign languages, people, and places became a part of the public, political, clerical, and even royal cultures of Tudor and Stuart England. An emerging class of gentleman adventurers (such as Sir Francis Drake or Sir Walter Ralegh) or well-traveled courtiers (including Sir Philip Sidney and Sir Thomas More) signaled this trend, as did the intense royal patronage of foreign travels by Queen Elizabeth and Prince Henry, the oldest son of James I. Fashions and tastes are often shaped by outside influences and novelties, but fundamental developments were guided by the specific experiences of wandering English and Scots. The English learned about dike construction from those who had been to Holland. An invigorated plan for colonization in Ireland was proposed in 1566 by Sir Henry Sidney, and may have resulted from the time he had spent in Spain, during which he learned about Spanish methods of colonization.[17] Travel became more frequent and emerged in the eighteenth century as the grand tour, an expected and formulaic ritual for the wellborn. It cemented the importance of continental relations, of languages, of mastery of foreign mores, of learning how to interact with foreign people and cultures.

These men who moved into public affairs began their careers as educational travelers and comprised the majority of those who left England and Scotland for reasons other than employment, although in many respects educational travel offered an apprenticeship for later public service. These privileged young men tended to travel with tutors on highly structured tours. They settled in carefully selected towns to learn languages and in some cases to read and attend lectures at universities, especially subjects such as law and medicine that were more difficult to study in England.[18] In his extended essay on travel in 1606, Thomas Palmer's intended audience was precisely this educational traveler, "the yonger sort of such noble gentleman as intend so recomendable a course."[19] Howell's *Instructions for Forreine Travell* had a similar reader in mind. Howell himself had been such a traveler, going off to the continent to complete his education after he received his BA at Oxford. Palmer's and Howell's imagined audience comprised men on their way to study in foreign universities, to learn languages, to acquire genteel skills. Such young men were especially in need of guidance because contemporaries believed that travel was dangerous business, undertaken seriously, and only by men of suitable education, rank, and age (and, it went without saying, wealth). Palmer believed that a traveler should be in "middle age," certainly older than twenty-five, when he would be less prone to the "slie perswasions of others."[20] Fynes Moryson argued that neither women nor married men should travel, even if laws permitted them to do so. Travelers should seek the permission of their parents and others in authority, as Moryson did before he left home in 1591 at the age of twenty-five or twenty-six. He received his parents' consent and a license from the Master and fellows of Peterhouse, Cambridge, where he was a fellow.[21]

For all its pleasures, travel was state business, and travelers of all sorts required the permission of the king or other highly placed officials. Educational travelers had to acquire licenses for time overseas and for permission to carry funds to support them for three years. Howell's book of travel instructions was organized around this customary time frame: he estimated that a traveler should be able to see France, Spain, Italy, the Alps, Germany, and Belgium in three years and four months (four months allotted for actual travels, and three years for time in residence).[22] If travelers wished to extend their stay, they needed to seek approval.[23] Moreover, if they wished to add new destinations, they similarly needed permission to amend their licenses. James Hamilton, the son of Viscount Claneboye in Ireland, received a pass from the king in August of 1633 for travels to Europe, but did not have permission to travel to Rome and wished, moreover, for an extension of his license, which he received.[24]

Licenses stipulated how much money travelers could take with them, since the government was also concerned about the loss of specie. Most recreational travelers came from families with sufficient resources to support their travels. But there were other ways of funding a voyage. Moryson's brother Henry contrived a bet on his safe return. This was apparently not an uncommon way of funding travel: a potential traveler without resources got himself insured. Henry put out £400 and anticipated £1,200 on his return to England, but his death in the Ottoman Empire made this a losing proposition for all concerned.[25] Fynes did the same thing among his friends, putting out £100 for his friends who gambled on his safe return.[26]

Procuring licenses and securing funds were the pragmatic prerequisites to travel. But manuals required aspiring travelers to make other careful preparations for their journeys, including intense self-scrutiny to determine the legitimacy and nobility of their calling abroad. Before they traveled, men should ask themselves whether their purpose was "their owne lusts and affections" or instead the real service of the commonwealth.[27] Moryson reiterated that he did not want to travel "to get libertie," of which he had abundance in Cambridge, but rather "to enable my understanding."[28] Travelers should probe whether they possessed the knowledge and judgment necessary to suit them to travel. They should prepare adequately, learning about the countries they planned to visit. And their choice of destination should reflect some awareness of self and state: they should "resolve to goe into such Countreys…which may afford them best gaine of knowledge and experience; either to reforme in them defects of nature, or to benefite most their Common weale."[29] John Wray, who traveled in 1605–1606, urged the traveler to "have a care for his own betteringe, & his countries service," by putting his time to the best use, missing no opportunity that might educate him.[30] Personal amelioration joined public benefit.

This same deliberate introspection and self-discipline were to guide travelers throughout their voyages. Palmer urged moderation in diet, exercise, and passions, and respectful treatment of those they met. Based on his own extensive travels, Moryson elaborated on these instructions. He assumed that these potential travelers were complete novices, reminding them, for example, to gather all of their possessions before they left their inn or hostel to be sure they did not forget anything.[31] His twenty-seven precepts and other advice scattered throughout his account governed the most basic behavior. Always carry a book. Be humble, patient, quiet, discreet, polite, and cautious. Follow your own preferences in diet, but wear whatever local clothing is popular where you travel. Howell agreed, "for as a Spaniard lookes like a bug-beare [monster] in France in his own cut, so a Frenchman appears ridiculous in Spaine." Wear your own clothing to bed because beds for travelers were generally filthy. Bring a compass, and climb the highest tower in a new city to get a good view. Such navigational advice was repeated in Howell's *Instructions*, which ordered potential travelers to know how to use a map and globe.[32] New travelers were eager for whatever wisdom experienced travelers might impart, and diarists sometimes recorded the counsel they received. In the 1660s the Scot John Lauder asked another traveler who was nearing the end of his travels how a man might make "the best use" of his travels. His companion advised him to remember his duty to God and to seek good company who could teach him about the customs of a country.[33]

Learning these customs required that travelers acquire habits of cultural accommodation. *The Merchants Avizo* from the 1580s urged travelers to be circumspect in their behavior and to adhere to local laws and customs.[34] Robert Southwell recommended that if people talked of something one did not like, the best idea was to talk loudly to someone about another topic. His commonplace book of 1660–1661 recorded some of the witticisms exchanged and topics of conversation, as if he could peruse his compilation for inspiration before a social gathering.[35] One anxious father who compiled a list of instructions for his wandering son in 1663 hoped he would learn about people. "Study persons as weal as things," he advised, and find out "how to accomodat yourself to [strangers] without giving offens or receaving any for escheweing of snairs and Affronts."[36] These manuals combined guides to etiquette with urgently needed advice for those who sojourned in lands that might suddenly turn inhospitable. To learn how to live with all kinds of people, Moryson recommended that travelers should start in Germany, where they would learn the custom of sharing a single cup at a table, and from that one communal cup, presumably, came acceptance of other new rituals.[37]

To help travelers from privileged backgrounds understand what this self-abnegation entailed when so little in their childhood training might equip them for such a demeanor, William Biddulph, a Levant Company chaplain, used the extended metaphor of a painting of a servant, which he ordered a traveler to study and to emulate. The traveler should have the feet of a deer, to be quick about his business; he should keep his hands wide open, to show he is faithful and generous. At home, men should dress well to show their status, but when abroad, they should dress simply, for their safety.[38]

Those who followed advice about cultural accommodation found that travel could offer a welcome period of anonymity. Men could try on different fashions, styles, and personalities, while those burdened with the expenses that came with noble birth could revel in a quieter life. The Earl of Tarras tried to travel incognito. Doing so relieved him of the expensive obligation to maintain appearances. But when he was in Paris in 1670, the English and Scots ambassador knew who he was, "soe that I am obledged," he complained to his father, "to spend in clothes & other extraordinaires which I needed not else to have done."[39] The accounts of Charles Somerset suggest the high portion of a budget that could be devoured by maintaining appearances through dress. In his travels in 1611–1612, Somerset spent £1,315 during less than a year abroad, £517 on lodging, transportation, and food, and the rest (sixty percent of his budget) on clothes and gifts.[40] A modest travel garb could promote safety in addition to stretching funds. Moryson dressed in old clothes during his travels in Germany to deter thieves.[41]

When men returned home still in their traveling togs, they could be unrecognizable. This ability of travelers to transform themselves into strangers made people mistrust them and frown on travel more generally: those who cast on new costumes so quickly might equally adopt new loyalties and faiths. Moryson's travel garb confused people twice. On his first trip home in 1595 to replenish his finances, called before the mayor of Dover, Moryson was dressed so meanly that the mayor's assistants were rude to him, and not until they asked his name did affairs smooth over. When he reached his sister's house in this same clothing, a servant almost seized him. Returning from his second travels two years later, he stayed at an inn in Gravesend, but in his long gown the watch thought he was an Italian or a priest, and not until he woke and spoke to the landlord, with his language able to contradict his clothes, was the watch dismissed.[42] Clothes made the man, and in this period when dress signaled status and ethnicity, they placed a traveler in danger. Outer garb, moreover, had a cultural power signaled in the sumptuary laws that ensured that apparel reflected social hierarchies. Clothes signaled and redefined identity.[43]

Manuals linked practical advice about garb and demeanor with an unspoken but necessary defense of the utility of travel. Moryson told new travelers to make careful notes each day on numerous subjects—including libraries, the prices of goods, state structure, and the source of a country's wealth. Somerset followed this practice by detailing who ruled each town he visited and what kind of authority these governors had.[44] Travel provided these young men with an informal study of political theory. Such knowledge was not only for a traveler's own edification, which was not insignificant since so many went into public careers, but also for the benefit of the nation.[45] Manuals enjoined travelers to visit learned men, always careful to take notes of what they discovered, and in order to keep this important information secure, to send their papers to safe places.[46] Because travel was a serious business of value to the state, travelers were advised to look carefully at their surroundings, at things natural (rivers or ports) and artificial (cities, universities, or buildings). A traveler must not be too obvious in his observations, lest he be mistaken for a spy. But in fact all travelers who followed the advice manuals were spies: these texts ordered travelers to learn whatever they could, and rather than wait until he was home to share his wisdom, a dutiful traveler should go first to the English ambassador in the country he visited.[47]

As the importance of information gathering and reporting might indicate, travel merged almost seamlessly in this period into commercial and diplomatic ventures. Much of the need was practical. Travelers' finances were arranged through letters of credit that connected them to English or Scottish merchants.[48] Several Scottish travelers in France in 1645 found their way eased by a network of Scottish merchants that included John Clark at the royal court in Paris, William Robertson in La Rochelle, and James Brown at Bordeaux. These merchants received travelers and their letters of credit, sent them on their way with letters of introduction, and amid their business correspondence they reported candidly their opinion of the young Scots they met. One traveler, Robert Gray, incurred the disapproval of James Brown, and according to William Robertson, who hosted Gray in La Rochelle, the young traveler returned the sentiment. Gray was dependent on the assistance of these merchants, as he hoped to travel to Italy; however, Brown reported (with a transparent vindictive delight), he had not organized his finances sufficiently in advance and did not have his credit arranged for his journey.[49] Merchants were also a valuable source of information for travelers, not simply a practical way to secure funds or to procure assistance. Howell recommended that travelers to Seville talk to the merchants there to gain useful information. "Their conversation is much to be valued," he explained, "for many of them are very gentile and knowing men in the affaires of the State, by reason of their long sojourne and actuall negotiations, and [law] processes in the Countrey." Likely the merchants would also have to extricate these nosy Seville travelers from prison, since Howell urged visitors to try to get a copy of the constitutions of the *Casa de Contratación*, the centralized customs and trade body that regulated commerce with the West Indies. He called this constitution "the greatest Mystery in the Spanish Government."[50]

The behavior of men during their travels reveals the extent to which they followed the instructions of travel manuals. They complied with one of the basic precepts, to record their experiences in diaries and letters.[51] Keeping a narrative account of one's travels was fundamental to the improvement of self and state that was supposed to accompany and justify travel. Some of the surviving diaries were clearly kept during travel itself. Thomas Abdie's journal was a minuscule book easily transported.[52] An anonymous diarist similarly carried a very small book on his journey to Portugal in 1661 and 1662.[53] A Scot on his journey to Egypt in 1655 carried a tiny volume measuring perhaps two by three inches.[54] These were all portable books, exactly what Howell had in mind when he told travelers to keep their book with them always.[55]

In keeping a diary writers both signaled the departure from the rhythms of daily life at home and created an opportunity for personal reflection on the world around them. For one Scots traveler, the journey commenced when he left his home in Scotland, and so he described the sights of England on his way to London. England was a foreign country to him, even if the two kingdoms were then united under a single monarch. He admired Newcastle, so "pleasantly seated," and he marveled at the library in Oxford before he reached London and toured the popular sights there.[56] Other writers commenced their journals with their departure for the port. One traveler to Naples started his account with his voyage to Gravesend,[57] another with his departure from Tower Wharf in London.[58] Somerset delineated his departure with incredible specificity: he left London on April 2, 1611, at 4:00 PM. The precise timing reflected in part one of Somerset's idiosyncrasies but also suggested the demarcation of this new experience, which commenced for him not on the continent, but in London, still on English soil, but at the moment of his departure.[59]

Their eagerness to record their journeys demonstrated the self-consciousness with which travelers approached their anticipated adventures. This, the diarist heralded, was a special episode in life, one to be chronicled, pondered, cherished, recorded for later study and entertainment, with even the shortest entry able to spark memories. Good intentions for faithful record keeping often went awry. One of the great nightmares of the travel diarist is falling behind. One traveler who apparently experienced this fate left three pages of his journal blank for a description of Rome, which presumably he intended to return to later but either forgot or decided it was simply better to stay up to date.[60] Some diaries were intended for the traveler's own reflection and benefit. Other writers labored to provide more descriptive detail for a clear (if now unknown) audience. An anonymous diarist who went to Lisbon in 1661 and 1662 kept his diary for another person's entertainment, and specifically addressed this person as "you" in his account.[61]

One quirk of these diaries is their emphasis on movement, which in fact misrepresents the main purpose of the educational traveler's sojourn overseas. Most of the wellborn men whose families supported their journeys to the continent were expected to study foreign languages and to acquire desirable skills and social graces. These were skills acquired through residence. On these long periods of stability the travelers were often silent. Months might lapse before a diary resumed.

Writing letters was as important as keeping a diary. Howell ordered travelers to write their friends monthly ("not in a carelesse perfunctory way"), and reminded them that if they wrote letters, they would also receive them.[62] Henry Erskine's letters to his father in the 1610s were exemplary. They described letters sent and received, detailed the financial arrangements for his travels and their anticipated itinerary, reported news of other Scots, and finally related news and gossip of affairs in Europe—battles, murders, marriages, the travels of royalty, exactly the sort of personal and political information an alert educational traveler should observe and report. In contrast, his younger brother Alexander's letters were brief, and each could be contained on a modern postcard. Alexander relied on Henry and on their accompanying tutor, John Schaw, to provide important news to their parents, but these pitiful and laconic epistles probably infuriated them nonetheless. For all that travel opponents feared how travel could transform people, the experience of travel by no means made the reticent loquacious. Walter Scott, the Earl of Tarras, explained to his father from France in 1667 that he did not write separately to his mother because—after at least two months away from Scotland—he had nothing to say.[63]

As the opaque letters of these taciturn sons indicate, not all travelers were thoughtful and reflective people, and many accounts contain formulaic recitations of meals, conveyances, mileage, expenses, and sights recorded only by name, with neither evaluation nor opinion. One French Protestant minister in Saumur, a city that was popular with Scots travelers, complained about the practice of rote recording of sights. He observed that most foreigners went abroad without knowing the reason why, and when they reached Saumur, all they did was to write down in their books where they went and what they saw.[64] Recording experiences could substitute for real engagement. Sir J. North's travel account was literally an accounting, a record of expenses that probably functioned as his journal. The expenses commenced in London in September of 1575, when he procured paper books, leather purses, a felt hat, and other sundries, and continued through the continent to Mantua.[65]

Travel was characterized by this paper trail. Travelers recorded their experiences in diaries. They wrote home; they maintained accounts; they carried letters of credit and their passports—sewn securely into their clothing, folded carefully in watertight leather pouches, hidden from thieves in their hats and their boots. And they also sought documents along the way to attest to their experiences. One surviving certificate for a stay in the Holy Land in 1635 illustrates the practice. Dated from a convent in Jerusalem, the Latin document detailed the sights seen by a Scot, William Fleming [*Guglielimum* (sic) *flaminium scotum*], including Mt. Olive and Mt. Zion, the places of the nativity and assumption, "and all other sacred and pious places, both within and outside the holy city, that are usually visited."[66] The list suggests that it was not sufficient to claim to have visited the Holy Land: the specific sights gave authority to the journey. Such certificates apparently served a range of functions. William Lithgow was presumably carrying just such an item, described as his "patent of Jerusalem," when he was accosted by bandits in Calabria. When the thieves read his patent, they instead paid Lithgow homage. Lithgow presumably had anticipated the protective value of this document, since he had acquired it on an earlier trip to the Holy Land in 1612 and carried it with him when he set out from England yet again. The clever voyager traveled lightly, so Lithgow's careful transportation of this precious item suggested its multiple values, in this case as a pass for safe travel, at least among those remarkably literate brigands who revered the pilgrim.[67]

Although travel offered young men the chance to see important historical, cultural, and religious sights, the justification for educational travel lay particularly in the skills a traveler could acquire. Foremost was language study. Travelers were supposed to prepare themselves before their travels in order to make the best use of their time overseas: they should know the rules of grammar and also Latin since it would help with the romance languages.[68] Because it was impossible to master all the languages that a traveler would encounter in his journey, manuals singled out a few. Palmer believed French, Latin, and Spanish to be the most important languages. Travelers and travel manuals also tackled the pedagogical issue of methods of language acquisition. Palmer understood linguistic facility to include more than the ability to speak, read, and write. The manner of presentation mattered as well. Palmer wanted travelers to "follow the most esteemed fashions both in framing the letters & sentences." Those who wrote letters should be sure to use "that kind of hand most common and commendable." Writers should follow national conventions, superscripting and subscripting letters, words, prefixes, and suffixes as customs dictated. Abdie perhaps followed this policy to make a new language second nature to him when he switched from English to French in his travel diary in the spring of 1634 after spending five months studying in Blois.[69]

In learning to speak and to write, most travelers arranged for formal language study once abroad. Manuals and experienced travelers had strong opinions on the subject. Travel guides recommended places to study where the language was purest (thus Siena, not Genoa, for Italian), instruction was safe and convenient, students would not be distracted by fellow countrymen, and—for some Protestant travelers—the reformed religion was secure.[70] It was especially important to avoid other English speakers in order to facilitate language study, "for the greatest bane of English Gentlemen abroad, is too much frequency and communication with their own Countrey-men."[71] In France, the Erskine brothers based themselves initially in Bourges, where Henry Erskine studied law and both brothers planned to learn French, but they later moved on to Saumur because of "the sindrie incommoditeis broght into them by the muntitude of scottisch men resident thair." Law was not taught in Saumur, so Henry was reduced to studying his notes from Bourges, but he explained to his father that this was no great loss, "for all the good that tetchin in the scooles dois to men, is only bot to gif them some progresse wharby they may understand the thinge they vide [see]."[72] An English traveler similarly left Blois in 1648 for Tours, "a place voide of English."[73] The goal for these serious students was language immersion, not consorting with English speakers.

But apart from this formal instruction, there were informal ways to learn languages, all dependent on the flexibility of travelers. Travel companions, for example, could teach foreign languages in addition to helping the English and Scots learn about foreign people.[74] Moryson advised travelers to talk to "Weomen, Children, and the most talkative people."[75] Howell directed those seeking the best knowledge of French to loiter by the grates at a nunnery because "the Nunnes speake a quaint Dialect, and besides they have most commonly all the Newes that passe." So central was this remarkable language strategy that Howell advised English travelers to bring "some small bagatels" to present to the nuns as small favors.[76]

Travelers communicated in ways that linguistically impaired travelers do today. They cobbled together hastily learned phrases, found a common language to speak in, and used exuberant gesture and vivid facial expression. The quickest language studies were those like John Lauder who threw themselves into the enterprise, willing to make a fool of himself and recording in his journal with a self-deprecating charm the occasions he made people laugh at his efforts.[77] Thomas Penson knew some Dutch because he had lived for three months in Holland. He had as well "a little French" and "some remnants of Latin." But he was imaginative in his schemes to enhance communication. He drew pictures in his diary of a pigeon, a fish, some eggs, and a sheep in order to communicate his food preferences, and his culinary cheat sheet included French translations of his requests.[78] If all else failed, he could simply point at his illustrations and his phrases.

Language acquisition was the starting point for the educational traveler, whose ideal itinerary included a stay in Paris after a lengthy residence in the provinces to learn French.[79] Travelers followed clear routes (see figure 1.1). France was the main destination for recreational and educational travelers, and it was the place they spent the most time acquiring skills, from languages to legal training to the adornments of a refined education—fencing, tennis, dance, musical instruments, riding, poetry, even the art of portraiture.[80] Schaw, who accompanied the Erskine brothers on their travels, planned to have them stay in Paris until they could "acqueir such pairts as ar fitting to be in men of thair qualitie."[81] Henry and Alexander Erskine studied tennis, dancing, and fencing in their travels. Alexander learned how to dance "verie properly and light," while he also learned to play "prettelie well" on his lute.[82] Abdie's financial accounts for his travels detail the skills he learned once he settled down in Blois in November of 1633: French, math, the viol, and dance.[83] If Britons later forged a national identity in opposition to France in this period—despite episodic warfare, commercial rivalries, and devastating defeats when English Protestants fought alongside French Huguenots—France provided the crucial training that enabled English and Scots men to immerse themselves in the worlds of politics and commerce at home.

After time in France, many students toured the continent. Educational travelers expected to see Italy and the Low Countries, and if possible,

Figure 1.1. Map of Western Europe as experienced by English and Scottish travelers.

Switzerland and parts of the Holy Roman Empire. When the Earl of Tarras wanted to stay on the continent despite news of his brother's grave illness, he wrote to his father in 1669 that he would obey him if he was ordered home, but that it would be a "fault not pardonable amonge travellers" for him to return to Scotland without seeing Holland and Flanders.[84] Schaw made a similar plea on behalf of the Erskine brothers in 1617; they hoped to make a tour of the Low Countries before their father called them home.[85]

Travelers like the Erskine brothers undertook educational travel not only for its immediate pleasures but also for its future benefits: all of these skills, from dancing to languages, would aid them in their quest for personal or political power at home. Travel through geographic space was thus linked profitably to time, to the future advantages travel might confer. Yet a traveler's sense of time was rattled as soon as he reached the European continent. The English and Scots (Julian) calendar lagged ten days behind the Gregorian calendar in use almost everywhere on the continent.[86] Moreover, the English still started the New Year on March 25: most of continental Europe started the new year on January 1. Finding out and recording the proper date was surprisingly difficult. Most travelers switched right away to new style dates as soon as they crossed the channel: any other strategy would have been profoundly confusing. One anonymous traveler attempted to record the date of his arrival in Dieppe, but was unsure of what that date might be. He wrote down June 30, which was the day it actually was in Dieppe, then crossed it out, and wrote it in again, in an effort to figure out new style dates or to commit himself to any single system.[87] A more experienced traveler grasped the concept more emphatically. December 15, 1648, "ther Crestmas day," he recorded laconically near Venice, and ten days later, "our Christmas day."[88] Some travelers double dated all letters to avoid confusion.[89] Others were careful at the start of their diaries to note which system they used: Lauder recorded that he traveled to Paris on May 6 French style, but April 26 according to Scots.[90]

Even once travelers sorted out the confusion of the date, other customs delineated the passage of time in new ways. Protestant travelers always commented on the many holy days observed in Catholic countries. In Orleans in the 1660s, Lauder witnessed a series of religious processions in June, starting with Saint Barnabas Day, followed soon by midsummer's eve, with bonfires for the birth of John the Baptist, and then quickly by a solemn day of commemoration for Joan, "the maid of Orleans." The impressed Lauder described the procession in detail.[91] If it seems self-evident that Catholic travelers sought to experience Christianity's holy days and associated festivals in special places, Protestants did the same to enhance their overseas experience. One traveler planned to stay in Venice through Carnival; others tried to reach Rome (or Jerusalem, for the most ambitious travelers) for Holy Week and Easter. France permitted English Catholics to experience the full rituals of the church calendar. Catholics immersed themselves in opportunities for public worship, while Protestants, especially Calvinists, gawked from a safe distance. A sacred ritual for some was a sightseeing opportunity for others. One expedient traveler attended mass at Fontainebleau simply in order to see the king and the Duke of Orleans.[92]

Travel writings exposed religious differences in large part because English-speaking Catholic travelers were disproportionately represented on the continent and because travelers of both faiths enjoyed similar and often identical destinations. Institutional educational opportunities could only be found outside of England for Catholic girls and boys, who flocked to the English schools and convents on the continent in high numbers. One 1602 report counted 500 English students abroad in Catholic schools; by 1604, there were as many as 2,000.[93] Ambassadors on the continent tried to keep track of the movements of this population, since the activities of English Catholics were always a source of royal concern, especially in the reigns of Elizabeth and James I. Catholics had difficulty obtaining licenses to travel, so English Catholics had to find creative ways to elude authorities. Some young Catholic women whose parents wished them to receive a convent education, for example, feigned marriage to gentlemen who were in the Low Countries in order to secure permission to depart England. The English consul in Lisbon fumed at these tactics between 1607 and 1617.[94] Travelers (Protestant and Catholic alike) visited these same colleges and merchants used them to arrange letters of credit.[95] Politics shaped the sex ratio of educational travelers: this Catholic population contained far more women than did the comparable population of Protestant travelers. It is likely that Catholic educational travelers were overrepresented abroad in light of the number of Catholic families in England itself and the paucity of educational opportunities for them. The displacement of English Catholics outside of England was part of a larger theme of exile among travelers: while many young people journeyed of their own volition, during the turbulent half-century before 1660, others were forcibly displaced for religious and political reasons.[96]

Religious differences were readily apparent among travelers. Catholics and Protestants revealed themselves immediately by their vocabulary. The Protestant Scots travelers universally referred to other Protestants on the continent as people of "the religion." Catholics referred to this same French population as Huguenots or heretics. The sights these travelers of opposing faiths saw consistently evoked different responses, at least among those travelers whose records went beyond the practical minutiae of travel. France, the starting point for all overseas educational travels, exposed these differences as if the kingdom was a litmus test of religious sensibility, a perspective Lauder revealed when he announced his arrival in France, "the land of graven images."[97]

All travelers through France, Protestant and Catholic alike, saw and remarked on tangible evidence of religious conflict, specifically the wars of religion. A young Londoner, Francis Mortost, journeyed through France and Italy in 1658 and 1659. He brought with him two historical reference points that helped him organize his thoughts about his travels: the recent wars and the ancient Roman world. In France he recorded the history of particular churches by listing who had control of them and how they had fared during the wars. In each town, he detailed the history, power, and location of the Protestant community. The churches bore signs of the ravages of conflict. In Orleans, he observed that the church of St. Croix had been greatly damaged by the wars.[98] Montpelier's fine churches and convents lived only in reputation, likewise devastated by the conflicts.[99] Although similarly dismayed by the damages of the wars, the Catholic traveler Sir Charles Somerset had found more to admire in his travels in France in 1611–1612. He described the relics he saw at great length, particularly in Paris at St. Denis; he saw ceremonies a Protestant would not, including a service for a young woman entering a Carmelite order; and in Paris he also went to see an anchoret (those hermits who sealed themselves into rooms attached to churches) who had been entombed for two years.[100]

Rome exposed religious differences even more vividly than France. When the Protestants Henry and Alexander Erskine visited Rome in 1619, they spent twenty-two days seeing the major sights, "as also the abominations of that place," which, their tutor assured their father, "confirmit" the boys "in that only treuth professed by the reformit church."[101] Travel hardened the anti-Catholicism of many ardent Protestant travelers. William Lithgow's time in the Netherlands revealed to him "the tyranny of the Spaniards dayly executed upon the distressed Protestants of Wiesel, over whom they domineered like Divells."[102] John Wray saw all the sights of Rome in 1606, but disapproved of the elaborate processions he witnessed during Holy Week. His insulting reference to the pope as "His Pope-shippe" succinctly conveyed his attitude toward the church and its head.[103] Mortost wrote of Rome in 1658 that it was a famous city "much renowned for those rare antiquityes yt are here to be seene more then in any other place," but made no reference to Rome as an important religious center.[104] Contrast this description with that of Somerset, a Catholic, who regarded every foot of Rome as "holie," washed with the blood of the martyrs. If the city had been under Roman rule the "seate of Infidelitie," for Somerset it was in 1611 "the seate of true religion."[105] And English Catholics unaccustomed by the middle of the seventeenth century to the public ritual life of the church marveled at what they saw. One anonymous observer of self-flagellating penitents in 1661–1662 thought their actions "disgustfull," and equally distasteful was the blood that spattered the faces of spectators. But his presence at Holy Week services in Rome enabled him to kiss the Pope's toe, an honor he had missed at Candlemas. If the Protestant Reformation, even in its gentler English guise, stripped the Reformed churches of much of the physicality of Catholic ritual, travelers outside of England could nonetheless taste, smell, feel, see, and hear that rich ritual world for themselves.[106]

As Somerset's characterization of Rome indicates, for Catholic travelers, a journey to Italy had special meaning. Lady Whetenall made her journey to Rome in a jubilee year. When she visited the Vatican library, she saw manuscripts that would be of particular interest to her. The librarians proudly displayed Henry VIII's defense of the Catholic church against Martin Luther. They also showed her letters from Henry VIII to Anne Boleyn in both English and French, "both nought being amorus letters," her companion reported, "yet her lad[yshi]p redd some of them that shee might see, and beare wittnesse, from what a sordid source the schisme of england came & our miseries now doe follow."[107] Sir William Karr, a Protestant traveler from Ireland, had seen the same items on display when he visited the Vatican's "famous librarye" in 1625.[108] For Lady Whetenall, these documents provided the historical roots of her faith's ordeal in England; for Karr, they were simply historical artifacts. Lady Whetenall also extracted important lessons about what she identified as "the unitie and universalitie of the catholike religion" in Rome when she saw Catholics of all nations, "Italians English french spanierds germans polacks duch hungarians grecians armenians" all worshiping in the same faith.[109]

Protestant travelers toured Catholic sights with skepticism. One Catholic traveler explicitly addressed this Protestant suspicion. Richard Lassels related the story of Mary's house where the annunciation took place, now located in Loreto (on the Adriatic coast) and brought there by the hands of angels, first from Nazareth to Dalmatia and then to Italy. Protestants did not believe this story, he wrote, but Catholics found to the contrary that nothing was impossible.[110] Indeed, doubt permeated the Protestant John Wray's version of the same story.[111] However inspiring sacred sites were, numerous competing claims (to the sites of the crucifixion or of the Last Supper) reminded travelers to trust nobody. As a consequence of the multiple sites he saw, the cleric William Biddulph devised a policy to help him sift inconsistent information. He divided the sights of Jerusalem into three categories: "apparent truths," "manifest untruths," "things doubtful." Only those events supported by reason or scripture were manifest truths.[112] Moryson believed that the special challenges Protestant travelers faced, particularly at the turn of the seventeenth century when he traveled, shaped their experiences, requiring of them a unique flexibility. He observed that the English were especially prone to adapt to local customs in food, law, language, and dress, unlike travelers from Germany or Italy. But he believed that this adaptability was in part the result of coercion: Protestants were forced to dissemble when they traveled among Catholics.[113] Continental travel inspired and required new habits of skepticism and new styles of accommodation.

National differences between Scots and English travelers were similarly exposed through their diverse experiences on the continent. Although united under a single monarch and although many features of their travels were shared, the Scots and English had their own distinct networks to support their travels. A common language was not a sufficient incentive for travelers to join together in their journeys. The sons of the Earl of Mar, Alexander and Henry Erskine, embarked in 1617 with their Scottish tutor and companion on travels that lasted over three years. Their finances were arranged through a Scottish captain, John Seton, who was based in Paris. Their social world centered around other Scots. When Henry wrote his father, he told him news both of Scots in their company and of those of whom he had heard reports.[114] These Scots supported each other. When the Lord of Pitmillie sickened and died while in Bourges, the Erskine brothers, their friend Lord Morton, and "all the rest of our contrey men" carried his body to Sancerre where he could be buried in the reformed religion.[115] They traveled in company with Scots, planning to go to Italy with three others, "al Scottis men."[116]

Isolated Scottish travelers conveyed a sense of elation when they met other Scots. Lithgow ran into a fellow Scot at Malta, to his "great contentment."[117] Another old friend, Mathew Douglas, met up with Lithgow at Messina, which was "exceeding comfortable," at least for Lithgow, who was moved to recite to Douglas a sonnet he had composed on Mt. Aetna.[118] In a dangerous moment in the Mediterranean the Englishman Sir Henry Blount announced he was a Scot, relying on ignorance about Scotland to enable him to travel safely, but the Scots travelers never reported such a masquerade.[119] They perceived no advantage in passing as English. Indeed, such a nationality could be perilous. One Scots ship was detained in Bilbao and all its goods confiscated precisely—its owners complained in 1608—because it was mistaken for an English vessel.[120]

If Bourges and Saumur were centers for Scots travelers, Anjou and Touraine played a comparable role for the English elite.[121] So did Blois, which one traveler remarked in 1648 was "full of English."[122] Travel in Europe provided ample opportunities for English men and women to reflect on English history and nationality, always refracted through personal and religious sensibilities. Lady Whetenall was interested in the history of Christianity in England, and attended particularly to the story of Marcus Aurelius's victory over the Marcomanni, news of which spread to Lucius, king of Britain, who grew interested in Christianity.[123] But travel in France also prompted some painful national sentiments, particularly at the Île de Rhé, a site of English failure in their efforts to support a Huguenot rebellion in France. One traveler in 1648 saw "(with shame and anger) ye colours wch were taken from us at ye ile of rye voyage hung up in ye church."[124] At the Île de Rhé ten years later, and thirty years after the actual event, Francis Mortost memorialized that same episode, commenting that this was the place "where so many English were slayne in ye tyme of ye Duke of Buckingham."[125]

Catholics and Protestants, Scots and English, had some qualitatively different experiences on the road, but there is insufficient evidence to speculate in any systematic way on the experience of women travelers in this period. While many women journeyed to the continent, particularly young Catholic women whose families sent them to study in convents, few journeyed as recreational travelers. Lady Whetenall was exceptional in this regard. Her voyage took place at her instigation: she persuaded her husband to permit it and to accompany her and her tutor, Richard Lassels. She was drawn to sights and stories that might be of unique interest to her as a woman, but she also experienced her travels as a Catholic whose journey to Rome was particularly urgent to her because it was a jubilee year.

Lassels recorded Lady Whetenall's travels in Italy in 1650, so we do not have her own impressions. She died on her journey, but before she became sick, she had requested an account of her travels to remind her of the things she had seen when she was finally back in England.[126] Lassels's record has a hagiographic quality (he was clearly fond of her and he wrote the account in part to comfort her grief-stricken husband), but it also offers hints of what Lady Whetenall herself found interesting on her travels. Lassels reported her favorite sights, or at least "the best things" that she saw.[127] "Shee was much taken," wrote Lassels of her trip to the Vatican, with the open gallery whose ceiling was painted by Raphael.[128] Lassels remarked frequently on the presence of English convents, which clearly were of particular interest to this Catholic gentlewoman who had herself been married (and likely educated) in the English convent in Louvain.[129] Lady Whetenall was also intrigued by stories of stalwart Catholic women: in his journal entry for Nieuport in Flanders, Lassels related the story of twelve Spanish women who were found among the dead, disguised in men's clothes and at the front of the army's ranks, after the battle fought there between the Spanish and the Dutch.[130] She disliked the thriftiness of the Doge at Venice, because he did not allow clean napkins for every meal.[131]

Lady Whetenall did have one experience unique to women travelers: she journeyed while she was pregnant. No travel manual covered this particular condition, although manuals had a great deal to say on the subject of maintaining health while traveling. In fact, no travel writer imagined a woman as his reader or imitator, and some, such as Fynes Moryson, advised specifically against women traveling. Lady Whetenall married her husband on September 5, 1649, and they set out on their travels six days later. She reached Rome for Lent and stayed, as almost all travelers did, through Easter. By the time she left Rome, she was "greate wth child," and so traveled by horse, rather than coach, which was regarded as less safe in her condition. In Padua, she fell ill and could not proceed. Her fever was all the more dangerous, Lassels recalled, because her pregnancy made doctors reluctant to treat her with the customary cure for a fever, bleeding. She gave birth to a stillborn child, and then died herself soon after, on July 6, 1650.[132] Dying in a Catholic country was a great fear of Protestant travelers, because of the danger of receiving the sacrament of extreme unction if they fell sick in Italy or Spain. This was obviously not a concern for Lady Whetenall.

Lady Whetenall's pregnancy, her interest in English convents, love of Raphael, and silent cheering for the women who fought for Spain, all attest to the deeply idiosyncratic and personal ways in which travelers experienced their journeys. They brought singular tastes and passions that guided the sights they saw and the destinations they pursued. The mathematician John Greaves traveled in the 1630s with his scientific instruments. He appreciated the historical context of the sights he saw, but he also liked to extract precise measurements. His commentary jumbled local lore and science, sacred myth and measured observations, all charmingly united in his account. In Lucca, he remarked on one miraculous hole (which he neglected to measure) "where a gamester sunk into the earth, for blaspheming and throwing a stone at our lady's picture."[133] At the church of Santa Croce in Rome he saw one of the nails of the cross and one of the thirty pieces of silver that betrayed Christ. Greaves described the size of the nail and estimated the weight of the coin. And as for the two thorns from the crown, they prompted him to digress into other thorns he had seen (and bought) in Egypt.[134] Dr. Edward Browne's professional interests as a surgeon revealed themselves periodically in his diary: he drew detailed diagrams of the curative baths he saw and described the process in detail.[135]

Charles Somerset, like many travelers, was a lover of music. His interests were broad and deep: today we would call him an ethnomusicologist. In Avignon he was struck by the variety of music he heard from the galley slaves there.[136] Dr. Browne conveyed his interest in music through the illustrations that decorate his diary. The cover has an image of a chest drum—an instrument Browne heard for the first time near Vienna—with details about how it was played.[137] In Budapest he heard a three-stringed instrument with a body like a large gourd called a "kimche" in Turkish, and he described in detail how the musician played it.[138] Lady Whetenall also delighted in music, and organized her visits to churches in Rome in order to hear music there. Lassels shared her passion, for of the nuns' beautiful music at Campo Marzio on St. Benedict's Day, Lassels wrote that it "was the onely thing next unto the jubily which made my journey up to rome a saveing journey."[139]

Whatever conventions shaped the outlines of travelers' observations, including those instructions in travel manuals about sights and conduct or the advice of other travelers, travelers ultimately had their own personal experiences, particularly in this period when what became formulaic conventions were only in the process of emerging. Travelers remarked on foreign practices in unique ways that reflected a range of cultural attitudes and assumptions. Howell urged travelers to be careful not to boast about England and believed that the English in particular suffered from this trait, tending "to undervalue and vilifie other Countreys."[140] The purpose of travel was emphatically not to solidify a sense of cultural superiority, or at least not to articulate such a conclusion. Travel, then, had the potential to dislodge people from unthinking loyalties or xenophobia.

One consequence of this process of detachment was that travelers displayed an ability to critique their own culture. Not all foreign customs put English practices, whether legal or familial, in a good light. Somerset and his near contemporary, Moryson, shared a fascination with laws governing inheritance: Somerset remarked on the partible inheritance practices of France, while Moryson railed against the injustice of primogeniture throughout his travels. Somerset was also interested in inheritance of wives and illegitimate children.[141] Both men were younger sons, frustrated by their inability to access their family estates, and their praise for foreign practices implicitly criticized English primogeniture. It was no accident that so many younger sons took the training and educations their fathers had provided for them, in lieu of real property, and joined Moryson and Somerset in voyages overseas. Travelers admired other customs as well. In the Holy Land, Lithgow observed the birth practices of the "savage women" on his way from Jerusalem to Cairo. They gave birth and went back to work on the third or fourth day. English travelers habitually commented—and complained—about the speedy post-natal recoveries of American and Irish women, taking women's ease in childbirth as an indication of their more "natural" state.[142] But Lithgow's analysis turned this interpretation on its head. He argued that the conduct of these women was in fact preferable to the practice of English women, who spent a month lying in, "putting their husbands to incompatible charges."[143] English views of strangers, especially of people who later became clearly located at the bottom of social and racial hierarchies, were not yet solidified. Praising Africans and deploring some Europeans in a passage cautioning travelers against prejudice, Thomas Palmer, who did not travel beyond Europe, admired Africans who regarded "bodily cleanliness and honestie a point of dutie."[144]

Those who traveled outside England brought back, as travelers always did, new technology, information, aesthetics, and diplomatic experience. They carted trunks laden with souvenirs—manuscripts, books, artifacts, weapons, and botanical specimens. Ships' holds carried live animals and occasionally dismantled ruins, all bound for private collections, university libraries, royal parks, and the cabinets of curiosity that were so popular across Europe. Travelers also returned to England with their diaries. Once home, travelers worked to demonstrate the public and political utility of their experiences in published and manuscript works. For example, in his unpublished manuscript, "Observations Regarding Trade," prepared for James I in 1620, John Keymer specifically credited his travels with his insights into how England's commercial prowess might be enlarged and secured: "I have diligently in my travells observed how ye countries heerein menconed doe growe potent…I thus mooved began to dyve into ye depth of theire pollices & cercumventinge practizes whereby they drayne & still covett to exhaust" England's own wealth. He surveyed trade practices in northern Europe, especially Denmark, France, and Amsterdam, and he remarked particularly on the influence his time in Bordeaux had on his understanding of trade.[145] In his observations and in his careful effort to turn travel into policy and profit, Keymer was exemplary. He embodied one of Palmer's instructions, that a traveler should "get knowledge for the bettering of himselfe and his Countrie."[146] No traveler was exempt from these obligations. Edwyn Sandys used his travels to write an extended essay on religious unity in *A Relation of the State of Religion and with what hopes and pollicies it hath beene framed, and is maintained in the severall states of these westerne parts of the world* (London, 1605). An ardent Protestant, Sandys returned from his continental travels unshaken in his core religious beliefs, certain of the errors of Catholicism and, adhering to the guidelines of Palmer's travel manual, he dutifully made his report for the improvement of Christendom.

The process of reviewing and editing travel writing showed the varied ways in which travelers came to terms with their experiences. Sometimes travelers used notes they kept during their travels to write more polished accounts later, which they shared with family and friends in manuscript or which they published ("as it is the manner of travellers") for the edification and entertainment of a wider public.[147] For these aspiring authors, the first challenge was to make sense of their notes. Moryson touched on this process when he described the year he spent living with his sister in Lincoln. He tried to organize his "confused and torne writings" from his travels but was distracted by a new job in Ireland.[148] As a result, Moryson's account (containing only a portion of his extensive manuscripts) appeared over two decades after his first travels.[149] Moryson was perhaps atypical in the length of the gap between return and publication, but delay itself was common, as travelers sifted through their notes and their memories and tried to determine how to shape their experiences for public consumption. Probably most travelers engaged in careful editing and even self-censorship. Henry Blount produced his account a year after his return to England; George Sandys's narrative was published about three years after his return. Thomas Herbert's account was printed after eight years, and only, he professed, at the urging of friends.[150] Some of these travel books went through multiple editions. Sandys's *Relation*, first published in 1615, went through five editions before 1641. Another popular published account was that of Blount, whose *Voyage into the Levant* enjoyed eight editions between 1636 and 1671. For sheer entertainment, few could rival Lithgow, who interspersed his narrative with his own verse. Five versions of Lithgow's travels were published between 1614 and 1640. Henry Timberlake's account of his travels to the Holy Land went through six editions between 1608 and 1631.

Review and revision often produced information that travelers added after the fact. Some sacrificed authority for entertainment, repeating stories that were specious and drawing on the accounts of other travelers, creating a travel canon with the publication of each original account. In the time-worn style of *The Canterbury Tales* and *The Decameron*, Thomas Herbert's method was characterized by his willingness to relate the stories told to him in his travels.[151] Thomas Coryate relied on published works, including a Latin book printed in Italy, to flesh out his descriptions of some Italian cities where he stayed only briefly.[152] John Wray similarly enhanced his manuscript account. Some of the material he added gave gravitas to his narrative, perhaps intended to please his father. He recited, for example, the sources of the French crown's revenue, and delineated the king's guard. Other information was more charmingly authentic, purely based on his own experiences: Wray described the effusive new friendship of a Frenchman, who would fawn all over a newcomer and talk incessantly unless his mouth were silenced "wth a Tenis-ball."[153]

One struggle for the travel writer and for the diarist who wrote simply for his own pleasure or to prod his memory later was to describe the foreign in ways that were comprehensible. In this period of the domestication of travel, a variety of indicators point to the increased familiarity of an English audience with the larger world. The numerous and popular publications about travel and the world were one measure. Another way in which travelers domesticated travel was in the frames of reference they employed. One traveler compared the buildings of the Palais Royale in Paris with those in Lincoln's Inn Fields in London; another likened the Via Appia in Rome to Edinburgh Street.[154] The Scot John Lauder observed that he saw a pole in Orleans as high as the tallest house in Edinburgh.[155] These comparisons, of which there are infinite examples in almost every travel record, point to how travelers made sense of their surroundings and made the foreign more familiar.

When English and Scots travelers cast farther afield for a simile to help English audiences understand their experiences, they often settled on the Irish—that most proximate and problematic, both familiar and foreign population. The exotic were found not only far from home, in India or Jerusalem or America, but right across the Irish Sea. Moryson, who went from his

European travels to Ireland, observed that "the Arabians" he encountered in the Holy Land "are not unlike the wild Irish, for they are subject to the great Turke, yet being poore and farre distant from his imperiall seat, they cannot be brought to due obedience, much lesse to abstaine from robberies."[156] Blount reached for an Irish comparison as well in his 1636 description of the mountain people he met while traveling toward Sofia with the Turkish army. They lived "like the wild Irish...upon spoyle."[157] While these points of comparison were common in published accounts, they appeared in manuscript diaries as well. Somerset observed during his travels in 1611–1612 that the headdress of women he saw in Dieppe was "in the manner much of the Irish rugg."[158] Making the exotic more familiar, even if only by comparison to a still foreign population, brought travel experiences from around the world into the more provincial worldview of English readers.

Publication enabled a traveler to legitimize his experiences in a number of ways, one of which was by inspiring others to follow his example. Such was one of the two explicit purposes for Coryate's account.[159] Moryson had a similar aim, combining entertainment with practical instructions for "unexperienced Travellers."[160] Although at its size his *Itinerary* was not something that a traveler could easily transport, a traveler might fruitfully copy Moryson's practical advice. Because travel was a controversial enterprise, travelers, especially those who published their accounts, often labored to explain their actions. Moryson defended himself against critics stoutly when he proclaimed that "the fruit of travell is travell it selfe"[161] (see figure 1.2). Sir Henry Blount likewise asserted the importance of travel, and most especially of seeing people whose customs differed from those of the English. He resolved to go to Turkey and explained his desire to observe the religion and manners there, to satisfy his curiosity about the sects who lived under Turkish rule, to witness the army in action, and to see Cairo. And so his great travel adventure began.[162]

Most travelers did not publish their accounts. Most did not make a career out of traveling, either by identifying themselves as travelers in their public persona or by traveling abroad again. But the experience of educational travel nonetheless followed them home in a variety of ways. Commerce, diplomacy, the church, politics, all were shaped by the men who returned to England with languages acquired overseas and new ways of thinking about the world and their place in it. Such was the logic that justified educational travel, and such was the response of these privileged men. Because travel was undertaken most often by young men of considerable financial and familial resources, it is not surprising that so many ended up with positions of political power: their birth destined them to such careers. But so did their travels prepare many of them for these occupations.

While many of the travelers profiled here wrote anonymous accounts, those who can be tracked attest to the varied avenues of public service these the fight and knowledge of ftrange , and vnfrequented kingdomes, fuch is the inftinct of his naturall affection. Nauigation hath often vnited the bodies of Realmes together, but trauell hath done much more; for firft to the Actor it giueth the impreffion of vnderftanding , experience, patience, and an infinite treafure, of vnexprimable vertues : fecondly, it vnfoldeth to the world, the gouernment of States, the authority and difpofition of Kings and Princes; the fecrets, manners, cuftomes, and Religions of all Nations and People. And laftly, bringeth fatisfaction to the home-dwelling man, of thefe things, he would haue feene, and could not attempt. Trauell hath beene in more requeft amongft the Ancients, then it is now with vs in the latter Age. Philofophers, Poets, Hiftoriographers, and learned Diuines, how they haue perigrinated to know the life of States, and the fafhions of farre Countries, would be an endles taske for me briefly to relate. Many (I confeffe) long to fee the remoteft Regions of the earth , but dare not vndertake the dangers of fight , the chargeable expences of a tributary iourney , the hard indurance of flint ftones, for a foft feather bed, the extremities of thirft, nor the parching heat of the Sun, hunger in the belly, nor the moift diftilling dew to be a humide couerlet to their tender skinne, with innumerable other infuing miferies. But *Ixion*-like, miftaking *Iuno*, would by a meere imagination, runne out the fleeping courfe of an endleffe peregrination. For my part, what I haue reaped, is by a deare bought knowledge, as it were, a fmall contentment, in a neuer contenting fubiect, a bitter pleafant taft, of a fweete-feafoned fowre, and all in all, what I found was more then ordinary reioycing, in an extraordinary forrow of delights.

But now to leaue the contemplation of attempts, I

D come

Figure 1.2. At least one reader seemed interested in the ways in which travelers talked about the value of their experiences. William Lithgow offered a defense of travel in *The Totall Discourse, of the Rare Adventures, and Painefull Peregrinations of long nineteene Yeares Travayles* (London, 1632), p. 9. In the margins of one of the Folger Shakespeare Library copies, a penciled note in a seventeenth-century hand remarked "the use of travell." By permission of The Folger Shakespeare Library.

men pursued. Many had careers that took them abroad again. The travel writer Howell had further continental adventures after his return from his travels in the 1610s. He was sent to Spain to recover an English ship that had been seized there, and nine years later he went as a secretary to the ambassador to the king of Denmark.[163] The laconic Alexander Erskine later represented his father's interests on the continent. In 1623, two-and-one-half years after he returned from his travels, a more mature Alexander Erskine wrote his father from the Hague, arranging financing and reporting on the Prince of Orange's activities.[164] Robert Southwell's first trip overseas was the one that produced the commonplace book cited previously: he became a career diplomat, first appointed in 1665 as the envoy to Portugal. Travel to the continent, moreover, prepared men for subsequent ventures much farther from home. Moryson, Blount, Greaves, Browne, Coryate, and Lithgow all started with educational trips in western Europe before the journeys that took them to Greece, Turkey, Egypt, Persia, or India. Henry Timberlake was active in the East India Company. George Sandys was deeply involved in colonial affairs for both the Virginia and Somers Island Companies, and lived in Virginia. Even a short trip to the European continent was enough to instill curiosity for more distant adventures, an indispensable attitude in this crucial period of English global expansion.

Others turned their attention to affairs at home, as indeed the travel manuals anticipated they would do: Howell in fact recommended in his *Instructions* that a young man should settle down to the study of the law after his travels.[165] Wray served in Parliament; Lauder was a Member of Parliament in Scotland; Thomas Herbert was a close servant of Charles I and was rewarded with a baronetcy. Fynes Moryson took a position with the English colonial regime in Ireland. George and Edwyn Sandys worked for the Virginia Company. William Karr (or Kerr), the Earl of Lothian, was involved in politics, as was Walter Scott, the Earl of Tarras. At the center of domestic politics in England and Scotland and in some colonial ventures were men who had traveled abroad, rubbing shoulders with those who had never gone far from home.

Were these people unusual or atypical in their willingness to expose themselves to foreigners and their practices? To some extent some of these wanderers, especially those who traveled solely for pleasure, were eager to experience a world unfamiliar to them. Moryson, for example, wrote that he believed "variety to be the most pleasing thing in the World…Such is the delight of visiting forraigne Countreys, charming all our sences with most sweet variety." Moryson went so far as to esteem nomads the happiest people of all for their frequent change of habitat.[166] This was in fact an astonishing perspective at a time when English colonial theory, first articulated in Ireland in the late sixteenth century, justified the displacement of people who followed their herds rather than pursue settled agriculture. Other recreational travelers set out on their voyages with a similar enthusiasm to see and experience the most remote and unfamiliar people and places they could. Like Spens, they were "borne to travell." Blount elaborated on this perspective. He explained his journey to Turkey in such a way, remarking that he had already spent time in Italy, France, and Spain, and these were all Christian countries that "did but represent in a severall dresse, the effect of what I knew before." Devout Protestants might have disputed his assessment of these Catholic kingdoms, yet Blount thought it did him little benefit to see familiar sites "with little acquist of new."[167] But the educational travelers, the young men profiled here, went to Europe largely because it was a crucial part of their education. They were not necessarily predisposed to any unusual cultural openness.

In 1617, when Joseph Hall tried to conjure up remote and improbable destinations to reveal the lunacy of letting travelers indulge their curiosity by going anywhere they liked, he named Mecca and the stables of the Mughal emperor in addition to the library of the moon. Must a traveler go to Jerusalem or Ajmer or Bengal just because that is his whim, Hall queried?[168] But over the course of the seventeenth century, English travelers made it to Mecca, and English traders brought the world and commodities of India home to England. If the moon still remained out of reach, the remote became pedestrian, the improbable and impossible became ordinary. The English went abroad, and the foreign came home to England.

By the time the play *The Antipodes* was performed in 1638, travel itself had become common enough that the play sought to temper the public fascination with the marvels and wonders of the foreign world.[169] *The Antipodes* contained the theatre's first "travel snob," the traveler who sneered at journeys within Europe in favor of more remote destinations.[170] It is easy to imagine the type of traveler the play mocked. Consider Lithgow's opinion on the four greatest cities of the world: Fez, Cairo, Aleppo, and Istanbul. Paris, London, Naples, all large European cities, did not make his list in favor of these more remote places.[171] Thomas Penson, whose travels in 1690 set him well outside this period in which travel became more common and familiar, was able to set his own reflections on his travels in the context of those who had gone before. Invoking the image of the travel snob, he did not want to be "one of those fooles who praise and admire all things they se because they are forreigne."[172]

As travel became more common, tourists' trips became more formulaic, and a travel canon shaped one's tours and expectations. Everyone who reached Naples, for example, marveled in virtually identical language at a grotto nearby. It emitted air so poisonous that tourists purchased dogs from heartless vendors to watch the beasts faint in the close air.[173] Published accounts by European travelers led novice tourists to count on expected sights, whether the wondrous egg hatchery in Cairo or the cheapest tailor in Paris.[174] Greaves's fascination with the hatchery led to the publication of

"The Manner of Hatching Chicken at Cario, observ'd by Mr. John Greaves" some forty years later.[175] By 1674, John Covel was able to enhance his enjoyment of Istanbul with a little handwritten pamphlet (not in his writing) that provided a guide to the city. It identified the main sights and told the traveler what was on each hill.[176]

The cost of such travel-facilitating texts, however, was a loss of the sense of discovery that earlier travelers had experienced. Travel became such a common enterprise that a father could reject the exhortations of early-seventeenth-century travel manuals for careful record-keeping. By 1663, one father whose son was heading abroad sought to temper the addiction to the travel diary. He urged his son to note remarkable occurrences and "the customs & manners of the peopel" and to write all this down in a "day booke." But he commanded his son not to be a slave to the daily regimen of writing. "Som days," he remarked, there would be nothing important to record, "and for the most part little but what you may read observed in print already."[177] Personal experience could only replicate, not elaborate on or alter, readily available texts. Travel had become so common that authors no longer bothered to justify it either in published manuals or in their own travel accounts.[178]

The most vivid indicator of travel's common acceptance was the rise of the "Grand Tour," that ritualized stay by elite British men in Italy without which no gentleman's education was considered complete.[179] Long appreciated as a phenomenon of the eighteenth century, the Grand Tour emerged with the travel writer and priest Richard Lassels, in his instructive *Voyage of Italy* in 1670. His Catholicism was not irrelevant to the power of his argument. While Protestant English travelers had long been interested in Italian travel, their journeys there were always challenged at times of political and accompanying religious conflicts. As a priest, Lassels had traveled Italy easily, able to see all of its religious sights and treasures. His advocacy of Italy as the important site for English travel emerged from his personal experience, but also built on the extensive experience the English had gained in the country by the middle of the seventeenth century. Lassels praised foreign travel for its importance in political training for young men. But it is clear that by the middle of the seventeenth century, travel had *already* emerged as a normal part of the education of the young gentleman: Lassels's comment did not recommend new policies but rather reflected current practice, as he indeed would know, based on his own travels, including his voyage with Lady Whetenall. Young men, both English and Scottish, in the first decades of the seventeenth century followed shared conventions in their scheduled travels and in their places of residence for language study. They learned new languages, they studied law, they mastered different national styles of sociability, and they took home with them not only their new knowledge of Europe but also their avid curiosity in the world beyond the shores of their island kingdoms.

2

The Mediterranean Origins of the British Empire

When medieval Christian cartographers mapped their known world, they placed Jerusalem at its center. On the farthest fringes of Europe, tucked at the bottom margin of the page (east was at the top in such projections), lay the small kingdom of England. These maps reflected a Christian worldview that placed the faith's most sacred site at the center of the universe. But the map's focal point in the eastern Mediterranean was not only the heart of Christendom, but also the international marketplace of the old world. Caravans journeyed west on the silk road bearing precious spices and silks; traders and their encumbered camels made a still more perilous and parched journey north across the Sahara desert with gold, ivory, salt, pepper, and slaves. All gathered in the Mediterranean. There, in markets scattered on coasts and islands, from Venice to Chios to Cairo to Istanbul to Tunis, merchants exchanged their wares. Goods bound for western Europe converged in Venice. The region monopolized long-distance European trade even in the wake of American discoveries and new sea routes to Asia. England's efforts to gain power in Europe and to engage in commerce around the world hinged on successful intervention closer to home in the Mediterranean, and the English accomplished this difficult task over the course of the seventeenth century. It was in the Mediterranean that the English acquired their first significant experience with large-scale, long-distance trade in an alien and inhospitable environment. The crucial skills learned there anchored and shaped subsequent English enterprises around the world.

The sixteenth century witnessed fluctuating power relations among the existing and emerging empires of the world, and the Mediterranean contained a microcosm of some of these volatile dynamics (see figure 2.1). The

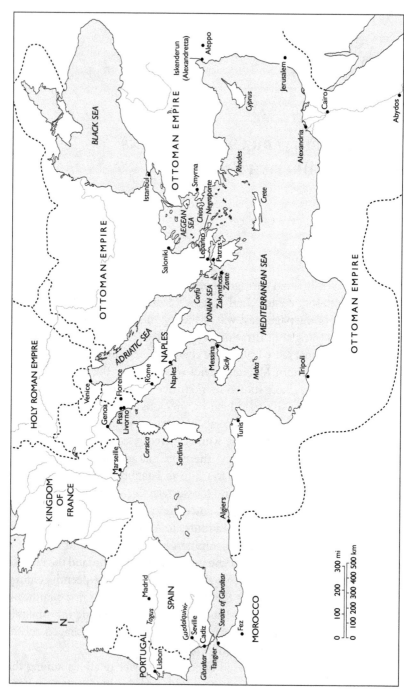

Figure 2.1. The Mediterranean

region contained portions of two major empires, the Habsburg Empire to the west in the Iberian peninsula and southern Italy, and the Ottoman Empire, centered in Istanbul but with territory swaddling three-quarters of the sea, stretching across northern Africa to the Levant and all the way around to Greece and north into the Balkans. Both empires pursued expansionary policies in the region while simultaneously engaged elsewhere—the Habsburgs in central and south America, Asia, and northern Europe, and the Ottomans on their extensive land frontiers.

Jostling for position and command over trade routes were smaller states, including two Italian ones: Venice was on the wane after repeated defeats by the Ottomans, and Genoa, too, was displaced after 1566 when the Ottomans seized Chios. North Africa contained four independent Barbary states (Tunis, Algiers, Tripoli, and Morocco). Three of these states—Tripoli (1553), Algiers (1555), and Tunis (1575)—accepted Ottoman dominion, but Morocco remained independent and all four states tended to pursue their own often predatory interests in the region. Land-locked Florence had seized the coastal cities of Pisa in 1406 and Livorno in 1421, and the latter commercial center eventually surpassed Venice as a free port. By 1661, one admiring Englishman praised Livorno as the "warehous of the levant."[1] All states vied for control over trade routes and were joined by pirates, making the region not only a marketplace but also a war zone. This unsettled, bellicose world deterred English trade with the region. Although the English had initiated direct trade to the Levant as early as 1511, a final English voyage in 1552 in the wake of clear Ottoman ascendancy had signaled the end of English commercial aspirations at least for a while. By 1538, after defeat of a Venetian and Habsburg alliance, the Ottoman Empire securely dominated the eastern Mediterranean.

The great showdown between the two main aggressors in the region occurred in 1571 at the naval battle of Lepanto. The Spanish defeated the Ottomans in a gruesome encounter that left 30,000 Ottoman mariners and soldiers dead, their bloated corpses clogging the sea. Overextended in Europe and the Americas, however, the Habsburgs were unable to take advantage of the opportunity their victory promised. The Ottomans were weakened but not at all disabled, as subsequent territorial acquisitions indicated; the Spanish were distracted; and, far from signaling Habsburg dominion, the battle created a power vacuum that opened the Mediterranean to aggressive European rivals, especially the English, French, and Dutch. And so in the last quarter of the sixteenth century, the English made their way back to the eastern Mediterranean. The sea's western kingdoms in France, Spain, Portugal, and Italy were already familiar to English traders, who had opened consulates at Naples and Marseille by 1461 in order to trade directly with the region. It was the east that had remained out of reach during the tumultuous and dangerous decades of Venetian, Habsburg, and Ottoman rivalry, and those markets enticed the English to return. Western Mediterranean markets also contained large—and rapidly growing—populations of Catholics eager to consume fish on the many fast days their faith required them to observe. English access to North Atlantic fisheries positioned them to bring cod, easily dried, preserved, and transported, to this hungry market.

If religious obligations created markets of believers keen for fish in the west, religious conflicts provided another powerful impetus for English trade in the east: in 1570, the Pope excommunicated Elizabeth I. This action liberated Protestant English merchants from Catholic prohibitions on trade with Muslims and, combined with Ottoman demand for armaments in the 1570s for their wars with Persia, led to a propitious reciprocal interest, culminating in William Harborne's trip to Istanbul in 1578 to initiate formal relations.[2] Among the many valuable domestic raw materials the English could offer the Ottomans was tin, a crucial component in casting bronze artillery. They also traded lead, always useful for deadly projectiles and armaments. With these desirable commodities, the English secured trading privileges from the Turks in 1580. At the initiative of two London merchants, Edward Osborne and Richard Staper, Elizabeth I chartered the Turkey Merchants in 1581, and this small cadre, many already experienced in the Barbary trade, monopolized commerce until 1588, when their charter was not renewed. A larger commercial consortium called the Levant Company was subsequently chartered in 1592.[3] The Company prospered, becoming, along with the East India Company, one of England's most powerful and profitable overseas trading ventures. Soon the English permeated the region, moving inland from the coastal ports to places such as Aleppo reached primarily by caravan.[4]

Other English companies traded in the Mediterranean as well, including the Venice Company (which despite its name was focused on the eastern Mediterranean), chartered in 1583 and absorbed by the Levant Company in 1592, the Barbary Company, chartered in 1585, and the Spanish Company. By the middle of the seventeenth century, the English had a number of trading posts abroad, including Levant Company settlements in Istanbul (1583), Aleppo (by 1586), and Smyrna (by 1620) in the Ottoman Empire, Barbary Company posts, an English consul at Messina and at Zante (Zakynthos), another in Patras in the Morea (Greece), a consul stationed in Negroponte by the 1660s, as well as numerous small communities of English merchants in Cairo and Alexandria, in addition to older merchant houses in Lisbon, Seville, Venice, Livorno, Naples, and Marseilles.[5] All were served by a steady stream of English ships, which transported cloth, tin, lead, metalwares, herring, and cod. These vessels returned home laden with currants (although dismissed as "trash" berries by one Levant Company ambassador, they were very popular in England), indigo, oil, alum, Malmsey wine, and cotton wool, which was essential for England's growing textile industry in Lancashire. Numbering in the hundreds in any given year, these ships carried thousands of merchants, ministers, statesmen, and mariners, all participating in these revitalized trades. Recreational travelers who were also eager to take advantage of the relative safety of the period to visit the region's famous historical and biblical sights joined them. Even men in the Mediterranean on commercial affairs paused throughout their journeys to sightsee, and they composed accounts of their adventures. Competing with these formally licensed merchants were hundreds of private English traders, privateers, and pirates who engaged in the coastal carrying trade (transporting soldiers, slaves, and other goods) and traded arms directly with the Ottoman Empire, enraging European rivals. All of these English merchants and mariners competed not only with other newcomers to the region—especially the French and the Dutch—but also with long established traders, including Venetians, Genoese, Armenians, and Spanish.

Thanks to all of this vigorous and expanding commercial activity, the Mediterranean trade bolstered England's economy in the sixteenth and seventeenth centuries, not to be eclipsed until the eighteenth century by trade with America and the East Indies.[6] Yet it was far more than prosperity that the English found in the region. There they acquired two indispensable building blocks for long-distance commercial success: organizational skills and a habit of cultural accommodation. In this respect, the Mediterranean defined English global expansion in the same way that the region had fashioned the Spanish empire. The Christian Reconquest of the Iberian Peninsula, accompanied by Spanish occupation and colonization of conquered territories and the forcible conversion of Muslims, shaped subsequent Spanish invasions of America and, more importantly, influenced how the Spanish incorporated indigenous people into their polity, their nation, and their faith. Moreover, the sugar and slave plantation complex that emerged in the Atlantic world had important Mediterranean roots: it was in the Mediterranean that the Portuguese and Spanish first learned how to cultivate sugar with enslaved labor. The Mediterranean shaped English expansion as well, although in different ways. It gave them commercial expertise and, even more crucially, instructed them in the habits of cultural exchange and accommodation that were essential for surviving and thriving in an alien land.

The first important pragmatic advantage that the English gained from their earliest trade forays in the Mediterranean came from the experience merchants acquired through their work in the Levant Company. Merchants learned in the Mediterranean how to secure trade privileges from a powerful empire, and they mastered the challenges of organizing a complex and multifaceted trade over long distances. The East India Company subsequently acquired its leadership and much of its capital from the Levant Company, and experienced Levant traders applied their knowledge to later trade efforts in the Indian Ocean.[7]

The second important lesson the English acquired in the Mediterranean was how to persevere in an alien and dangerous land, and this lesson served them well in their subsequent ventures around the globe. Because the English lagged behind their competitors, William Harborne instructed the first English consul at Tripoli in 1583 to observe the French and Venetians closely and to imitate the French.[8] This advice pointed to the multiple challenges the English confronted as traders, not just in the Mediterranean but in other parts of the world, where they so often arrived late and last. They were also vulnerable as Christians and, especially, as Protestants: the English returned to the Mediterranean precisely at the moment that English and Spanish rivalries intensified, and these animosities were always exacerbated by religious differences. The English were generally less safe in the Christian kingdoms of the Mediterranean (which were universally Catholic) than they were in those governed by Muslim rulers, who may have afforded Christians fewer privileges than Muslims but did not prohibit religious practice.

When they started voyaging to the Mediterranean in large numbers, the English acquired for themselves valuable survival skills that derived from their position of weakness.[9] As travelers, ministers, ambassadors, mariners, and merchants insinuated themselves into new trading worlds, they mastered a commercial demeanor defined by its style of accommodation and dissimulation. In the Mediterranean, large numbers of English traders and tourists confronted for the first time a world they found alien and perplexing. From their vantage as outsiders, they remarked with interest on the status of other minority groups (Jews, Orthodox and Uniate Christians of all types, as well as ancient Christian sects). They also perceived the region as a place of exotic eroticism, from the homosocial world of the Knights of Malta to the cloistered worlds of the harem. They labored to assimilate this world into their existing familiar intellectual frameworks, but little could prepare them for the three main challenges the region posed: captivity, forced or voluntary conversion from Protestantism, and enslavement. Although the English had acquired extensive experience trading in the Baltic, for example, no trading partners there posed the challenges the English confronted in the Mediterranean, The Muscovy Company signaled that awareness when it recruited Sebastian Cabot from the Mediterranean in 1550 to train its merchants in crucial skills associated with the region: how to feign support, to lie, to dissemble, to get along in whatever way was necessary. In accommodating foreign norms, the English embraced a habit of dissimulation that enabled their overseas ventures to thrive.[10]

To be sure, when possible and expedient the English embraced a style of rule generated and sustained by violence. They were ultimately able to employ force in the Mediterranean to gain control over shipping: although their tenure at Tangier (from 1661 to 1684) was thwarted, the capture of Gibraltar in 1704 finally ushered in a new era of English dominance in the region, if only at the Straits. But such a path was not inevitable. Between 1580 and 1660, the English could not indulge in military aggression if they hoped to thrive in the region. Instead, they relied on the culture of trade, a style dictated by an acquisitive spirit inclined toward accommodation in order to extract the most advantageous terms of exchange. In India, in Japan, and elsewhere we find the English adhering to this Mediterranean model. And, indeed, we find it in America, where the English first ventured for purposes of trade, and where many of the first colonial leaders came with experience in the Levant. This Mediterranean model endured for generations in places where the English were a minority and where trade depended on local alliances, from the cold waters of Hudson Bay to West African trading ports.

A WORLD APART

Although the Mediterranean obviously encompassed a range of religions, people, cultures, and economies, from the Catholic kingdoms of southwestern Europe to the Muslim strongholds of the Ottoman Empire, this chapter treats the region in its entirety since that is how the English perceived and experienced it. And for the English, the Mediterranean included Lisbon: although the city faces the Atlantic, English travelers through the region associated it with the cultural and social norms and religious challenges of the Mediterranean. Anyone venturing from England to the eastern Mediterranean by sea looped first past Lisbon, through the Straits, and then traveled through the entire sea, stopping at coastal ports and islands along the way. The Levant Company cleric William Biddulph noted the growing unity of the region as early as 1609. If the voyage of Ulysses was once remarkable, nowadays "his travels would be counted nothing…for he travelled but betwixt Venice and Egypt which is now a common voyage."[11] The English clearly appreciated the differences between the Mediterranean's many polities, yet the region posed universal challenges to English Protestant travelers.

Travel within the Mediterranean had its own rhythm, its own calendar, its own peculiar and varied conveyances, its own cosmopolitan companions. Tourists there followed a distinct schedule. They tried to reach Rome or Jerusalem in time for Easter so that they could witness religious spectacles there during Christianity's biggest holy days. In 1606 John Wray dallied too long at Naples during Holy Week and had to make "the more hast to returne to Rome" by Easter.[12] While travel within western Europe was generally land and river based, men navigated the Mediterranean by water, and even there the means of conveyance was novel.[13] They journeyed on a range of ships, many on galleys manned by slaves. Some Turkish galleys could be enormous, carrying as many as 700 to 800 passengers, far eclipsing the largest English passenger ships that held at most 250 cramped people in voyages across the Atlantic.[14] They rode camels on caravans in the eastern Mediterranean, accompanied by Jews, soldiers, pilgrims, slaves (a category that the English employed loosely and broadly and that encompassed an enormous range of people and laborers), and other companions the English described vaguely as "Arabs" and "Bedouins." The merchant Henry Timberlake recorded his own entourage, including the "Moor" who had accompanied him through-out his pilgrimage to the Holy Land in 1601, and the "2 wild arabians with 2 dromedaries" he hired to take him to Cairo.[15] Of his uncomfortable camel conveyance, another pilgrim grumbled that "when I was mounted I wished my self down again."[16]

In adornment and companionship the region proved equally alien. Trav-elers in the Mediterranean changed into local garb to enhance both their comfort and their safety. In western Europe the English and Scots traveled with other people of their own nation, or occasionally with other north-ern European Protestants, but in the Mediterranean they acquired a diverse entourage. As George Sandys traveled the Holy Land, he enjoyed the com-pany of Italian, French, German, and Portuguese travelers. A Scots traveler headed to Jerusalem in 1656 accompanied by "jews egypians and greeks," whom he dismissed as no company at all.[17] Fynes Moryson and his brother ventured through the Mediterranean in the 1590s on a boat filled by people of all nations and faiths, including Italians, Turks, Persians, and even people he thought were Indians. All, he remarked, prayed privately, a prudent and diplomatic solution to the variety of rival faiths.[18] In Jerusalem, Protestant pilgrims stayed at special houses for European priests and pilgrims and consorted with Catholics. This was truly a world apart, with its unfamiliar conveyances and its diverse inhabitants highlighting the differences from northwestern Europe.

English and Scots travelers were overwhelmed by the urbanism of the Mediterranean and, in the Ottoman Empire, by the cosmopolitan nature of the cities they visited. Merchants set up trading posts in Istanbul and Smyrna, Madrid and Lisbon, Venice and Livorno. Some of the metropolises tourists visited were enormous. Istanbul, described by Fernand Braudel as an "urban monster," had a population of 700,000 at the end of the sixteenth century. Naples reached 280,000 by 1595. Henry Blount said of Cairo that it was "populous beyond all proportion." In 1600, London's population was approximately 200,000 (and growing fast, thanks to immigration from other parts of the kingdom). But other English ports from which these Mediterranean-bound travelers sailed were tiny in comparison. Bristol's population hovered around 12,000 at the turn of the century.[19]

The heterogeneity of these cities, especially in Ottoman territories, was even more bewildering to English newcomers than their size. Biddulph, a Levant Company chaplain, was struck by the people he described as Jews, Arabians, Moors, Greeks, Armenians, Turks, and others whom he saw at Aleppo in the early years of the seventeenth century.[20] Serving there some twenty years later, the chaplain Charles Robson observed traders of all countries (except Spain) and along with these international men were those "of all Religions."[21] George Sandys listed and described some of the populations he encountered in Cairo—"Moors, Turks, Negroes, Jewes, Coptics, Greeks, and Armenians."[22] The assiduous efforts of English observers to categorize the people they saw conveyed their desire to make sense of unfamiliar groups and also their inability to understand the heterogeneous nature of the Ottoman Empire, which was distinctive among all European powers in the period for the legal and economic privileges it extended to all its subjects. No population was barred from any profession. All religious groups were permitted to enforce their own religious laws on followers; there were no legal ghettos demarcating residential zones for minority populations. While the Ottoman Empire did not extend equality to all, it did organize its laws and mores around the reality of its diverse, multicultural, multireligious, polyglot population.[23]

The English turned their attention to the other marginal minorities of western European society. Wherever they went, English travelers remarked on Jewish populations. Since Jews had been expelled from England in 1290, most English had had no direct contact with Jewish people or practices. Their views of Jews varied depending on the status of the English and the relative privileges afforded Jews in different locales. In general, they demonstrated more sympathy for Jews in Catholic countries, where Jews suffered a range of legal and social penalties, than in the Ottoman Empire, where the privileges afforded Jews were the same as those given Christians. The exception to this pattern was in those Catholic jurisdictions (specifically Italian cities such as Rome and Venice, and the papal territory of Avignon) where Jews, but not Protestants, were allowed to worship freely. No monolithic anti-Semitism shaped English assessments; rather, responses ranged from compassion to jealous hostility.

In southwestern Europe, English travelers generally regarded Jews as oddities and often as objects of sympathy. From Lisbon, the English consul Hugh Lee reported with pity in March of 1609 that as many as sixty Jews had been taken by the Inquisition during Lent.[24] Their arrest was in anticipation of the great Easter *auto da fé* on April 12, at which, Lee reported, about seven people were burned. (*Auto da fé* is Portuguese for "act of faith," and the term described the public rituals of penitence orchestrated by the Inquisition, sometimes culminating in the execution of heretics.) It is little surprise that Lee soon reported that fear of the Inquisition encouraged Jews to leave.[25] Travelers visited synagogues and wandered through Jewish quarters. The trader Laurence Aldersley spoke respectfully of the Jews he saw in Venice in 1581, reporting that he found them "very devoute." He viewed their ritual of carrying the Books of Moses around the synagogue as comparable to Catholic rituals with the cross.[26] Francis Mortost visited the Jewish community in the papal territory of Avignon some eighty years later, where he sympathetically described the people as "very poore & much slighted by the Inhabitants." Like many travelers to Avignon, he remarked on the yellow hats Jews were required to wear.[27]

In the eastern Mediterranean, where both Jews and Christians occupied distinct minority positions within the Ottoman Empire, English hostility toward Jews expanded. There was no doubt that Jews still suffered legal disadvantages in the Ottoman Empire. George Sandys admired the "invincible patience" with which Jews in the Holy Land endured a life of "wrongs and contumelies."[28] Christians and Jews alike were vulnerable to violence on the street during times of Muslim festivals in Istanbul.[29] Those who traveled by caravan recorded the different tolls that voyagers paid. Muslims paid the least, and Jews the most. A Scottish traveler in 1656 noted that at one toll the Jews had to pay eighty-eight medines (small silver coins used in Egypt and the Ottoman Empire) and the Christians fifty-two medines. A few days later his Jewish companions had to pay thirty-eight medines to the Christian's thirty for their lodging. And Jews had to pay a special fee to enter Jerusalem, which he explained resulted from "their cruel usadg of our saviour."[30] For all his occasional sympathies, George Sandys was also critical of Jews: he did not like the singing, jumping, nodding, and weaving that he saw in their worship, and accused them of being liars.[31] When the English found themselves in conflict with Jews in court and over matters of trade, their sympathy soon evaporated. They relied on pernicious stereotypes to foster and justify their hostilities. One observer wrote that Jews were known as "fraudulent and false-hearted people."[32]

Thomas Roe, the English ambassador at Istanbul in the 1620s, complained to the English merchants of the difficulties he believed they faced in their dealings with Jewish merchants, "having had experience, that none of that Nation will give testimony, one against another." Roe resolved that all contracts with Jews or Muslims must be in writing. He urged the same policy, moreover, on all other "christian ambassadors" in the Levant.[33] But in the case of the Jewish merchants Roe was plagued by prejudices: he complained to the English merchants that he was "abused and affronted by a base Jewe with peremptory and saucy language before ye great Vizier." This "rascally Jewe" threatened Roe's status: it disturbed Roe that a Jewish merchant "should be countenanced against an Ambassador."[34] For all his suspicion and mistrust of the Jewish merchants, the interpreters who made English business possible in the Ottoman Empire were often Jewish, as in the case of one valued father and son pair who worked for Roe.[35] Moreover, English merchants in Ottoman cities hired Jewish prostitutes, or so Fynes Moryson reported from Aleppo in the 1590s.[36]

What fueled English antipathy toward Jews in the Ottoman Empire was the legal position of Christians there. Moryson admired the Ottoman courts for the way all men of any rank fell under their purview, but warned that Christians could not testify against Turks.[37] English and Scots travelers perceived themselves as always vulnerable to the whims and demands of others. William Lithgow observed that it was important to give janissaries whatever they wanted, because they would take it anyhow by force, especially goods of a Christian, whom they regarded as no "more than a dogge."[38] Janissaries were soldiers of Christian backgrounds who were taken as boys from their homes, converted to Islam, and served the Sultan as an enslaved soldier elite. As Lithgow's interpretation suggests, travelers often believed that attacks on them were connected to their weak legal position and their religious status. Still, there were some tangible indicators of low status. In Istanbul, the scientist John Greaves visited the Hagia Sophia in the 1630s and remarked on the gallery where Christians were permitted to stand—apart from the worshipers.[39] Their travels in the region gave the English experience living as outsiders, symbolized no more vividly than at the gate of Jerusalem, that most holy city that Christians could not enter without special permission.[40] It was a vivid contrast to the history of crusader victories, which might have provided another model for English interaction in the region. Instead, constant reminders of Christian weakness made this other model ultimately irrelevant. All Christians faced the more overt hazard George Sandys identified when he reported that a Christian within five miles of Mecca—which of course held a special place in Islam—would be killed.[41] In this context, the English regarded *any* privileges extended to Jews as an affront to their own fragile status.

Jews were only one of many unfamiliar religious populations that English and Scots Protestants confronted in their Mediterranean travels. In Egypt and the Holy Land travelers were likely to encounter a wide range of people who defined themselves as Christians, some of the Orthodox church, others of the Uniate church, still others regarded by Protestants as heretics. Their attitude toward these coreligionists generally suggested intellectual curiosity and respect. When possible, the English observed the rituals of other faiths.

In Thessaloniki in 1669, Dr. Edward Browne attended the christening of two Greek children.[42] A Scots traveler noted the Maronite Christians in Bethlehem; the Levant Company minister William Biddulph saw Maronites near Tripoli in a village he called Hatcheeth and conversed with a man he identified as the patriarch.[43] Biddulph rejoiced in the worship he witnessed. He heard services of the "ancient Christians called Zazarites" in Syriac, "both read and sung very reverently." He thought the English could learn from these people, who used set forms of prayers in their services. He also saw some Druze near Mt. Lebanon.[44] George Sandys detailed the customs of the Copts and Armenians he encountered in Egypt. The Copt he hired as an interpreter on his journey from Cairo to Jerusalem presumably offered him more information about the faith.[45] Sandys described "Ethiopian" forms of Christian worship in Jerusalem, including Nestorians reading scripture in the corner of the church.[46]

As they marveled at the multiplicity of Christian practices around them and at the ways in which these ancient practices brought them closer to the historical Jesus, so did they remark on the sexual practices they both observed and imagined. Travelers were interested in cloistered communities, polygamy, the harem, eunuchs, and homosexuality, and so, it seems, were their readers. One horrified and fascinated reader wrote in the margin of a prurient description of men pandering their wives in Sio, "an abomination."[47] What made these observations more than salacious entertainment was the political content of the commentary. Observers consistently connected sexual practices with political power and with population growth, and joined a condemnation of aberrant (to them) practices with a larger critique of the states within which such practices endured.

The sexual activity of women intrigued English travelers, although in most instances they were forced to conjecture wildly given the reclusive lives of many Mediterranean women. Of the women in Lisbon, one member of an English diplomatic entourage noted honestly in 1662, they were seldom seen in public.[48] The women in Algiers, another traveler reported in 1655, went about covered in white veils, "all covered to their eyes and nothing you shall see but eyes and eyebrowes."[49] More speculative still were tales about the Muslim women of Turkey, particularly those in the sultan's seraglio. William Lithgow dismissed the sultan's harem as his "cabine of leachery," but the truth was that male travelers from Britain had no real understanding of this cloistered world.[50] Such ignorance only fueled lascivious imaginations. One writer who lived at the English trading post in Istanbul in the 1620s or 1630s reported that the women of the seraglio were prohibited particularly problematic vegetables ("radishes, cucumbers, gourds, or such like meats") that might invite "beastly and unnatural uncleaness" unless they were sliced.[51] Women outside the seraglio were equally prone to libidinous impulses, according to the same author, who was convinced that the Turkish baths seduced all to carnal improprieties.[52] George Sandys agreed, noting the "unnaturall and filthie lust" of the baths.[53] English observers pondered the political meaning of polygamy. Conditioned by their own religious faith to reject the practice, travelers were nonetheless familiar with its importance in Old Testament households. Shedding any moralistic judgment, Blount believed that polygamy was politically pragmatic and helped account for the strength of the Ottoman Empire. He thought that polygamy contributed to population growth, "which is the foundation of all great empires."[54]

As Blount's observation indicates, travel turned some into amateur demographers. Sexual practices logically explained to some observers a small population. One traveler to Italy in 1661–1662 thought that this "most detestable custome" of homosexuality, which he understood to be pervasive in Italy, helped explain (as did the plague) the generally unpopulated nature of the countryside around Pistoia. That Naples was so populous was, he recorded in surprise, "a miracle in Italie."[55] Henry Timberlake believed that Christian fear of Turkish sexual depredations encouraged the early marriage of their children, as young as ten years old: only marriage could protect boys from the practice of pedophilia.[56]

For these English and Scots critics, it was an easy connection between homosexuality among adults and pedophilia. A Scot in the slave market at Cairo in 1656 remarked that a beautiful boy was worth as much as a girl because of the preference for men there for "hansom boyes wanting a beard."[57] While traveling in a caravan with a group of Ottoman troops headed for Poland, Blount described the sexual practices he heard of, taking particular note of the young boys who were attached to officers as "their serious loves."[58] Two men observed that sodomy was punished as a crime but paired such commentary with remarks about how pervasive the practice was. George Sandys said sodomy (for which eight pages were punished with drowning while he was in Istanbul) was "an ordinary crime, if esteemed a crime, in that nation."[59] On Malta Lithgow saw a Spanish soldier and a boy of Malta burned for sodomy, and reported that in the wake of this punishment, 100 "whoorish boys" fled to Sicily.[60]

The English were similarly fascinated by eunuchs. Blount interrogated one in Belgrade who threw Turkish children in a river as part of his "secret revenges" against the Turks for their "marr[ing] his game."[61] One Englishman in Istanbul in the 1630s believed that boys were willing participants in their castration, for otherwise "they would be in great danger of death" from the operation.[62] This attitude reflected a disconcerting but not atypical lack of sympathy for these men. Moryson dismissed their "black harts" because of their apostasy.[63] But for all the peculiarity of eunuchs, these castrated men formed one end of a spectrum of male homosocial groups that travelers encountered throughout the region. The Knights of Malta, for example, invariably inspired pages of description from every traveler who stopped among them in the Mediterranean.[64]

In their manuscript and published accounts of the Mediterranean—east and west, Catholic and Muslim—Scots and English visitors described it, as a place where all sorts of appetites could be satisfied and all sorts of domestic living and sexual arrangements were sanctioned, whether homo-social communities of men, women gathered under the protection of eunuchs but the sexual partners of a single man, or homosexual relations. All of these dynamics reinforced the connection between sexuality and commerce, since concubines could be purchased and eunuchs were generally victims of the slave trade, boys who were castrated because of the high price they would command in the marketplace. George Sandys considered wives in the Ottoman Empire as mere slaves, "for little difference is made betweene them."[65] The sexual commodification of people reached its nadir (or its apogee) in the slave markets, where one Englishman remarked that "lustful appetites" prompted some buyers to procure slaves.[66] Hiring prostitutes (which seems to have been common among Englishmen in Levant Company trading posts) did not provoke similar political or sociological commentary.

The English linked sexuality with religious practices and with political power. The two most powerful institutions in the region, the Catholic Church and the Ottoman state, could be diminished when attached to sexual practices that seemed to undermine their menacing authority. Edwyn Sandys made the connection explicit in *Europae Speculum* (1629), a text intended to survey the state of religion and to investigate the possibility of religious unity among Christians. Sandys provided an unrelenting attack on the "errors" of Catholicism. His disgust for the faith led him to dismiss Italy altogether. "The whole Countrey," he wrote, "is straungely overflowen and overborne with wickedness, with filthinesse of speech, with beastlinesse of actions; both Governours and Subjects, both priests and friers." People vied to outdo each other in turpitude. The pope, Sandys insisted, encouraged incestuous marriages and a criminal had only to call himself a mendicant to get away with any crime he wished.[67] As outsiders in Muslim and Catholic polities, penalized in legal status and unable to worship freely in Catholic nations, English Protestants called on time-honored ways to indict the sacred and civic structures around them, associating them with unnatural and perverse sexual practices, and thus bolstering their own moral position in a world in which they were vulnerable and marginal figures. But they made these critiques in writing, not publicly, and were normally politic and prudent in their dealings with the people of the Mediterranean.

MAKING SENSE OF THE MEDITERRANEAN

The eastern Mediterranean in particular occupied a complicated spot on an English voyager's conceptual map of the world. It was both apart from and within Christendom. The domination of Islam and the military power of the Ottoman Empire rendered this world alien and often frightening to Christians from western Europe. In many ways contemporary sources make clear the perceived opposition between Christendom and the world of the Ottoman Turks. To John Greaves, a scientist who traveled to Turkey, the differences were stark. "The condition of this Place," he reported in a letter from Istanbul in 1638, "requires a more speciall protection then yt of Chrdome being exposed to so many dangers."[68] And Levant Company traders planning to return to England demarcated the regions clearly when they spoke of "returning for Christendome."[69]

However replete with exotic, bewildering, and sometimes distasteful practices, the Mediterranean was not entirely unfamiliar to English newcomers. In a myriad of ways this world was knit firmly into a familiar context comprised of classical learning and scripture. Biblical knowledge made more geographically remote parts of the Mediterranean more familiar to some than Christian Europe. Few men and women in England knew much of Scandinavia or Poland or indeed many places outside their parish borders, but they knew the stories of the Old and New Testaments, the accounts of early Christian martyrs, the letters and ordeals of the apostles, all of whom inhabited the Mediterranean world. One minister conveyed this view of the special place the eastern Mediterranean occupied in Christian history when he wrote that Antioch was "the fort of Christendom."[70] The biblical sites of the western Mediterranean were enshrined in a child's religious education. Travelers through France or Italy might remark on a range of sights linked to biblical history: the cave where Mary Magdalene allegedly lived for thirty-three years near Marseille; and in Rome the drops of blood, the indentations in rocks, and the coliseums that attested to the spectacle of the bloody and grisly death of early Christian martyrdom. Yet, the well-read English Protestant traveler and trader, and even the non-literate mariner, recognized the historic and biblical importance of sights in the eastern Mediterranean.[71] Protestant pilgrims reached Jerusalem overcome by emotion, singing exuberant psalms in the case of the Scot William Lithgow, as if they were finally reunited with an old and sorely missed friend.[72]

For the most elite visitors, an intense study of the classics joined their familiarity with the Bible to prepare them to see and process places that fit into their expectations. Tourists and merchants alike collected souvenir stones at sites they believed to be Troy. They remarked on the harbor of

Rhodes and sought remnants of the Colossus; they saw the sites (often multiple and competing) of the crucifixion, the last supper, and the house of the good thief crucified with Christ; and they recited suitable classical verse as an homage to islands of mythical and historical importance.

The regular list of sites found in any traveler's account makes it clear that this region offered a secular pilgrimage to men trained rigorously in the classics. In the typical account, all these features got jumbled together: myth, history, sacred site, travelogue, ethnography. George Sandys provides abundant examples of such an eclectic and erudite approach, but one will suffice. He wrote of the island of St. Maura, formerly called Leucadia (and now Lefkada), which information took him to the story of Artemisia, and thence to tales of the sacrifices of Apollo, and finally on to the story of a city inhabited by Jews, who were welcomed by Bayezid II after their expulsion from Spain. But Sandys was not done after this excursion into history and myth, as he then launched into some verses by Sappho and Menander.[73] William Lithgow's colorful account of his own remarkable travels showed a similar collapsing of historical time, itself a common feature of travel in the Holy Land. Like Sandys, he moved seamlessly from the modern to the ancient, from the reported arrival of mutinous Christian slaves in Abydos to the story of Xerxes building a bridge over the strait (in 480 BC).[74]

Those whose memory was unreliable or who had not attended dutifully to their schoolmaster's lessons might still manage, as one traveler in Rome did, to speculate that the story he heard of a man fed to a lion in an amphitheatre "may bee ye bondslave androclus of whom I rememb to have read."[75] The less studious travelers tried to show what little learning they could command by dropping the ancient names of places, as one visitor did at Milan (or Mediolanum, he pointed out) and as others did at length in Tunis (near Carthage, the home of Queen Dido).[76] Where their education or preparation failed them, they relied on their companions or hired professional interpreters to assist them, but with varying results.[77] Henry Blount worked hard in Egypt to get information about a table of Isis he saw in Cairo and hoped to see more antiquities beyond the pyramids, including the spot where Moses parted the Red Sea, but had trouble finding out where the location might be.[78] The cleric Charles Robson was intrigued by some of the sights he saw on his way from Iskenderun to Aleppo, particularly the foundations of large cities and a church steeple, but the janissaries who provided protection for his journey could not tell him what these remains were.[79]

Such was the awe these ancient remains inspired that even adventurers paused to enjoy—and loot—the sights. Sir Kenelm Digby sailed the Mediterranean as a predator, one of the many unofficial traders who engaged in the coastal trade and challenged the Levant Company's monopoly. Digby was a privateer with permission to attack French ships, but sometimes he got distracted from his official mission and found occasion to launch attacks indiscriminately. Between fights, chases, and slaving raids in 1628, Digby rested at the sacred island of Delos, where he spent a day "in search of antiquities." A few days later, he occupied his men, trained as mariners and fighters, in carting away antiquities from Delos, "which they did with such eagernesse as though it had bin the earnestest businesse that they came out for." He kept 300 men hard at work dismantling, transporting, and loading what he believed to be a ruin of a temple of Apollo.[80]

Captivated by the world they were exposed to, some travelers engaged in laborious enterprises to translate the texts, engravings, and monuments they saw. They simultaneously engaged in acts of cultural translation, but their understanding was incomplete, their perceptions influenced by the conditioning impact of education, their views skewed by expectations. Clinging to the coast and to ports as they journeyed through the region by water, their understanding could be only superficial. The illustrations mariners and travelers included in their travel accounts emphasize this perspective from the water: surviving images show coastlines, views of port cities, with indications of good watering holes. Their coastal travels led them to quick and often critical judgments of a world transformed from the ancient one they had studied.

Those who admired classical Greece deplored the modern society they encountered. The traveler and travel writer James Howell remarked that Greece, formerly "the nource [nursery] of all speculative knowlege, as also of policy and prowesse, is now ore whelm'd with barbarisme and ignorance, with slavery and abjection of Spirit."[81] Lithgow agreed, finding the Greeks "wholly degenerate from their Auncestors in valour, vertue, and learning."[82] Even the language, the minister Charles Robson reported, was "degenerate from the true and ancient."[83] A Scots traveler in Egypt was similarly dismayed by the decline he saw in Alexandria, noting in particular a crumbling wall and the absence of any old buildings.[84] He reported at Gaza the evidence of the former glory of the place, embodied in the pillars and pieces of marble that lay in the streets.[85] Robson's perception of decay was fueled by his failure to find the "famous primitive Church" at Smyrna, where it was instead "all buried under the beastly new Turkish Smirna."[86]

Robson's critique of the new city matched his loathing of Ottoman power in general. He marveled at the riches of Syria, which he found "unhappy in nothing but the cursed Lords of it, the Turkes."[87] As a Levant Company chaplain, Robson had to learn to live in this polity he abhorred. Other observers indulged in similar critiques. George Sandys characterized the Ottoman Empire as a tyranny sustained by armies of slaves.[88]

Yet of course this complex and powerful empire was not dismissed so easily, and many English commentators found much to admire. Henry Blount believed that Turkish justice, "Severe, Speedy, and Arbitrary," was necessary in a polity of different people with no common interest.[89] He thought that the Turks were justified in their harsh rule because Egyptians were known to be "malicious, treacherous, effiminate, and therefore dangerous."[90] Sandys himself wrote that the current empire was "the greatest that is, or perhaps that ever was from the beginning."[91] Whatever the English might say about the decline of ancient powers, it was clear that a new power had emerged. References to cowardly and pitiful Turks were contradicted by the Ottoman Empire's hold on the region. Even in a century when the power of the empire began to wane, its strength—signaled in its geographic scope, its population, its urban and architectural wonders—remained evident. Thus in a special appendix published in 1650 containing "som directions for travelling into Turky and the Levant parts," James Howell proposed that "the Turks dominions" were "next to Christendome…[the] fittest to be known."[92]

CHALLENGES: CONVERSION, CAPTIVITY, AND ENSLAVEMENT

Their admiration for the sights of the region and their desire for commercial success did not make the English immune from the great perils of the sea. The Mediterranean remained hazardous because of a trifecta of captivity, conversion, and enslavement. In the Mediterranean, the English were a vulnerable minority, deprived of privileges both as Protestants in Catholic parts of the region and as Christians in those areas under Ottoman control. All who traveled by sea in the region, whether statesmen, tourists, mariners, or traders, were vulnerable to capture by pirates. Protestants endured an extra peril from the Inquisition, the ecclesiastical courts established by the Catholic church to identify and punish heretics and to enforce conformity. And the English feared the possibility of conversion to Islam or (for Protestants) to Catholicism. Dangers ebbed and flowed, with times of concentrated danger for Protestants in the Catholic southwest and with recurring hazards for Christians in the Ottoman world.

Protestants faced considerable risks in places controlled by the Habsburg crown (Spain, Portugal, and southern Italy) well into the seventeenth century. The frustrated tourist Fynes Moryson lamented in the late sixteenth century that wars made it impossible for him to visit Spain.[93] In times of conflict, an Englishman was in peril in an enemy's territory, but even in times of peace the Inquisition posed a threat to both life and livelihood.[94] In 1605 England signed a treaty with Spain ending some twenty years of warfare and granting more freedom to English merchants in Spanish territories. The English, for example, were supposed to be allowed to engage in some

Protestant worship. But even though the Pope himself had approved the treaty, as had the Spanish crown, the Inquisition chose to follow its own path of prosecution. English visitors and merchants who strayed outside very narrow parameters of conduct, or who neglected to exhibit proper reverence for public Catholic rituals, might find themselves interrogated by the Inquisition. Protestants who failed to raise their hats when the angelus was rung, or who ate meat on fast days, or who did not raise their hats when the host passed by in a street procession (a matter specifically addressed in the 1605 treaty) might be reported to the Inquisition.

In the first years of the seventeenth century, Pope Clement VIII shifted from a policy of terror to one of trying to draw converts to the faith, but people were still caught by the Inquisition, as the English merchant Hugh Gurgeny discovered in 1606 and the Scots traveler Lithgow did in 1621.[95] Twenty years later, English travelers and traders could move more freely in the region, but Howell still recommended that the casual traveler to Spain confine himself to Madrid, "for I know no other place secure enough for a Protestant Gentleman to live in" thanks to the safety provided by the presence of the English ambassador.[96] Because of the many hazards—physical, diplomatic, and spiritual—facing Englishmen in Spain, few visitors there had real freedom of movement, but rather remained under close scrutiny and supervision of English consuls and ambassadors.[97]

Although historians have tempered the old view of the Inquisition as an arm of terror by setting it in a larger context of Iberian jurisprudence, contemporary English travelers and merchants had no such perspective. To Protestants the Inquisition was already a court serving a religion identified with idolatry and operated by the minions of the antichrist. In fact, by the middle of the sixteenth century the Spanish Inquisition affected more foreign than Spanish Protestants, since the domestic population had been expunged. Although foreign traders generally secured privileges that enabled them to work freely, English mariners and merchants were often uniquely vulnerable because many had been baptized as Catholics during Queen Mary's reign (1653–1658), regardless of subsequent Protestant upbringings, and were considered fair game as heretics and apostates.[98] The horror of the possibility of torture and execution was greatly disproportionate to the number of English actually ensnared in the Inquisition, but those most likely to come into contact with Inquisition officials—mariners and merchants—were the people best equipped to carry news around Europe and back to England. The very nature of the Inquisition—its secrecy and celerity in seizing the accused, the hidden names of accusers, the failure to tell the accused their offenses—stood at odds with the English justice these sailors and traders might have experienced, either before a civil court or even the harsh but public justice found aboard a ship.

If only a few Englishmen (and the occasional Scot) found themselves entangled in the Inquisition, their stories, whether published or circulated informally, were spectacularly graphic and lurid. The English merchant Hugh Gurgeny, imprisoned by the Inquisition between 1606 and 1608, invoked precisely that pervasive childhood fear when he spoke in his own defense in Lisbon. His helpless frustration emerges from his lament: "It puts me beside myself that I should have been dragged into this dangerous abyss of Spain of which every boy in my own country has heard."[99] Lithgow recalled his close calls with "the hunting of these blood-sucking Inquisitors" when he was at Rome.[100] His luck ran out in Malaga, where he was imprisoned by the governor as a spy before being handed over to the Inquisition (see figure 2.2). For the English, the Inquisition rivaled the Jesuits in inspiring conspiracy theories, leading one consul in Lisbon to believe that the Inquisition was plotting to remove him from office.[101] Richard Hasleton, who endured five years of captivity in North Africa in the 1580s before falling into the hands of the Inquisition, recalled that he found the Christians who ran the Inquisition more cruel than the Turks.[102] This juxtaposition of Catholic cruelty and relative Muslim charity was a recurring theme of the period.

Southern Italy ultimately became such a common destination for English and Scottish recreational travelers that it was enshrined in the Grand Tour, the formulaic continental travels of the elite young man. But in this period, Rome and Naples remained dangerous, although precisely because of their danger, prestigious and desirable destinations.[103] Licenses from the English government for continental travel often specifically prohibited travel to Rome. Those who wished to venture there had to seek special amendments.[104] One hopeful tourist wrote in French to William Graham, the Earl of Strathern, for letters to help him in his planned trip to Italy in the spring of 1632. He possessed "an extreme desire" to see the country, and felt such an urgent need to visit that if something prevented his journey he would spend the rest of his days "in bitterness and sadness."[105]

Capture by the Inquisition raised a specter of helpless terror for Protestant Englishmen, who knew neither their offense nor the temporal nor corporal limits of their ordeal. In contrast, capture at sea by slavers and pirates followed a more familiar narrative, one known to mariners and part of popular culture, immortalized in English ballads and chapbooks, the cheap pamphlets marketed by peddlers.[106] Captivity was an enduring, endemic threat in the region. Pirates were not unique to the Mediterranean, of course. Voyagers found them at sea and encountered their bandit equivalents on land wherever they traveled. As one traveler remarked in 1661, Ostend in northern Europe was "peopled by piratts."[107] Yet pirates were a particular menace in the Mediterranean, a region shaped by a culture of piracy and ransom. Piracy intensified in the wake of the uncertain settlement after Lepanto,

Figure 2.2. This print, from *Rare and most wonderfull things which Edward Webbe hath seene and passed* [1592], f. D1r, illustrates the powerlessness Protestants often felt when confronted with Catholic officials. By permission of The Folger Shakespeare Library.

when no jurisdiction could claim dominance of the region and pirates joined licensed traders to benefit from the myriad opportunities of the sea and the vessels that traversed it. In their wake, pirates left stripped boats floating at sea like ghosts; in 1628 Kenelm Digby found one such vessel adrift with a cargo of two corpses inside.[108]

Pirates based in North Africa were the prime threat for most Mediterranean voyagers and residents. These predators were a diverse lot. One fleet of eighteen ships sailed from Algiers in 1600; thirteen of the captains were Christians, including one Englishman and one Welshman.[109] Of these, some, like the Englishman John Ward, converted to Islam.[110] Some of the English who embraced the slaving opportunities of the region were infamous among other Europeans in such ports as Algiers, Iskenderun, and Istanbul in the 1580s for their willingness to trade in Christian slaves.[111] Other men enjoyed the licensed piracy that was a crucial arm of the early modern state. English enthusiasm for piracy in the Mediterranean posed serious diplomatic and commercial challenges for legitimate English traders there, forcing English ambassadors and consuls to make formal apologies and concessions.[112] Insurance rates reflected the enhanced danger of the region. Dutch ships in 1634, for example, were insured for their voyages to the Barbary Coast at rates as much as four times higher than voyages to Danzig or Riga.[113]

One consequence of piracy, beyond the plunder of goods that increased financial losses to merchants, was the capture of passengers and mariners. The extent of Mediterranean captivity was considerable, equaling the Atlantic slave trade until the middle of the seventeenth century. The historian Robert C. Davis has estimated a total of between 1 and 1.25 million Christian European captives along the Barbary coast between 1530 and 1780. Some cities, such as Algiers, contained as many as 25,000 captives in any given year between 1580 and 1680, although only a fraction was English. In 1640, for example, 3,000 British captives languished in Algiers.[114] Captives provided important revenue to their captors, who included hundreds of European pirates, either from the funds raised for their ransom or because they could be sold as slaves or put to work. The regions of the most frequent pirate raids in Italy and Spain were encumbered by the burdens these "almost annual events of terror" imposed: their economies sagged under the onerous protection money and ransoms required to preempt raids and liberate captives, while expensive fortifications similarly diverted resources.[115] Towers remain to this day along Mediterranean coastlines where residents watched for raids.

When they voyaged to the Mediterranean, English traders and travelers threw themselves in harm's way. Although the degree of peril varied from year to year and from place to place, sailors, merchants, and travelers knew that an attack by pirates off North Africa could result in enslavement and labor in the galleys. Tales of narrow escapes and redemption were staples of Mediterranean travel accounts. In 1634 Blount traveled on a French ship from Egypt to Sicily that had already been taken twice by Turks but ransomed each time.[116] William Lithgow described this procedure some twenty years earlier. He traveled from Corfu on a Greek ship toward Zakynthos with forty-eight passengers. A Turkish galley appeared, and the passengers debated their options. Most wanted to surrender and arrange for their friends to pay their ransoms, but Lithgow, who held little hope that his distant friends could liberate him, pushed the shipmaster to fight, and a battle ensued. Lithgow's boat escaped thanks to a storm.[117]

The redemption of captives became a central occupation of English ambassadors and emissaries, whether in Lisbon, Algiers, or Istanbul. Formal diplomatic relations with rulers in the Mediterranean were always complicated by the need to wrest both trade privileges and English captives from local authorities. From the earliest English embassy to the Ottoman Empire, Elizabeth I requested the liberation of English captives held as galley slaves. Emissaries arranged prisoner swaps and purchased freedom. The numbers were considerable, as best they can be pieced together. The Royal Navy reported that 466 English and Scottish ships had been taken by corsairs between 1606 and 1609. The English consul in Lisbon wrote in 1615 that at least fifty English captives lingered in the Portuguese galleys, some for as long as five years. In 1623, the Levant Company ambassador in Istanbul devoted much of his energies to securing the release of Englishmen held as slaves by the pirates of Tunis and Algiers. He reckoned that in the space of the two years before he reached Istanbul in 1622, more than one hundred ships and 1,200 Englishmen (which would include mariners, merchants, and travelers) had been taken and enslaved. As many as 8,000 Englishmen, along with more than 400 ships, may have been taken by Barbary pirates between 1616 and 1642, of whom perhaps one-third were ultimately released. Many captives were liberated through formal diplomatic channels; still others were freed piecemeal by the private efforts of mariners in the region. John Weale reported from Algiers in 1655 that his ship "cleered" all of the "English and Irish slaves," and liberated some Dutch "slaves" as well.[118]

Flight from captivity was often prompted by the horrors of galley labor, which probably rivaled sugar production and mining as the most onerous, life-threatening work a man could perform. While Spanish and Italian institutions existed for the sole purpose of redeeming their own nationals, English efforts to rescue prisoners were more intermittent. It was probably this recognition of the English state's difficulty in liberating captives that prompted Henry Thornton, a trader in Aleppo, to bequeath 100 dollars "for redempton of poore captives" in 1640.[119] Still, prisoners were usually left to their own devices. One successful escape was reported in 1640 by twelve men who had been held at Algiers. They seized weapons and a boat and set out to sea, rowing toward Majorca for three days. Without food or drink, they prayed for deliverance, which miraculously appeared in the form of a turtle sleeping in the sea who unsuspectingly rested his head in the boat. The English ate the turtle raw, and the next day reached Majorca.[120]

Some Englishmen experienced multiple captivities in a variety of jurisdictions. The soldier and adventurer John Smith is certainly the best known of this group. While legendary for his American captivity by the Powhatan Indians and his alleged reprieve by the child Pocahontas in 1607, Smith had been held as a slave just a few years earlier in the Ottoman Empire. Smith remembered the humiliations and hardships of his enslavement years afterwards, recalling how he and his companions were sold "like beasts in a market-place," before he was purchased and marched off to Istanbul with a chain around his neck. An Ottoman Pocahontas, Charatza Tragabigzanda, tried to come to his rescue, sending Smith to her brother to learn "what it was to be a Turke" until she was old enough to determine her own future. (Smith's implication was that this woman had fallen in love with him.) Unfortunately, her brother abused Smith, shaving his hair, stripping his clothes, and putting Smith at the bottom of the pecking order, the "slave of slaves to them all." Smith finally escaped, finding comfort as he always claimed to do in the kindness of foreign women, and ultimately sanctuary in Transylvania, where the solace of friends rendered him "glutted with content, and neere drowned with joy."[121]

Far less fortunate was Edward Webbe, who was taken prisoner first in Russia (where he worked for the Muscovy Company) as an adolescent for five years. Ransomed, Webbe ultimately made his way to Alexandria as a master gunner, but his ship was seized by some Turkish galleys. Webbe's enslavement resumed, this time in the hands of Turks. He spent five years in the galleys, "wonderfully beaten & misused every day," manacled to his oar, and subsisting on black bread and "stinking water." Webbe was released from the galleys only by offering the Turks his skills as a gunner, which landed him in the midst of an attack on Persia. After his martial adventures, Webbe was returned to prison in Istanbul. There an attempted escape garnered him and his companions, all Christians, 700 blows each. The English ambassador, William Harborne, ultimately secured Webbe's release in 1588, along with twenty other Englishmen. Webbe took a peculiar route home to England, traveling through Italy where he was arrested as a spy. He finally returned to England briefly before continuing his military career in France in the service of Henry IV, vanishing from view after 1592.[122]

Most Englishmen were not enslaved, of course, yet travel in the Mediterranean gave them an intimate familiarity with the institution of slavery. Some traveled on galleys that were manned by captive or convict labor, a crew that might easily include captured English mariners or traders. Fourteen English prisoners were redeemed from the galleys in Lisbon in 1608, "delivered out of the inquisition in the Indies."[123] English travels were everywhere eased by people who occupied various dependent statuses that these foreign travelers associated with slavery. Domestic services were performed by such laborers, from diving to fetch mussels for dinner in Egypt to preparing food and clothes.[124] Throughout the Ottoman Empire, English travelers acquired janissaries to safeguard their voyages.[125]

In the Ottoman Empire, the association of Christians with the institution of slavery highlighted their degraded status. Fynes Moryson was mistaken for one such Christian captive in Istanbul in 1596 and a woman offered to buy him. Adding to the insult, the woman offered four times as much for the English ambassador's servant, and Moryson, who believed that a man of his status was certainly worth more than a servant, was quick to explain that he was in a weakened condition from a long illness.[126] One Christian tried to buy Sir Henry Blount in Bosnia.[127] William Lithgow feared being captured into slavery in Algiers, where he saw many Christian slaves, and he refused to go out in public unless he had several Christian slaves to guard him.[128]

Travelers and traders visited the large slave markets of the region. William Biddulph remarked with some disapproval that those markets sold people "as ordinarily as we doe cattle in England."[129] One Scot described the great market place in Cairo, where in 1656 he saw "all sort of comodties men woeman boyes and girles both black and whyt." He remarked on the prices each person commanded, and repeated what later became a central canard of English justifications of the slave trade, that parents sold their children and parted with them "wth all litle truble as we doe wth our horses."[130] In Istanbul the anonymous author (probably Robert Wither) of "A description of the Grand Seignor's seraglio" described the degrading experience of the slave market, where slaves' bodies were prodded and probed, while they were interrogated about their backgrounds and skills.[131]

The Mediterranean was the first region where large numbers of Englishmen acquired intimate experience with slavery, both as a condition that might befall them and as a status of the laborers who attended them. Many English merchants and mariners participated themselves in slaving voyages in the region. So it is no surprise that the first metaphors of enslavement that the English devised were those of being held by Turks like slaves. No critique of slavery emerged from this experience: Thomas Phelps came close in his *True Account* of his captivity (1685), but his intent was to call attention to the plight of other English captives, not to indict slavery itself.[132]

In fact, the first English critiques of slavery seem to have been derived from religious conviction, not from personal experience as captives. As early as 1634, a colonist on the English settlement of Providence Island in the western Caribbean argued that Christians should not keep slaves. Samuel Rushworth posed a real problem on the island, where slaves were a large portion of the population. His employers believed that his public attack on the institution made slaves "disaffected" to the Company's service and encouraged them to run away. The governor was ordered to take action against Rushworth, who was shipped home. Other religious radicals joined in their objections to the institution, and the North American colony of Rhode Island signaled this commitment in a 1652 act abolishing life-long slavery.[133]

Rushworth's was a lone voice in the English Caribbean protesting the institution, in a region where the English were just beginning to become slave traders and slaveholders. And the Rhode Island General Court's efforts to turn enslaved Africans into indentured servants proved shortlived. In the Mediterranean, the English who were confronted with slavery and captivity had already developed clear ideas about who should—and should not—endure this status. Their efforts to redeem English, Scots, Irish, or Dutch captives from their galley service signaled their disapproval of slavery for other Protestants or for those who were subjects of the English crown. Blount pondered this question in his 1636 account of his travels. He wondered if some might be born to be masters, while others were born to serve. He concluded that the people most likely born to command were the Turks.[134] In a few decades, the English would join rivals in their aggressive pursuit of the Atlantic slave trade, and sought in the Atlantic to achieve the right to command that Blount thought the Turks had won in the Mediterranean.

Intimately connected to captivity and enslavement was another hazard of the region, conversion. No polity in the Mediterranean supported English Protestantism, although some jurisdictions were less hostile than others, and everywhere travelers, especially the young, might be attracted to new faiths or converted by force. Thus travel manuals advised voyagers to be well instructed in their faith, lest they be "sun-burnt" in the "torrid Zone," where competing faiths might be found.[135] Yet many who traveled overseas were young and weak in their knowledge. Particularly vulnerable to conversion, all agreed, were those boys taken by the North African pirates and held as slaves or captives in Muslim regions. These children (some as young as ten, mostly adolescents) were indispensable on merchant ships, training as mariners and performing chores for officers, sailors, and passengers. Some were likely also children shipped overseas by their parents or masters to learn trade languages. While adults were permitted to retain their faith, captured boys were forced (the English understood) "to turne Turke."[136] A traveler in Tripoli in 1650 reported that the governor came to the English ship "and tooke a boy out of our boat and soe card hime a shoor and turnd turke" but acknowledged "the boy was willing before to goe."[137] The English were at times at a loss as to what to do with these boys. Efforts to recover English captives in Algiers in 1620 made provisions for all boys, both those who were Christian and those who had "turned turk and would revolt," to be sent aboard the English ship.[138] Religious rituals eased these converts back into Christian union.[139]

Although not forced to convert, adult captives faced powerful incentives to do so. Robert Adams told his father in 1625 that he was beaten every day to convert or to obtain his ransom.[140] Converts to Islam did not escape slavery, but could generally escape onerous service in the galleys. As many as four percent of all captives converted, and the newest captives were the most likely to do so.[141] One of the most celebrated and wellborn converts of the period was Sir Francis Verney, who by the age of twenty-four had squandered his ample inheritance and by 1608 left England for good. After a pilgrimage to the Holy Land, he joined the English pirate John Ward. In Tunis he converted to Islam. Piracy was always a perilous occupation, and Verney himself was captured at sea by a Sicilian galley and endured two years as a galley slave. He was redeemed by an English Jesuit on the promise that he convert to Catholicism, which he did, but he soon died in Messina in 1615. An English merchant brought home with him some of the eclectic souvenirs of Verney's multiple religious faiths, including a pilgrim's staff from his travels in the Holy Land, a turban, and a Turkish robe.[142]

Those who did convert were visible to visitors in the region. One man who traveled through the Mediterranean to Tripoli in 1650 socialized regularly with English converts (renegades, as he styled them) who came on board the ship. His first encounter with them was at his arrival on February 22, when the governor of Tripoli came on board ship "with 9 ore 10 of his runnagadoes with him." One "runnagada" from Kent came to dinner with the ship's master. Other converts, including an Irishman and an Englishman from Dover, came for meals, and stayed all night playing cards with the ship's master. On shore the author talked to a captive, a man from Dorset, and was able to buy him out of captivity, and the ship's company held a collection to raise funds to buy another captive his freedom.[143] Blount recorded his conversations with converts (not English, in this instance) in Turkey in 1634. He "did much converse" with them, thanks to their knowledge of Italian, and particularly inquired why they left their faith (or "fell off," in his term). "Generally I found them Atheists…these hate us not otherwise than in shew, unless where they find themselves abhorred for their Apostacy."[144] Familiarity with converts and some understanding of the circumstances of captivity which led to their conversion did not necessarily produce much sympathy for their situation. Evidence of the contempt with which they were regarded at least by some mariners can be seen in a fight aboard an English ship, when a bosun struck another man and insulted him, calling him "a ronagat roge."[145]

In England the head of state was also the head of the church. As a result, taking a new faith made the English traitors as well as apostates. When pressured by the Inquisitors in 1608, the English merchant Hugh Gurgeny explained that he could not convert to Catholicism because of the political and legal consequences at home.[146] To their peers, apostates were dangerous not only for their rejection of a faith indelibly associated with national identity, but also for their ability to tempt others down similar paths. So led was an Englishman named William Trednock. He was redeemed from captivity in Tunis, and during his ordeal apparently did not convert, resisting the many practical allures of Islam. Yet in Istanbul in 1650 he became acquainted with "an English Renegade," who persuaded Trednock to convert to Islam, an action that infuriated the English captain who had gone to the trouble of liberating him.[147] Trednock's subsequent absence from English records suggests he assimilated into his new Muslim world and separated himself from the English community in Turkey.

ADAPTATIONS: A MEDITERRANEAN SURVIVAL GUIDE

To weather the hazards of the Mediterranean, travelers and traders adopted very distinctive strategies, but these behaviors themselves required Englishmen to deny and subvert their religious and national affiliations. Travel accounts and traders' instructions were replete with practical advice for Christians and, specifically, for Protestants who needed to navigate their way through the region. A range of techniques could help ensure safety in threatening environments. It was, for example, important for visitors to avoid controversial subjects. Nothing was more controversial than religion, so Protestants generally sought to avoid the subject altogether. James Howell adjured Englishmen to "entertaine none at all touching Religion, unlesse it be with Silence."[148]

The English normally tried to maintain a low profile. In the first decade of the seventeenth century, William Biddulph emphasized the pragmatism of such a strategy for those who hoped to live in Turkey. He thought it was possible to live safely among the Turks as long as the foreigner did not interfere "with their Law, their women, nor their slaves."[149] Fynes Moryson demonstrated this eagerness to remain invisible when he adopted two contradictory strategies in Italy in the 1590s in his efforts to avoid Inquisition officials. He sought to escape detection as a Protestant when he was in Italy by moving frequently, not least because he was in Italy during Lent when his conduct might come under greater scrutiny.[150] He later opted to settle in San Casciano, near Florence.[151] William Lithgow hid in Rome for three days.[152]

In the 1620s, one English minister was so alarmed by the prospect of the Inquisition that, even though there was none at Livorno, he resolved it was unsafe to remain there, and traveled on to Pisa.[153]

At times more overt acts of deceit were necessary. Some Englishmen tried to pass as Catholic. One man studying in Italy left his lodging house each morning at the time of mass in order to let his landlord believe he was Catholic. Others attended mass, trying to mimic the actions of the worshippers around them. Moryson worked strenuously in his travels in Italy to acquire multiple national identities: he spoke German, Italian, and French. Rarely did he speak English. Once when he encountered another traveler in Italy who claimed to be Dutch, the two men tried to speak in Italian, French, and Dutch before it became clear that both were English. Moryson and the English merchant talked privately where no one could overhear them.[154] Henry Blount adopted a similarly deceitful strategy at one precarious moment in the Mediterranean when he announced that he was a Scot to an audience that knew nothing of Scotland but which associated Englishness with Protestantism.[155] In Catholic countries at times of conflict or diplomatic strain with England it was always advisable for the prudent Englishman to avoid detection, so in the 1590s Moryson dressed in "disguised poore habit," in addition to adopting another nationality.[156] Henry Timberlake advised pilgrims wishing entrance to Jerusalem to tell the Turks in charge that they were French, since he thought the Turks did not know who the English were.[157] Passing as Catholic could make life easier and safer for travelers. When asked by the Spanish mariners who navigated his felucca (a small sailing ship used in the eastern Mediterranean) if he were Lutheran, George Sandys prevaricated. He denied he was Lutheran (meaning he was no Protestant), which altered their conduct, for around Scylla, where he was, "they detest the English, & think us not Christians."[158] At a similarly dangerous moment during a voyage at sea in 1581, the trader Laurence Aldersey rejected the prevailing pattern of deceit and instead refused to kiss an image of Mary and claimed his faith proudly, but he was protected by two kindly friars.[159]

While English travelers endeavored to mislead those around them through their actions and their words, they relied as well on dress. The English minimized risks by adopting the garb of the place they traveled, both to avoid offending people and to blend in to their surroundings (see figure 2.3). Green was a sacred color to the Muslims of the Ottoman Empire. Both George Sandys and Moryson remarked on this sumptuary law and noted the consequences of non-compliance. In fact, Moryson's doublet was lined with green fabric, but since he wore it during his entire time in Turkey, no one saw the lining and he did not encounter any legal difficulty for his sartorial choice—although the stench of the well-worn garment must have caused

Loe here's mine Effigie, *and* Turkish *suite* ;
My Staffe, *my* Shaffe, *as I did* Asia *foote* :
Plac'd in old Ilium ; Priams *Scepter thralles*:
The Grecian *Campe defign'd* ; *loft* Dardan *falles*
Gird'd with fmall Simois : Idaes *tops, a Gate* ;
Two fatall Tombes, *an* Eagle, *fackt* Troyes *State.*

Figure 2.3. William Lithgow in his Turkish costume. William Lithgow, *The Totall Discourse, of the Rare Adventures, and Painefull Peregrinations of long nineteene Yeares Travayles* (London, 1632). This item is reproduced by permission of The Henry E. Huntington Library, San Marino, California.

discomfort to those around him. Another less fortunate European was beaten, reported the English ambassador, for wearing green shoestrings.[160]

In the Ottoman Empire, Moryson tried to avoid any challenges by wearing correct clothes, European clothes being offensive to Turks. So he and his brother purchased long coats and gowns from a Flemish merchant in Venice before journeying east.[161] Sir Henry Blount similarly followed the advice of the travel manuals and changed his clothing to ease his travels, dressing primarily in Turkish garb and remarking particularly when in his words he "shifted into Christian habit."[162] He blended in so adeptly that he was arrested in Rhodes as a spy.[163] Like all other travelers in the Holy Land, George Sandys and his party dressed as pilgrims, donning what the trader Timberlake referred to as his "pilgrimes weeds" for their voyage from Cairo to Jersualem.[164] In their willingness to accommodate local preferences, these travelers emulated the habits of the European ambassadors Moryson saw in Istanbul. The English, French, and Venetian ambassadors wore the clothing of their own countries indoors, but when they ventured out, they put on Turkish clothes.[165]

In their conduct the English similarly tried to accommodate themselves to local mores and to local expectations for the behavior of a subservient population. The prudent Englishman was prepared to prostrate himself to stave off violence. In Egypt George Sandys and his companions were "abused by a beggerly Moore," but fled to another man who seemed "of good sort." They won his favor by kissing his gown: he protected the Englishmen, but they were later berated by the "beggarly Moore," who amused onlookers by attacking the Christian travelers as "dogs and Infidels."[166] Within the Ottoman Empire, Christians suffered legal disadvantages and always had to be prepared to defer to Ottoman officials. Moryson particularly warned that Christians in Turkey could not carry a sword, should not quarrel, and should avoid looking a Turk in the face lest they invite a beating.[167] Never, warned William Biddulph, should one strike a blow, no matter the provocation.[168] Visitors reported with lurid fascination the gruesome torments awaiting malefactors wherever they traveled, with the tortured bodies of criminals offering tangible reminders of the need to stay out of view. Moryson remarked on many of the hazards greeting travelers, having experienced several himself. Near Jerusalem, his party encountered an Ottoman horsemen who, seeing Moryson and his brother, wheeled his mount about and inquired of Moryson's janissary, "why doe not these dogges light on foot to honour mee as I passe"? Moryson and his brother quickly "tumbled" off their mounts and bowed in a suitably respectful manner. Moryson praised the prudence of this conduct, "for woe be to that Christian who resists any Turke."[169] Likewise, Henry Blount, donned in Turkish clothes, was accosted by four riders in the Ottoman Empire who suspected he was Christian. Their clue was his head, Blount reported—whether his hairstyle or his covering. Only Blount's submissive manner—his smiling face, his gentle voice, his obeisance—saved him from the violence an Italian merchant experienced when he had two of his ribs broken.[170]

As these tales suggest, Englishmen in the Mediterranean had to be prepared to swallow their pride to save their lives and their goods. What is striking about these accounts is the authors' willingness to accommodate local norms. Obviously practical considerations of personal security governed much of this conduct, but even this real threat was, apparently, not a sufficient explanation for men who denied their nationality and disguised their religion (especially problematic for the English, with their national church turning apostates into traitors). Henry Blount addressed precisely this concern when he justified declaring that he was a Scot in order to ensure his safety by denying it was "any quitting of my Countrey, but rather a retreat from one corner [England] to the other [Scotland]," a reference to the common king who ruled both countries after 1603.[171]

Travelers and traders in the Mediterranean (at least those who recorded and especially those who published their thoughts) were sometimes forced to justify their behavior when they seemed to place safety and convenience ahead of faith and nation. Moryson, who lived in a monastery while he saw the sights of Jerusalem, defended himself against attack in his account of his travels. He proclaimed his easy conscience yet warned readers of the need for "outward reverence of the body" during Mass, which he faithfully attended. Indeed, Moryson insisted that no one more fully detested Catholicism than did those who witnessed its mysteries in action: observing the Mass, he recorded, only made him want to laugh.[172] In contrast, Biddulph lambasted those who put themselves in the position of cooperating with Catholic rituals. He argued that the well-prepared traveler could avoid such a predicament, a potential "shipwracke of conscience," with adequate money and letters of introduction, which allowed Biddulph and his companions to be excused from the confessions and masses newcomers to Jerusalem were otherwise obligated to experience.[173] But Biddulph was a minister, thoroughly equipped for his travels. Other young men were not so fortunate. To see what they hoped to see, to get where they needed to go, to trade their wares, they followed a different path.

For those who journeyed in the Mediterranean, deceit was important both for minor advantages—better sightseeing—and for major considerations—saving life and limb. Blount justified the practice. He praised the advantages of being, he claimed, the only Christian traveling on a Venetian galley, recalling that he "became all things to all men, which let me into the breasts of many."[174] Moryson made the case for dissimulation vigorously: should a traveler know how to swim, he advised, it was best not to broadcast the ability, lest others drag the swimmer down in a shipwreck.[175] Far from apologizing, Moryson believed it was the *obligation* of a traveler to dissemble in order to benefit most fully from his travels. "He that cannot dissemble," he warned, "cannot live."[176] The prudent traveler and the ambitious trader had to be prepared to disguise and occasionally deny their religion and their nationality. For some people travel might have solidified a sense of nationalism, as men learned who they were in opposition to other cultures. But in the Mediterranean travel and trade required men to subordinate their pride, their national affiliations, and their faith. Identity—the way in which an individual both perceived and presented himself, the extent to which his behavior reflected cultural norms of his home society, the conditioned responses of childhood—all required intense and immediate reevaluation amid the hazards of the region. Habits of xenophobia or cultural superiority were deadly in such an environment.

This style of dissimulation was not limited to the Mediterranean, but it was forged there first and most deliberately by the unprecedented number of travelers, traders, ministers, mariners, and statesmen who journeyed to the region after the Battle of Lepanto opened the waters to northern European traders. People came with apprehension, and rightly so, given the risks of travel there, but fueled by cupidity or curiosity, they found ways to circumvent the hazards of the region. The survival strategies of accommodation, adaptability, and deceit that the English cultivated in the Mediterranean from their position of political weakness and religious vulnerability provided one crucial style of expansion that anchored the trading ventures the English soon turned to around the world and would, in turn, help to animate an empire.

3

ENGLISH OVERSEAS MERCHANTS IN AN EXPANDING WORLD OF TRADE, 1590–1660

The world of long-distance commerce was, by necessity and design, a cosmopolitan one. Tangibly centered around the circulation of goods, commerce also required the circulation of people to identify and to procure desirable commodities from abroad and to export English goods to new markets. Glimpses of this cosmopolitan world were especially evident in London. A visit to the City's Royal Exchange, built in 1568 specifically for the needs of London's community of international merchants, prepared any trader for what lay beyond England's shores. There, merchants from all over Europe and beyond gathered to swap commodities and the news of the world. In a drawing he made of the Royal Exchange in 1644, the Czech artist Wenceslaus Hollar depicted crowds of men gathered in the large open courtyard, garbed in diverse and distinctive national costumes. In Hollar's view, the men cluster in small conversational groupings, animated, gesturing, exchanging news and doing business.

The docks where trading vessels landed their goods were similarly vibrant places. English mariners died in high numbers on long ocean voyages, the victims of scurvy, infectious diseases, and misfortune, and English merchant ships always sailed home with sailors acquired along the way. When John Saris left Japan in 1613, his East India Company ship carried a crew of fifteen Japanese, forty-six English, and five men simply described as "Swarts," a word denoting a dark or swarthy complexion and likely referring to sailors hired in India. While the Japanese sailors probably did not travel far from home, the East India Company always had to feed and house Indian mariners who made it to London.[1] And the mariners themselves brought back pets, including monkeys and parrots, whose cries added to the babel of voices heard at the port.[2] But above all, these vessels carried foreign goods that were coveted by English consumers—textiles such as luxury silks and colorful calicos, spices, both necessities (salt and pepper for food preservation) and luxuries (like nutmeg and mace), and dyegoods for the vital English textile industries. The visual and tactile and olfactory presence of new commodities generated a festival for all the senses and brought distant lands into the domestic setting of English households.

The bustle of activity at the Royal Exchange and the city's docks reflected the arduous labors of London's established and emerging trading companies, those joint-stock partnerships of investors who pooled their capital to fund risky and expensive long-distance trading voyages. Over the course of the seventeenth century, the nature of English trade shifted, not so much in its total volume but rather in markets and merchandise. Economic historians consider the first half of the seventeenth century in England "an age of statistical darkness": until the Navigation Acts of 1651 and 1660 required the compilation of trade statistics, sketchy and inconsistent records impede systematic comparison of trade flows. The best one can discern is overall trends. From 1600 through the 1640s, English trade with traditional markets in western Europe declined, replaced by trade with ports in Africa, Spain, and elsewhere in the Mediterranean. The main export continued to be English cloth, although broadcloths (sold primarily to northern Europe) declined in favor of lighter fabrics (sold in the Mediterranean). Imports consisted primarily of textiles (raw materials and finished products), timber, wine, and foodstuffs. Over the course of the seventeenth century, East Indies trade assumed a growing importance.[3]

At the center of this process of commercial reorientation were the overseas trade companies, composed primarily of merchants but with some gentry investors as well. These companies formed sometimes to fund single, specific enterprises—such as Martin Frobisher's three voyages to search for the northwest passage (in 1576, 1577, and 1578), Humphrey Gilbert's two Newfoundland voyages in 1578 and 1583, or individual privateering ventures. Other companies joined like modern-day land developers to promote investment in remote places, such as Virginia, or in the Caribbean. Such was the case for the Providence Island Company, whose twenty members hoped to develop lucrative economic activities on their three small islands (Tortuga, San Andrés, and Providence) in the West Indies. Some, like the Baffin Company with eight members, or the Cavendish Company with four, were small operations, while others, like the Virginia Company, swelled with 1,684 members during its short life span.[4]

In this period companies also received royal monopolies to pursue trade in specified portions of the world. The first charter of the East India Company, for example, permitted the Company the exclusive right to trade with countries that lay beyond the Cape of Good Hope and the Straits of Magellan. Among the largest of these overseas companies were the Levant Company (chartered in 1592 after some false starts, the Company had some 572 members before 1630, centered around trade in the Mediterranean), the short-lived Spanish Company of the late sixteenth and early seventeenth centuries (with 1,096 members, focused especially on the wine trade), and the East India Company, which boasted 1,318 members in its first three decades.[5] The East India Company was especially important because, from among the other trading consortiums at work in London, it emerged, took the lead, and altered the practice of trade.[6] But the companies contained overlapping membership, as investors diversified their portfolios, thereby hoping to reduce risks and maximize returns, so the expertise of one company was easily transferred to another. Thirty percent of the members of the East India Company also belonged to the Levant Company; similarly, almost forty-two percent of Levant Company members owned shares in the East India Company.[7] Some individuals, like Sir Thomas Smythe, invested in numerous companies, in his case including the East India, Virginia, Levant, Muscovy, French, Northwest Passage, and Bermuda Companies, along with other sporadic overseas investments.[8]

It is possible to discern England's transition toward a world of trade beyond western Europe in part from the impressive organizational activities of these enterprising merchants in London. But their profits depended on men who traveled abroad, inserted themselves in foreign communities, and brought back their treasures. These traders, dispersed around the world, show how the English constructed a trading empire, one personal commercial connection at a time, and they demonstrate that globalization—a process underway in the early seventeenth century—was about people, not inanimate forces. This chapter follows these global merchants in some of the major venues where they plied their trades. It looks at the diverse experiences of newcomers and seasoned hands, at hiring practices, and at the different strategies merchants employed in trading settlements in order to emphasize the personal skills and the improvisation and adaptability central to overseas trade in this period. The varied responses of English traders to the worlds they encountered around the globe were emphatically pragmatic. Overseas trading posts existed to facilitate commerce, and the best way for merchants to insinuate themselves in local trade networks was to ingratiate themselves with their hosts in whatever manner that might require, whether through respect for a distasteful religion or the acceptance of offensive diplomatic practices. A rigid xenophobe was unlikely to become a trader. At the same time, it is clear that some merchants did not simply tolerate but rather delighted in the opportunities they encountered, from new languages, new holidays, new people, new fashions, new plants, new food, and new friends.

Men who engaged in long-distance commerce acquired extensive trading and traveling experiences that exposed them to unfamiliar customs, to foreign communities of other traders (with whom they found both alliances and enmities), and to local inhabitants. The English generally lived together either in shared houses or separate neighborhoods for foreigners (see figures 3.1 and 3.2). In the terminology of the time, these clusters of merchants and their warehouses were called trade factories, and the merchants and the men who represented them were known as factors. They were expected to adhere to standards of conduct dictated and regulated by trade consuls or ambassadors. Commercial cultures were similarly shaped by the mores of a host society. Efforts to balance these competing pressures, one demanding flexibility and accommodation, the other insisting on continuities with English conventions, generated a range of innovative cultural practices and a willingness to adapt to new circumstances that traders transported around the globe as they ventured from one enterprise to the next.

The diverse ways in which merchants integrated themselves as outsiders and foreigners into unfamiliar communities reveal that there was no single English style of interaction with foreign people.[9] Foreign governments gave English trading companies formal rights (known as capitulations) that permitted them to trade. These privileges included access to commodities, the right to residence in stipulated places, freedom to trade in restricted areas, permission to worship freely (although privately) in their own faith, and the retention of legal rights (for punishing their own malefactors according to English law, for example).[10] In the same way that foreign rulers dictated the constraints within which English traders could operate, foreign people and cultures shaped how English merchants comported themselves overseas. This was especially the case where the English were numerically and diplomatically weak, as they were virtually everywhere in the early seventeenth century, and where they were latecomers who had to follow the trade patterns other Europeans had already established. In some posts, English merchants lived gently and discreetly, both a part of and apart from the dominant host culture. Elsewhere, the English sought to immerse themselves in the varied opportunities of foreign ports. The English devised different relationships with the people they encountered in Europe, in East and South Asia, and in the Middle East, and they similarly had complex and ever-shifting relations with competitors from other parts of Europe. The ability of the English to accommodate these different expectations reflects the adaptability, the essential—whether forced or voluntary—cosmopolitanism that was central to trade relations.

In the overseas trading post, merchants immersed themselves in foreign worlds. Formal travel literature written specifically for merchants advised

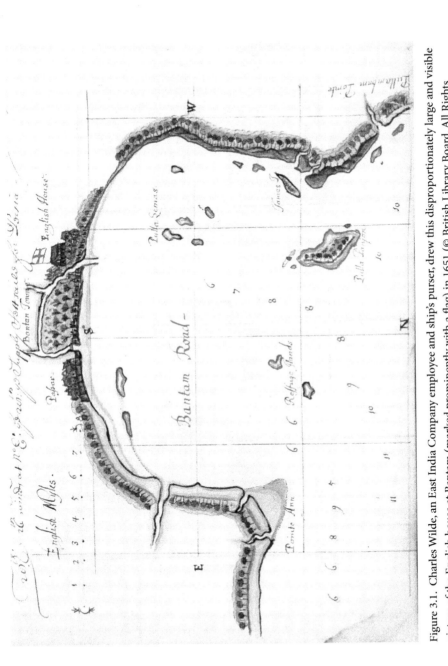

Figure 3.1. Charles Wilde, an East India Company employee and ship's purser, drew this disproportionately large and visible picture of the English house at Bantam (marked prominently with a flag) in 1651 (© British Library Board. All Rights Reserved, Sloane 3231, p. 86).

Figure 3.2. Cornelis de Bruyn, a Dutch painter and traveler who set out from the Hague in 1674, illustrated the trading post at Smyrna, and carefully identified each building. The center of the city is clustered to the right, in the densely settled bulge; the foreign trading houses were all lined up in a row to the left near the customs house. The English house was again distinguished by its large flag. Cornelis de Bruyn, *A voyage to the Levant* (London, 1702). By permission of The Folger Shakespeare Library.

a circumspect and pious approach to work overseas, building directly on skills acquired in the Mediterranean. *The Merchants Avizo* (London, 1607) typified this message. Written in the 1580s for those merchants who traveled to "Spaine and Portingale" or elsewhere (in other words, the places of greatest danger for Protestant English merchants), the author urged fidelity to the rituals of faith and prayer, but also gave traders practical advice about the demeanor most likely to further success. Be "lowly, curteous, and serviceable unto every person," the author advised, "for though you and many of us else may think, that too much lowlinesse bringeth contempt and disgrace unto us: yet assuredly…that there springeth of no one vertue so great fruite unto us, as of gentlenesse and humilitie." He also recommended that merchants comply with local laws and customs. Although he insisted on regular prayer—morning and evening, before and after meals—he was sensitive to the dangerous contexts in which the English worked and instructed them to say these prayers "silentlie."[11] The advice merchants offered to each other echoed this theme of humility and restraint. In 1639 Philip Williams, a trader in Istanbul, supplied another merchant who was on his way to Livorno in Italy with a collection of instructions. He urged him to remember his duty to God by beginning each day with prayer, to behave himself in a civil and orderly fashion aboard ship and in port, to keep the company of men from whom he might learn, and, most particularly, to listen, and not to speak.[12]

These exhortations to private worship, to silence, and to the submersion of one's pride composed pragmatic advice for men eager to facilitate trade in unfamiliar places. Merchants needed to acquire cultural understanding in order to do business, and they required strategies to enable themselves to perch in foreign ports. While what men wore, how they dressed and ate, with whom and how they socialized might seem like private choices, for these enterprising traders, personal attributes facilitated commercial relations. In this era when many English merchants were the first of their nation to open new markets, the first to assess new commodities, the first to persuade foreign merchants that they wanted to buy English goods, the first to cement trade relations with strangers, the first to blunder their way through unfamiliar diplomatic rituals, men had to rely on their social acuity to establish trade. Sometimes the English reached places where there was little prior knowledge of England at all; such was the case in 1613 when English merchants sailed to Hirado, in Japan. In these situations, merchants became ambassadors, not simply traders.

Successful merchants had to be willing to acknowledge their cultural ignorance and to be guided by European competitors and by their foreign hosts in diplomatic and commercial conventions. One false step might imperil an entire venture; thus merchants had to be prepared to place their pride secondary to other interests, and they had to learn quickly whom to trust. If they did not master the history and meaning behind religious practices, they soon ascertained the culturally appropriate ways to demonstrate respect for indigenous traditions. If they did not value the erudition of indigenous priests, they knew to mask their disdain. They played the roles of gracious host and guest constantly. In pursuit of these goals, they required a social competence—measured in their enthusiasm for new pursuits—which must have made the best of these traders charming companions. Richard Cocks, who led the English trade factory in Japan from 1613 to 1623, worked strenuously to read the preferences of his Japanese friends, visitors, potential patrons, and customers, and organized entertainment at a moment's notice. He threw together banquets and waited all night if he thought guests might appear. Cocks even organized an impromptu chamber ensemble composed of a ship's carpenter and a sailor to divert Japanese music lovers.[13]

Merchants needed, moreover, to be quick studies. However little they might have probed the depth of the new societies they encountered, they rapidly mastered at least a superficial knowledge of local tastes. They needed a keen awareness of commercial preferences—what people wanted, what they wore, what they ate—and compiled lists of commodities they thought would sell. In one such list for Japan, Captain John Saris detailed fabrics and minerals but also recommended "Pictures paynted, som lascivious, others of stories of warrs by sea and land, the larger the better." Saris apparently had a personal interest in "lascivious" images and books, since the censorious East India Company publicly burned his collection of such items. Thomas Roe likewise wrote quite sternly to the East India Company in 1617 of the type of goods that were marketable in India, and particularly urged that wares "must be made by Indian patternes." He warned the Company not to send allegorical pictures as presents to the Royal Court. Jahangir and his attendants studied with considerable concern one East India Company gift that depicted Venus and a satyr. After he observed the intense conversation that this painting inspired, the troubled ambassador speculated that Jahangir "understood the Morall to be a scorne of Asiatique, whom the naked Satyre represented, and was of the same complexion, and not unlike; who, being held by Venus, a white woman, by the Nose, it seemed that shee led him Captive."[14] Roe thought it best to avoid gifts apt to be misconstrued. Responding to cultural cues, merchants learned trading preferences slowly, through trial and error.

English merchants acquired this information in matters ranging from diet to art to clothing by befriending local merchants, by meeting their families, by observing fashions and tastes, and by visiting people in their homes. Conventions of buying and selling introduced people to foreign tastes in deeply intimate ways. The English house at Japan was simultaneously a residence, a storehouse, and a showroom. The head of the factory entertained visiting merchants and brought out his wares for display, a system that enabled traders to scrutinize each other's reactions to the goods offered.[15] Once new-comers learned the body language of strangers, they could read a gesture, an expression, as easily as they could an overt comment.

Merchants on their first tours overseas were often so preoccupied with the challenges of establishing their own reputations that they tended to focus entirely on the networks that linked them home to England. Newcomers functioned in two overlapping worlds, the first the local one of the trading post and the second an international world of maritime commerce, in which reputations traveled with the letters that accompanied each vessel from port to port, linking a remote outpost to an employer in London through the umbilical cord of correspondence. Two rare surviving letterbooks of two new traders trying to make their way in Levant Company trading posts reveal the competitive and insular nature of commercial culture. The Levant Company's factors were generally men who were apprenticed to a mem-ber of the Company in London. They typically spent three years learning the trade in London, before their employers shipped them overseas for the remaining four years of the typical seven-year apprenticeship. Apprentices received a percentage of the goods they traded, and most engaged in per-sonal trade, apart from their masters' business.

Those first months and years in Levant Company trading posts were busy ones. As newcomers, these men were intensely focused on connections with England and on getting a stake as traders. They were thus perhaps less engaged in or distracted by the new foreign world around them than were established traders. One such factor, Philip Williams, ventured to the Otto-man Empire in 1639, reaching Smyrna (Izmir) first before traveling overland to Galata, the Istanbul neighborhood containing the main Levant Company trading post. In Istanbul, the English merchants sold English cloth, lead, tin, and drugs (which they procured in London from the East India Company) and purchased such goods as mohair, silk from Persia, carpets, gold, nut-meg, and cinnamon. Almost twenty years later, Richard Lakes journeyed to the English trading post at Aleppo. Lakes had completed his seven-year apprenticeship in London with a man named Thomas Rich, and in Aleppo he hoped "to seeke [his] fortune" and with the help of his friends to "advance [him]selfe to a competent estate."[16] Located some eighty miles inland from the Mediterranean coast, Aleppo was the terminus of the long caravan routes from Persia and Mesopotamia, reached by camel from the port at Iskenderun (then known by the English as Alexandretta). English merchants there purchased cottons and raw silk, especially important in the growth of the silk industry in England.

Both Lakes and Williams maintained letterbooks with copies of most of the letters they sent, a crucial practice among merchants whose business depended on faithful record keeping. Their letters give us a unique perspective on the ordeals of new traders and their search for employment, which depended on their ties to patrons in England and on their ability to establish their reputations in Turkey. They had connections in England, but each man lacked both the extensive networks that came with age and fathers who might launch their business. Williams anticipated that he would stay away from England for four or five years, although he ultimately married and settled at Livorno. Lakes envisioned a stay of seven years yet he embarked without enough business to sustain him. Their early years in the Mediterranean were characterized by unrelenting efforts to rally friends and supporters in England to their sides, to defend reputations that had already been damaged by conduct at home, and to succeed in trade.

Their first task was to secure their professional livelihood, to make sure they had enough business not only to occupy themselves but also to become known as competent merchants. Both set to work writing letters home to those who might stake their business. Williams seems to have been better prepared for his undertaking than was Lakes. He had knowledgeable friends and relations to offer advice, and he reached Istanbul with his trade connections already intact. He represented a number of family and friends abroad, trading cloth for his brother and uncle, and doing business for other associates. But a general depression in the area diminished his success. In Istanbul he found business greatly depleted, "soe that here wee live in a miserable time & place." Although counseled by an uncle to stay in Istanbul for two or three years, Williams lamented the state of trade, and planned to go to Livorno for four or five years to make his way there.[17]

For Lakes, establishing himself as a factor was a much greater struggle, largely because of personal difficulties. He reached Aleppo after an easy voyage in 1658, and quickly reported home to his mother that "this is a brave healthful place, but something too Expensive to live here an Idle person, soe that if you can advance yor sonnes interest, p[er] the Recommendation of any frendes imploymt I shall take itt for a greate favour."[18] A letter to his brother the same day revealed that he had departed with insufficient funds for either brother "to bee [their] owne M[aste]r."[19] Lakes felt this poverty and its accompanying dependence keenly in Aleppo, a place boasting a range of recreational opportunities for those who could afford them. If only, he told another friend, he could get a pack of beagles, "I should have rare hunting here." The city proved too expensive a place for him to live in his reduced circumstances.[20]

The poverty of purse that made it difficult for Lakes to enjoy the Aleppo trading post was accompanied by a paucity of information. Ill-equipped with instructions from his former master, Lakes pleaded for people to intervene on his behalf in his quest for employment. When boats sailed from Aleppo,

Lakes fell into a frenzy of letter writing, making sure that he reached anyone who might help him or who might know someone who could. "Show mee all the frendshipp you can," he implored Ralph Lee, a friendship to be expressed by Lee giving him business. When Lee gave him commissions, Lakes called him his "cheife friend."[21]

Death haunted the small English post in the summer and fall of 1659. It had been "very hott and sickly," Lakes wrote his mother, with four English dead by the beginning of September.[22] Outside of England, merchants often confronted harsh and unfamiliar disease environments. Barring epidemics, life on dry land was generally less hazardous than the miseries of the sea voyage, but some trading centers were unhealthy, especially in Asia, and merchants organized their lives accordingly. Thus when the English consul in Aleppo fell ill in 1626, his creditors "were urgent wth him" to recover their debts. Experience, presumably, had taught these creditors the risks of waiting for repayment once a man fell ill.[23]

The unhealthy disease environment in places such as Aleppo offered the newcomer Lakes opportunities, and the pragmatic and ambitious factor seized on them. In July he had been appointed the assignee of his friend Richard Godfrey's estate. "It will be no matter of Benifitt," he explained to his mother, "but however may gaine mee some reputation, which I value att high esteeme."[24] Another death the following year offered even more tangible opportunities for this enterprising man. In the same letter in which he informed Samuel Bernardister of his brother's death in Aleppo, he asked for Bernardister's business in place of the deceased brother.[25] Lakes was able to piece together small commissions—£100 from his master, Thomas Rich; some tin; some money. But these small amounts of business gave Lakes no sense of satisfaction or accomplishment. The accumulation of disappointments made him question his decision to go to Aleppo. He thought he had friends in London who would provision him and provide him with business, but he began to think he had no friends at all.[26] Instead, he wrote to England in February of 1660 that he had "rubbed out allmost 2 yeares, and had little imploymt." Yet he remained optimistic that the remaining years would be more profitable.[27]

The search for business required a preoccupation with reputation, both that established in England and a new one emerging in the Levant. The two were inseparable. Philip Williams made the connection immediately on his arrival in Galata, where he saw his cousin, Philip Gyffard, who was awaiting orders out of England. Williams reported that he hoped to find his cousin a master in Turkey, but Gyffard's gambling habits in England made the task harder.[28] Geographic distance from England in no way liberated men from the web of personal relations that shaped business connections in this period. Factors tended to be acquaintances and relations of merchants, and men's characters were of vital importance. Lakes wrote his master, Thomas Rich, begging for pardon for anything he might have done. "I will therefore freely confesse," he wrote in one characteristic lament, "that I was very leud, debaucht and otious person." His biggest crime, he revealed, was his "too much love of wine and Compa[ny]."[29] He even implored his master's daughter to intercede on his behalf. His failure to secure business shattered not only his pocketbook, but also his pride. In Aleppo, the traders viewed Rich "as one of the best principles a factor can have," and it chagrined Lakes, indeed it "cutts [his] very heart," that Rich gave him no commission at all when he was known for giving large commissions to others.[30] Lakes particularly deplored the public humiliation he endured: everyone knew his failure to secure business. Lakes's difficulties in Aleppo gave him ample opportunity to lament a misspent youth, which made men loathe to trust him with their fortunes. He fell into the habit of starting his letters simply by offering blanket apologies to the recipient for any behavior that might have caused offense in the past.

Philip Williams also fretted about his reputation in England. His cousin wrote about the "censure" of him at home because of his conduct toward a woman, and Williams conceded "my carriage to her was not as it should have been," but insisted that his enemies made too much of it. From his distance of thousands of miles he worried about the story being spread about him while he was helpless to stop it. His inability to make enough money to support himself deeply shamed Williams. He was forced to write his brother William of his "negligence" at Istanbul and the great expense it caused him. Unable to satisfy his creditors, Philip asked his brother to pay one debt for him, but implored him to "bee private in it for it shames mee extreamly to think of such an extravagant expence." In the closed and intimate world of the trading factory, everyone knew the business of other factors. Williams's debts could not be long hidden, and his failings humiliated him. Small wonder that he also wrote his brother asking him to let him know what was due him of the family estate: "pray sr hasten to let mee see an acc[oun]t of what I may call *mine owne.*" His words conveyed both the urgency of the sentiment and the need to have something tangible of his own in a world where he labored for the business of others and accumulated only debts for himself. Williams's exile promised to last, he assured his brother, until he made back in Livorno what he had squandered in Istanbul. Fortunately in Livorno he had enough business that he sent to England for an assistant, and he expanded his network of family partners to include another brother-in-law. Thanks to the assiduous labors of Williams's relations and supporters in England, the East India Company decided to give Philip some of their pepper to trade in 1642, and his business achieved a secure footing.[31] Indeed, he even married the eldest daughter of the English ambassador to Istanbul, Thomas Bendysh, in 1646, which was a sure sign of his social ascent. In contrast, Lakes's disappearance from view suggests that his own career foundered.

Preoccupied with their own success, dependent as it was on new and emerging reputations, Lakes and Williams illustrate the ordeals of newcomers, whose attention remained fixed on English patrons, relatives, and fellow merchants. These factors were forced to familiarize themselves with a new trading culture while simultaneously relying on their connections at home for sustenance. They were novices, unable to immerse themselves in the international communities of Istanbul or Aleppo until they had secured their trade networks at home and established their independence—becoming, as Lakes put it, his own master, or, as Williams yearned, to know what he could call his own.

Investors based in London relied entirely on their representatives overseas for the success of their ventures. Factors who were lazy, dishonest, disreputable, clumsy, or xenophobic imperiled a venture, as the East India Company discovered when one Peter Wadden, sent from Japan for his "leude behaviour," proved untrustworthy for any kind of work. "As one good for nothinge," he was sent home to England from Batavia in 1621.[32] The Levant Company was similarly affronted in 1618 by John Adams, a factor in Aleppo who served a Mr. Finett. He was derided as a "lewd and loose fellow" and was shipped away at the first chance.[33]

The large overseas companies faced an awkward predicament in their necessary dependence on their distant representatives and in their reluctance to trust these men. This tension came to the fore in the hiring mechanisms and goals of the East India Company, whose unique commercial strategy placed special responsibilities on its employees overseas. The Company's first goal had been to procure pepper and spices (nutmeg, cloves, and mace, which the English had previously purchased in the eastern Mediterranean) directly from India, Sumatra, Java, and Borneo. But the East India Company's operations soon spread beyond pepper. One challenge the East India Company faced (as did its rival, the Dutch East India Company) was that there was little interest in Asia in English commodities, although the English fleet sailed with goods like woolen cloth, lead, and tin. As a result, the English learned to satisfy commodities exchange through two strategies. First, the Company diversified its exports. It shipped out large quantities of bullion and provisioned the fleet with other exports acquired in European trade. Second, it engaged in the local carrying trade within Asia, in which English ships transported goods within the region rather than relying on a balance of Asian and European commodities. This dependence on the carrying trade (called the country trade) was a departure from other English chartered companies. The Company's system required an extensive chain of trading posts throughout the region, with each one staffed by merchants who sought local commodities to ship on to other ports in Asia or possibly to Europe. Developing new trading relations was a process of trial and error, and the East India Company regularly closed trading posts, as it did in Japan, when business failed to thrive. There were two major waystations for the Asian trade, one in Surat (in India) and the other at Bantam, on Java. But joining these larger posts were numerous smaller settlements dotting isles and coasts around the Indian Ocean, the Chinese coast, Indonesia, and Japan.[34]

The East India Company's multipronged trade strategy required considerable innovation, flexibility, and shrewdness by traders and made the Company especially reliant on its overseas merchants. Unlike other companies, the East India Company tended to hire only men who had experience overseas, not novices such as Lakes or Williams. Yet ideas prevalent at the time about the way in which travel outside of England shaped a man's identity and undermined his loyalty meant that these men were perceived as unreliable. Debates over which traders to hire reveal this tension between the desire for loyal employees and the advantage of experienced traders.

The Levant Company and the Mediterranean in general offered an invaluable training ground in long-distance trade for new traders, but merchants who sought employment with an English trade company regarded the East India Company as the pinnacle of accomplishment, not least because such positions brought merchants the opportunity to pursue lucrative private trade. One imaginative supplicant for employment rendered his application in verse, but most men appeared more formally before the Company, either in person or through a letter, armed with the recommendations of Company members or bolstered by their own impressive trade experiences.[35] They recited the languages (usually at least three) they spoke and explained how and where they had acquired experience in trade (generally in the Mediterranean, but also in the West Indies and occasionally in the Indian Ocean with rival trade companies). At a meeting on December 16, 1613, for example, John Sanderosse outlined his credentials. Raised in Istanbul and Aleppo, he spoke Turkish and Italian, and he singled out his expertise with the commodities the East India Company might most value, including drugs, indigo, silk, and especially spices, the Company's dominant import. The same day Richard Battye applied for a position as factor. He had spent three years working in Middelburg (a major marketing center for English cloth) and one in Barbary. He spoke Dutch and understood Portuguese. Any Company meeting revealed men of similar accomplishment whose linguistic facility and trading experiences attested to their ability and their willingness to insinuate themselves into local commercial networks. Typical was William Squier, who had lived in Spain, Portugal, "and sundry other places." He knew navigation and sought employment "as one well experyent wth

those of subtile wytte havinge beene brought up amongst the Moores & Por-
tugalls." The East India Company lauded his skills and determined him "fitt
for one of their principall factors." Two other Company members praised
Richard Gipps as "a good linguiste," having previously gained proficiency in
Portuguese and "Morisco," by which he presumably meant Aljamiado, Spanish written in Arabic script and spoken by Moriscos.[36]

The range of experiences was breathtaking. Mr. Wentworth had acquired
navigational expertise with Sir John Hawkins and Martin Frobisher; Mr.
Besbitch, a merchant and accountant, had lived in Madrid and had been to
the West Indies. One Dutchman spoke Persian, Malaccan, and Portuguese
after thirteen years in India with the Dutch, while another Dutchman had
spent seven years in Java. Samuel Saltonstall had practiced physick in Ireland and York; James Freeman had recently been in Greenland; and Richard Whitlock boasted five languages (Italian, German, Turkish, Flemish, and
Latin) in addition to English.[37]

These few examples hint at the varied nationalities of applicants. Not all
applicants were English, and even those who were English subjects had lived
outside of England for such extended periods that their fidelity to England
might be called into question. Ironically, a lengthy sojourn abroad might
qualify a man with the right skills for the job, but it also made Company
members worry about complex personal ties that embedded traders in foreign and rival nations. Captain Edward Gyles first appeared before the East
India Company in September of 1614, boasting a long list of credentials
as navigator, soldier, and trader. In November a Company member raised
an objection to Gyles's application: his wife was a Spaniard who lived in
Spain—a Catholic subject of a rival monarch. Gyles explained this awkward
marital predicament by describing "howe casuallie he attayned unto her to
better his fortunes." He further emphasized his plans to move his wife from
Spain to England. The Company found his explanation of a marriage for the
sole purpose of financial benefit to be adequate, as it doubtless reflected the
avenue of advancement pursued by many Company members. Pleased by
Gyles's proposed solution, the Company agreed to consider his employment,
and he voyaged to India.[38]

More troubling to the Company was the career of William Carmechell,
a Scot with three years' experience in the East Indies with the Portuguese
and at the time of his application employed in the Low Countries. These
jobs would seem to provide Carmechell with the perfect credentials for East
India Company employment, but his situation was a complicated one. He
had a wife and three children in Goa, which was under Portuguese control.
His initial application met with considerable doubts because of his Portuguese service, which raised questions about Carmechell's religious affiliation. In November of 1614 the Company concluded that Carmechell's case

was "too dangerous for them to meddle with." In May of 1615, Carmech-ell renewed his suit, but with no greater success. Company members were troubled that he had sought employment with the Portuguese, "favoringe a stranger rather then his owne Prince, to whome by Nation, education, dutye and religion hee was bound." Moreover, the Company wondered how suc-cessfully he could work for the English, which employment would make the Portuguese his enemies, with his wife and children their pawns. For all his experience, the Company rejected Carmechell.[39]

Company members who turned down these cosmopolitan traders acted in part on political and economic theories of the period that connected a nation's political power with its commercial might. Enhancing a nation's trade was a patriotic act, however much commerce might line a merchant's own pocketbook. And those who traded for other nations revealed a suspi-cious lack of fidelity to their own sovereign.

These concerns about loyalty were particularly pronounced in the cases of those English subjects who through circuitous routes sought the protec-tion and employment of English trade companies overseas. The Englishman Thomas Harod made it to Japan on a Portuguese ship. He hoped to find employment in Hirado with the new East India Company trading post there, established in 1613. Hirado, northwest of Nagasaki, was a longstanding trade entrepot. The Portuguese had reached Hirado in the middle of the sixteenth century. The Dutch arrived in 1609, and by the time the English appeared four years later, they were just beginning to piece together the commercial potential of the port. For their part, the English spent ten years trying to make the trade flourish, but ultimately failed. Thomas Harod acknowledged his "follie" of Portuguese service and hoped to be taken in by the Company not out of his own need "but for conscience & love of his countire."[40] Richard Cocks, the head of the English factory in Japan, elaborated on Harod's story. He had been imprisoned by the Inquisition at Goa, and had just reached Japan, but was eager "to see his native cuntrey."[41]

But for all his advocacy of the displaced men who washed up in Hirado, Cocks remained troubled by men whose careers took them out of English service. His background had perhaps encouraged this apprehension. Cocks was in his forties when he reached Japan, an experienced trader who had launched his career as an apprentice to a clothworker in London. He spent some five years in France as a factor, buying and selling goods there on behalf of merchants based back in England. From his location in Bayonne, Cocks served as an informal spy for the English government, keeping track of movement in and out of Spain.[42] He brought his expertise in commerce, his knowledge of fabric, his perspicacity, and his discretion to his job in Japan, and his acute judgment—and chronic suspicion—of the European men he met in Hirado reflected this training in the worlds of trade, diplomacy, and espionage. When a Dutch ship reached Hirado in June of 1617, the four or five Englishmen on board triggered Cocks's curiosity. In response to Cocks's query about their nationality, one mariner confirmed Cocks's apprehension. "One of them," he recorded in his journal, "a talle fello, stood staring as yf he had byn agast, and tould me he was dowbtfull whether he might tell me he was an English man or no."[43] In the seventeenth century, English people believed that a person could be transformed by external factors and, indeed, by his very garb; wearing foreign clothes might fundamentally change a man. Travel could alter an individual, shaking his sense of self at its very core. So this vague mariner, either unsure who he was or reluctant to tell Cocks, helps us understand the heart of the problem for the large trading companies that relied on loyal employees far from their control, thousands of miles away. How could men be loyal when the very experience of leaving home, necessary for their business, undermined their attachment to home?

For the English in Japan, there was no better illustration of the slippery loyalty of the trader than William Adams. Adams had served for eleven or twelve years with the Barbary merchants until he went into the service of the Dutch in the East Indies. He washed up in Japan in 1600, where he became a valued member of society, took a second wife and had two children, and lived, in his own words, like a lord, supported by the shogun with eighty to ninety "husbandmen" as his "slaves or servauntes."[44] When the English contemplated trade in Japan, Adams's presence was a crucial linchpin. Indeed, he had initiated contact with the East India Company, writing traders at Bantam from his new home in Japan about opportunities there. Well placed at court, multilingual, adept in Japanese commercial practices, Adams helped establish the English trading presence there. But Adams's loyalties seemed uncertain to the English newcomers. He had worked for the Dutch, spoke the language, and continued to have relations with the Dutch who traded in Japan and who preceded the English there. Where, the English traders worried, did his loyalties lie?

John Saris, the East India Company employee who led the first traders to Japan in 1613, mistrusted Adams. He was, nonetheless, completely dependent on him as an interpreter, a helplessness symbolized graphically when Saris's first letter to the shogun landed in Adams's hands for translation. Saris deplored the "great libertie" which the country offered Adams, "whereunto he is much affected." Saris suspected Adams of being more drawn to both the Dutch and the Spanish than to "hes owne nation." He particularly urged Cocks not to trust Adams with money, but warned him of the fine line he must walk, fearful of alienating Adams yet not wishing Adams to take advantage of English helplessness. He urged Cocks to use Adams as a "linguist at corte." Adams's position was further strengthened because of his family connections. Married to a Japanese woman, he had a brother-in-law who was engaged in Adams's business.[45]

Cocks was more appreciative of—or perhaps more apprehensive about—Adams's talents, for he warned another merchant, Richard Wickham, to be careful on his voyage to Siam not to offend Adams.[46] An interpreter whose fidelity was uncertain was dangerous for any international trade venture, and Adams was far more than an interpreter. With his former Dutch employment, his Japanese wife and her family, his familiarity with Dutch and Japanese customs, Adams had too many options to cast his future entirely with the uncertain English venture and to imperil his hard-earned status in Japan.[47] In fact, for all these English anxieties, Adams secured more advantageous terms for English trade from Tokugawa Ieyasu than the Dutch enjoyed, and it took the Dutch trade two years to recover.[48] These multiple and competing attachments—to old and new employers, to sovereigns of different nations, to incompatible religions, to family—were natural products of the cosmopolitan careers of traders. The East India Company explicitly preferred "grave staid men," with all of their problematic experiences, to "younge greene heads" who lacked sufficient maturity and probity to serve companies and merchants reliably and competently.[49]

Shrewd traders exacerbated this tendency toward cultural malleability with the long-standing practice of sending young boys (either their sons or apprentices) overseas to learn languages in order to facilitate trade. So important was this practice that when the head of the Japanese trading post feared that Japanese distrust of Christians would prohibit him from placing an English boy "to learne the Japon tong," he mentioned it specifically in a letter to another merchant at Patani.[50] Companies, parents, and masters sent boys away from England to study trade languages. The East India Company agreed in 1614 to send John Gooding, a thirteen- or fourteen-year-old boy who already knew Dutch and French, to Surat to learn the language.[51] The Scot John Portis had been sent by his father into Spain to learn the language, and ended up with a career that spanned the globe.[52] Adolescents were not only well positioned to absorb a new language through this strategy of full immersion, but also were susceptible to the attractions of a new culture. From Lisbon the English trade consul Hugh Lee wrote of his concerns about the boys studying Portuguese. Settled in Portuguese families and required by them to attend Mass, the children ended up converting to Catholicism.[53]

In placing these young boys in foreign homes to master new languages, English and Scottish merchants replicated domestic practices of childrearing. By the age of fourteen or fifteen, English boys and girls were sent away from their biological families to reside elsewhere, acquiring the skills deemed suitable for their gender and station. In apprenticing their children, parents hoped they would model themselves on a master or mistress. Young boys sent outside England to live in non-English and non-Protestant households had a greater challenge. They were supposed to acquire a new language, but *not* model themselves on their host family or culture. These were difficult tasks to separate for boys who were linguistically and culturally isolated and far from family and friends. Religious conversions, marriages, and new political and social allegiances were sometimes the unintended results.

For all the social and political costs of cultural conversion, trade companies were eager to teach English boys foreign languages because of merchants' enormous vulnerability when matters of trade were left in the hands of non-English interpreters. Without reliable English polyglots (and an English polyglot was by definition not entirely faithful because of the methods employed for language acquisition), the English depended on a range of other linguists. In Japan Adams hired an interpreter named Migell for the English, but Richard Cocks did not trust him. Migell roamed too freely, "leaving mee," Cocks raged, conveying his profound linguistic isolation, "without any one that could speake a word." Cocks then hired a Christian Japanese boy named Juan who presented himself for service and could speak Spanish after having spent three years working for a Spaniard in Manila. While the English found him somewhat more dependable, his prior Spanish service continued to trouble Cocks.[54]

Literal interpretation was only one part of a larger process of successful cultural communication crucial for profitable commercial exchange. Adult traders found themselves drawn to the dominant cultures they encountered: learning about these new cultures in order to facilitate trade also introduced merchants to appealing new faiths and practices. For the most part trade consuls endeavored to curtail these inclinations toward cultural immersion. A glimpse at two trading communities, one in Lisbon and the other in Japan, in the first two decades of the seventeenth century conveys the diverse strategies English merchants pursued in their quest for safety and commercial success, and demonstrates how English trading practices were shaped and constrained by indigenous cultures.

Lisbon was a city that had long been familiar to English traders, who by the early seventeenth century had traded there for centuries. Unlike most overseas merchants, the Lisbon traders were never part of a company. They sold cloth in addition to leather goods, iron, pewter, and brass, and they procured wine, bullion, and commodities from Portuguese trade with the Indies, Africa, and Brazil. Although in the sixteenth century English merchants lived in Portuguese houses, by the early seventeenth century they tended to rent rooms in boarding houses. They lived clustered together in a geographically constrained community, governed by a trade consul they selected.[55]

For all its geographic proximity to England, however, religious differences and international rivalries made Lisbon a perilous place for Protestant English traders. Protestant merchants in Catholic countries required papal licenses, and even treaties failed to provide sufficient safeguards for merchants.[56] English merchants who traded with Spain complained about the chilling effect the Inquisition had on commerce. Merchants and mariners were confined to their ships until the officers of the Inquisition inspected the men and their goods and searched for forbidden items such as prayer books. Insufficient observance of Catholic rituals by a single mariner might condemn an entire crew to interrogation and punishment, and the complaints of merchants communicate a sense of panic in the face of such collective retribution. Moreover, the actions of the Inquisition injured national pride. If, for example, a merchant had cause to take legal action, and if the English monarch were referred to in such legal documents as the "defender of the faith" (the title bestowed on Henry VIII by the pope in 1521 in the wake of his attack on Martin Luther, before Henry himself saw the appeal of a break with Rome) the officers of the Inquisition carefully crossed this title out.[57] In the years before the Anglo-Spanish Treaty was ratified in 1605, insufficient respect for Catholicism prompted deadly retribution. Complaints lodged between 1584 and 1600 reveal the range of hazards English mariners faced. Walter Bet, a ship's carpenter, failed to take off his hat or to kneel when the Host passed by on the opposite side of the river in Seville, for which he and the whole ship's company were seized, and he was burned to death. Cutbeard Tollarde, a gunner, refused to kiss a holy picture carried in a street procession. He, too, was burned. John Gimekins saw fit to criticize the sexual behavior of Catholic priests to a friar, and burned for his frankness. Other individual examples abound.[58]

The Anglo-Spanish Treaty was supposed to clarify the freedoms available to English merchants, yet the officers of the Inquisition continued to inspect ships and their crews carefully for contraband goods, especially books.[59] The English perceived the Inquisition to be an opportunity to punish people for offenses that might have little to do with religion, an impression reinforced by the policy of seizing the goods of the accused.[60] In the years following the Anglo-Spanish Treaty (which included Portugal in its terms, since the kingdom was part of the Habsburg Empire from 1580 to 1640), the Englishman who was most vested in protecting the privileges of the English merchants in Lisbon was Hugh Lee, who spent twelve years as the English trade consul and who represented the English community, which contained only twelve merchants in 1610 in addition to apprentices and the sons of merchants.[61] Although their community in Lisbon was small, by the early seventeenth century, the English were the most prominent of the foreign merchant communities in Portugal.[62] Lee complained that the articles specifically intended to protect the English from the Inquisition were ignored, and indeed were neither printed nor evident in the laws of Spain and Portugal.[63]

Lee was occupied with matters of trade, but he also labored to protect his Protestant colleagues from the lures of Catholicism and the threat of the Inquisition. The spectacle of the Inquisition was visible to the merchants, and Lee wrote of those *auto da fé* he saw or heard reports of, including one in 1609 when seven people were burned.[64] Trade and faith intersected because the Inquisition confiscated the goods of anyone who was imprisoned by it; whenever an English merchant was seized, the consul had to leap into action to safeguard his goods.[65] In fact it is only by understanding the religious context of the city that we can make sense of Lee's apprehensions.

Two cases from after the Anglo-Spanish treaty illustrate how this English community functioned and why the consul labored to maintain the insularity of the English merchants. The first ordeal was that of Hugh Gurgeny, an English merchant seized by the Inquisition in September of 1606.[66] The Inquisition had initially resolved to deport Gurgeny from Portugal for failing to doff his hat when the Host passed in the street, for arguing with Catholics and trying to convert them, and for criticizing Catholic customs. At this juncture, an English Jesuit in Lisbon, Thomas Flood, singled out Gurgeny as his special project. Because Gurgeny's mother had been Catholic, Flood intervened, and encouraged the Inquisition to arrest Gurgeny rather than implement the deportation order. The Inquisition justified Gurgeny's subsequent trial as a heretic by claiming that Gurgeny was in fact a member of the Catholic church because of the manner in which his Catholic mother had had him baptized. Gurgeny faced execution in the *auto da fé*. The matter provoked considerable anxiety among the English merchants, in addition to the terror it caused poor Gurgeny. He ultimately converted to Catholicism after a lengthy ordeal, and after three years in prison he lived the rest of his life in obscurity in Portugal, forever separated from his English connections by his conversion and his need to buffer himself from potential accusations of religious laxity.

The second incident—more alarming to Lee, perhaps, because of its voluntary nature—was the conversion of the merchant Richard Drap to Catholicism in 1610. Although Drap tried to keep his new faith secret, Hugh Lee learned of it and urged authorities in England to summon Drap home from Lisbon. Lee worried that Drap would entice younger merchants and apprentices to emulate his conversion, complaining that "he doth soe pleaz the younger sorte that frequent his place, that they holde hym the most wisest fellowe that useth his place, whereby they are very prompt to be ledd by hym." Drap had carried a candle in a religious procession, thus joining in the festive rituals of his new faith.[67]

Drap's public activity is noteworthy in its contrast to other descriptions of English engagement with Catholic practices. Normally the Protestant English observed these rituals from a distance: testimony before Inquisition courts describes the English looking at processions through windows of buildings along parade routes, lurking obliquely on the margins, both literally and metaphorically. They were required by the Inquisition to demonstrate their public respect for Catholic rituals, doffing their hats even from inside buildings as processions passed, but these displays of respect were carried out by outsiders who practiced a faith clearly regarded as inferior by the host culture. When Drap was able to carry his candle, to join the procession as an active participant, he vaulted to the center of the action. And as a new convert, he would be celebrated and feted by the Catholics he joined, especially because of the triumph his conversion signaled in a period in which religious wars drew blood. The English in Lisbon were required to live quietly outside of a Catholic culture, but Drap publicized his beliefs. Had the other merchants followed his example, Lee worried that English trade in Lisbon might suffer from the mixed loyalties of Catholic merchants. As a result of these perils, the English in Lisbon were characterized by a cautious insularity, and Drap's momentous conversion and public participation in the rituals of his new faith were precisely what consuls such as Lee dreaded and sought to prevent.

Although wherever they ventured English merchants and factors comprised a minority population in countries with unfamiliar religious and cultural practices, they did not everywhere demonstrate the trepidation of the apprehensive Lisbon consul. In marked contrast to the dangers that greeted Protestant English merchants close to home in Lisbon, those traders who went to Japan flung themselves into Japanese culture. As in Lisbon, the English population in Japan was small, so clearly size was not the variable shaping an English trading community's culture. Even well established trading communities contained modest numbers of Englishmen: the largest Levant Company factory in Istanbul in 1649 contained thirty men.[68] When the Japan post was first established in 1613, it was staffed by seven Englishmen, and while the numbers increased and fluctuated over the next decade, the population remained small. Moreover, the English in Japan dispersed to pursue trade opportunities for the East India Company's carrying trade in the region, further reducing the size and the cultural impact of the English community even more and making individual Englishmen particularly reliant on Japanese women and men for companionship. The absence of regular contact between Japan and England—a Company ship might arrive once a year—contrasted with the communication possible between England and Lisbon. Formal Company correspondence and personal and chatty letters among the different merchants in Japan—frank, graphic, surprisingly revealing—make it possible to sketch the contours of the private lives of English traders who established residence in Hirado.[69]

It was officially, of course, a world centered around trade connections, on commodities (especially English broadcloth), on trading favors, on winning friends and patrons and clients and customers. But to accomplish these goals, merchants immersed themselves fully in Japanese life, and Japanese women were at the center of this process. The role of women in trading posts was complex. Commerce was an extension of, and often the impulse toward, diplomacy. Women were central to diplomatic exchanges within Europe in an era when relations between states were routinely cemented by the exchange of marriageable sons and daughters. Diplomacy existed in many cases to foster commerce, but outside of Europe legal unions were not always central to this commercial dynamic. Only one account survives of one of the major long-distance trade companies contemplating marriage as a diplomatic extension of commerce, and when the company rejected the scheme, it signaled a commitment instead to informal sexual and romantic relations in overseas trading posts.

Iskendar Muda, the Sultan of Acheh, had asked James I for an English wife in 1614. Only the year before he had allowed the English to open a trading post at Acheh, and promises for future control over pepper supplies accompanied this proposal, which the East India Company debated. One ambitious father presented his daughter to the Company as "a gentlewoman of most excellent parts, for musicke, her needle, and good discourse as alsoe very beautifull and p[er]sonable." Her father offered to escort her to Sumatra, and to stay with her there.[70] He dismissed objections from some clergy, who were concerned about the propriety of the match, the number of wives the king might already have (and how they might treat a newcomer), and the fate of the woman's Christian convictions once in Sumatra.[71] The Company ultimately abandoned the project, but the serious consideration the proposal received in multiple court meetings reveals the centrality of women in rituals of commercial and diplomatic exchange. The rejection of the scheme likewise pointed to a different direction, toward informal unions. Although marriage continued to cement diplomatic ties within Europe, it did not accompany the extension of English commercial networks around the globe in these decades.

Informal unions were pervasive because English overseas companies generally forbid merchants to travel with their wives. These policies stood in contrast to those of the Dutch East India Company, which permitted employees to marry and to bring wives with them and even sent single Dutch women to the East Indies for merchants to court. Captain John Saris of the East India Company remarked on the Dutch factory at Bachan, in the Moluccas, where he saw thirty soldiers, "the most of them maryed, some to the counterye women [meaning women of the region], and some to Holland women."[72] In 1614, an English captain challenged the East India Company's policy. William Keeling petitioned the Company for permission to bring his wife, Anna, with him to the English post at Bantam in Java, and prompted a thoughtful debate among Company members. Although there was some sympathy for the Keelings, "being both younge and not fittto bee p[ar]ted for soe longe tyme," Keeling's case sparked some resentment because he had not indicated his interest in bringing his wife with him when he was first hired. Some Company members believed the presence of Anna Keeling was necessary because so much time apart from her might damage Keeling's soul and the "quiet of his minde." Others were hostile to Keeling's petition, fearing his wife's presence would keep Keeling's attentions too much on her and would "soe hinder the maine busynes that hee is employed for...of passinge from porte to porte," seeking out new opportunities for the Company's country trade and unable to stay in any one place with his wife.[73]

Keeling traveled without his wife, but wrote from Bantam in March of 1615 complaining about the policy banning wives. He insisted that the Company would benefit from their presence, "both for their health and saufetie of the companies goods, and faithfulnes in their busines, for prolonging their lives, prevention of scandall to or religion, and many other consideracons of consequence." He advocated hiring only married traders. Very few of the men in Bantam, "notwthstandinge there best endevors to live wthout the companie of woemen," could resist temptation, which in his view induced "the greate disorder of the factors nowe liveinge at Bantam."[74] One enterprising man, Mr. Steele, circumvented East India Company policy altogether: he secretly married before he left for India, and his wife traveled as a maid on the same voyage. Captain Martin Pring confessed in 1618 that he "cannot but admire Steele's foolish insolence, who has attempted what Capt. Keeling durst not presume to do." Yet he wondered how well Steele could perform his service to the Company, "with a clog at his heels."[75]

The "disorder" at Bantam that Keeling perceived and derided was, he argued self-servingly, the consequence of the official ban on wives. Levant Company employees also spoke frankly of prostitutes in their midst, which prompted at least one fight among the merchants, and in 1600 John Sanderson referred to the traders in Istanbul as a company of "whoremongers."[76] The main exception to this policy seems to have been the Levant Company's willingness to permit consuls and ambassadors to bring their wives with them. Otherwise, until employers changed their policies (as the East India Company did in the 1660s), merchants were denied the companionship of wives, and married and single men alike pursued alliances, both short- and long-term, with the women they met overseas. Such was the case in Japan.

Japanese women were part of the diplomatic rituals surrounding the opening of English trade relations in 1613. As the East India Company ship rode at anchor, the daimyo (or local feudal lord), Matsūra Takanobu, brought both men and women to greet the newcomers, so many milling about the deck that the English themselves could not go on board. Japanese boats thronged the English vessel as people came to gawk and admire. Later, the ruler returned, boarding the *Clove* with four women, clad in silk, "well faced, handed, and footed…very curteous in behaviour, not ignorant of the respect to be given unto persons according to their fashion." These women, at first shy, were ordered by the daimyo "to bee frollicke," so they sang songs (reading music as the English did) and played a stringed instrument like a lute. After two hours' recreation, the visitors departed.[77] The publicly paraded women whose garb and skills signaled their careful training in social graces foreshadowed the centrality of women in the lives of the English merchants in Japan and in their access to Japanese culture.

Correspondence among the merchants who traded in Japan suggests that every one of the East India Company employees who lived there for more than a few months quickly established long-term liaisons with Japanese women, who not only offered companionship, but also helped traders learn about the culture they had joined. The most accomplished traders were those who were culturally bilingual, who understood the social cues around them. Women assisted in this process, as they did in so many trading communities around the world.[78] Most, if not all, of these women were already Christians, and so were predisposed to have interest in and sympathy for foreign Christian visitors. The first Christian missionaries had reached Japan in the 1550s and at their height had converted about 300,000 people. As Christians, these women occupied a minority status, but some regions of Japan such as Nagasaki were Christian strongholds, and Christians had access to political and commercial positions until their persecution began in earnest in 1616.

The traders spoke of the women they acquired through purchase or negotiations with families in the sexually violent language of the age. Richard Cocks wrote Richard Wickham of the twelve-year-old girl he bought for three taels (worth about fifteen English shillings at the time) for five years' service. Her contract required her to repay the sum at the end of five years, or else to "remeane a p'[er]petuall captive." Of her youth, Cocks remarked that she was "over small yet for trade," but assured Wickham that he would suffer no sexual deprivation, since he had another woman in the offing, "I think a gentel woman of your accoyntance," who was "more lapedable," or ready for mature sexual relations. Sexual unions were not necessarily permanent, nor were they monogamous. The women, moreover, lived in separate accommodations, paid for by the Englishmen. William Eaton seems to have had two women: Kamezō, with whom he had two or possibly three children, and Oman, whom he seems to have given or sold to another man, probably Richard Wickham, in a move that dismayed and angered Oman's protective mother.[79] The merchants also shared women. The trader William Nealson's woman, for example, had previously been Wickham's companion. Cocks cast off his woman, Matinga, after he heard rumors of her infidelity with several others, including Nealson, who brashly and tactlessly recorded his conquest in riddles and verse. The puzzle was hardly cryptic: "Read this reversed," he instructed Wickham, "*ad dextro ad sinistro*: OIGNITAM."[80]

But for all the overt commodification of women and the sexual violence that marked the traders' private correspondence, their letters also convey affection and appreciation of the women's skills. Wickham referred to Nealson's woman as his "language tutor." In the same letter in which Wickham extolled her practical skills, he also presented her with a pair of stockings, a token signaling his affection or gratitude.[81] Wickham's gift to Nealson's woman was part of a common pattern among the merchants. When trying to curry favor, they also sent presents to their consorts' mothers and other family members.[82] The Japanese women who became so central to the lives of English merchants doubtless initiated Englishmen not only in the Japanese language, but also in a panoply of customs crucial to English success. The English trusted their women to transport and receive their goods.[83] They traveled with their women around Japan, likely relying on the women's assistance to navigate the country. When they had set off without their women and were lonely, they sent for their companions.[84]

Most of the men of the factory were legally single, but William Adams had a wife and children in England in addition to his wife and two children in Japan. His will divided his estate evenly between his two families.[85] However unsanctioned these relationships were by English law (which punished bigamy harshly), the merchants conveyed their perception of the legitimacy of these unions by referring to women as "wives."[86] Other words might suffice—traders commonly used woman, whore, and wench. But instead these merchants dignified these relationships with the legal status and permanent connection conveyed by *wife*.

The social and religious rituals of home accommodated, embraced, and even legitimated these new and legally unsanctioned families. The merchants remembered each other's families with small gifts and conventional courtesies, sending presents and greetings in letters. In May of 1616, Richard Wickham sent William Eaton's daughter two summer kimonos commissioned by her father as well as a present for Richard Cocks's woman.[87] Cocks was a thoughtful man who regularly bought presents for the children of the English traders, including puppets for the children of Adams and a silk coat for Eaton's daughter Helena.[88] They paid sick calls when members of the extended English trade family were ill.[89] They reported to each other on the births and deaths of their children or the illnesses of their women.[90] They arranged rituals that legitimated their children. Henry Smith, the purser of the *Royal James*, had a son born in Japan. The child's birth must have been welcomed by his father's friends, who supervised his baptism. Arthur Hatch, the chaplain of the *Palsgrove*, christened the baby and named him after his father. Two English merchants, William Eaton and Joseph Cockram, served as godfathers, while a Japanese woman, Maria (or Mateyasu), the companion of Edmund Sayers, acted as godmother.[91]

All of the English left Japan by 1623, when the East India Company abandoned its trading post there, for reasons having nothing, it seems, to do with English efforts to understand local trading practices or with their commercial skills but largely because of structural and official impediments to trade. The English would clearly not be able to succeed in this venture if they were not able to provide commodities the Japanese wanted—especially Chinese silk of a high quality. Although Cocks's friend Li Tan promised repeatedly to help Cocks penetrate this market, he failed to do so. A second major challenge the English faced came in 1616, when Tokugawa Ieyasu's successor, Hidetada, banned all foreigners from free travel and trade around Japan, thus overturning the generous trade concessions the English had won in 1613. Stuck in Hirado, the English could not supply markets, and the Japanese in turn complained about the inadequacy of English goods. The decision to close the factory, made by the English based at Batavia, was part of a larger restructuring of trade in the region, and English traders at Ayuthia and Patani were similarly ordered to abandon their ventures, at least for the short-term.[92]

English arrangements to depart were complicated by family ties in Japan. When the English trader Eaton left, he arranged for his son William to follow him home on a Dutch ship. The boy attended Trinity College, Cambridge, and secured the legal status of denizen of England in 1639.[93] The boy's mother, Kamezō, who stayed in Japan with Eaton's daughter and possibly a second son, wrote to Cocks from Hirado in January of 1624, expressing her concern about the safe arrival of the party. She implored him to look after her son, and Kamezō's mother joined her in her good wishes and expressions of anxiety about the boy.[94] Edmund Sayers left his daughter Joan behind with her mother, Maria, in Japan, but received a letter in January of 1624 telling him that they were well, and Joan and Maria apparently sailed later to Batavia.[95] The English trading post in Japan did not last long enough for this population of children to mature and to join their fathers in their business enterprises, as was the case in other trade factories. If the example of the Dutch is anything to go by, these half-European, half-Japanese children and their mothers ultimately suffered considerable hardship in Japan.[96]

East India Company merchants and mariners seem to have strewn their children around the Indian and Pacific Oceans, leaving, in some cases, other men to provide for their care. Richard Welden referred to a "young daughter" he found and retrieved when he was at Boeton in 1614 (he did not want to leave her at risk of becoming a Muslim or a slave), while Thomas Kerridge reported to the East India Company in the same year of the two children left behind in Persia by John Midnall. Midnall at least left his goods to the children in his will.[97] Cocks was thwarted in one effort to provide for an English child. An East India Company employee named James Turner, a man dismissed scathingly by Cocks as "the fidling youth," impregnated a Japanese woman when he was in Hirado. Cocks gave the woman (whom he characterized as a prostitute) money to support the child, thus hoping to prevent her from committing infanticide, but she elected to kill the child as soon as it was born anyhow, "it being an ordinary thing here."[98]

The long-term liaisons the English created with Japanese women in Hirado and elsewhere were clearly matters of choice and strategy. Sex was easily available in Japan: English mariners enjoyed all the entertainment on offer when Company ships came to port—a source of considerable stress to Cocks, who was hardpressed to control the ships' crews.[99] That the English who were resident in the factory pursued different kinds of partnerships indicates that they perceived benefits (emotional, physical, commercial) in these relationships. Moreover, the terms of relations were shaped and dictated by the Japanese. Family members intervened when they disapproved of English behavior: William Eaton had to placate the mother of his Japanese woman, Oman, when her mother feared he would trade Oman to a man who would take her out of Japan.[100] This pattern of Japanese control over English access to family members was replicated in English efforts to hire young boys to help at the factory. Richard Wickham had a reputation for beating his servants, and he found it difficult to find parents willing to put a child into his care. Parents apprenticed their sons with careful restrictions, forbidding the English to take their children to certain destinations, including Bantam and England.[101] English access to labor and to women was constrained by Japanese preferences and terms.

Of course, not all English merchants understood or embraced the culture of the Japanese trading post. Richard Watts, the purser of a ship that reached Hirado in 1621, wrote with frank disapproval of the conditions he found. He deplored "this sinefull Sodome of Jappon," and said of the English house there that it "is more liker a puteree [whorehouse] then a m[er]'cheantes' factory, everie man for the p[ar]'te afected to his owne pleasure or his private p[ro]fitte."[102] But Watts's offended sensibility was perhaps the response of a new arrival, and probably of a man little familiar with East India Company trading practices after only two years in the Company's employment—and one writing home to find favor with his employer in London. Different trading communities had their own distinct cultures: part of the chameleon quality of the merchant rested in his ability to adapt to widely divergent local mores. In Japan, the head of the Hirado trading post, Richard Cocks, was not inclined to restrain the traders from pursuing long-term sexual and companionate relations with Japanese women since he had women of his own and these women were absolutely central to the ability of the English traders to navigate their way in an unfamiliar world.

Even without women as cultural informants and interpreters, everywhere they went, English merchants found local people to help them comprehend the myriad unfamiliar practices—"the customs of the country"—of new trading worlds. These friendships were indispensable. In India, Thomas Roe, the English ambassador in 1616–1617, befriended the viceroy of Patna, a man of seventy years, who instructed Roe "much of the Customes of this Countrie."[103] Roe struggled at first with these practices. He clearly misunderstood some aspects of diplomacy and commerce as they were conducted in the court of the Mughal Empire, disliking the "barbarous custome" of the public performance of all business.[104] Assistance in navigating these practices was crucial, but it was difficult to acquire sufficient knowledge to conduct business without being cheated or without losing face. Richard Cocks displayed some wares at the English house in Hirado to some customers who took items but paid only what they thought was right, not what Cocks demanded. Cocks sought advice, unsure whether this might be "the custome of this Countrey or no," as he had heard it was the case at Nagasaki (where these traders were from) with the Chinese and Portuguese. He was told that such was indeed the practice at Nagasaki but only because the Chinese and Portuguese had no trade privileges. Cocks, who had the right to trade, should have been paid the price he demanded.[105]

Without such instructions, the English would commit a range of social and diplomatic gaffes, all of which might imperil commercial success. Foreign business practices assaulted English sensibilities, making private affairs public and placing important power in the hands of underlings. In Japan, the English resented the role that Japanese military leaders and retainers played in diplomatic rituals. As representatives of the English crown, trade consuls sought the status of a visiting monarch, but foreign customs required more submissive behavior than a stand-in monarch might desire. Adams recorded a close call when the English commander of the new post at Hirado, John Saris, wanted to deliver a letter to the shogun's court himself, placing the letter into Tokugawa Ieyasu's hand. Although Saris was told that such was not the custom and that the letter would instead be placed into the shogun's hand in Saris's presence, the Englishman took offense. He insisted that he would retreat to his lodging if he could not deliver the letter personally. The shogun's secretary admonished Adams for his failure to interpret Japanese culture satisfactorily. Finally Adams mollified Saris and all was done as Japanese custom required.[106]

The English readily absorbed a range of local mores and practices in their overseas trading posts. Foremost was the importance of the "gift," which could soothe any diplomatic exchange. What Roe dismissed pejoratively in

India as bribes were gifts to secure reciprocity and to signal affection and dependence. When Roe came to negotiations empty handed, his hosts were perplexed, and Roe consistently interpreted this confusion as greed. For his part, Jahangir much preferred Roe to the merchants who had represented the East India Company in previous years, but he puzzled over the "little, meane, and inferiour" presents Roe had to give compared to these other men.[107]

In India, Roe adapted to the style required, paving his way with presents, but he clearly found these customs frustrating and peculiar and occasionally insulting to his status. When the king tried to give him an elephant as a present, Roe objected, taking offense and grumbling that he had no use for an elephant, "neyther was it the Custome of my Nation, especially of my place, to ask anything."[108] Although the budget-conscious English usually communicated an initial dismay at the expectation of giving and receiving gifts, wherever they went, they eventually adapted. After all, such practices furthered commercial ties. After the *qadi* who governed Aleppo ordered that all "franks" (meaning western Europeans) must vacate the area in 1633, the English determined that a voluntary present might help the *qadi* change his mind.[109] When the English got control of Tangier in 1661, their budget for holding the city included "donations" to the commander of the country nearby, and another sum "to be paid according to Custome" to rulers and people at the entrance of the Earl of Peterborough into the city.[110] Merchants learned quickly that it was better to pave their way with presents and gentle words than to try to bully their way into new places. When the English went to Tongking (the modern city of Hanoi) to open trade relations in 1672, they were guided by pilots they regarded as incompetent. But "rather than to give them any Disgust," the English showered them with coins and presents, including a pair of spectacles for one old man, perhaps a silent statement on his piloting skills.[111] During their first weeks in Japan, the English learned daily of men who should receive presents, and of what sort. The English merchants consulted and drew up lists in which they detailed the presents and their value, with recipients garnering baskets of goods, and the discovery of overlooked people requiring the English to consult anew.

The English learned not only from inhabitants of host countries, but also from other experienced traders. Trading ports were international places: the English were usually only one of several European nations to establish trading posts and in this era they generally lagged behind competitors. Their bonds with these rivals spanned from armed conflict to deeply affectionate relationships. To communicate with these associates Englishmen wrote letters in Italian, Spanish, Dutch, and Portuguese.[112] These missives sustained the commercial relationships the English established with other traders, for whom they performed favors and wrote cordially expressing their desire for renewed friendship when their globetrotting paths crossed again.[113]

These trade relations sometimes grew into real friendship. Cocks befriended the Chinese merchant, Li Tan (whom the English called Andrea Dittis), who rented the English their house in Hirado (and who seems to have duped the friendly and gullible Cocks into an overreliance on Li Tan's extravagant and expensive promises of trade from China). They traveled together and socialized together. When Dittis purchased some cloth from the English house, he obviously told Cocks exactly how he planned to use it: it was pink broadcloth, to make stockings or boots for his daughter. The color mattered, as did the use of the fabric. It was the kind of conversation between men who assumed that the other was interested in the purpose—an interest that was confirmed by Cocks's careful diary entry.[114]

For the English in Japan, Dutch merchants provided an indispensable guide. Cocks was surprised when he dined in Hirado at the Dutch traders' residence to see his Dutch hosts serve the guests on their knees. At the end of the meal, the head of the Dutch post, Hendrik Brouwer, emulated his traders, serving his Japanese and English guests drinks on his knees, "which seemed strange to me," Cocks observed. When he later asked Brouwer about his behavior, he was told it was "the fashion of the Country."[115]

Anglo-Dutch relations were always complicated by shared enemies (their mutual effort to dislodge the Spanish and Portuguese), a shared commitment to Protestantism, and ardent commercial rivalry. Competition led to some frightening and acrimonious incidents, including the day in Hirado in 1619 when the Dutch attacked the English house three times. In the wake of seizing an English ship in 1617, the Dutch ripped the English flag into pieces and used the scraps as toilet paper.[116] Several years of hostility at Ambon in the Moluccas came to a head when the Dutch killed ten English merchants, ten Japanese employees, and one Portuguese man at the trade factory in 1623.[117] The Dutch pretext was an English plot (whose details were extracted through torture, first of a Japanese accused of spying for the English and subsequently of the English merchants themselves) to overthrow the Dutch. The "massacre" had little impact on English trade aspirations since the East India Company had already decided to close its factory at Ambon before the Dutch attack. Inveterate and intermittent enemies found it prudent to set aside hostilities in times of need, while many merchants made friendships that transcended language barriers and circumvented trade rivalries and international conflict. Trading life was both embedded in European conflicts and set apart from them.

Communities of merchants overseas evinced a range of strategies in their efforts to accommodate the demands of a new culture and to ensure the financial success that justified their existence. Those traders with the most extensive experience outside of England and especially outside of Europe adapted with ease, enjoying the opportunity to savor new cultural practices, while newcomers, often preoccupied by their own commercial success, tended to focus on the other English merchants around them and remained wedded to commercial and patronage bonds with English investors and employers. For all the diversions that surrounded them, the business of the trading factory—the logic behind its existence—also kept traders focused on themselves and each other. They socialized together, fought, drank, gambled, gardened, exchanged books and women, played with their children, admired ancient and religious sites, and all this while they competed fiercely for business, watching the actions of others for any competitive advantages.

These were hybrid worlds, where traders simultaneously embraced new customs and adhered to familiar rituals. Christian holidays marked trading calendars as surely as they did the passage of time at home. The traders at Aleppo observed unspecified festivities at Christmas, noting during Christmas and the New Year in 1634 that their seasonal observations delayed their work.[118] They observed the holidays somewhat grudgingly, as one Aleppo merchant suggested when he complained that "it is Christmas tyme wch I must somewhat respect."[119]

In Japan, the English similarly marked their holidays with special meals, but their observances embraced Japanese neighbors. On Christmas in 1615, Japanese neighbors in Hirado sent the English presents "per reason of Christmas."[120] Four months later, some neighbors invited themselves to the English house for dinner, "it being our Easterday," and the English hosted twenty-four for dinner.[121] The English also enjoyed observing Japanese festivals, especially the Buddhist festival of Obon. Cocks marveled at the processions with lanterns to burial spots, after which the Japanese asked "their dead frendes to com and eate with them."[122] Although that struck Cocks as strange, he was able to understand other customs more easily, such as a pilgrimage women made to a fertility god, which he likened to pilgrimages barren women made in France to seek help from the image of a saint.[123]

As a result of these ritual exchanges, some curious Japanese acquired an interest and, remarkably, a liking for English cuisine. Soon after his arrival, Cocks recorded that the old daimyo requested (and received in a catered meal) English pork and beef, prepared with turnips and onions.[124] If the diet was unfamiliar, so were the habits of eating. Cocks feasted at the English house with guests in two different styles: "They dyned after the Japan manner, and supped after the English."[125] This accommodating spirit was hardly unique to the Japanese trading post, but rather central to some of the first English commercial exchanges in the late sixteenth century. William Harborne, who helped to open English trade with the Ottoman Empire in 1578–1579, sat on the ground to eat with his Turkish hosts.[126]

If some English merchants and factors overseas were homesick, dismayed by their distance from friends, eager for the creature comforts of home, and repulsed by the unfamiliar customs and people around them, others were cosmopolitans who seized these new opportunities. They communicated their enthusiasm in a variety of ways. Estate inventories offer clues about these diverse interests, particularly those inventories that detailed the books men owned. Companies equipped men for their voyages with religious tomes and some staples of the travel literature, including the works of William Perkins, Foxe's *Martyrs*, and the indispensable travel accounts compiled by Richard Hakluyt.[127] But merchants brought their own private libraries with them and acquired new works, collecting manuscripts and books on their travels. No English trader had a more extensive library in Aleppo, according to surviving estate inventories for the traders there, than did John Kynnaston, who left over forty books in 1638. Journals, ledgers, and daybooks helped record his trade activities, while his prayer books and Bible anchored his spiritual life. Language study and communication in Aleppo (where the lingua franca was Italian) were facilitated by his Italian Bible, his Italian dictionary, and a description of the world in Italian. Numerous moral and religious books suggested Kynnaston's interest in self-examination and self-improvement, while his many histories, his copy of Purchas's *Pilgrims*, John Speed's *History of the World*, and several other volumes indicate that his interest in the world outside England transcended his own residence in Aleppo. His knowledge of his new home in the Ottoman Empire was enhanced by his copy of a Turkish history.[128]

Richard Cocks was one of the great readers of the Hirado settlement. His interests were obviously well known, as another merchant, George Ball, wrote Cocks from Bantam that, "understanding you are given to history," he was sending him via Richard Wickham two books "contayning the Cronacells of England from Brutt untill the Powder Treason, wherin you maye see the shire, hundred & parrish where you ware borne."[129] Cocks shared his books, loaning his "Turkish History" to one Englishman "to passe away the tyme" on a voyage.[130] In March, he shared the same work with William Nealson, while he loaned Wickham, about to depart for Macao and an inveterate reader who possessed at his death seventy-nine books, his copy of Augustine's *City of God*.[131]

The range of books men owned and their interest in collecting books and manuscripts as they traveled reveal the curiosity that defined some of the most experienced merchants and presumably had driven them to pursue careers in foreign trade. This cosmopolitan sensibility is particularly evident for those with repeated overseas experiences, and thus most apparent among the men of the East India Company trading posts. The Hirado merchants were inclined to throw themselves into the new opportunities and customs—medical, spiritual, botanical, judicial—of their transformed world. The English surgeon in Japan, although admittedly "being in his pots" (or drunk), sampled Japanese prognostication when he asked a conjurer when John Saris would return from Edo to Hirado.[132] A sick Englishman sought a second opinion from a Japanese physician, although he found the medicine did not work for him. He returned to the English doctor, thus offending his Japanese practitioner.[133] The English frequently attended cultural performances. Richard Cocks was impressed by the plays he saw in Hirado, although he found the music abrasive.[134]

Cocks proved to be a great experimenter during his ten years in Japan. He rented a garden in Hirado for the equivalent of five shillings a year. In it, he planted potatoes (a plant indigenous to South America) and fruit trees. His plants reflected the world of reciprocity he lived in. Friends heard of his interest and sent him samples. In March of 1616, Cocks received fifteen fruit trees from a Buddhist priest for his orchard, and the trees clearly flourished, since eighteen months later Cocks arranged for a man to come and trim them.[135] Signaling his identification with his adopted home, and possibly greater facility with the language, sometime during 1620 or 1621, Richard Cocks started adding Japanese dates to every diary entry. Thus April 14 became Sanguach 3 in 1621.[136]

Cocks even intervened in the Japanese judicial system. In December of 1615, he tried to spare the life of a sixteen-year-old boy who was to be executed for stealing a boat. The daimyo granted Cocks's request and sent a messenger to tell the executioner to wait for the formal pardon, but the executioner went ahead with the punishment.[137] At times, Cocks succeeded in his intervention, and after he saved one Japanese man, the daimyo gave him to Cocks as a slave. Cocks's efforts were not simply those of a man trying to persuade himself that he had power in an alien culture. The Japanese perceived Cocks as someone who could act effectively within a quick and punitive legal system. In April of 1616 some Japanese came to Cocks for help for a friend whose husband had stolen money and run away. Although this woman had already been seized, Cocks and his Chinese friend Andrea Dittis intervened, and she was kept from prison.[138] Cocks's life at the English trading post in Japan expanded and elevated his social status, giving him a cultural power in Hirado that likely exceeded what he would have known as a merchant in England.

Cocks's intrusion into the practice of justice reflected cultural confidence. It also revealed Cocks's familiarity with the ways of Hirado—doing favors, asking favors. He also embraced Japanese rituals of gift giving. One tradition involved men sending their daughters with presents. Sometimes these were infants—Cocks received babies in the arms of their nurses. But always he gave them presents in return. The children of English merchants were absorbed in this custom. William Eaton's daughter Helena, accompanied by her nurse, presented Cocks with a "blanket for a present, Japon fation."[139] Cocks also engaged in another practice: people brought their children to him and asked for names. At her parents' request, he named one twenty-day-old girl, the daughter of his interpreter, Elizabeth.[140]

This English queen's name for a Japanese child illustrates the cultural mixtures of trade communities and of the people who lived and worked within them. These trading posts were multifaceted, places where merchants traded and places where traders learned new ways of understanding the world. Merchants looked to other Englishmen for diversion and support while they simultaneously looked outward to the new worlds in which they were immersed; successful trade required both of these traits. For every cosmopolitan Richard Cocks, there was a timorous trader writing home with laments of the miseries of his lot. Yet it was men like Cocks who ventured repeatedly from one port to another, and it was such men (by virtue of their willingness to travel) who were able to shape trading cultures around the globe. Their willingness to adapt to the uncertainties and opportunities of foreign commercial centers helped reorient English trade in the seventeenth century. The nation's growth thus hinged on men with global interests. The English procured foreign commodities and created global trade networks because individual men deliberately adapted to unfamiliar customs. They fulfilled personal and company commercial ambitions by accommodating local mores, whatever that might entail. This was the world of overseas trade, one defined by the cosmopolitan interests of its most skilled practitioners.

4

Virginia, 1607–1622

In late April 1607, three English ships carrying some 108 passengers and a score of mariners tacked into the Chesapeake Bay five long months after the fleet had left London. Their voyage shared the features of so many transatlantic crossings from northern Europe in this period. Storms delayed their departure from England, forcing the fleet to dawdle along the coast of Kent in what must have been miserable conditions for those passengers who were prone to motion sickness. With fair winds, the ships finally sailed south toward the Canaries in preparation for their southwestern route into the Caribbean and then up the North American coastline to their destination. More storms marked the end of the trip, causing the sailors to lose their way and framing the voyage as it had begun, in a tempest. Those seeking God's will in the natural world must have wondered with some trepidation at His plan for their American venture.

But there were mortal plans to worry about as well: what economic activity would sustain this new venture? Virginia was launched in a world of trade whose center still lay east in the Mediterranean and Asia. The men who invested in the Virginia Company of London had secured a monopoly from James I to pursue profitable enterprises along the southern coastline of North America, but the source of these imagined profits was unknown. Jamestown even had a twin whose parallel development reveals the uncertainty of the era's new projects. In the winter of 1607, an English venture got underway with 120 men in southern Maine, at the mouth of the Kennebec River. This was the Sagadahoc settlement, and it endured only one dismal winter: all European enterprises in North America were plagued in this period by the terrible cold winters of the Little Ice Age. When the king signed the charters for the two Virginia Companies (of London and of Bristol) and their projects in 1606, it was unclear to observers which one might flourish, or what economic activities might sustain either enterprise. Virginia Company investors envisioned their Chesapeake settlement in multiple ways: as a trading post, characterized by the amicable and cooperative relations English traders employed around the world; as a place where the English could extract minerals; as a chance to emulate Spanish successes by capturing their own Tenochtitlán, the populous and fabulous Aztec capital claimed by the Spanish in central America; and as a base for the quest for the elusive northwest passage.

The wide reading, knowledge, and experience of investors, employees, and settlers alike shaped these varied goals. Forty percent of the Englishmen who invested in the Virginia Company also owned shares in other companies. Their most popular investments were in the East India Company, which forty-six percent invested in, followed distantly by the Irish, Levant, and Northwest Passage Companies.[1] When they turned to their Virginia enterprise, and when they drafted the charter for their Company, they emulated other prototypes, including charters for the Muscovy Company and the East India Company.[2] Even the physical space of Virginia was defined by competing commercial interests: the boundaries of the new charter stretched south to thirty-four degrees N latitude, which was the northern limit of Spanish exploration in Florida, and north to forty-five degrees, which kept the Virginia enterprise well away from the lucrative Newfoundland fisheries.[3] The English crown and the Company's investors viewed Virginia, like all overseas enterprises in this period, as part of a multipronged geopolitical strategy designed to undermine Spanish power and to divert Spanish wealth to English strongboxes.

The Virginia Company's early goals revealed multiple paths to profit. It signaled its expectations for lucrative trade in the orders that accompanied the first fleet by instructing the men to select a treasurer to manage the many warehouses that would be stuffed with "goods, wares and commodities."[4] The instructions given to the first fleet in 1606 and three years later to Sir Thomas Gates, the new governor of Virginia, identified three further ways to enrich the venture, and all were embedded in the diverse experiences the English brought with them from other enterprises. They were first to explore rivers in order to find the northwest passage.[5] Second, the English hoped to secure tribute from Indian subjects. In this aspiration, the English revealed their expectation that another great indigenous empire awaited discovery. Spanish examples were always foremost in the minds of Virginia's literate and cosmopolitan inhabitants. Governor Edward Maria Wingfield's interest in the Spanish was so pronounced that he was even accused of plotting with them against the settlement. In his defense in 1608, he admitted that he had "alwayes admyred any noble vertue & prowesse as well in the Spanniards (as in other Nations)" but reiterated his distrust in them.[6] The Virginia resident William Strachey fueled this expectation of tribute from Virginia's Indians in his own writings, believing that the English would do better to adhere to the Spanish example of conquest and tribute than to condemn it.[7]

Yet the people of the Chesapeake proved inadequate for English tribute needs. Some 15,000 Indians occupied the territory they called Tsenacommacah, a number more than sufficient to satisfy English visions of Indian tributaries. While subject tribes were accustomed to paying tribute to Wahunsonacock, their paramount chief and the leader the English called Powhatan, English efforts to force tribute payments were generally thwarted. Moreover, the tribes were not sedentary. John Smith was the first to realize that people who were fully prepared to shift their place of settlement, to "fly into the woods," could not be relied on as a steady source of labor or tribute.[8] The Spanish model dictated a relentless search for gold and hopes for a Chesapeake El Dorado. These aspirations toward Spanish emulation did not fully erode until the 1620s, a period when the grim economic realities of the region—with no tribute populations or mineral deposits or lucrative tropical crops available—intruded.[9]

And, finally, the Virginia Company believed that it could rely on men's labor to procure marketable commodities, including naval stores such as pitch, tar, and timber, or grapes for wine.[10] Investors anticipated that they would find the precious metals that Spanish rivals appropriated in central and south America, or perhaps commodities for lucrative marketing in Europe. Laborers would be required to extract these commodities, but the vision was limited to extraction.[11]

The story of Virginia's early years is a tale of death, of experimentation, of trial and error, and, ultimately, of the success of plantation agriculture and of England's first permanent colony. In light of the goals that shaped it, however, the colonization that came to define the enterprise emerges as a surprising form of economic and social organization, even if this kind of relocation of English men and women to America was precisely what the vocal English promoter Richard Hakluyt and others had called for since the late sixteenth century. Yet for all of this lip service to the benefits idle and underemployed Englishmen might accrue by American residence, the commercial companies that sought profit from American investments were unsure where profits might lie.[12] Settlement was only one possibility, and an expensive and inefficient one at that. In fact, everything central to English expansion in the late sixteenth and early seventeenth century—the pursuit of commercial advantage over rivals, the desire to dislodge the Spanish and Portuguese from their territories—should make us wonder why a small group of Englishmen might want to travel three thousand miles to farm and especially to cultivate tobacco—a crop the English did not know how to plant.[13] Viewed at the time, Virginia was an embarrassing failure, one whose weakness made the English vulnerable to Spanish rivals in North America, although it turned out that the real vulnerability was to Indian attack. Amid politically charged accusations of mismanagement in the wake of a deadly attack led by the Powhatan leader Opechancanough in 1622, which killed one-third of the English settlers, King James himself disbanded the Virginia Company and took direct control of the colony.

In order for Virginia to succeed as a colony, it had to fail in all of its original goals. This chapter explains Virginia's ultimate development as a colony by looking at why trade aspirations foundered in the Chesapeake. To do so requires recapturing lost conceptualizations of a world where the English were weak and vulnerable, and where, thanks to extensive experience traveling and trading in just such perilous places, from the Mediterranean to the Indian Ocean, they knew precisely how to comport themselves within such a power dynamic.[14]

By 1607, when the English reached Virginia, the people of the Chesapeake were already familiar with Europeans and the English were already accustomed to different ways of interacting with strangers around the globe. The Company's experienced investors and employees tried to apply their knowledge to Virginia, but the terrain ultimately proved too different and the challenges of adaptation too severe to recreate the conditions that sustained trade elsewhere.[15] There were cumulatively a series of departures from the possibility of the amicable relations pervasive in trading cultures: 1611, when the English undertook an aggressive policy of defense and settled new towns, primarily in response to external, European threats; 1614–1616, when the colonist John Rolfe married Pocahontas and perfected hybrid tobacco cultivation, twin turning points in opposite directions, one toward interracial harmony and the other toward agricultural practices that precluded or at least challenged cohabitation; 1618, when the Virginia Company sought to diversify the colony's economy, turning it away from tobacco and encouraging European migration. Opechancanough's attack in 1622 embodied an indigenous effort to curtail expanding English settlement. It similarly inaugurated the clear commitment by the English to an adversarial and violent model of habitation, marked by the separation of populations and the vast exploitation of appropriated land. In short, Virginia came to define an intensive style of colonization that characterized English settlement in North America and the Caribbean and that departed from the trade model pervasive almost everywhere else the English went. Virginia may have established a pattern of colonization in North America and in the Caribbean, but it was an anomaly among English overseas ventures at the time.

As was so often the case when the English reached new trading posts in places such as Hirado or Bantam or Surat or Aleppo, other Europeans had been there first, and indigenous people were already familiar with them. This was also true in Virginia, and prior knowledge contributed both to English expectations about the people of the Chesapeake and to Indian assumptions about the English. For indigenous people in the Chesapeake, knowledge of Europeans predated Jamestown, reaching at least as far back as 1560, a time of Spanish forays in the region. The Chesapeake was a place of strategic value for the Spanish in their effort to maintain their exclusive claim to Florida, which was part of the territory given them by the pope in the Treaty of Tordesillas in 1494. This treaty divided the new discoveries in the Americas between Spain and Portugal. But other kingdoms had long rejected the principle of the division. King Francis I of France purportedly asked to see the will that made Spain's monarchs Adam's sole heirs as outlined in the papal bull. Subsequent rivals such as the English and Dutch whose Protestant faith led them to reject papal authority in any guise perceived no need to respect the pontiff's division.[16] By the 1560s, the Spanish had to fight to keep the land given to them as other Europeans competed for American riches. Pedro Menéndez de Avilés, the governor of Florida—as the Spanish called the entire swath of American territory north of the Gulf of Mexico—was eager to fortify the region in the 1560s in order to keep out English and French rivals. He pursued the land's development for the two years he remained in Florida. He also believed that the Chesapeake was close to a passageway that led to the far east and its commercial riches.[17]

The Spanish had sailed through the region in 1561 and picked up a captive, a man whose Indian name was Paquiquineo, and who was later known after his conversion and baptism as Don Luis de Velasco.[18] He was the first (as far as we know) of many Chesapeake Indians who were ultimately taken to Europe, either voluntarily or as captives. Don Luis lived among the Spanish in Spain, Havana, and Mexico City. He converted to Christianity. He seems to have contrived to persuade the Jesuits he met to settle a mission near his old home. Here his interests coincided with missionary ambitions among the order, which participated in Spanish conquests and occupation of Florida.

Once Don Luis led his mission companions to the place they called Ajacán, however, he abandoned them, returning to live with his people who, the Jesuits reported, had thought him dead and were "greatly consoled in him." The Jesuits imposed their Christian vision on the Indian response to Don Luis' return, insisting that they thought he had risen from the dead and descended from heaven. Don Luis may have found a warm welcome among his kin, but his Jesuit companions arrived at what they described as a time of prolonged famine.[19] Historians are unsure what exactly caused this famine, but it was likely connected to an extensive drought in the region, coupled by the shorter growing seasons of the Little Ice Age that gripped the planet, freezing the waters of the Thames and spelling doom for count-less colonial enterprises. Possibly epidemics caused by Eurasian diseases also played a role in disrupting agricultural cycles. Jesuit demands for food from a population already straining to sustain itself forced the Jesuits to beg their superior in Havana for supplies.

But Paquiquineo had his own resolution in mind. He seems to have elected to reject many aspects of his recently acquired Christianity once he returned home. He adopted, for example, his people's practice of polygamy, despite the direct criticism of the Jesuits.[20] According to the report of the single survivor, a child named Alonso, he instigated the murder of the Jesu-its in 1571.[21] This violence terminated Spanish missionary attempts, but not Spanish incursions. A year later, the Spanish took their revenge, although not on the people directly responsible for the attack. Instead, they hanged several Chickahominy on board their ship, in full sight of shore, and slaughtered and wounded scores of those standing along the coast. The Chickahominy bore an understandable animosity to the Spanish for years in the wake of these murders, or so they later told one Jamestown resident, Ralph Hamor.[22] The Spanish returned in 1588, taking two more boys away with them, and con-tinued to make occasional visits to the region.[23] So far, from an indigenous point of view, Europeans had proved undesirable and predatory visitors, the violence of their appearances mitigated only by their brevity. Little of what they had seen other Indians experience, however, persuaded the Powhatans that they should immediately fear Europeans when more of them washed ashore in 1607.[24]

Indian knowledge of Europeans and their technology was enhanced by those Chesapeake Indians who, like Don Luis, visited Europe in the very early years of English settlement. The information these visitors and spies gathered was important in helping Indian leaders shape their diplomatic policies. Initially, Europeans kidnapped Indians in order to force them to learn European languages to facilitate trade and exploration. These captives also assisted in investors' public relations efforts, and to that end the first captives from the Chesapeake paddled a canoe in the Thames. But Wahun-sonacock also sent his own emissaries, and the historian Alden T. Vaughan has argued that more Chesapeake Indians visited England voluntarily, as travelers, spies, and emissaries, than by force. Wahunsonacock had sent Namontack as early as 1608, but complained later that he did not learn enough from this spy. This accumulated knowledge, whether from captives or emissaries, bilingual Indians or Englishmen, shaped indigenous responses to the English in their midst. Wahunsonacock, for example, insisted in 1610 that the English show him the respect enjoyed by the "great werowances [or leaders] and lords in England" by bringing him a coach and horses, to enable him "to ride and visit other great men." So he had been told by Indians who had been in England.[25]

For Indians, the story of what became the English settlement in Virginia had a long preface, reaching back to the first Spanish incursions in the 1560s. What of the English? When and where did Virginia begin for them? Historians have answered this question by looking to Ireland, Roanoke, the Caribbean, and all around the Atlantic. Historians have especially turned to Ireland and the English conquest there that began in the 1560s to make sense of English colonization in North America.[26] In Ireland, as part of their occupation of the rebellious kingdom, the English resettled loyal English families to establish models of fealty and to control the Irish. Pockets of English settlement dotted the Irish landscape. The colonization of Ireland was a crucial component of a more urgent enterprise, conquest. Inspired by Spanish examples, Sir Henry Sidney suggested a plan for colonization in order to make England's tenure more secure. It was not a model for harmonious cohabitation, and thus it was diametrically opposed to the assimilationist style of trading cultures. When Sir Humphrey Gilbert first presented the scheme to Queen Elizabeth, she was apprehensive, worrying that such an adversarial approach might hinder reconciliation between the English and Irish.[27]

In Ireland the English learned to assume the mantle of conquerors. Conquest and colonization there involved thousands of soldiers possessed of a suitably ardent and bloodthirsty religious zeal, the displacement of the indigenous population, and the migration of ultimately 100,000 Protestant settlers from Scotland and England before 1641 to reshape the economic and cultural geography of the kingdom. English occupation of Ireland also gave the English an opportunity to fit the Irish into an emerging ethnography in which the Irish were understood to be at a lower stage of human development than the English, and could be profitably and violently yanked toward civilization with the improving and edifying example of English settlements in their midst. Historians have seen in this brutal conquest a useful rehearsal for North American enterprises, although in fact these colonization efforts failed in Ireland, so it is unclear why the English would seek to adopt a model of failure for their new exploits.

Ireland would be a useful rehearsal only if the English ventured to North America expecting to establish colonies in the Irish model. No evidence suggests that they did. The Irish connection might explain the *timing* of English intervention in the western Atlantic, since the English were distracted closer to home and thus latecomers as settlers (although not as fishermen or traders) to America. Perhaps it also tells us something important about the cultural expectations about Indians that some English brought with them overseas. But the oddity is that Ireland has become a canonical assertion of fact as formative in English invasions of America despite the pronounced absence of direct evidence that the English drew on Irish experiences or models at Jamestown or elsewhere.[28] Some people went from Ireland to America (primarily to Roanoke) but some (such as the Roanoke settlers Thomas Harriot and John White) went the other way, making Ireland "an alternative colony to America for certain Englishman."[29] If the English sometimes compared the people of America to the Irish, they also understood the Irish in light of their reading about America, thus using the catch-all insult of the sixteenth century, "cannibal," to describe the Irish. These two enterprises in Ireland and North America were part of a larger struggle against Catholicism, a struggle with many different strategies and manifestations, including trading posts, Irish conquest, and Caribbean piracy.[30]

None of the Virginia Company's original aspirations nor the experiences employees brought with them depended on the large-scale relocation of English men and women that defined English settlement in Ireland. One source of modern confusion about the Company's goals is that the Virginia Company used the word "colony" to describe its enterprise. William Strachey spoke of the settlement as "our Colony," despite his admission that it contained "but of a handfull of men."[31] One puzzle, then, is to determine what these men meant. As Karen Kupperman has observed, in this period a colony was a place for making gold.[32] Participants also used the language of commerce, referring to their undertaking as the "business." When the Virginia Company used "colony," however, it was always paired with "plantation," the word most frequently used in the period to describe forms of settlement that modern readers might associate with colonies (which is why colonists were known as planters). The Company's instructions for the new government reiterate the words "Colony and Plantation" in tandem, and the Letters Patent speak of the "severall colonies and plantations."[33]

The pairing of words suggests that each had different meanings: the attributes that historians now associate with colonies were, in the seventeenth century, the attributes associated with plantations (which was the term used to describe English settlements in Ireland). The configuration of colonies was less certain. Only in their propaganda efforts to shore up the faith of a skeptical public in the future of their visibly faltering venture did the Virginia Company use colony primarily in the sense of plantation. In 1610, the anonymous author of the Virginia Company's *True Declaration* wrote that "a Colony is therefore denominated, because they should be *Coloni*, the tillers of the earth, and stewards of fertility."[34]

The very first Englishmen in the western Atlantic pursued not colonies but fish, a high-protein commodity in enormous demand in Europe, especially in its portable dried form. These fishermen stayed only seasonally. They were later joined by men interested in acquiring commodities, characterized in the Caribbean by the theft of foreign ships and goods and on the mainland by clumsy exchanges as the English sought new world treasures, especially pelts, through licit and illicit means. There was extensive English activity in the Caribbean, including 300 different voyages between 1550 and 1624 comprising as many as 25,000 sailors on 900 ships.[35] Many of these voyages engaged in plunder and raids on Spanish settlements. The English also learned about crops there, including tobacco, cotton, and indigo. In their voyages along the North American coast, English mariners and merchants engaged in the casual trade of English goods. However casual the trade, the American populations suffered mortality rates as high as ninety percent in the most devastating outbreaks that resulted from contact with Europeans and their unfamiliar pathogens. None of these ventures required permanent habitation of any sort.

As part of these coastal visits, the English had explored the North American coastline before their attempt to establish Jamestown. James Rosier took part in a voyage to New England in 1605 that included men who "had beene...in sundry Countries, and in the most famous Rivers, yet affirmed them not comparable to" what they saw in New England. "Some that were with Sir Walter Raleigh, in his Voyage to Guiana, in the Discovery of the River Orienoque, which eccoed fame to the worlds eares; gave reasons why it was not to be compared with this, which wanteth the dangers of many Shoalds and broken grounds, wherewith that was encombred. Others preferred it farre before that notable River in the West Indias, called Rio Grande: some before the Rivers of Burdana, Orleance, and Brest in France."[36] If Rosier's companions give us any hint about the kinds of men who found themselves on ships to the Chesapeake, we can imagine that the region was visited and later populated by well-traveled individuals.

Beyond their casual coastal visits and explorations, the English also attempted settlements. On the barrier island at Roanoke, the English established what they hoped to be a base for plunder of Spanish ships: the settlement's location was dictated by tantalizing proximity to Spanish shipping lanes through the Caribbean and across the Atlantic. With this predatory goal, the colony required men with extensive military experience, and in fact it is Roanoke that provides the most persuasive example of a possible Irish connection. Several of the men at Roanoke, particularly leaders such as Ralph Lane, Sir Richard Grenville, and Arthur Barlowe, had prior experience in Ireland, and the expectations of these men and their quick recourse to violence help explain the degeneration of English relations with the Roanoke Indians.[37] This experiment failed, famously abandoned during the three years the colony's governor, John White, spent in England on his resupply mission. White was unable to return to North America because of the attack of the Spanish Armada in 1588, which occupied all available English ships.

By the time he reached Roanoke, the inhabitants (including his daughter and granddaughter) were gone. But the settlement there encouraged the English to sail north into the Chesapeake to explore. They took one trip there in 1603 (when five English were killed on shore) and another before 1607 (with another skirmish).[38] It is difficult to know how to assess the impact of these prior European experiences in the region of the Chesapeake on the Europeans who settled at Jamestown in 1607. The English seem to have known nothing of the Spanish mission, and their interest in the Roanoke colonists remains clouded in mystery, worried as they were about the bad press that might result in England if the fate of the colonists proved too dismal.

Within the Atlantic alone, from Ireland to the fisheries of Newfoundland to a series of thwarted settlements in Guyana, the English already had a range of strategies to draw from in their new venture in Virginia. But as the preceding chapters have illustrated, Englishmen traveled *east* from England in equally large numbers, and experiences there were equally formative, whether in trading ventures or military encampments. The Englishmen who settled Jamestown brought a world of experiences with them to match the Virginia Company's diverse goals. Some came from Ireland, others from the Caribbean, from pirate raids, from thwarted settlements, from Istanbul and Aleppo and the East Indies. They had traveled by caravan and caravel and camel; they had bowed before sultans and kissed the rings of sheikhs. They had witnessed or negotiated complex treaties and they had endured life-threatening perils. They had seen elephants and monkeys and terrifying serpents. They had survived typhoons and hurricanes, droughts and floods. They had beheaded enemies and experienced slavery and written treatises on agricultural production. Virginia was one of many adventures for them, and one for which they were well-equipped.

In their eastern voyages, some English who later ended up in Virginia served as soldiers, for example, fighting on the continent during the Eighty Years' War, the protracted effort of the Spanish subjects of the Netherlands to expel the Spanish between 1568 and 1648, in what John Pory described as "that university of warre the lowe Countries."[39] Some of these soldiers then found their way *west* across the Atlantic. This military background was crucial for men such as Thomas Gates, Edward Maria Wingfield, Lord De La Warr, John Smith, and Thomas Dale, just to name individuals who led the Virginia settlement in its first five years of existence All of them fought in the Netherlands, and Dale, Gates, and De La Warr also had served in Ireland.[40] John Bargrave conveyed the ecumenical and opportunistic interests of such men whose colonial service was an interlude amid other actitives: "after 10 yeares service in the warres in the summer tyme and at my study in the wynter," he developed an interest in Virginia, and acquired a plantation there in 1618.[41] The Virginia Company hired these captains not to fight an unknown indigenous enemy but rather to discipline English inhabitants and to fend off the anticipated attacks of a familiar adversary, the Spanish. Early trade forays into the region's interior, led by these military men, reveal the amity that the English pursued, as they wooed Indians and especially their children with free trade goods.[42] If the Indians who lived around the Chesapeake Bay knew something about Europeans, the Europeans who tried to establish a profitable settlement at Jamestown knew something about the opportunities and challenges of a world of trade, travel, and adventure.

Setting Virginia in the context of the many simultaneous ventures the English pursued around the world casts a different light on an old story of failure and mistakes. It has been too easy for historians, focusing primarily on the outcome of tobacco-intensive settlement, to characterize the early years at Jamestown as a series of blunders as men fumbled their way toward the ultimate goal of plantation agriculture: men with unrealistic expectations and inadequate skills attempting to reap impossible riches from an unyielding land. It is a tale of stupidity and recklessness, populated by gentlemen who would not plant or engage in manual labor; deluded fools seeking gold mines; ragged and impoverished vagrants and waifs rounded up from city streets and shipped thousands of miles away; thirsty men who settled on brackish water, sickening themselves by their choice of habitation while better informed indigenes watched in wonder. No image has proved more enduring than that of starving men bowling in the street, the sight that greeted Dale when he reached the colony in 1611. In fact, the most celebrated images of Virginia's disasters center around food, or its absence: one Mr. Collines allegedly salted his dead wife's corpse in order to survive during the famous "starving times."[43] The familiar and striking icons of the colony's catastrophic misfortunes make the settlement a series of ghastly cautionary tales, particularly if one expects these men to settle down, finally, and plant some tobacco. All of these exploits and misjudgments emerge as dead ends and ludicrous fantasies, not as realistic pursuits.

Yet it is important to find another way to describe these early years, to think not in terms of foolish and deadly mistakes that emerge so clearly in hindsight but rather in terms of the expectations the English brought with them—as logical, we have to believe, as the expectations Indians had about what these uninvited arrivals might do in their new home.[44] These were not ill-prepared men with reckless visions.[45] It was imperative for their survival that each group, English and Indians alike, try to understand the other, and their frequent failure to do so reflects neither a wilfull ignorance nor a narrow ethnocentrism but rather the tenacity of prior understandings and expectations. When necessary, gentlemen and those unaccustomed to manual labor could plant. Governor Wingfield boasted in 1608 of the thirty-seven chickens he raised "by (his) owne huswiferie."[46] The minister Alexander Whitaker similarly marveled with transparent pride at the corn he was able to plant with three others, despite his lack of experience, sowing enough during "the idle howres of one weeke" to last for one-quarter of the year.[47] That he made this boast in 1613 in a promotional text designed to enjoin others to follow him to Virginia reinforces English acceptance of acclimatization to new circumstances. The English could adapt, and indeed they did, departing from all of the Virginia Company's original expectations, experimenting with agriculture, and fashioning a new type of overseas settlement, one rooted primarily in English responses to the indigenous economies they found and in the gradual dismantling of prior expectations.

Although Virginia ultimately developed as a place of English settlement, in its first few years it adhered more closely to a trade model. Such were the hopes of the London investors. They wanted to establish settlements capable of procuring the commodities that the English otherwise were required to import from southern Europe, including fruits, dyes, olives, and sugar.[48] Trade was important not only to sustain the enterprise, but also to legitimate it. William Strachey justified trade with the Indians by comparing that trade with England's "rich and necessary Trades into Turkey, and the East Indies."[49] Strachey argued that the law of nations allows men to trade, which permitted trade in Virginia. Although the Indians were ignorant of these laws, "we that are Christians doe know how this lawe (enriching all kingdoms) gives priveledges to Ambasadours, keepes the Seas common and safe, layes open Ports and Havens, and allowes free scales and liberal accesse" for those who wished to import and export excess goods. In Strachey's vision, trade would elevate the Indians.[50] Moreover, he wanted English rights to this new land to depend on its proper acquisition through purchase. "Every foote of Land which we shall take unto our use, we will bargayne and buy of them for copper, hatchetts, and such like commoditytes," which would then let the Indians turn around and sell goods to their neighbors.[51] Trade justified English presence in the region and legitimated their access to foreign territory—theirs not through theft, but through exchange.

Strachey's infusion of morality into commerce echoes the complex motives guiding colonial and commercial ventures in this period.[52] The Virginia Company was a business enterprise, one involving high risk and considerable uncertainty. Motives for profit were always intertwined in this period with language concerning the good of the state, in the same way that people conceptualized travel outside of England in terms of its public utility and benefit. These motives were inseparable, and it hardly misrepresents the interests of Virginia Company investors to suggest that they readily linked concerns about domestic economic hardship, England's trade balance, the loss of specie, the benefit to indigenous Americans if they could be liberated from the horrors of Catholicism, aspirations for personal profit, and nationalist hopes for England's strength.

The first English inhabitants busied themselves identifying lucrative commodities. Christopher Newport sailed home with samples of ore, and Gabriel Archer insisted that the English could produce as much clapboard as could be sold in England, a kingdom with an alarmingly inadequate supply of timber for fuel, construction, or shipbuilding.[53] John Smith's accounts describe his own preoccupation with trade as he traveled the country exchanging commodities. The Company echoed the business hierarchies of trade settlements in designating one leader as its "cape merchant," clinging to the title well after the settlement's inhabitants started planting tobacco in earnest.[54]

In their hopes for trade to be convenient, easy, and profitable, the adventurers were likely misled not only by their expectations but also by their experiences as they traveled to Virginia through the Caribbean. Francis Perkin described his visit there to a friend in England in 1608. He stopped at Dominica, where "we spent the whole day there trading with the savages." The Dominicans boarded Perkin's ship laden with wares, foods such as potatoes, bananas, cassava bread, hens, and other items including linen and parrots. They traded for useful goods for their personal use or to exchange to their own trading partners.[55] In Perkin's recollection, the English did not even have to get themselves to shore to get the goods they desired, and all departed the exchange content with their loot. If the English expected the people of Virginia to be similarly prepared to accommodate English commercial needs, they were mistaken. The Caribbean had limited utility in this respect as a model for Virginia.

Commerce was similarly undermined by a problem familiar to all English ventures, private trade by merchants or sailors on their own behalf, with their own goods, not on behalf of employers in London. Like any trading consortium, the Virginia Company preferred to monopolize all commercial exchanges, and worried about this leakage by unauthorized entrepreneurs. The Virginia Council's original instructions to the new government in the colony urged leaders to be sure that the mariners "do not marr your trade," because the sailors sought only whatever gain they could get, and not the long-term goals of the Company, and the risk of their selling and buying goods at low, quick, prices was the hindrance of trade "for Ever after."[56] The leakage was immediately apparent: some sold for profit, but others, John Smith reported, stole Company goods to sell to the Indians for food, an obvious rebuke of English aspirations to self-sufficiency.[57] Observers blamed trading difficulties on precisely this problem. When Strachey reached Virginia in 1609, he reported that the Indians asked for too much copper to pay for the commodities the English so desperately needed, and Strachey blamed the mariners for their insistence on an "East Indian increase, four for one, all charges cleared."[58] Governors repeatedly sought to quell these ambitious amateur merchants.[59]

As was true in all East India Company and some Levant Company trading posts, life for the English in Virginia was routinely truncated by death. Virginia's early years were so deadly and debilitating that the survival of the venture was wholly uncertain. New arrivals died at high rates, as many as forty percent succumbing in their first year in residence, largely because of the hostile disease environment they joined; colonies were as lethal to newcomers as cities were in this period. This deadly pattern endured for decades. Virginia's English residents died of familiar endemic sicknesses (like smallpox or measles) that plagued people in England but also from maladies spawned in their new American setting: salt poisoning from drinking brackish water, malaria, malnutrition, and the dysentery (what they aptly if gruesomely called "bloody fluxes") that resulted from poor sanitation. And the English starved. In the terrible winter of 1609–1610, the population plummeted from 500 to 60.[60] They expected the Indians to provision their food needs, and neglected to plant corn for themselves. Indeed, how could they, when the Virginia Company failed to send experienced farmers? Instead, the men and boys of the first fleet (no women reached the colony in 1607, and even by 1620 men outnumbered women by a ratio of about seven to one)[61] included gentlemen (men who by definition would not engage in manual labor), specialized craftsmen (who in this era of tight guild regulations performed only the job they were trained for) and unskilled laborers, an inauspicious collection of people poorly prepared to labor for their own survival.

High mortality and private trade were customary impediments to successful and profitable trade and they plagued all commercial enterprises. To smooth trade relations, the English in Virginia adopted numerous strategies central to trading culture. They placed boys in Indian communities to learn languages. These boys could serve as hostages to good English behavior (if the English cared about the fate of the children) but the policy was also consistent with trade practices. One young boy placed among the Powhatan Indians in 1609 to learn the language experienced an apparent cultural conversion in the same way that a trader's apprentice placed in a Portuguese household might convert to Catholicism. Henry Spelman spent a year with the Indians, returned to England, but then sailed again to Virginia where he worked as a trader and served as an interpreter for the colony. In 1619, the Virginia government accused him of treasonous loyalty to Opechancanough. His familiarity with Indian ways explained his actions to contemporaries, who recorded that he "had in him more of the Savage then of the Christian."[62] Moreover, John Rolfe speculated that Spelman's fault derived from his "Childish ignorance," an interesting evaluation of a man of Spelman's age (he must have been at least in his early twenties), and possibly an indication that the English believed that Spelman's maturation was atrophied by his residence with Indians.[63] Spelman's language skills were too valuable to permit his execution, so he was demoted and bound to serve the colony as an interpreter for seven years.[64] Spelman was not alone in his cultural preferences. The child Thomas Savage, also delivered by the English to the Indians as an interpreter, was befriended by an Accomac leader who gave him land on Virginia's eastern shore, and he settled there as an adult in the 1620s.[65]

The English pursued a second strategy common in trading communities: cultural assimilation and commercial advantage through sexual alliances. The most famous wedding in early Virginia might have been such an alliance, the marriage of the settler John Rolfe and the Indian Pocahontas. The Spanish conquistadors had quickly established a pattern of using indigenous women from noble families to cement their authority at the top of preconquest hierarchies. Tecuichpotzin, the daughter of Moctezuma II, and renamed Doña Isabel by the Spanish, was married five times in succession by Hernando Cortés to bolster Spanish authority over the toppled Aztec Empire.[66] These Spanish marriages were characteristic of the first generation of Spanish invasion. When Spanish women finally started to migrate to America, Spanish men dispensed with their legal marriages to powerful Indian women and married other Spaniards instead.

The English, then, had at least two models of sexual alliance available to them in their own American adventures. They could adhere to the familiar model of the trading post, pursuing informal or formal, long-term or short-term sexual alliances for companionship, advantageous family connections, and practical benefits. Or they could emulate the Spanish model of marriage for diplomatic and strategic purposes. Some of John Smith's friends apparently suggested the latter possibility when they proposed an alliance with Pocahontas in order to "(make) himself a king." Smith understood the Powhatan inheritance system, and knew that he would gain no right to the territory through such a marriage.[67] Governor Thomas Dale apparently entertained this idea as well. Ralph Hamor described a mission to persuade Wahunsonacock to marry another daughter to Dale. The daughter, it turned out, was, like Dale himself, already married, and despite Hamor's suggestion that she be reclaimed from her marriage for this English match, Wahunsonacock demurred, replying that the English already had one of his children.[68]

Informal sexual alliances are difficult to trace in Virginia records. The East India Company traders may have written frankly about their women and children, but Virginia visitors and residents were not similarly candid—or, at least, their correspondence on these subjects has not survived. But certainly such unions existed. Strachey's extensive vocabulary lists offer us a clue: one

Algonquin phrase he included was "to lye with a woman."[69] Another hint comes from a letter written in 1612 by the Spanish ambassador in London to Philip III of Spain, who heard news from "a friend, who telles me the truth," about affairs in Virginia. Some of the men in Virginia were thinking of marrying Indian women, he reported, and some forty or fifty were already married. He was apparently incorrect about the marriages, but might well have been accurate about the English pursuit of and partnership with Indian women. He reported that the cleric Alexander Whitaker was critical of the sexual behavior of some of the men at Jamestown. Interest in Indian women was hardly unique to Virginia. Some twenty years later, the inhabitants of Providence Island, an English settlement off the coast of Nicaragua, proposed to their employers in London that they bring Indian women to the island from the Mosquito Coast, a plan the Company rejected.[70]

The case of John Rolfe illustrates a slight departure from the trade model. Although some relationships endured for years in trade settlements, and men fathered children whom they recognized and named and provided for in their wills, these relationships were also entered into casually, and men cast aside old partners and acquired new ones. Rolfe had no interest in this kind of informal sexual union. He wanted to *marry* Pocahontas. She has become one of the most celebrated names of seventeenth-century North America, yet much about her remains obscure.[71] Historians do know that she was the daughter, apparently a favorite, of Wahunsonacock, the paramount chief of the region. Sent as her father's emissary to the English to secure the freedom of Indian captives, she quickly grew acquainted with the English, and became a playmate of children at the English settlement. John Smith later claimed that it was Pocahontas who rescued him from execution, but the veracity of this account remains disputed: Smith was famously rescued by women in many of his life's mishaps, with an Ottoman Pocahontas liberating him from slavery in the Ottoman Empire. He embellished his colorful life history and added this account of Pocahontas's rescue only after she had acquired some fame of her own during her visit to England in 1616.[72]

Pocahontas was someone the English knew well during her childhood, or at least as well as these adult English men who came from a culture that valued children little and small girls even less would bother to get to know any American child. They came to know her better when they kidnapped her and imprisoned her in 1613. During her captivity, Pocahontas lived with Alexander Whitaker, a minister who had been eager for the opportunity to convert someone to Christianity and who—it seems—was kind to his pupil. Pocahontas was instructed in Christianity. She donned English style clothing, encumbering her limbs with long skirts, and she apparently came to know John Rolfe very well. Within the constraints of her life in captivity, she chose to convert, and at her baptism in 1614 she took the name of Rebecca.

And again within the constraints of captivity, isolation from her family, and total immersion in English culture, she consented to marry Rolfe. With the Powhatans and English at war, Pocahontas's and Rolfe's marriage in 1614 (the second for each party) cemented an alliance which brought about peace.

Rolfe apparently agonized over his desire to marry Pocahontas. Rolfe and his first wife had traveled to Virginia in 1609 on the ill-fated *Sea Venture*, which wrecked on Bermuda. Rolfe's wife bore a daughter there, but little Bermuda died, and the mother soon followed, leaving Rolfe a widower. After almost a year on Bermuda, these resourceful people built a new ship for themselves and found their way to the American mainland. Their ordeal inspired William Shakespeare's *The Tempest*, and prompted the Virginia Company to settle and develop Bermuda in tandem with Virginia.[73]

As Rolfe, comfortably established in Virginia, contemplated this second marriage, he labored to separate his motivations from carnal desire—"so farre forth as mans weakenesse may permit." Instead, he pursued this match "for the good of this plantation, for the honour of our countrie, for the glory of God, for my owne salvation," and for Pocahontas's conversion. And yet these noble goals were immediately followed by the frank admission that it was she "to whom my hartie and best thoughts are, and have a long time bin so intagled and inthralled in so intricate a laborinth." Rolfe's language revealed his distress over his attraction to Pocahontas: he prayed faithfully to God for cures from "so dangerous an ulcer." He had biblical examples in mind, thinking of God's displeasure when the sons of Levi and Israel married "strange wives." He marveled that he should "be in love with one whose education hath bin rude, her manners barbarous, her generation accursed, and so discrepant in all nurtriture frome my selfe," and concluded at times that his love was sparked by the Devil. Rolfe resolved his quandary with the commitment to support her conversion. It would be unnatural and uncharitable to decline to assist so needy a soul. Assured that his conscience was "clean from the filth of impurity," he trusted his motives were honorable. If it were sex alone he wanted, he stated frankly, he could satisfy his desire with far more suitable partners.[74]

Rolfe's interest in marriage was a pattern that the English in general did not elect to follow in Virginia, although elsewhere English traders found numerous advantages to establishing sexual alliances with indigenous women. But his conviction that marriage was a desirable and viable arrangement points to yet another road not taken in early Virginia. It is obviously absurd to argue that sexual alliances necessarily led to harmonious relations between people of different cultures, particularly when these encounters were embedded in asymmetrical power relations, as was the case, for example, for enslaved women and their masters or overseers. Yet in those many instances in the early seventeenth century when the English reached outposts as a weak and dependent population, sexual relations provided an entrée to unfamiliar societies and into the kin networks that sustained trade and livelihood, and a quick way to learn about the languages, cultures, and customs that would further trade. Such had been the case at Hirado in Japan. In Virginia, the English were weak, and the potential that sexual alliances might further a dynamic more akin to that of the trade community was real. In the case of Rolfe's and Pocahontas's marriage, the alliance cemented harmonious relationships for a while, but simultaneous activity revealed the real incompatibility between English ambitions for their settlement and indigenous use of the land and waters of the bay.

A FAILED TRADING POST

The English soon departed in Virginia from the trade model pervasive around the globe. They did so for two reasons. First, the English inhabitants failed to act like good traders: all of the lessons that traders learned and applied in other parts of the world had too little resonance in what the English regarded as the much more alien world of Virginia. Second, various pressures, both internal (hunger) and external (security from enemies and pressure from the Virginia Company for a diverse and profitable economy), encouraged the English to occupy land in new ways and to pursue more adversarial relations with the Powhatans. Even if English investors brought to their Virginia enterprise an understanding of what made trading ventures successful in other parts of the world, that did not mean that this knowledge could be successfully or easily applied in Virginia. To be sure, the language of trade permeated the first years of settlement and experimentation, and in some ways the English acted like traders. But these patterns were rapidly, even immediately, overlaid with other responses to unfamiliar places. In the end, the population that achieved the greatest cultural understanding of the other was the Powhatans, and they deployed their knowledge in an effort to constrain and destroy the English settlement.

The multiple meanings the English and Indians brought to exchanges immediately complicated trade. The Company expected its employees to pursue opportunities for commerce. Here the English drew directly on the trade model so central to English expansion and wealth in this period in Asia and Europe. And in the Powhatans, they found willing trade partners eager for metal goods, which were of great practical utility in all sorts of daily activities, including hunting, food preparation, and farming. The Indians also valued European textiles, and in return for these products offered the corn that sustained the English and pelts for export. Yet the Indians had their own mechanisms of exchange. Indian alliances were secured with gift exchanges, and so chiefs sought to establish alliances for precisely that reason. English "trade," then, operated within a particular indigenous idiom, one requiring ritual surrounding it and a different cultural logic from the commodity exchange the English envisioned.[75] The Powhatans saw the English as people of great richness because of their abundant goods; they were therefore expected to give generously. The English followed a different economic philosophy, one which maintained that the universe contained only a fixed amount of wealth. So they pursued a different logic, one in which their goal was to benefit as much as possible from any exchange with the least possible expenditure of goods.[76] These conflicting philosophies were problematic for an amicable trade relationship and similarly challenged the English ability to implement the Virginia Council's instructions not to offend the Indians.[77] Incompatible ideas extended, of course, well beyond trade. In Powhatan eyes, the inability of the English to feed themselves attested to their helplessness and inferiority. That the English simultaneously saw themselves as superior to the Indians bore no reflection of their relative ability to survive in their shared environment.[78]

The accommodating culture of the trading post was similarly thwarted by English efforts to impose rituals drawn from other contexts, rituals that emphasized English power and dominion, not their adaptation to indigenous norms. Take, for example, the odd case of Wahunsonacock's coronation, a peculiar ceremony arranged by the English in 1608. It echoed the custom of "Surrender and Regrant" that the English started to use in the sixteenth century to extract loyalty from Irish rulers. In these rituals, the English compelled Irish lords to submit to English authority, but then bestowed new authority upon them. The ceremony for Wahunsonacock similarly sought to place Wahunsonacock in a tributary role.[79] The English insistence on "crowning" Wahunsonacock and on regarding him as the main Indian authority reflected their misunderstanding of Powhatan politics. Like most Indian leaders in the region, Wahunsonacock in fact had modest power over the daily activities of his people. This English confusion had violent consequences for Anglo-Powhatan relations, since the English regarded all Indians who failed to comply with a treaty made between the English and any single leader as savage and treacherous, both justifying reprisals and shaping English perceptions of Indians as unscrupulous people unbound by law and treaty.[80]

Smith's description of his first meeting with Wahunsonacock emphasized the chief's authority. Wahunsonacock greeted Smith "with such a Majestie as I cannot expresse, nor yet have often seene, either in Pagan or Christian."[81] Yet Smith described the subsequent coronation in comic detail. The English sought Wahunsonacock's compliance by promising him support against his enemies, the Monocans. Wahunsonacock, who had witnessed feeble English efforts to sustain themselves in Virginia, replied that he did not require their help. Wahunsonacock also refused to play his subordinate role by insisting that Captain Christopher Newport travel to *him*. And so Newport did, sending ahead the presents procured for Wahunsonacock. Only at the urging of Namontack, who had been to England, would Wahunsonacock consent to don the scarlet robe given him for the occasion, and further farce ensued when Wahunsonacock refused to kneel. "At last by leaning hard on his shoulders," John Smith recalled, "he a little stooped, and Newport put the Crowne on his head."[82] And so a man who was not a king was crowned by an authority he did not recognize.

The departure from the culture of trade continued. Englishmen were capable of drawing on a wide range of demeanors when they encountered foreigners. They could subordinate their pride, their nationality, and their religion if it were necessary and expedient to do so, as they had learned in the Mediterranean. They could work to make themselves charming companions, as they did in Japan. Jamestown emerged out of this malleable trade context but quickly took a different turn. Virginia failed as a trading post for reasons well beyond failed diplomacy and the more apparent challenge of insufficient desirable trade goods. The Englishmen in Virginia first and foremost failed to act consistently like traders. Traders needed to settle among their trading partners, but the English were ambivalent about this prospect in Virginia. At Jamestown, their first conduct vacillated between the diplomatic caution and obsequiousness of the new head merchant and the bullying of a soldier or a timorous stranger. John Smith had two dimensions to his Indian diplomacy: he hoped to avoid warfare, and he tried to instill fear.[83] Neither goal suited the imperatives of a long-term trade relationship.

Rather than prepare for midnight banquets, as Richard Cocks did in Japan, ready to welcome all comers, the English in Virginia hid in their fort, afraid to leave to get food or fresh water. The London Council's first orders to the settlement's leaders in 1606, before the English had even established themselves in Virginia, urged them to make strenuous efforts to prevent Indians from seeing any kind of English weakness, whether poor marksmanship or sickness. The Council similarly warned the English to settle away from any woods that the Indians might use as cover in an attack.[84] Their inability to distinguish at first who were friends and who might be foes increased their anxiety. Appearances were forever deceiving them. Ralph Hamor encountered an Englishman named William Parker who looked so much like an Indian that Hamor knew him only by his language—and even language might not be a clue once some English and Indian boys had become fully bilingual.[85] And language failed the English in another way. John Smith, captured in the Ottoman Empire, was able to communicate with his owner in

Italian. In the Chesapeake, with no established trade pidgins or lingua franca in place, the English relied on their child-interpreters, boys like Savage or Spelman, who too often identified with their Indian hosts.[86]

Jamestown was unlike any trading post the English had established. In trading ports, the English socialized with other Europeans, even those who were trade rivals. Wherever they went, other Europeans were in residence and could teach the English the customs of the country. With no prior European inhabitants to lend the English the assistance they counted on in foreign trading posts, Indians shaped how the English learned about the region, serving as guides and as local experts about the mineral wealth of the region.[87] Indians also worked as cultural interpreters for those English who wrote about the Chesapeake, as Thomas Harriot did at Roanoke and William Strachey did in Jamestown, both relying heavily on native informants. In Virginia, the English who sought lessons in other European endeavors in America had only their reading and some largely irrelevant lessons from the Caribbean, Roanoke, or the fisheries to rely on.

A trading and extractive venture populated by men ill-prepared to act like traders was destined for trouble. These were also traders without access to that most crucial component of commerce: marketable goods. John Smith had alerted the Company to the dearth of commodities in one of his first reports. When he wrote home to the Virginia Company in 1608, he compared with frustration his experiences trying to get commodities in Virginia with the easier efforts of the merchants of the Muscovy Company in Moscow. Smith warned the Virginia Company against great expectations from Virginia, for "though your Factors there [in Moscow] can buy as much in a week as will fraught you a ship, or as much as you please; you must not expect from us any such matter." Smith offered a blunt assessment of the English participants in the Virginia venture, whom he dismissed as "but a many of ignorant miserable soules, that are scarce able to get wherewith to live, and defend our selves against the inconstant Salvages: finding but here and there a tree fit for the purpose, and want all things els the Russians have."[88] As no lucrative commodities appeared, and no Indians presented themselves willing to pay tribute in the marketable goods the English coveted, original expectations receded, and Richard Hakluyt's imperial vision, centered around commodities produced by English workers, ascended.[89] If the Indians would not willingly trade for the corn the English desired, the English turned to force. Moreover, faced with this unreliable supply of food, the English had to grow their own, and that required land. After enduring a turbulent period known even then as the "starving time," the ill-chosen assortment of men at Jamestown finally—but only under the draconian discipline of a new governor, Thomas Dale—settled down to feed themselves, planting corn under penalty of death for noncompliance.

In its earliest years, when the English in Virginia were most interested in finding commodities and trade goods, the settlement was weak, and could have been easily destroyed. But it was not: Wahunsonacock could not see how these helpless men incapable of feeding themselves could pose a threat to him. Moreover, in the midst of expanding his own confederacy, he identified possible advantages of an English alliance. Pedro de Zúñiga, the Spanish ambassador in London, urged Philip III in 1607 to do just what Wahunsonacock would not: "It will be a service to God and Your Majesty to expel those rogues from there, hanging them while so little [effort] is needed to make it possible," just as the Spanish had done to French Protestants who settled in Florida in 1565.[90] And this was precisely the attack of which the English were most concerned. They dreaded the arrival of the Spanish, the "strangers" whom Governor Thomas Gates had been warned in 1609 were one of his two great enemies (the other being the Powhatans).[91] They oriented their forts to the sea, where an enemy might approach. And so they did. In 1611, a Spanish ship sailed into the Chesapeake, asking for a pilot and leaving three men behind as hostages.

The fear of Spanish attack encouraged the English to devote more resources to fortifications. The Virginia Company sent Dale to Virginia in 1611 for precisely this reason. After the Spanish ship sailed into the river and anchored at Point Comfort, Dale cast his gaze first at the weak English, with bodies "so diseased and crazed" that little work could be expected of them, and then at the "subtle, mischievous, Great Powhatan," and knew a third menace when he saw it. He recommended strategic locations to command the rivers. He established new settlements at Henrico and Bermuda Hundred, which the English expected to be more easily defended from Spanish attack than was Jamestown.[92] Dale built his new fortified towns precisely where the Indians did not want them, exaccerbating hostilities in Virginia. This was not the first nor the last time that English territorial expansion antagonized the Powhatans. When the English had dispersed from Jamestown in 1609, they built their fort at Nansemond on the site of an Indian temple.[93] Together, Dale's changes placed more emphasis on the importance of soldiers to protect the colony.[94]

By 1615, there were numerous indicators that a trade model would never take hold. The English failed to find the commodities that made trade profitable. They neglected to comport themselves as traders should, failed in Indian diplomacy, and fortified themselves in palisaded villages. They seized Indian territory, and their need for corn put new demands on indigenous land. Hostilities were intermittent between 1609 and 1614; in periods of peace, the two parties traded. Further pressure on land came from the actions of none other than John Rolfe, the man whose marriage suggested more harmonious possibilities, because of his experiments with tobacco. Even before the English sought to plant their own tobacco, they enjoyed consuming the plant in Virginia. Strachey recorded numerous words and phrases related to tobacco use in his extensive Algonquian vocabulary lists, compiled between 1609 and 1611 while he lived in Virginia. "I have noe Tobacco," "I must putt Tobacco in yt," "The Tobacco is good," and "the tobacco is naught" were phrases Strachey thought useful enough to record for the edification of future visitors and of readers in England, in addition to including the words for tobacco bag, tobacco pipe, and the wishful instruction, "Fill the pipe with tobacco."[95]

Tobacco was popular in England (despite the opposition of James I and many others), but English consumers depended on Spanish tobacco. Trinidado was the preferred weed, celebrated in a contemporary song and noted for its wonderful physical effects and medicinal value, making the smoker dizzy, sweaty, miraculously curing all ills.[96] The English tried to smoke the local Virginia variant, but could not stomach it. John Rolfe experimented with the plant and produced a hybrid. Moreover, he learned how to harvest tobacco (possibly with the assistance of his wife), hanging each leaf individually in Indian fashion. By 1617 the crop dominated colonial trade with England.[97]

Rolfe's experiments led to a tobacco craze so furious that colonists once again neglected to plant food crops. Cheap and able-bodied workers, including indentured servants, apprentices, and wage laborers, were abundant in this period for Virginia and all other English overseas commercial and military ventures as the English population grew amid stagnant economic opportunities at home. And the colony finally thrived. Or, more accurately, it began to generate some profits for farmers and investors. Englishmen still died at high rates and the colony's population grew feebly despite the infusion of newcomers, reaching some one thousand people by 1622. Tobacco also placed pressure on land, as colonists sought to put more into production, and further strained indigenous subsistence economies. Rolfe himself had come to believe that the Indians held title to their lands, and that it was incumbent on the English to purchase it, but this philosophy competed with other ideas that the English held that people derived their title to land from their efficient and appropriate use of it. The English prized agriculture over the range of activities (including hunting, fishing, and gathering) pursued by the Indians of the Chesapeake, and believed that their use of land gave them superior claim.[98]

In the wake of Rolfe's experiments with tobacco, Virginia Company members pondered the direction of their American investment. Their reforms, called the Sandys reforms after the Company's leader, Edwyn Sandys, centered on the settlers' personal conduct (gambling, idleness, drunkenness, violation of sumptuary laws) and on diversifying the colonial economy.[99] Dale had sought a more diverse economy as early as 1611, when he requested a permanent population of mariners in Virginia who could engage in the fur trade with Indians further afield and could also fish.[100] But not until the emergence of tobacco monoculture did the Company focus so fully on the settlement's economic structure. The Company tried to limit tobacco production and force people to plant corn, but tobacco was the only reliable lucrative crop the colonists could produce. With all of their spare time focused on food production, they had little time or energy left for the economic experimentation the Company pursued in new industries such as glass, silk, wines, and dyes.[101] The Company also shored up its funding through a national lottery.

To stabilize and diversify the colony's economy, the Company shipped thousands of new migrants to Virginia, many on vessels with inadequate supplies, and with similarly insufficient reserves in Virginia to tide them over for their first year.[102] The Company recognized the difficulty it had attracting the numerous people it envisioned because of scarce supplies, and these people were crucial elements in the Company's vision of the "flourishing State" they hoped the colony would become.[103] In contrast to the painstaking recruitment and interviews commercial companies exhibited in their quest for suitable overseas traders, the Virginia Company's attitude was considerably more casual. But their interest in launching new industries encouraged the Company's aggressive pursuit of suitable men. They cast their eyes east toward the European mainland. John Pory urged the Company to look in the Low Countries for men experienced at managing flax.[104] In 1620 the Company discussed a scheme to bring Dutch millwrights from Hamburg to go to Virginia to build mills, and by June, four carpenters were ready to embark.[105] They were joined by other Europeans. In 1621 the Virginia Company sought to hire some French vintners from Languedoc to go to Virginia to plant vines and to raise silkworms. One English adventurer planned to bring four Italians and their families to the colony to set up a glassworks. He hoped to make beads and glass, with the beads specifically targeted for the Indian trade.[106] Captain Norton and his Italian companions sailed to Virginia in 1621. We know little about how these Italians fared in the colony: we can safely assume that they were Catholics in a jurisdiction that officially allowed no accommodation of their worship but that must have made some private arrangement in order to recruit them to the colony.

The Virginia Company recognized the expertise that foreigners provided in the production of desirable commodities and crops, and so sought men who had been in the East Indies. One such hire was Robert Carles, who after sixteen years in the East Indies and even more in the West Indies was an expert in a whole range of coveted crops, including rice, sugar cane, indigo, and cotton, and had even written a treatise on cultivating these plants.[107] These continental Europeans and global traders contributed to a cosmopolitan presence in the colony at the same time that the colony moved in a new direction, away from the commercial and cultural heterogeneity of the trading post and toward intensive agricultural settlement.

The surprise, in retrospect, is the tenacity of the alternative vision of the trading post. Even as the English started planting corn with more enthusiasm, colony leaders *continued* to believe that the colony's prosperity might yet lie in trade and mineral extraction. The minister Alexander Whitaker reminded those who read his sermon, *Good Newes from Virginia*, in 1613 not to be discouraged by adversity, but rather to look to the tenacity of the Spanish and Portuguese, who struggled before they flourished and profited in the West Indies. He listed Virginia's commodities and praised its interlocking network of waterways, making riverine transportation of goods easy, as advantageous, he noted, as it was to the people of that great trading powerhouse, the Low Countries. With ore nearby, evidence of other metals such as iron, steel, and aluminum, and the south sea certainly somewhere off to the west (it was just a matter of finding it), Virginia in Whitaker's mind continued to harbor the multiple paths to prosperity first envisioned by the Virginia Company in 1606, reaffirmed in 1609, and echoed in Whitaker's aspirations.[108]

For all the fear that kept inhabitants sequestered in their fort, early residents were enthusiastic about the trade prospects of the region. William Strachey, who reached the colony at a particularly low moment in its fortunes, precisely when the inhabitants were in the process of evacuating themselves from their American deathtrap and turned back only at the appearance of the new governor, was nonetheless exuberantly optimistic about the advantages there. "If the business be continued," he wrote, "I doubt nothing…but to see it in times a country, an haven, and a staple fitted for such a trade as shall advance assureder increase" than the English trade with the Mediterranean. Strachey had arrived to find the colonists starving, and—afraid to go into the woods for firewood—burning instead the houses of the dead. The Indians killed some English soon after his arrival as well.[109] Yet he optimistically wrote with continued hopes of the "business" and believed that Virginia might eclipse the Mediterranean.[110]

The reasons for the failure of trade and the new direction of the colony had everything to do with indigenous economies and viable commodities, but deceit, as Strachey's self-deception attests, played a role as well. The English distorted their knowledge of and experiences in Virginia in order to shape public perceptions of the place. They sent back reports exaggerating and misrepresenting the bounty of the country, repeating rumors of gold mines and of passageways to Asia. The English also lied to the Powhatans, with the pattern commencing as soon as they arrived. Wahunsonacock asked John Smith what the English were doing in the Chesapeake, and Smith prevaricated, telling him that the English had fought the Spanish and washed ashore by bad weather, biding their time only until Captain Newport could ferry them away.[111]

Successful trade relations hinged on quick and, if possible, deep cultural understanding. Such understanding best existed among the Indians in Virginia, not the English. The attack launched by Opechancanough in 1622 permanently transformed Indian and English relations, clarifying and solidifying growing cultural divergences. It certainly made an indelible impression on the English. One-third of the colonists were killed. His attack recognized the clear shift in the settlement's economic enterprise. By 1622 Virginia had become a new kind of English overseas enterprise, a colony based on export agriculture, and that transformation required an accompanying alteration in indigenous economies. No longer even trying to perch gently like traders, adapting to the world around them, the English instead sought dominion. And their dominion was aided by another deviation from English experiences in trading posts overseas: the high mortality of indigenous people. While the English succumbed to disease, the Indians died at far higher rates as they confronted unfamiliar pathogens—smallpox, diphtheria, measles, influenza. Indian plans to curtail English settlement took place amid the dislocation of calamitous epidemics.

Opechancanough's attack in 1622 took the English by surprise in part because during a period of intense missionary activity by the English, and apparent acceptance by the Indians, Opechancanough had lulled them into a belief in Indian acceptance of their presence. Despite English fears of Indians, and a commensurate desire to separate themselves from them, Indians lived among the English.[112] The Indians had become dependent on convenient English commodities and were forced to conform to English methods of exchange in order to get them. Some Indians worked for the English—learning English in the process—in order to procure desired trade goods.[113]

Indian knowledge of England furthered this process of cultural comprehension. Uttamatomakin, one of Wahunsonacock's emissaries to London who had traveled there in 1616 with Pocahontas, proved invaluable in shaping future Powhatan diplomacy. He returned home after his journey and spoke against the English: he was particularly repelled by their religious intolerance.[114] There is a story—apocryphal, it seems, and the kind of condescending anecdote that the English liked to invent about Indians—that Uttamatomakin tried to count the English he encountered in order to deliver an accurate reckoning to Wahunsonacock.[115] The story tells us that he tried to notch a stick for each person he met, but that he quickly gave up at the vast numbers. The larger point—Wahunsonacock's urgent need for accurate information about the English—nonetheless remains important. The report of such a populous kingdom, capable of replenishing any diminution of the colony's population, would have been vital information that helped guide Indian strategies. Uttamatomakin's news confirmed a fear the Powhatans had from the very earliest appearance of the English: how many were there? John Smith's *Map of Virginia*, first published in 1612, included an Algonquian sentence translated into English that conveyed this concern: "In how many daies will there come hether any more English ships?"[116]

The attack in 1622 liberated the English from pretensions of amity. To be sure, it posed a public relations problem for the Virginia Company, but imaginative interpreters explained the advantages of the attack. One writer proclaimed that the massacre would actually end up being good for the plantation. Whereas before English hands were "tied with gentlenesse and faire usage," now they were "set at liberty by the treacherous violence of the Sauvages." Again the Spanish precedent came to the fore: drive the Indians on their enemies, the author urged, as the Spanish had exploited fights among Indians. He credited these divisions for giving the Spanish two kingdoms, those of Peru and Mexico.[117] Even as the English embarked on their own style of American settlement, one characterized by its departure from Spanish precedent, they drew on the useful examples of their rival. English reprisals for the 1622 attack lasted two years, and there were two more major conflagrations with Virginia Indians during the seventeenth century, but it was clear by 1622 that the English were well on their way to developing a new kind of overseas venture. By the middle of the seventeenth century, the Virginia settlement came to be defined by extensive export agriculture and intensive English migration. None of the many English models available in 1607 predicted this outcome. No one in the settlement's first years could have anticipated that the colony's prosperity (and the Powhatans' downfall) would come with a dried leaf and a puff of smoke.

STILL LOOKING BACKWARD: THE ENDURING MEDITERRANEAN

And yet, while the Virginia settlement solidified its departure from all original goals and demonstrated the evolution of a new kind of English overseas venture, not a trading post with a few English merchants living in an international community but rather a settlement defined by the displacement of an indigenous population and its replacement by English settlers, older frames of reference endured. It is impossible to see the world as Virginia's first English inhabitants perceived it. The vast majority was not literate; the few who wrote rarely reflected on their perception of themselves and the world they lived in. But clues help us to see how the English assimilated this strange American world into preexisting conceputalizations. What is startling to realize—in light of what we know happened in Virginia—was how slow residents and visitors were to reshape their worldview to accommodate the real circumstances around them. This remained a world oriented toward the East, toward the ancient heart of Christendom. Before Christian Europeans "discovered" the Americas, their world maps placed Jerusalem at the center. These two-dimensional maps shifted slowly as new geographies came into view. But the *mental* map shifted slowly as well. The eastern frame of reference is intriguing in its Virginia application because it reinforces the legacy of an eastern orientation (toward the European continent, and toward the trade cultures of the Mediterranean) in English exploits to the west even after new circumstances emerged that made eastern models irrelevant. People who went to Virginia and who experienced cultural innovations there turned to other foreign places in order to explain their American world to others. They used comparisons that would resonate with readers. And the world they evoked was that of the Mediterranean.

The first men to make the comparison were those who had been in both places, so the frame of reference is hardly surprising. The practice was evident as early as the 1580s, when the English established their settlement at Roanoke. There, Thomas Harriot reported, the people ate maize, called "Guinney wheate or Turkie wheate" by the English.[118] In Jamestown, the Turkish comparisons expanded well beyond staple crops. In his *Historie of Travel into Virginia Britania*, a text which was never published but circulated only in manuscript at the time, William Strachey drew regularly on Turkish comparisons to describe the Algonquins of Virginia. Since Strachey had spent a year in Istanbul, his knowledge of the Ottoman Turks was extensive by English standards. He compared Wahunsonacock's justice to Turkish justice; he distinguished between Wahunsonacock's living arrangement with his many wives, who lived scattered in his domains, and the Sultan's seraglio. He compared the winter clothing of Indian men and women to Turkish (and Irish) trousers. As the Turks spread a carpet for visitors, so too did Indian chiefs spread mats for their own guests and supplicants. Like the Turks, the Powhatans drank water, and they played a pipe like that of the Greeks. Ritual life also reminded him of his other foreign experiences. He described a dance, with its shouting and stamping and sweating and yelling like that of dervishes in their mosques.[119] But even men who had not lived in both places made a similar conflation. Mediterranean metaphors spread into the language used to describe the Algonquin Indians, characterized in Virginia Company records as late as 1620 as "infidels," the language of Christian and Muslim opposition, not as heathens, as Indians were often called elsewhere.[120]

Obviously, no one confused Istanbul with Virginia. Istanbul was the largest city in Europe, a polyglot, polyethnic, multireligious trading port of some

700,000 people. In 1622, Virginia as a whole contained just a thousand Europeans, and each could be counted in the list of the living and dead compiled after Opechancanough's attack. The differences could not have been more stark. John Pory's letters indicate the difficulty he had linking his two experiences. He had lived for several years in Istanbul before he journeyed to Virginia. The "solitary uncouthnes" of Virginia, particularly compared "with those partes of Christendome or Turky where I had bene" struck him forcefully, as did his sense of isolation. Pory lamented the paucity of news, which "did no a little vexe" him. Those eleven ships that arrived—and Pory's careful count suggested how significant these events were—came "fraighted with ignorance." The sensory stimulation of the "Christall rivers, & odoriferous woods" proved some comfort. Yet he chafed at the solitude of Virginia, and took care "to have some good booke alwayes in store, being in solitude the best and choicest company."[121]

Despite the glaring differences between rustic Jamestown, with its newly built homes and palisaded fort, and Istanbul, its urban skyline defined by the spires of minarets, those who had lived in both places continued to draw on Mediterranean people in order to understand and to explain Virginia. The delayed assimilation of new circumstances is immediately apparent if we look at what some Virginians said and wrote about slavery. The Mediterranean gave the English their first extensive context for slavery, an institution with which they acquired considerable familiarity: they saw slave markets, were accompanied by slaves, rowed by slaves, captured and sold into slavery, and threatened with enslavement. Some became slave traders there. When the English in Virginia wrote about slavery, they did so in this Mediterranean idiom. In 1620, the Virginia Company in London learned about a man who was defaming the colony by saying that the people there were "used with more slavery then if they were under the Turke."[122] The incantation of slavery appeared whenever someone wanted to find the most damning way possible to critique the colony. In the 1620s, critics of Sir Thomas Smythe's control over the Virginia Company and the colony drew on the metaphor of slavery to condemn the treatment of English in the colony. They claimed that Dale's strict laws, sent over by Smythe, had created great misfortune and kept the colony in "extreme misery and slavery" for all of Dale's tenure. Slavery functioned as a code, a single word conveying horrors no Englishman should have to endure.[123]

As late as the 1670s, fifty years after the first enslaved African reached Virginia, the image of Mediterranean slavery remained dominant.[124] When a minister recorded the tale of Thomas Hellier, a servant in Virginia who murdered his master and mistress in 1678 and was executed for his crimes, he sought to extract a cautionary tale not just in Hellier's violent solution to his servitude but also in Virginia's social dynamics. The clergyman chastised those Virginia masters who abused their servants, treating them not as fellow Christians, but rather employing tyranny, "as Turks do over Galley-slaves, compelling them unmercifully beyond their strength."[125] Even after seventy years of settlement—and by the 1670s a greater familiarity with enslaved Africans—the Mediterranean metaphor was the most powerful indictment this clergyman could muster, and it showed the tenacity of this model. The endurance of the Mediterranean frame of reference is especially intriguing because we know that English laborers worked alongside others—Africans—who endured real enslavement. Another servant, James Revel, described his ordeal in Virginia in lengthy verse, and pointed to the paired labor of English and African: "We and the Negroes both alike did fare/Of work and food we had an equal share."[126]

These Mediterranean comparisons were obviously not sufficient to turn Indians into Ottomans, indentured servants into galley slaves, or Jamestown into a Levant Company trading post, whatever the aspirations of investors or the hopes of some English inhabitants. As was the case around the globe, wherever the English went, indigenous conditions—defined in Virginia's case by the failure of trade and the opportunity for agriculture—shaped how the English occupied new territory. In this instance, the colony that developed in Virginia turned out to be the first successful English colonial experiment in the Americas. It introduced the English to new and violent ways of claiming and exploiting territory overseas, and provided a crucial model of coercion and aggression that the English drew on in later ventures. But when the colony of Virginia had evolved into a new kind of English settlement, one with export agriculture, high rates of European migration, and ultimately an enslaved population of non-Europeans, inhabitants and observers nonetheless understood this new venture in the context of what they had known before. And what they had known before was not only English, and not only Christian; these models did not prove relevant, it seems, as the English made sense of the new slave-based society they had created in North America. Instead, they embedded this North American colonial experiment fully within a global and multipronged effort to enhance English power and to diminish that of its rivals, part of a strategy that reached back into the sixteenth century and reached outward toward the Mediterranean and beyond.

5

ALL THE KING'S MEN

Governors, Consuls, and Ambassadors, 1590–1650

Virginia's emergence as a lucrative agricultural settlement populated by English men and women revived interest among English investors in colonies as viable avenues to profit. Small forays at Sagadahoc (1607), Bermuda (1609), Guyana (1609), Newfoundland (1610), and Plymouth (1620) were soon overshadowed in the 1620s and 1630s by intense colonial activity in the Caribbean and on the North American mainland and by the large-scale migration from England that sustained these ventures. These settlements required leaders, and as early as the 1620s a cadre of men emerged who had experience governing multiple colonies. These civil authorities resembled another emerging population who sought to govern globally dispersed communities of English subjects: ambassadors and trade consuls.

Governors, ambassadors, and consuls led two different types of overseas enterprises: precarious ventures in regions newly claimed by the English (whether predatory or agricultural or military) and trading posts. Each commercial community had a consul, sometimes selected and paid by the merchants themselves, and many overseas trading companies also appointed ambassadors to represent their interests. Trading centers all around the world, from Bordeaux to Cairo to Surat, had an English consul in residence. But the lines between consul and ambassador, and their different tasks, were not yet fixed. Consuls might be paid by merchants, but they also communicated regularly with the English secretary of state about foreign affairs and monitored the behavior of English overseas residents, serving in that respect as ambassadors did. For their part, ambassadors were generally appointed (and always paid) by trading companies but the crown occasionally intervened in their selection. Other settlements—strategic outposts, pirate bases, colonies—required their own leaders, men who came to be called governors after an initial period of shifting titles.

Governors in the first decades of the seventeenth century came primarily from military backgrounds; consuls and ambassadors generally had commercial careers, although there were important exceptions to both patterns. They rarely moved from one position to another, and in this respect, the personnel demonstrated a stark dichotomy between commercial and colonial ventures. Nonetheless, these leaders were embedded in a single overarching process—the expansion of English commercial and strategic interests overseas and the encroachment on territories or trade claimed by others—and confronted similar challenges. In the struggle for English power at home and around the world, the governor and the ambassador shared a common goal, one the soldier and colonial governor Nathaniel Butler articulated forcefully in the 1620s when he remarked on the special power of the English monarch "to humble the Spanish king."[1]

Ambassadors, consuls, and governors bring into focus some themes central to understanding English expansion in this period. They reveal the important military component in both colonial and commercial ventures, although the target and purpose of military action varied. Their successive appointments illustrate the value (perceived and real) of knowledge and expertise transmitted from one place to another. The care in their selection suggests how important England's reputation was to the crown, merchants, and investors, especially since the conduct of governors and ambassadors shaped foreign perceptions of England. These officials represented the crown in varied ways that reflected the unique local challenges of governance, the competing demands of crown, employer, and the English abroad, and the personality of individual men. These leaders also illustrate one way in which the English state projected itself overseas, indirectly, through these representatives, who served private employers while also serving the crown, and who always wrestled with the tension between being company men and the king's men.

The international context of commercial, extractive, and colonial activities required these company leaders to have diplomatic and political responsibilities and they possessed similar and overlapping skills. They needed authority, derived from formal license or personal attributes, to control the populations of English they lived among. These leaders also needed sufficient status to negotiate with indigenous leaders, whether Wahunsonacock, Mustafa I, or Jahangir. They ruled the English overseas: colonial governors regulated primarily Europeans, but over time some Indians and Africans fell under their jurisdiction. Consuls and ambassadors were in charge of the English "nation," as these merchants called themselves when they met in a body. All of these men carried out the functions of state leaders. They dispensed justice, sometimes after first having to create a body of laws; they collected fees and taxes; they sought to regulate worship in a fractured religious polity; and they represented the crown's interests to foreign leaders. Whether pursuing advantageous commercial relations or securing a tenuous English foothold in newly claimed territory, and whether or not trading companies had any aspirations toward territorial governance, these leaders represented the English state and—at times—carried out state functions.[2]

THE GOVERNORS

Since colonies were an innovative enterprise for the English in the early seventeenth century, colonial leaders represented a new kind of civil authority. The novelty of administering overseas settlements is apparent in something as simple as titles. The first Virginia leaders, for example, were called presidents. In the contemporary English context, presidents were appointed men with administrative power over geographic regions. The quick shift from the language of president to that of governor revealed a new understanding about some of the challenges of overseas leadership. The term *governor* derived from Tudor military usage: governors were men who commanded military garrisons within conquered regions. The English had deployed this model in France, and transferred it to England and Ireland (where the governor also acquired extra-martial responsibilities for agriculture and civil society) and ultimately to America. These men were military administrators, and the model of garrison culture they recreated was derived from the Netherlands, that "university of warre" where so many of these men had served.[3]

Colonial officers and governors came almost exclusively from military ventures. The era saw a reign of captains: Lane, Newport, Gates, De La Warr, Smith, Dale, Butler, Standish, Bell, Hunt, Riskinner, Stokes. The importance of military service—which in this period meant primarily service on the European continent—is impossible to overstate for the perceived viability of Atlantic and Caribbean experiments and the defense of trade in the Indies. Most of these military governors gained experience in the Eighty Years' War. Some men served in English regiments (gathered by English officers, such as the Earl of Essex), but others served directly for the Dutch governing body, the States General. For those who were captains of companies, the opportunities were lucrative, offering numerous ways to line one's pockets, but especially by paying soldiers (called "dead pays") who did not exist.[4]

In these volatile times, those seeking military adventures had ample venues to test their skills. John Smith first learned his soldiering in France, at Havre de Grace. When peace came in 1598 with the end of France's religious wars, he journeyed to the Low Countries with the English company of one Captain Duxbury, and served there. He viewed his stints as educational: he learned "to ride a Horse and use his Armes, with such rudiments of warre, as his tender yeeres in those martiall Schooles could attaine unto." With his marketable skills and four like-minded Frenchmen, Smith set out to see the world.[5] In this interlude of peace, many other English soldiers left the European continent to serve in Ireland. Concern about what soldiers might get up to in peacetime encouraged the colonial promoter Richard Hakluyt to propose their availability for colonial service lest they be "hurtfull to this Realme" without gainful employment.[6]

Military experience and particularly the ability to build fortifications were essential in a world in which European rivalries were endemic. English ventures placed English subjects in dangerous locations. The logic of territorial acquisition—for profit, for strategic advantage—dictated this peril. The English selected Roanoke for settlement because it provided a good privateering base for attacks on the Spanish fleet and settlements, and the same logic guided the English acquisition of Providence Island almost fifty years later (the Spanish agreed with the island's strategic value for such predatory ends, and after repeated attempts finally seized it from the English in 1641). Europeans in the Americas anticipated assaults from their multiple rivals. When the Spanish ambassador Pedro de Zúñiga wrote Philip III from London in 1608 that the English were fortified in Virginia in order to carry on piracy, he hoped that Philip would respond by destroying the settlement.[7] Even if English invaders also confronted overt hostilities from the indigenous people they flung themselves among, they oriented their fortifications to the sea.

The selection of these military men, witnessed in some of England's earliest North Atlantic ventures, was a deliberate choice to impose a particular kind of order on uncertain settlements. These officers arrived ready to work. Captain Thomas Dale strengthened Virginia's defenses and established new fortified towns in 1611; Captain Nathaniel Butler got to work on Bermuda's fortifications once he arrived in 1619; Captain Nicholas Riskinner sailed to Tortuga in 1635 with ordnance and munitions and a good supply of men, ready to fortify the island against Spanish attack. So urgent were matters of defense that the Providence Company ordered Captain Robert Hunt, the new governor of Providence in 1636, to ensure that the island's inhabitants were "very regmentlie excercised, especially upon the first comeing to p[er]sons to the Island till they be brought to a p[er]fect knowledge of the use of armes."[8] Although these men followed company orders, they also made their own contributions. Dale added fifty-one articles to Virginia's martial laws, all concerning military crimes. In the quasi-military regime of Virginia, all inhabitants, including women and children, were subjected to discipline considered brutal even by the standards of the day, vulnerable to the death penalty if, for example, they were so reckless as to pluck an ear of corn or pick a flower.[9]

Men whom historians associate first with other personal qualities such as religious piety or familial connections often secured their initial employment in part because of their military skills. Like so many of his peers, John Winthrop Jr. (later the governor of Connecticut) had continental adventures before he journeyed west across the Atlantic. He was part of the large English campaign under the Duke of Buckingham to relieve the besieged Huguenot stronghold of La Rochelle in 1627, and participated in the humiliating debacle at the Île de Rhé lamented by English Protestant travelers in later years. When he was recruited for his father's Massachusetts venture in 1631, he was appointed to organize the colony's defenses against Indians, and as part of his responsibilities inspected the English fort at Harwich.[10] The New England colonies may have valued piety, but, sandwiched between French and Dutch territory, they knew the importance of good fortifications and defense, and recruited men with relevant skills.

Martial experience was not the only attribute employers sought. Although Thomas Dale seems to have worked his way up from soldier to officer, some of these officers were gentlemen who possessed the social authority that employers hoped would enhance their leadership.[11] His employers characterized Captain Riskinner, bound for Tortuga in 1635, as "a Gent[leman] of birth and a souldyer."[12] Philip Bell, who governed Bermuda, Providence, and Barbados, came from a privileged background, and it did not always serve him well. His earliest experiences on Bermuda alerted him to the challenges he might face. He reached Bermuda in late 1626 or early 1627, and found his predecessor, Henry Woodhouse, at the center of considerable criticism. Bell sought to navigate this awkward situation from the perspective of his gentle birth. He recognized that Woodhouse had oppressed the people on Bermuda. Bell urged Woodhouse to get on the first ship and thereby evade the island's assembly and its humiliating interrogation, believing that "one of his place" should not face such dishonorable questioning. Woodhouse refused and the Bermuda assembly censured and fined him. Although Bell begged Woodhouse to make a submission to avoid the further degradation of imprisonment, Woodhouse was adamant. For his pride, Woodhouse ended up imprisoned in the colony's capital. While Bell avoided the poor judgment that dogged Woodhouse, he nonetheless found his position as a governor to be in conflict with his status as a gentleman. He resented his employment under merchants and the need "to live in such a slavishe subjectione to such meane & base minded men as the citizen part of the Companye are & doe showe themselves."[13] Overseas investors and their control over remote colonial leaders could overturn long engrained social hierarchies, contributing to the frustrations of wellborn governors far from home.

As companies courted the same type of military men for colonial ventures, one important consequence was that a cadre of professional colonial governors emerged, fully evident by the 1620s. Like Bell, these men went from colony to colony. Nathaniel Butler was the governor of Providence and Bermuda. Robert Hunt governed Providence Island in the 1630s, and fifteen years later was put in charge of the Assada plantation off Madagascar. These men possessed skills so urgent to colonial success that they often enjoyed competing offers. The Providence Company made a hard sell for Captain Riskinner, promising him provisions for himself and his family if he would go to Tortuga, as well as five or six slaves when he got there. He was accompanied by extensive munitions, including powder, shot, match, thirty swords, pistols, and muskets, and, to bring the sounds and sights of martial display to this English outpost, a drum and a flag.[14]

These military governors of the 1600s–1640s differ in important ways from the "governors-general" of a slightly later period. The captains who worked as governors were privately employed, serving at the pleasure of the various overseas companies and only as long as their patrons and supporters retained a voting majority. They constructed fortifications not against a subservient dependent population (as governors did later in India or Africa) but initially to fend off foreign European attack. They regulated the behavior and work discipline primarily of the English, not of non-European subordinates, although the quick turn to slavery in some places introduced a new threat and an internal enemy to these already precarious outposts. The important shift in governing personnel and in their links to central state authority came in the 1650s, particularly during Oliver Cromwell's Western Design, a military campaign aimed at Spanish holdings in the Caribbean. In the first four decades of the seventeenth century, the careers and activities of the military governors in the western Atlantic reinforce the importance of military power in private hands: this pattern endured for the East India Company until 1857.[15]

The fleeting nature of their employment illustrates this pattern. For many soldiers, work as a colonial governor was an interlude. These were, after all, soldiers of fortune, willing to serve different masters. Sir Thomas Gates interrupted his military service in the Low Countries, where he commanded a company in Dutch service, to govern in Virginia, but later died back in the army. These soldiers were valuable in colonial ventures, but they were also recruited by trading companies, which in this period created their own armies. Companies deployed these private armies sometimes against indigenous people (and potential trading partners) and mostly against European rivals. Such armies could be used for defensive and offensive reasons, whether preying on the Spanish or fighting off rivals and predators.[16]

Thomas Dale was one such man. He left military service in the Netherlands in 1611 to accept a position in Virginia, which he described as "the hardest task he ever undertook."[17] But Dale's duties were hardly complete on his return to England in 1616, as he traveled with an entourage of Powhatan companions, including Pocahontas, then known as Rebecca or Matoaka, and helped to usher them around England. He subsequently returned to the Low Countries, but not in a timely fashion. Before his departure for Virginia, he had married, and on his return to England after his long absence, he tarried with his sickly wife for some six months rather than return expeditiously to his regiment. He conceded that his delay "may pass for current with good and honest husbands, though not with my Lords the States in matter of service."[18] He seems also to have found time to get his portrait painted.

Dale was held in such esteem that he was paid by the States General even while he was in Virginia, although seven years was certainly longer than the States had permitted.[19] But Dale showed an odd loyalty to the people who had released him from service and paid him despite his lengthy absence. From Holland in January of 1618, he wrote the East India Company and alerted them to the Dutch East India Company's plans to challenge the English in the Indies.[20] So important was this kind of reliable intelligence about trade rivals that in 1620 the East India Company hired a spy for the large sum of £200 per year "to live at Amsterdam, and gather what light and knowledge he can."[21] Although he was due about £1,000 for his Dutch military service, Dale almost lost the entire amount because of the nature of his hasty departure, "*sans dire adieu*," the English ambassador reported: "The liberality which was used towards him being very extraordinary, and his departure so sudden, even the very day of the receipt of his money, deserves some civil excuse." The ambassador tried to soothe these troubled waters but appealed to James I's secretary for assistance, since the States believed that the king had required Dale's service.[22]

The East India Company hired Dale to help them build fortifications and to counter Dutch competition in the Indies. He survived long enough to fend off the Dutch fleet in one "cruell blody fight" at Jakarta in December of 1618.[23] Once in East India Company service, however, Dale did not limit his military action to the Dutch. He also seized a Portuguese galleon and demanded restitution for English losses. Dale failed in his effort to repel the Dutch from their stronghold at Bantam (on Java) and in his alliance with the king there. But he exacted such revenge as he could for English losses whenever he encountered them, and he used the same strategy English soldiers employed in North America. At Engano (on Luzon in the Philippines), he saw the skulls of sixteen or eighteen Englishmen (or so he believed), and in retaliation he killed two people and burned some houses and trees.[24] He died at Masulipatam in August of 1619 with the "contempt of death" that honor demanded, and his corpse was subsequently "enclosed and housed in a form of tomb, which," the merchant William Methwold reported four months later, "is almost finished."[25] The global nature of Dale's career linked European contests and their Protestant armies against the Catholic Spanish with America and Asia. It reflected the shifting focus of English energies, as Spanish power waned and the English confronted a new rival in the form of the Dutch.

CONSULS AND AMBASSADORS

As Dale's global career suggests, military officers were indispensable in places where the English were newcomers and faced likely rivalries, whether in the Indies or in the Americas. New and established trade companies in major metropolitan capitals or other long-standing commercial entrepots required a different kind of man at the helm. In selecting its first ambassador in 1614, the East India Company determined that it must send "an Embassadour of extraordinarye Countenance and respect" to the court of the Mughal emperor Jahangir, in order to further its commercial interests, to secure the firm treaties that promised continued prosperity, and to subvert the machinations of the Jesuits whom the English always believed plotted to undermine English trade. Following a lengthy debate about likely candidates, the Company determined that "none were esteemed soe fitting for that service as Sir Thomas Roe, yf hee may bee had." Company members described Roe as a man "of a pregnant understandinge, well spooken, learned, industrious, and of a comelie personage."[26] In short, he possessed the traits deemed essential for a royal and commercial emissary to a distant and, to the English, confounding court and potentate.

Roe was an interesting choice for the Company's first ambassador. Unlike many other men appointed to such positions in other companies, he did not come to his job by rising up in the ranks of the trade factory. In contrast, the Levant Company's first few ambassadors all had experience working for the Company in the Ottoman Empire before their appointment. Edward Barton had been a secretary for the first ambassador and had perhaps as many as ten years experience in the region. Thomas Glover had been sent as a child to Istanbul and acquired valuable language skills. He also served as secretary for two ambassadors. Paul Pindar had spent fifteen years in Venice, worked as a secretary to the ambassador, and was the consul at Aleppo before he got the position of ambassador. In short, these were men with germane experience for the job.[27]

So if Roe was not a merchant, why then did the East India Company select him for such an important office, and why did the Levant Company later break its own pattern and follow suit? His personal connections were important. He came from a prominent London family: Roe's grandfather had been Lord Mayor of London, as was his uncle in 1608. Moreover, the East India Company's governor, Sir Thomas Smythe, was a patron of Roe. And Roe was a man of many skills. He studied at Oxford and then read law in the Middle Temple, where he acquired a reputation as a charming conversationalist. In the parlance of the time, he was praised as a "wit." In 1601, Roe entered the service of the crown. He survived the transition from the court of Elizabeth to that of her successor, James VI and I, with a position in the household of James's daughter, the Princess Elizabeth. Knighted sometime between 1603 and 1605, Roe benefited from the trust of the new monarch, who sent the young courtier to Spain.[28]

Overseas activities captured Roe's interests as early as 1607, when he was appointed to the Royal Council for Virginia, but Roe's own initiative came to the fore in his first Atlantic venture three years later. His close acquaintance with Prince Henry (James I's first son, who had been an enthusiastic supporter of colonization and exploration until his greatly lamented death in 1612) and Sir Walter Ralegh dictated that those interests would focus on South America. In February of 1610, this "right valiant Gentleman," almost thirty years of age, sailed for the Amazon with three goals: the search for El Dorado via a new route, the quest for mines on the Orinoco River, and a more aggressive policy toward Spain.[29] After a two-month journey, Roe reached the mouth of the Amazon, and proceeded to travel up the river some 300 miles, farther than any other English man had at the time (or so at least Roe believed). His forays were facilitated by his pragmatic use of local Indian vessels. He navigated the Wiapoco and Orinoco rivers, spending some thirteen months in his explorations.[30] After his return in the summer of 1611, he funded and equipped several expeditions to inhabit and cultivate the Amazon under the direction of his two agents.[31]

Roe returned to England to a variety of domestic political duties, but was summoned overseas again, this time by the East India Company, and he left London in February of 1615 for Surat.[32] The king's commission to Roe made clear the important responsibility he bore to conduct himself appropriately. James I ordered him "to be Carefull of the preservaccion of our honour and dignity … as well in your speeches and presentacion of our letters as in all other Circumstances." But James revealed some sensitivity to the challenges of a foreign setting, where English customs might not apply. He tempered his instructions, adding "as farre as it standeth with the Custome of those Countries."[33]

Armed with his letter from the king, Thomas Roe, the first East India Company ambassador, reached a land where ambassadors were something of a joke, "it beeing become ridiculous, so many having assumed that title, and not performed the offices."[34] So Roe's first weeks in Surat were occupied by strenuous jostling for position, prestige, and suitable acknowledgment of his office and status. He refused to be subjected to the demeaning, invasive customs inspections other English traders had endured, at one point threatening to draw his sword and to brandish his pistols in order to protect his English companions from the customary physical search.[35] Roe demanded that he be received with the same respect his king was due. He refused, for example, to visit lesser political figures (the governors) in Surat until he had seen the emperor first. His vociferous complaints about his treatment in Surat and his threats to register his displeasure at the royal court prompted frantic, conciliatory offers of horses, an elephant, and a flag-bearing entourage to escort him. An impatient Roe remarked of these gestures, "I was no baby to be abused one day, and pleased with a Pageant the next."[36] When he finally reached the Great Mughal's court, he claimed privileges denied Jahangir's own nobles. The emperor permitted Roe to follow English customs in bowing to the king, and Roe was placed above the local nobles at court. Yet his status required constant vigilance from a gauntlet of what he viewed as petty assaults and gratuitous offenses. He particularly railed against the many slights sent his way by Jahangir's son, Khurram (whose pride, Roe remarked, exceeded Lucifer's), and he carefully recorded all his triumphs, major and minor.[37]

After he returned home in the fall of 1619, Roe resumed an active position in the Virginia Company. He attended his first meeting in November of 1619, and a few months later purchased back five Company shares he had previously sold to another man.[38] He held property in Virginia, a farm managed by a partner, Andrew Jacob.[39] Roe even held a share of land in Bermuda.[40] Although he never ventured to either colony himself, he did play an important role in Virginia Company affairs in London. His status alone made him an asset to the Company, and his title secured his place among the first men listed in any record of Company meetings. Roe's familiarity with the royal court and the king's support of him—James I had recommended Roe to the Virginia Company for its new treasurer in 1620—positioned him to bring petitions and requests to the king's attention. In 1620 Roe presented a petition concerning fishing in Cape Cod.[41] In that same year the Virginia Company appointed Roe as one of "fower learned gentlemen professors of the Lawe" to draft new laws for the colony.[42] Since Roe had studied at the Inns of Court and had experience administering justice as the leader of his Amazon expedition and in running English affairs in India, he seemed an ideal choice.

As it turned out, Roe was unable to fulfill his Virginia Company responsibilities. In 1621, the Levant Company summoned him as their ambassador to Istanbul, where they hoped Roe would transact business as he had in India: regulating English affairs abroad, protecting trade, and securing favorable treaties. The Levant Company was particularly eager to hire Roe because of his experience in India, where he had learned both to handle commercial affairs and to conduct diplomacy in a state composed of "heathen Princes."[43] The Levant Company worried that a series of weak ambassadors had damaged English prestige in the region and hoped that Roe might salvage English honor.[44] Thomas Smith, a Levant Company chaplain, later credited Roe with restoring "the Respect due to Ambassadours, which had been utterly lost for several years before, by a succession of insolent Vizirs."[45]

The Levant Company's preoccupation with the ambassador's reputation reflected a number of concerns. The importance of a man's reputation lay not only in the internal qualities it embodied, but also in the ability to deploy one's reputation, to be regarded by others as a person of status and power, to get favors. In other words, status and reputation enabled ambassadors, consuls, and governors to get their job done. Those without these weapons were ineffective among the English and similarly weak when dealing with foreigners. One Levant Company secretary's abilities made the ambassador, a man who had apparently risen to the level of his incompetence, look inadequate in comparison. In 1603 John Ker was full of praise for Thomas Glover, who served as the ambassador's secretary: "He is a man all sufficient." Ker elaborated: Glover was familiar with the ways of the Turks, and knew their laws. He was able to read and write and had a "perfect understandinge of all their languages," thus freeing himself from reliance on the dragomen, or interpreters, others required. Glover's sterling qualities eclipsed the ambassador, who made the English "hange the heade and blushe at the open reproches and scornes of th'other nations."[46] The merchant John Sanderson recognized Glover as a man who was on his way up, and the ambassador as someone who was in over his head.[47]

Ambassadors fought to secure their own reputations, but they also needed some support from authorities at home. Roe wrote the Levant Company complaining about problems with the Venetian consul at Aleppo and his "insolence" toward the English. Roe sought guarantees from home that the English had the same right to trade in Turkey as in other countries, and hoped "that I may conclude my tyme with that reputation I have hitherto mayneteyned, and wch I cannot loose, but by beeing forsaken by yor Ho[no]rs."[48] For ambassadors, far from the social and political context in England in which their reputations acquired meaning, it was a constant struggle to maintain the status they sought. Roe couched his complaints to authorities in the Ottoman Empire in the context of these assaults on his dignity. In 1623, Roe criticized the treatment the English endured at the hands of one Ottoman official. When Roe sent him copies of the commercial treaty to remind him of the rights the English had secured, the official claimed they were counterfeit. "Of this Insolency, never before heard of nor done in any Civill Nation," Roe reported, "I complayned to the great vizier," but Roe received no satisfaction.[49]

This striving was useless if men could not deploy their reputations for the good of the English. In 1611, one English merchant, Simon Dibbins, was arrested in Istanbul after a fight between some Englishmen and some Turks. The ambassador sought to rescue the man, "offering to pledge for him," but he was pushed away and his men were beaten. Dibbins was hanged at the ambassador's gate, the head and the heels stolen from the corpse, and the rest of the body buried by the English.[50] The English consul at Aleppo was himself imprisoned in 1629 because of claims made against English property that the English refused to pay.[51]

James I's charge to Roe in 1615, reminding him to preserve the king's honor and dignity, points to the challenges that these royal representatives faced. Roe confronted this tension explicitly. He juggled two competing claims on his time and energy in India. His first charge was to attend to "the preservaccion of (the king's) honour and dignity." The second charge was to bolster the East India Company's trade. The East India Company, of course, placed commerce and profits alongside the delicate honor of the king, and Roe conceded that his awkward position impeded his progress. In one letter home in 1616 he wrote frankly:

> I assure your Honor it is not fitt to keepe an Ambassador in this Court. I have shuffled better out and escaped and avoyded affronts and slavish Customes clearer then ever any did…But his Majestie commanded mee to doe nothing unwoorthy the Honor of a Christian King, and noe reward can humble mee to any basenes…I know one that might creepe and sue would effect more busines then I.[52]

Although he refused to "creepe and sue," Roe nonetheless found the demands of his position to batter his pride. The only reason he tolerated the daily assaults on his dignity was because he served "for a publique cause, wher are divers dispositions to please, diverse opinions to satisfye."[53]

Roe's lament points to the complex nature of his job. Now we might think of an ambassador as a political and patronage appointment, but for these commercial companies reliable and profitable trade was paramount: when the monarch interfered and attempted to select the ambassador, it always roused company opposition, especially since it was still the company that was obligated to pay the ambassador's salary. The financial pressure of supporting an ambassador heightened tension with the crown. When James I raised duties on imports, the Levant Company protested that they could not support their ambassador if they had to pay these fees. James was indifferent to their troubles, and told the Company that if they wanted an ambassador, they had to find the money for him. The ambassador went unpaid for a while as a result.[54] Financial pressure meant, first, that poorly qualified men might buy their office, and, second, that ambassadors paid some of their own expenses out of pocket and then sought to recoup their expenses through private trade and other perks. The Levant Company sought to avoid an expensive investment in a new officer and his new gifts for local leaders when it attempted to keep Roe on at his post in 1625, in the face of royal pressure for a new consul of the king's choice.[55] And companies always urged their employees to practice economy. In contrast to his strenuous efforts to visit Jahangir's court as soon as he reached Surat in 1616, in Istanbul Roe was finally summoned by the impatient and insulted vizier to pay his respects. Reluctant to waste the present he had brought from England on a man he believed was soon to be removed from office, Roe had dawdled in his diplomatic rounds.[56]

ENGLISH STATES OVERSEAS

For all their responsibilities to private employers and patrons, ambassadors and governors also sought to represent the crown's interest—Roe's "publique cause"—in all aspects of their job. Their responsibilities as state representatives were myriad: to carry out diplomacy, to communicate English policy to foreigners and English alike, to settle religious or political or personal disputes among the English, to create a church and the legal institutions of civil society where they did not exist, to protect the English from attack. These duties required them to serve on behalf of the crown, but also to build functioning societies where they lacked the local elites that customarily governed in England. Distance from England—from financial networks, patronage, employers, supplies, information, military support—limited their ability to carry out their jobs.

Diplomacy was perhaps the most direct way to express the wishes of their sovereign. Roe's greatest accomplishment in Istanbul was the peace he secured between England and the pirates of Tunis and Algiers. Pirate attacks so disrupted English trade with the Ottoman Empire, Roe wrote in a series of instructions for a letter to one vizier, "that either those knaves must be suppressed or wee must trade wth an Army, or not attall." Roe asked permission for English ships to retaliate on the main pirate towns.[57] He ultimately secured concessions protecting English shipping and he arranged for an exchange of slaves and captives on both sides. And he secured peace, with all hostility "annulled and blotted out of memory."[58]

Part of an ambassador's responsibility centered around clarifying English policy both to the English and to foreigners. As the best positioned men to do so, governors and ambassadors tried to sort out fact from fiction as rumors circulated overseas. In 1622 Thomas Roe called the merchants together in Istanbul to clarify a rumor that had reached them by way of the English at Aleppo that James I had granted toleration to Catholics and liberty of conscience. Roe had previously tried to point out the absurdity of these rumors, and he finally summoned all the merchants so that he could read out loud copies of various relevant writings from the king to the Archbishop of Canterbury, explaining that the king had released recusants from imprisonment but had not extended religious toleration to all. He enjoined the merchants to do their part, rejecting any similar rumors when they heard them. And because Roe's job included representing English affairs to foreigners, not just to English subjects far from home, he had these documents translated into French and Italian, and delivered to the other ambassadors in Turkey.[59]

The balance of a governor's or ambassador's time was devoted to managing the internal affairs of colonial or factory life. Governors and ambassadors traveled around the world, and had to be ready to assume the varied and unpredictable responsibilities of command in addition to overcoming the inconveniences and the challenges of setting up a new household. When he reached Istanbul, for instance, Roe found the ambassador's house to be empty, "nothing no not a stoole, except some old picture." The previous ambassador insisted he had nothing during his tenure but what he had purchased from his own predecessor, Paul Pindar.[60] The Levant Company sought to remedy the desolation of the ambassador's residence at least by providing a proper conveyance. In 1622 the Company sent Roe a coach and a coachman.[61]

As they attempted to put their own houses in order, however, governors and ambassadors were in the service of the whole community. The Providence Company's instructions to Philip Bell in 1631 reveal the heavy duties of a leader of a new colony. He was to issue an oath to the settlers, arrange lodging for the minister, organize all of the people on the island into families, each with a "Cheife," ensure pious behavior, watch against such vices as profanity or drunkenness or idleness, keep men from planting tobacco, but make them plant corn, and try also to get them to plant some sugar cane. All this, while building habitations for all, a church, and fortifications, and keeping an anxious vigil for Spanish threats.[62] His previous experiences on Bermuda must have comforted him somewhat: he knew it was possible to establish a colony, but he also knew how difficult it could be, and Bermuda never faced the foreign threats Providence came to know.

Nathaniel Butler's *Historye of the Bermudaes* provides a detailed account of his activities on the island as governor. His first energies went toward the island's fortifications, but he also engaged in other building projects, including a new church, a new house, a new prison, a new well, and, in St. George's, a big stone house, the state house, which still stands (see figure 5.1). He pressed men into public service, including some passengers bound for England whose labor Butler required before they departed. Butler used his building projects in part to set an example. Such was his hope when he constructed "a new fayre house of hewen stone" in St. George's. He made it with a flat roof, as he had seen in other countries that were at the same latitude as Bermuda, "and he built it of that substance and forme also, by waye of example and envitement of others to doe the like, as most proper for the nature of the place and climate," a structure good for keeping out the wind and the rain during hurricanes, and also easy to keep cool.[63] Butler sought to enforce morality on the island, but had, the minister Lewis Hughes conceded, a real challenge ahead. Butler's own officers drank too much, and the people who lived on the main (St. George's, the town, was on a separate island) were out of Butler's sight and did as they pleased.[64]

When English ships arrived, ambassadors and governors not only fell into a frenzy of letter writing and letter copying (assisted by their secretaries and scribes) in order to have documents ready when the ship sailed but also arranged to have arriving supplies unloaded, inventoried, and secured, while alerting people to the need to get their goods (whether crops or commodities) to port. Ships brought newcomers who required assistance, particularly those who landed in sick or weakened condition. Ships also brought recreational travelers, some of whom ambassadors formally received. Armed with a letter of introduction from their father, the Earl of Mar, Henry and Alexander Erskine were entertained by the English ambassador in Venice, John Wilton, on Christmas Day in 1618.[65]

An ambassador was supposed to know how many English were in residence, and the numbers could be large. The English ambassador in Venice reported that there were seventy English there in 1612.[66] Ambassadors struggled to maintain the Protestant faith of travelers in Catholic countries, although with varying degrees of success.[67] They also monitored the movement of English subjects, as the consul Hugh Lee did in Lisbon, noting especially those Catholics who had escaped England through subterfuge.[68]

Ambassadors performed a range of practical services for visitors. Then, as now, ambassadors could provide protection for travelers. In Paris at the time of the St. Bartholomew Day's massacre of Protestants in 1572, for example, at least one English tutor was killed and the formal protection of the ambassador was essential for the survivors.[69] Officials struggled to extricate travelers from prisons. They helped arrange burials; they located doctors for sick

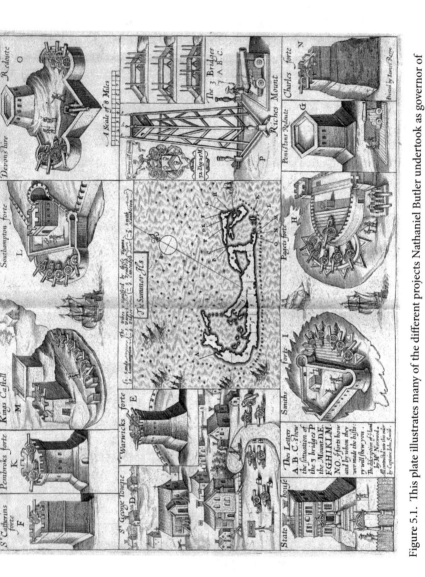

Figure 5.1. This plate illustrates many of the different projects Nathaniel Butler undertook as governor of Bermuda, including the state house (which still stands), fortifications, and other public works. John Smith, *The generall historie of Virginia, New-England, and the Summer Isles* (London, 1624), plate between pp. 168–169. By permission of The Folger Shakespeare Library.

travelers; they loaned money and clothing; they helped arrange letters of credit; they held mail and delivered it. Fynes Moryson regretted his failure to ask the English merchants or ambassador in Istanbul for a janissary to guide his brother and him in the Holy Land in the 1590s, thus forcing their dependence on Catholic hospices instead.[70] In Aleppo, the English consul George Dorington looked after the two brothers, handling their bills of exchange and loaning them money. No doubt he also procured the "Jew Physician" who attended the Morysons when they fell ill there. When Henry Moryson died, the consul helped with the burial and further assisted Fynes in recovering his brother's confiscated goods.[71]

The high mortality of overseas settlements meant that the care of the dead was a constant preoccupation. Governor Nathaniel Butler spent his own money to build a suitable memorial for the heart of Bermuda's first notable decedent, Sir George Somers, who had decided to settle there after his initial wreck on the *Sea Venture*. Although Somers's body was shipped home to England (an extravagance available only to the most elite decedent, and always difficult to accomplish since mariners disliked sailing with a corpse on board), his heart and bowels remained buried in Bermuda. Butler built a "smale monumental tombe" for these remains.[72] Edward Barton, the Levant Company ambassador, was buried in 1598 "(according to his always desier) under an olive tree before the enterance into the monastary one the topp of Calcose Ile," an elaborate undertaking requiring his successor's energy.[73]

English consuls similarly assisted foreign travelers by providing safe conducts for passengers. Roe produced one such document in Istanbul for a Greek priest, Theodoro Coredalio, who was on a voyage to Venice, calling on those who met him on the way or on those who might offer him passage on a ship to assist him. Roe invoked his own personal status, "Sr Thomas Roe knight," in addition to his office, "Ambassador Resident for his sacred Ma[jes]tie," in his letter.[74]

In addition to recreational travelers, an arriving ship might bring slaves or servants for a governor to allocate according to his employer's instructions, always a delicate process involving as it did the bestowal or withholding of favors and patronage. One vessel brought an unusual passenger to Bermuda: an Indian woman from Virginia. She had traveled to London in 1616 with John and Rebecca Rolfe, and the Virginia Company sent her from England to Bermuda, where they hoped Nathaniel Butler would find a suitable husband for her, and ship the newlyweds along to Virginia. Butler quailed before the responsibility of finding this woman an appropriate match ("a harder task," he complained, "than they wer aware of") but rallied. He found her "as fitt and agreeable an husband as the place would afforde," and hosted a wedding feast, at his house and at his own expense, for at least 100 guests. They dined on local produce. Among the guests were strangers who had recently arrived. Butler hoped to enhance Bermuda's reputation by spreading word of the made-in-Bermuda feast and its tasty island fare back to Virginia. He also sought to bolster Virginia's security by treating this Indian woman as well as possible, that the Indians of the mainland might be encouraged to continue in their friendship with the English. Butler was always aware of events in Bermuda's sister colony, and when he heard through letters from Virginia that the people there were hungry, he sent them some corn.[75]

As stand-ins for the crown, governors and ambassadors regulated civil and ecclesiastical affairs. The convention of describing each gathering of English merchants abroad as a "nation" reinforced how the ambassador replicated the sphere of the king's rule in a mini-England overseas. The governor was also invoked in the same Book of Common Prayer liturgy that named the sovereign. Nathaniel Butler complained from Providence that, amidst the religious upheavals the island experienced in the 1630s, when he was at odds with the colony's main minister, the clergy did not pray for him specifically when he was away from the island, an affront to his status.[76]

In the same way that a monarch could establish the religious settlement in England, colonial governors could influence a colony's religious settlement. With the latitudinarian sensibility of Elizabeth I, Nathaniel Butler resolved a religious conflict on Bermuda in the 1620s. There were two ministers there, Lewis Hughes and Samuel Lang, neither one of whom would use the Book of Common Prayer in services, a practice that revealed each man to be a dissenter from the established church. Moreover, they could not agree on how to administer the sacraments. The quarrel spread among the island residents, who worried whether the sacraments were legitimate. Butler devised a solution, ordering the ministers to employ the form of sacraments that was used on Jersey and Guernsey, which was the same order used in Geneva and in the United Provinces and by Huguenots. The ministers consented, and Butler himself made the English translation out of his French books.[77] As Butler's creative solution indicates, a thoughtful governor could temper religious conflict. Governor John Winthrop Jr. of Connecticut was opposed to the violent persecution of Quakers that marked the neighboring colony of Massachusetts in the 1660s.[78] His opposition earned the gratitude of his brother, Samuel, himself a Quaker, who wrote from Antigua that he had "been much comforted to hear & read of thy tendernesse to persecuted friends in New England."[79]

In their role as mini-sovereigns, governors guided civil affairs. They placed currency into use: Governor Tucker of Bermuda paid the islanders in "hog money," made by the Somers Island Company for use in Bermuda. These coins featured a hog on one side, probably because of the hogs—left by the Spanish—which ran wild on the island when the English arrived.[80] In the new polities characteristic of this period, much of a governor's responsibilities included educating men in the administration and enforcement of English law. Like other governors, Nathaniel Butler held assizes and assemblies on Bermuda. He provided lengthy and detailed instructions to his jurymen on crimes and their definitions.[81]

A governor could do more than create and define the law. He could determine whether to enforce it, thus using the autonomy of his office to innovate policy. In the 1660s John Winthrop squelched witch executions in Connecticut. Although he believed in witchcraft, he doubted allegations against accused witches, and single-handedly worked to infuse skepticism into the legal process, protecting the lives of accused women and men in the process.[82] But Governor Daniel Tucker on Bermuda abused his power during his tenure between 1616 and 1619. When Tucker took over, he imposed the martial discipline he had previously experienced in Virginia under Thomas Dale's tenure. Tucker even brought with him a copy of Dale's laws, and consulted it faithfully.[83] Tucker's harsh regime was all the more troubling in its contrast to what had come before. His predecessor, Mr. Moore, was a carpenter by trade, a man with practical skills and the right temperament for governance but deficient in formal education.[84] Tucker tried those who criticized him for mutiny and rebellion, and hanged a Frenchman who got drunk and spoke "saucely and arrogantly" to Tucker.[85] Tucker was so adamant about the authority of his position that a woman who made the mistake of criticizing the governor for hanging the Frenchman was also indicted and condemned for mutiny and rebellion, and survived only by a suspension of her sentence.[86] His conduct earned him the enmity of numerous island residents, including Lewis Hughes, who wrote his supporter Sir Nathaniel Rich to voice his complaints. Tucker was "too wrathful and furious in his passions towards every bodie, and wedded to much to his owne will, which doth discourage many and makes them wearie of dwelling here."[87]

In contrast to the severity of martial discipline he found in place when he arrived on Bermuda, Butler pursued a gentler course. He was sensitive to the unique challenges of colonial living, and reprieved three boys condemned to hang for stealing food, "since it might well be, that either the cruelty, povertie, or at least want of fitt government in their masters, wer chiefe occasions and motives of this ther pilferinge." And he cast the blame beyond the children's masters, accusing the investors in England of a poor choice of men.[88] He even made a journey through the island, much like the royal progress of a monarch, inspecting crops as he went, and giving advice about the care of tobacco and corn.

Although trade consuls did not have to create a new society from scratch, even to the point of organizing strangers into "families" with "Cheifes" as Governor Philip Bell did on Providence in 1631, they still had to manage affairs among the English merchants. In Istanbul in the 1620s, Roe settled disputes, recorded wills, executed estates, secured debts, and fined miscreants, keeping one-third of the fines for himself.[89] He issued oaths of loyalty to the local interpreters who helped negotiate treaties.[90] Ambassadors and consuls had some recourse when merchants disobeyed them. They sought to extract good behavior through a system of fines and by regulating conduct at court. Thomas Bendysh, the Levant Company ambassador at Istanbul, ordered one factor, George Hanger, to pay a fine of $2,000 in 1649 for his "fractious demeanour and carriage." Hanger's opposition to Bendysh might suggest that the fine was motivated only by personality conflict, but Bendysh also accused Hanger of behaving badly enough to prompt complaints from Turkish ministers, thus putting all of the English in danger.[91] Consuls could also imprison merchants.[92]

But for all Governor Tucker's violence or Ambassador Bendysh's fines, these officials did not have the authority of their sovereign. They were constrained in their activities, bound from above by the demands of their employers and checked from below by the ambitions of merchants and colonial inhabitants. Nathaniel Butler complained about the flawed instructions, the "equivocations, contradictions, oppositions, and defective expressions," which came in the Somers Island Company's letters to him. They "seeme rather to ensnare than informe me," he griped. He never got the important information he required, nor did he get answers to the specific questions he asked. The Company wanted him to focus on vines and sugar cane when he preferred to expend his energies building a strong blockhouse to safeguard women and children in case of a Spanish invasion. He requested supplies that never came, and instead the Company dumped ten convicts from Newgate on Bermuda.[93] He was unable to take the initiative he desired in those instances when his projects took time away from the Company's goals, which as the appeal for sugar indicates were often more focused on a quick profit than on long-term defenses. The gap between company orders and local circumstances shaped the reality of a governor's or ambassador's life and required adaptation and ingenuity.

Butler's concern about a governor's authority appeared in a treatise he wrote in 1626 on another topic altogether. In "A Designe upon the west indies fleet by the way of the Bermudoes, and how to be managed," he praised the strategic value of Bermuda. The Spanish fleet passed close by, and he proposed that an English fleet lie in wait in Bermuda's capacious harbors. Perhaps speaking from his experience as a colonial governor, he insisted that all men should serve under the admiral of the fleet, so that the governor would have no responsibility for them, and similarly stipulated that the governor have jurisdiction over any islanders who committed offenses against members of the fleet. His special attention to the allocation of jurisdiction in a pamphlet on international strategy suggests his experience and frustration in dealing with precisely these matters and demonstrates the link between the smooth workings of a small colonial polity and foreign affairs.[94]

There were other checks on a governor's power, centered around two problems: first, how expansive was a governor's authority, and, second, what was its locus. In dealing with colonists, the military leaders were given a new kind of authority. Thomas Gates of Virginia, who first served as governor from 1609–1610, was the first colony leader who was permitted to act alone, not with the support of the council.[95] Some early leaders were expected to share power. Six men occupied a rotating governorship of Bermuda from 1615 to 1616, casting lots "to see who first should begin the playe," and the Providence Company originally thought it would appoint two governors to split responsibility for the settlement when the enterprise began until Daniel Elfrith urged the Company to give Philip Bell sole responsibility on the island.[96] So the commitment to a single leader (whether elected, as in some New England colonies, or appointed, as in the proprietary and joint-stock colonies) was slow to develop, and reflected in part the uncertainty about how investors in England might impose their will on their distant holdings.

When Butler, armed with a commission from the Somers Island Company that had hired him, reached Bermuda in 1619, he reported in his *Historye* that "the first act he did as Governour was to let them at the towne understande that he was so."[97] He had to combat the feelings of men who believed that the *people* should choose their govenor. Captain Kendall, the acting governor before Butler arrived, had fueled this belief during his year in office. Butler complained of Kendall's leniency. "One of the effects therof is that the inhabitants here might and wer to choose their owne Governour." Kendall told Butler "that he did more relye upon his election that waye, than upon any commission he had from Cap: Tucker," his predecessor. One islander, John Yates, agreed, and he complained about the way governors were selected. He believed that the people, not the investors, should make the decision. Butler's fury is palpable across the centuries. "This ill-sounding opinion I have and shall crush and roote out by all means."[98]

But even if Butler railed against the need for the governed's consent, it was a necessary feature to these societies. Governors and consuls relied on the cooperation of the men they worked and lived among in order to secure their posts. When Josias Forster received his commission from the Somers Island Company to serve as governor in 1650, he reported that to everyone's surprise he was "freely and peacably admitted to the Place without the Least interruption, contrary to the expectation of many here amongst us." His reception was especially surprising in light of the recent eviction of Governor Turner from his office and the general political turmoil of the war years.[99]

The slow evolution of the office of governor was matched by the uncertainty about who or what made an ambassador or a consul, and how much authority these men had. The case of George Dorrington, the Levant Company consul in Aleppo, illustrates the problem. The Levant Company ambassador in Istanbul was reluctant to follow John Sanderson's advice to make George Dorrington a consul in Aleppo "without authoritie out of Ingland" in 1596.[100] Dorrington was in fact made a vice-consul, but the merchants at Aleppo wrote him a letter accusing him of numerous violations of Levant Company policy and asked him to resign. Dorrington had neither read the Company's orders and statutes to the merchants, nor made them available for their own study. He failed to keep a register of letters, and the merchants had no faith in him as an arbiter of conflicts. His reputation was so low in the city that he was "publiquelie a man defamd... Turks caulinge you a Jewe, and Jewes say you ar a Turke, and Christians reproche you by the name of both Turke and Jewe." Dorrington used a translator "so simple of witt and ignorant in languages" that he made himselfe "a laughinge stocke."[101] Rejecting this misfit, the merchants gathered to elect a new consul for their factory.[102]

Thomas Roe discovered the limits of his authority when he sought to alter the mechanisms of governance of the English merchants in Istanbul in 1622. The first English court he held established his guidelines. Roe guaranteed every man free speech and opinion "in decent and fitt tymes," provided there was also "due regard" to the honor of the king, the laws of England, "and respect to his L[ordshi]ps quality and the place."[103] At that same meeting, he tried to push a representative form of government on the English nation in Istanbul, but the merchants resisted, perhaps sensing the authoritarian proclivities of their new ambassador, demanding instead a direct democracy, "that *every man* might come" to court.[104] Roe's difficulty extracting suitable deference from the Levant Company merchants abroad obviously continued, for he had an act passed in March of 1625 providing for fines should any Englishman "give any evill words or uncivill language" in any court or assembly "before his l[ordshi]p."[105] A few weeks later Roe ordered that any man planning to speak in the court or assembly "shall with due Reverence and respect to his l[ordshi]p and ye place, stand upp, and with his hatt off direct his speech only to his lp in fitting and civill manner."[106]

The contentiousness and disrespect Roe's policies addressed were characteristic of trading posts everywhere. Ambassadors and consuls complained repeatedly about independent and unmalleable traders. From Lisbon, Hugh Lee wrote that he thought the "savages in Virginie" could not be more "incivill" than the merchants of Lisbon, one of whom had punched him in the eye.[107] In Aleppo, Thomas Hodges brought charges of battery against Randolf Eaton, who he claimed had hit him even in front of the consul.[108] The ambassador himself proved no deterrent. The merchant John Sanderson slugged his nemesis William Aldrich right in front of the Levant Company ambassador, Edward Barton.[109]

These conflicts might be easy to dismiss as distortions of ambassadors and consuls, who resented any challenges to their authority and who complained regularly to company officials in London. Exacerbating tensions for consuls and ambassadors was their inability to collect their salary. Although these men were often hired by London companies, financial arrangements required the merchants—the men they were supposed to govern—to provide their salaries. Not until 1825, with the creation of the Consular Service, did the government pay British consuls.[110] In Lisbon, the merchants paid the consul's salary, which explained in part Hugh Lee's frustration: in 1615, he could not get paid.[111] The consul in Lisbon had special trade privileges in order to supplement his salary, but Lee maintained that after twelve years in Lisbon, he had gone into debt.[112] Thomas Roe similarly struggled to collect his salary in Istanbul.[113]

Clearly connecting conflict with disobedience, Roe described the merchants at Surat as men more eager to argue for display and sheer delight than to carry out any of his orders.[114] Yet evidence from different trade factories suggests that the merchants were a disputatious lot: the culture of the trade factory required merchants to accommodate foreign norms, but they had no compunction about pursuing their own wishes within the safety of the English nation. The chancery books for the Istanbul factory are full of the merchants' accusations against each other, their attacks on other merchants for lying, and their attempts to discredit witnesses by accusing them of bad behavior.[115]

John Sanderson's frank characterization of the "contentious crue" at Istanbul suggests the kinds of men that found their way to trade factories. There was Mr. Garaway, who "died with wenching"; the unfortunate Charles Merrell, who was shot on his way to Aleppo by a janissary who was aiming at a pigeon; Barli, who died as a beggar; one Harman, whom he dismissed simply as "a knave and a roge"; Tient, a "knave graver"; and finally Midnall, "the cocould."[116] "I assuer you," he wrote a friend in London in 1600, "heare ar a jolly sett of divers devells, fooles, maddmen, antiques, monsters, beasts, whoremongers."[117] But merchants also blamed consuls and ambassadors for animosity. In 1639 the English trader Philip Williams faulted the ambassador for conflicts in Istanbul. His harsh behavior made men "more weary of ye place then ever ye jewes did, & for my part I wish my selfe in a more quiet clymate, where such buzzing of contentions may not affright mine eares, wch never were acquainted till I came hither with other then peaceable speeches free from violent & unsavory passion."[118]

These quarrels point to the small and constrained worlds the English lived in overseas. Social misunderstandings disproportionately damaged feelings in these insular enclaves. The Levant Company chaplain John Covel recalled one such incident in his journal in 1670. He toured Tunis (or Carthage, as he called it), where an English consul, Mr. Earlesman, attended to English affairs. The admiral of Covel's fleet had invited Earlesman to dine on board, but the letter of invitation failed to reach him until after 10:00 PM. The admiral, meanwhile, had held dinner for the consul, who later came to apologize but the admiral, having believed his invitation to be spurned, took umbrage and decided to weigh anchor that night. Nothing could be done to appease his hurt feelings.[119]

One ambassador, Thomas Smythe, sought to preempt conflict within the small commercial community of Muscovy merchants on his voyage to Russia in June of 1604. Before boarding the ship, Smythe gathered the merchants around him, and exhorted them to amity. Although they were strangers to each other, Smythe urged the merchants "to love and delight each in other, express your loves in helping and cherishing in time of distresse, sicknes, or distemperature." When some fell ill while others thrived, Smythe urged "the strong to helpe the weake, as fearing daily hee may fall into the like need." Like the message contained in the "Model of Christian Charity," the famous address delivered by the Massachusetts Bay governor John Winthrop to his companions on his first voyage to North America in 1630, Smythe hoped to create a community out of strangers. In case this first speech was not sufficient, Smythe addressed the men again before the ship left Archangel, telling them to show love and courtesy to each other and to avoid prostitutes.[120]

Amid the conflicts in colonies and factories, governors and consuls pursued the support of their patrons in England while their opponents tried to circumvent them. This process involved one of the central responsibilities of a distant representative—making reports on overseas affairs—and permitted governors and ambassadors to shape the news employers in England heard. Governors and ambassadors were often the most informed eyewitness investors had to overseas affairs, with the most extensive knowledge of their domain. Consuls and ambassadors wrote faithfully to their employers and to the secretary of state. For their part, governors reported on colony affairs, announcing the need for provisions or the challenges of subsistence, the paucity of supplies, and the abundance of rats. They even used their privileged vantage to report on other colonies, as Butler did in a highly partisan tattletale on Virginia, which he had visited on his way home from Bermuda in 1622. In his screed, he deplored the colony's lack of fortifications and observed that a ship could sail up the river and ride at anchor, firing its cannons and destroying the English houses.[121] Governors and ambassadors appeared at company meetings in London on their return home, ready to answer questions and respond to charges against them.[122]

But any literate Englishman had the same opportunity as these highly placed men to write home with his own version of affairs. Governors and ambassadors alike struggled to maintain their jobs and their reputations while their rivals and enemies maligned them. The Levant Company ambassador Henry Lello, whom John Kitely dismissed in 1607 as a "foggie cloud," attacked his replacement, Thomas Glover, once Lello was home in England. Lello accused Glover of bigamy, of beating a servant to death, of hitting his wife, of fathering a child by one of his maids, of sodomy with a boy, of leaving his wife's corpse unburied and stored in the buttery, and, finally, of excessive adornment (too many jewels and feathers) before the Sultan.[123] In Lello's view, Glover was a belligerent, rapacious, bisexual, excessively bejeweled adulterous pedophile with unfortunate tendencies toward fashion *faux pas*. John Sanderson, a Glover supporter, stopped speaking to Lello, although both men walked daily at the Royal Exchange, carefully keeping to different paths in their strolls.[124] Any man in power suffered the same verbal abuse. Nathaniel Butler's enemies presented a full "catalogue of divers wrougns and injuries" he had allegedly committed to the Virginia Company in London, and he went to the trouble of answering every single complaint.[125]

To protect their reputations, and perhaps also to satisfy personal inclinations, several of these men distinguished themselves as self-promoters: overseas service enabled them to redefine themselves abroad, but they left nothing to chance, crafting their own image in print and in portraits and securing others to assist them. The three Sherley brothers, Thomas, Robert, and Anthony, illustrate the opportunities for self-definition. Their careers began on the continent in military service, and they subsequently shed their attachment to the English state, becoming citizens of the world and serving a variety of masters. In their military ventures, Englishmen generally fought alongside men of other nationalities. This service might have played an important role in dislodging the English from unthinking national attachments. The first stage in this process was the acquisition of a pan-Protestant sensibility, as the English fought side by side with other Protestants against the Catholic Spanish. But soldiers who ventured farther afield discovered a broader definition of Christian, one able to encompass Protestants, Catholics and even Uniate Christians. When John Smith joined the wars against the Turks, he found himself "both lamenting and repenting to have seene so many Christians slaughter one another."[126]

Perhaps as a consequence of such experiences, Anthony Sherley converted to Catholicism early in his travels. He sailed to the West Indies on one expedition, and ended up in Persia, where he secured an appointment by the Shah as his ambassador to Europe. His brother Robert married a Persian woman and also worked as the Shah's ambassador, dressing in Persian garb when he performed this service and also choosing to be painted by Anthony Van Dyck in his Persian clothes when he was in Rome in 1622.[127] Thomas Sherley, whose career looked tame only in comparison to those of his brothers, went on several privateering voyages and endured 33 uncomfortable months in captivity in the Ottoman Empire. A travel writer in his own right, Thomas commissioned the writer Anthony Nixon to compose a pamphlet about the brothers, and it is possible that he also encouraged *The Travels of the Three English Brothers* (1607), a play about him and his brothers Anthony and Robert.[128] The Sherleys ensured that their reputations were solidified in print in multiple genres, and in expensive portraits. Other governors and ambassadors shared their interest in self-promotion, and it is no accident that these officeholders are the best illustrated population among the overseas travelers.

Many others ensured that their own version of events under their jurisdiction reached the public eye by writing "histories," or so they called them, demonstrating what historians have long suspected, that governing a colony or serving as an ambassador pale next to the opportunity to be a historian. John Smith did this multiple times, intertwining his inflated personal biography with the histories of the places and people he had visited. Other colonial governors followed suit. John Winthrop's journal had such a formal role: he titled the second and third notebooks "A continuation of the History of N. England," although he never sought to make public his record in his lifetime. Still, his journal enabled him to settle scores with his opponents, and his later editorial marks indicate that he used the text to compose a formal account of his time in power. Winthrop's acquaintance and New England neighbor William Bradford similarly wrote a history of the Plymouth Colony, which he governed. Nathaniel Butler composed a history of Bermuda, and although he wrote about himself in the third person, his favorable depiction of his activities reinforces the self-aggrandizing aspect of the text. Thomas Roe joined the enterprise as well, contributing chapters to a larger and preexisting history of Turkey.[129]

Writing gave these men the power to make permanent their own version of their rule, but it also provided them with an outlet for their occasional loneliness. Within these small worlds, the men at the top were especially isolated, unsure whom to trust and reluctant to confide in underlings. Governors and consuls sought to relieve their solitude in part through the entourages they brought with them. They were often able to appoint an entirely new staff to accompany them, as Thomas Glover did when he was appointed as the new Levant Company ambassador.[130] An ambassador's choice of staff theoretically guaranteed him their loyalty and good service, both essential attributes in the complex political worlds in which ambassadors lived and worked. Ambassadors could appoint ministers. They could bring servants. Governors and consuls could take their wives with them more easily than could merchants. Thomas Bendysh traveled to his embassy in Istanbul in 1646 with his wife, one son, five daughters, a physician, and an interpreter.[131] And in some instances, companies dangled the presence of a wife as bait to keep a governor content. When Philip Bell threatened to leave Providence in 1631, the Company resolved that it would try to get in touch with his wife and ship her to the Caribbean in hopes of encouraging him to stay on the island.[132]

Despite this companionship, some men regarded their overseas tours as hardship posts. Although Thomas Roe embraced his enterprises with enthusiasm, referring with wonder to the portion of America he saw as "the newest and strangest land," he occasionally regarded his time overseas as an exile.[133] The result was a sense of displacement that led to occasional homesickness. He referred to himself as a "banished freind" in one letter from India, and invoked the phrase again a few years later from Istanbul.[134] Roe wondered why no one wrote him save his employers. Speculating on his mother's health, he queried with a dramatic flourish, "is it not the bottome of oblivion to be forgotten by the womb that bare mee?" He begged a friend "to rowse up" his mother that he might know whether or not she lived."[135] The physical discomfort of his stay in India increased his distress. He found India a place of great inconvenience, a country with "no temperate or quiett season," offering only brief respite from the plagues of fires, floods, heat, and flies, and his frustration and impatience with the cultural barriers to his trade mission permeate his journal.[136] Even closer to home, from the relative proximity of Portugal, Hugh Lee took his plight in Lisbon to heart. He believed that other English merchants in other locations lived and labored in better conditions—he particularly singled out the consuls in Turkey and Italy.[137]

In their isolation, foreign visitors sometimes provided easier companionship than other English residents. In Bermuda and Providence, Nathaniel Butler insulated himself with foreigners. Seventy Spanish men, women, and children were shipwrecked on Bermuda in 1621, and Butler took care of them and protected their few surviving goods from the island's scavengers.[138] On Providence, he entertained two imprisoned Spanish friars and dined with them on Easter day in 1639.[139] Although the law of the sea required Butler to assist these distressed people, his hospitality separated the governor from the islanders in both instances. Butler's care for the shipwrecked Spaniards incited criticism from the people on Bermuda, and his socializing with Catholics was an open affront to the puritan ministers and colonists on Providence.[140]

Trade factories offered merchants more steady companionship than the occasional shipwreck might provide a colonial governor. These commercial entrepots were convivial places: men dined with people of other nations, attended religious services of different traditions, and sampled new food and new fashions. This sociability was what had enabled Lee to compare his miserable isolation in Lisbon to the greater comforts of other postings. When Thomas Glover's wife died in Istanbul in 1612, the Dutch ambassador, the

Hungarian agent, and a French colonel all followed her corpse from Pera to its grave.[141] International bonds forged in collective commemoration of the dead helped men cooperate for political and commercial ends. English ambassadors formed valuable alliances with other Europeans. In Istanbul, the French ambassador was imprisoned in 1617, and the ambassadors from England and the Low Countries threatened to leave Istanbul if he was not released.[142] These social interludes, whether with shipwrecked Spaniards or French traders, illustrate the cosmopolitan opportunities governors and ambassadors might find in places as remote as Bermuda or as urbane as Istanbul. Yet the cosmopolitanism of governors and ambassadors was always constrained by their need to represent their employers and their crown, and to do so with visible signs of English office, whether their garb, their authority, or other trappings, from the coach and coachman the Levant Company provided Ambassador Roe to the flag and drum the Providence Company sent with Governor Riskinner.

It was also constrained by international rivalries and personal affinities. While Roe enjoyed a friendship with his Dutch counterpart in Istanbul, everywhere Roe traveled, he encountered Spaniards and Portuguese who garnered his steady mistrust. His activities in South America, India, and Istanbul revealed fully his intense anti-Catholicism and his dislike of Spanish and Portuguese competition. He welcomed his activities in both South America and India as timely opportunities to alter King James's conciliatory attitude to Spain. He wrote from Trinidad in 1611 that all the sailors he encountered hoped for opportunities to compensate their losses by Spanish raids.[143] In India he struggled to counteract the power of Portugal's Jesuit ambassadors and requested permission to attack the Portuguese.[144]

Roe was also uncomfortable among the people he met in India. His marvel at the extremes of the country never overpowered his reservations about his new hosts, and he warned newcomers to reach India "stronge and in health" in order to arrive more advantageously "amonng their enemyes."[145] While this characterization of his hosts as his enemies might seem a strange and potentially destructive attitude for an ambassador to harbor, Roe's wariness helped him endure the many frustrations of his position. He summed up the whole culture in a single passage to the East India Company's minister in Surat: "Religions infinite, lawes none. In this Confusion what can bee expected?"[146] In all his time in India, Roe described only one man with real admiration and affection. This was Mir Jamaluddin Husain, the viceroy of Patna, a man who had served as an ambassador and was "of more understanding and curtesye then all his Countriemen." After some conversation with this man, Roe concluded that "hee was a good-Natured and right harted ould man."[147] Only another man such as himself, predisposed to enter into another's worldview, qualified as a friend.

TRANSPLANTS

Many of their activities in individual ports, factories, or settlements required governors and ambassadors to be flexible, imaginative, creative, and adaptable, hosting weddings, leaking rumors, resolving personal and commercial disputes. They forced men to test themselves, and those who thrived in such conditions pursued other opportunities to do so. One consequence of this repeated movement was the occasional transmission of useful and relevant experience from place to place. A glimpse within the Caribbean demonstrates how connections of personnel might have shaped colonial developments.

Take the familiar example of the emergence of slavery in the English Caribbean. Historians primarily explain this shift from indentured labor to slavery as a story of Barbados, and especially as a story of sugar with its connection to bound labor. In this narrative the migration of sugar and its producers first across the Atlantic, then north to the Caribbean from Brazil, explains the transition in Barbados in the 1640s from English indentured labor to African slaves. But there is another way of understanding the pace and ease, if not the timing, of the rapid emergence of slavery on Barbados. Barbados was not the first English island to experience slavery and of course slavery itself was not at all unfamiliar to the English. The English had an earlier, albeit abortive, experience with slavery on the islands of the Providence Company patent, particularly Tortuga and Providence. On Tortuga the English planters actually abandoned the island in 1638 in the face of concerted slave resistance, and Providence contained a slave majority in the 1630s.[148]

The loss of these islands to the Spanish in 1641 would seem to sever the connection of this historical precedent from the subsequent emergence of slavery on Barbados only a few short years later. But there was an important link between Providence and Barbados in the form of a colonial governor, Philip Bell, who started his career as governor of Bermuda, and went from there to Providence in 1631. He was replaced as governor in 1636, and left Providence itself in 1637. He led a group of settlers to St. Lucia in 1640, but by 1641 Bell was on Barbados as the colony's governor.[149] Bell was no doubt one of many people who ended up on Barbados after Providence was evacuated in 1641, but the lack of extant records makes it difficult to track these patterns of migration. Bell, then, is the most visible and tangible link between the two places.

Bell's sojourn on Providence accompanied the island's commitment to slaves, not solely as a replacement for English servants but particularly as a form of wealth stolen from rival nations by English ships and brought to Providence. But Bell did not require a stay on Providence to learn about slavery: Bermuda contained slaves as well, and Bell had brought some of his slaves with him to Providence in 1631. In his second colonial post Bell faced considerable challenges from the island's bound laborers. The greatest resistance came after he left the island, when some enslaved men rose in rebellion in May of 1638, while others embraced chronic resistance as maroons, runaways who established permanent communities outside English settlement. But if Bell's time as governor did not witness armed rebellion, he did preside over another important process. The years of Bell's governorship and residence were precisely the years of the island's shift from indentured to enslaved labor, centered especially around 1634–1635 when the four-year terms of English indentured servants expired and planters insisted on their right to use slaves. The Providence Company also charged Bell with silencing the lone voice raised in opposition to slavery on the island, that of a colonist whose conviction that Christians should not hold slaves was believed by both islanders and investors in London to make slaves "disaffected" to their service. Bell and the island council were ordered to proceed against this man.[150] His experience perhaps facilitated and even accelerated the identical process on Barbados a decade later.

The transition to slavery on Barbados in the 1640s has everything to do with sugar, but perhaps there are also explanations for the shift that lie within English colonial experiences within the Caribbean region, as English colonists gained knowledge of enslaved African laborers in sequential island homes, and transported that experience from one island to another. The English overseas could see the advantages slavery brought them and could simply buy people who were already slaves. Yet the English in the colonies needed to learn strategies on an intimate and domestic level for incorporating enslaved African captives into households, as indeed they did in the 1630s, regulating households by number and by race, precisely the kind of responsibility generally placed in the hands of governors in these new settlements. On Providence in 1636, Africans were deliberately dispersed in the households of the island's officers and planters, and two years later were allocated in specific ratios of two English to one African.[151] Tangible prior experience with slavery proved valuable, as men accustomed to defining and bolstering this new institution in one locale could transplant and replicate that knowledge elsewhere.

The sequential migration of governors in the first half of the seventeenth century aided the survival of colonies by transporting experienced men from one fragile outpost to another, and it similarly facilitated the English adoption of chattel slavery in the Caribbean and North Atlantic. The migration of men also changed the individual. The ingenuity and adaptability of governors, consuls, and ambassadors were invaluable traits. They helped men to navigate political turbulence in outposts and in England and to devise solutions to unanticipated problems. Thomas Roe's peripatetic and well-documented career illustrates the process of individual maturation and transformation. What distinguished him from some of the other men profiled here was the *extent* of his engagement with a variety of commercial and colonial opportunities: he was a large investor (East India and Somers Island and Virginia Companies), an adventurer (Guyana), an active company member (Virginia Company), and a trade ambassador (India and the Ottoman Empire). He came from a privileged background in England, grasped the multiple enthusiasms of the age, and exceeded any of his contemporaries in sheer diversity and depth of experience. Roe perceived a world in which opportunity existed equally to England's east and west. However replete Roe's service was with dangers and frustrations—embodied most fully by debilitating disease environments and by those he regarded as feckless servants, arbitrary customs officials, and willful and neglectful potentates—his international labors clearly excited and engaged this skilled man.

Roe's commercial, diplomatic, legislative, and colonial adventures in South America, England, India, and Istanbul illustrate the merging of private, state, and commercial interests. Roe's first mission overseas to the Amazon was a privately funded venture with a mixture of personal ambition (to find mines and El Dorado) and public mission (to persuade the king to terminate his peaceful policy toward Spain). In his embassy to India, these commercial interests were solidified with formal state support, although it was the support of the most passive kind, signaled only in the letter from James I authorizing Roe's mission. His salary was always paid by the private joint-stock companies that employed him, but royal sanction was essential for the success of their negotiations overseas and for some protection from attacks at sea. Thomas Roe moved seamlessly among these different types of activities—he was an adventurer in his Guyana voyage, a proprietor of subsequent settlements along the Amazon, an investor in his membership in the East India, Somers Island, and Virginia Companies and in his support for the search for the northwest passage, an ambassador and trade representative in the domain of the Mughal emperor and the Ottoman Empire. And his ventures overlapped. He had employees working for him on the Amazon while he was an ambassador in India; he held shares in the Virginia Company while he explored the Amazon and followed Jahangir through his domains, and again while he worked in Istanbul. For Roe there seemed to be no distinctions between the types of endeavors he tried. Some provided greater creature comforts, as was the case when he served the Virginia Company from the convenience of his residence in London. Some promised greater fortune, and some offered the possibility of spectacular public renown: had he found mines on his Amazon voyage, Roe would have achieved fame to rival Walter Ralegh. But Roe could not have predicted which venture would succeed and which would not. And so a Dutch report in 1615 observed that Roe's enterprise on the Amazon "will, in the course of time, be of greater benefit and consideration than that from the East Indies."[152]

For all his global interests, Roe was always able to reintegrate himself into English society. After each venture, his horizons had been broadened, his knowledge deepened, his skills sharpened, his prestige enhanced, but he was never displaced at home. He returned to positions of power, many derived from his adventures overseas. Roe's forays tested and stretched him. They changed him from the convivial London wit who delighted his friends to the cosmopolitan man who could charm a foreign emperor. They matured him from the brash Amazon explorer who boasted of his discoveries to the shrewd and steadfast diplomat who connived to secure lasting treaties using local customs when necessary. From the energetic adventurer hoping to antagonize Spain in South America Roe grew to become the man whose greatest diplomatic legacy outside of his continental diplomatic accomplishments was the guarantee of peaceful sailing for English ships in the Mediterranean. Small habits hinted at his frame of mind. In Istanbul Roe adopted a new dating system, accounting for the ten day discrepancy in the Julian and Gregorian calendars. It first appears in a letter signed "8/18 January 1621" (1622, new style), but Roe continued this habit later in his life, well after he had returned to England.[153] He also embraced the perspective derived from placing a familiar place or idea in the light of something less familiar. "Things compared, though contrary, or alike in nature, doe illustrate one the other," he wrote, in his introduction to a document about England's great rival, Spain. For Roe, comparisons were intrinsically valuable, bringing one phenomenon into clarity in proximity with another.[154] Perhaps it was this conviction that clarity came through the juxtaposition of the foreign with the familiar that encouraged him to seek new opportunities outside of England and thereby to obtain a clear perspective on both his kingdom and himself.

Roe and the other men profiled here served at the pleasure of English employers and of their sovereign as they tried to represent English interests abroad. Their diplomatic efforts forced them to understand as best they could the mores and values of another society, reaching beyond conventional rivalries, as Butler did when he hosted two Catholic priests on Providence. The challenges and oddities of governance in peculiar worlds far from the routines of England compelled them to improvise and adapt, to know when to dispense with rules and policies from England in favor of the necessities dictated by circumstances on the ground. Their military and commercial skills and expertise helped to secure new colonial settlements and new trading ventures. In a world where their sovereign was weak, they represented the crown as best they could within the varied constraints of their position.

But their importance lay well beyond the personal qualities and official authority such men brought with them around the world, and Roe's writings point to how governors and ambassadors acquired such a long-lasting influence. Through their published and manuscript writings, circulated among men such as themselves and, once published, unleashed on a wider reading public, they influenced subsequent efforts. Ralph Lane, the governor of the abandoned colony at Roanoke (in modern-day North Carolina), wrote about his explorations there in the 1580s. His account was read by Captain John Smith, and it informed his expectations for the settlement of Virginia some twenty years later. Lane had urged his men on in their search for mines, insisting that they keep moving as long as they still had a dog to eat, and Smith encouraged his men in the same vein. Edward Winslow, a leader of the English settlement at Plymouth in 1620, had read Smith, and put his knowledge to work in New England. Smith's prolific works spread around the world, inspiring colonial efforts in the East and West Indies. Other accounts, edited and packaged in Hakluyt's and Purchas's huge compilations, spread the knowledge of colonial and commercial leaders, each man building on the expertise of his predecessor, adding to it with his own painfully acquired knowledge, and cumulatively creating a manual for rule in overseas settings—and thus a manual for empire.[155] Highly placed, often with the best access to employers and sometimes their sovereign, and respected for their experience and perspective, they could influence English policies on matters ranging from likely places for settlement or trade to diplomacy with foreign rulers. With their published histories, their manuscript accounts, and their celebrated exploits, governors and ambassadors were also able to shape subsequent ventures as successors and emulators sought guidance from their prior experience. And so they came to see the world's multiple possibilities, and of their own—and England's—opportunities within it.

6

MADAGASCAR, 1635–1650

> He that is Lord of Madagascar may easily in good time be Emperour of all India.
>
> —Richard Boothby, merchant, 1646

If every overseas venture began as the glimmer in the eye of an imaginative, ambitious, and optimistic proprietor, Madagascar had a longer gestation period than most. The colony had two false starts, in 1636 and in 1639. These thwarted beginnings ultimately spawned two substantial efforts to fund and equip colonial expeditions: the first at Augustine Bay on the southwest coast in 1644; the other near the island of Nosy Be (then known as Assada), off Madagascar's northwest coast in 1649. Both efforts failed quickly. The first plantation suffered high mortality, insufficient supplies, poor seasonal timing, and adversarial relations with the Malagasy who lived there, while the second plantation (attempted twice) faced similar challenges. The few surviving settlers were evacuated within weeks of settlement. In the context of European colonization schemes around the globe, these failed ventures were the equivalent of the blink of an eye.[1]

Few historians know of these English ventures, largely because those interested in colonization have focused on the many contemporary successful English colonization efforts in the Atlantic and those interested in the Indian Ocean have understandably emphasized what has seemed to be the dominant story of English activity there, trade. Yet the two Madagascar plantations illustrate the overlapping interests of colonial investors, officers, and agents and the circular connections between trade and settlement in the early decades of English expansion. Sir William Courten, who had first held a patent granting him the monopoly to develop the West Indies before he lost it to the Earl of Carlisle, later secured a similar patent for Madagascar. Robert Hunt, who had previously served as governor of the Caribbean colony of Providence, promoted and led the second colonization party on

Assada. These Caribbean connections affected the structure and goals of the two Madagascar ventures. The earliest plans for Madagascar were focused on Indian Ocean trade and the best way to expand it by following Dutch examples and establishing permanent settlements. But in 1640 a shift by promoters toward American comparisons changed expectations about colonial settlement, and the second vision was modeled explicitly on Barbados. In the case of Madagascar, trade ambitions and colonial conquest went hand in hand (see figure 6.1).

Schemes for the colonization of Madagascar had been in the imaginations of a prestigious and powerful group of Englishmen for almost a decade before settlers voyaged there in 1644. What enabled these men to imagine a colony on Madagascar was growing English familiarity with the region (see figure 6.2). The first English voyage stopped there in 1591.[2] French, Dutch, Portuguese, and English traders broke up their lengthy and debilitating voyages to the trading factories of the East Indies with sojourns on Madagascar, where they repaired their ships, purchased cattle, and ate freely of the abundant fruit—using, according to one visitor, the island's monkeys (he was probably talking about ring-tailed lemurs, which dwell in the spiny forests of the arid south) as their food tasters.[3] The English were most familiar with the area Europeans called Augustine Bay, where East India Company ships bound to India stopped to replenish their supplies and refresh their passengers on the journey out and back. During one salubrious stay in 1630, after only five or six days, the sick were "perfectly cured."[4]

Although the English knew about Madagascar, interest in colonization there followed a long, often aborted path from imagination to charter to settlement. The East India Company claimed a monopoly over trade in the region, but that monopoly was challenged in 1635 when Sir William Courten organized a rival trade association.[5] His consortium received a valuable grant from Charles I that gave them the right to establish trade at Goa, China, Japan, Malabar, and other parts of the East Indies. In other words, the Courten Association received the right to trade anywhere that the East India Company had not established trade or fortifications. The intent was, in the face of stagnating trade with the east (which Courten and his allies blamed on the inadequacies of the East India Company), to enable a second company to pursue commercial opportunities.[6] Part of the Courten Association's critique of the English East India Company was that it had missed opportunities to secure greater revenue by pursuing permanent settlement as the Dutch had done. The consortium therefore sought a different approach to economic activity in Asia, aspiring, as one participant recalled, "to settle Factories and plant Collonies after the Dutch manner."[7]

When the Courten Association advocated Dutch models, it was Batavia they had in mind, pointing once again to the emulation and competition

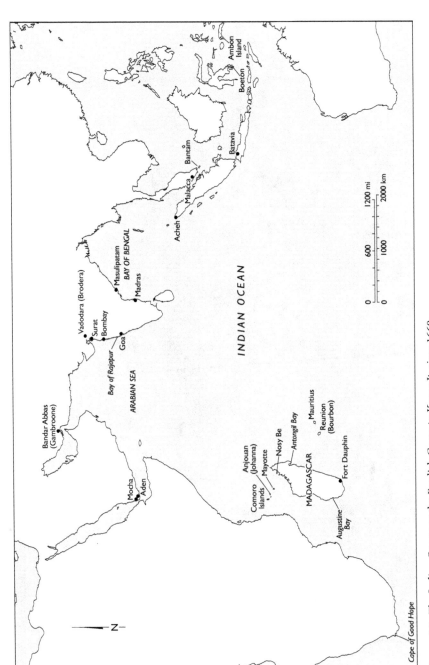

Figure 6.1. The Indian Ocean as the English Came to Know It, circa 1660.

Figure 6.2. This map, published in London in 1598, shows English access to information about Madagascar well before any interest in settlement there. Augustine Bay is in the lower right-hand corner. *The Description of a Voyage Made By Certain Ships of Holland into the East Indies* (London, 1598). This item is reproduced by permission of The Henry E. Huntington Library, San Marino, California.

characterizing English and Dutch relations in this era. Located at the site of old Jacatra on the island of Java, Batavia (as it was renamed by the Dutch) came under Dutch control after some English merchants tried to assert trading rights there in 1618. It soon became a densely inhabited place. The population grew from 2,000 in 1620 to 8,000 in 1624. The Dutch presence was tiny, consisting primarily of men who worked for the Company. These men took wives from elsewhere in Asia who acquired the European status of their husbands on marriage. Men affiliated with the Company spoke Dutch; everyone else spoke Malay or Portuguese. The city was the capital of Dutch activities in Asia and possessed an institutional vitality not shared by contemporary English trade factories.[8] It was, in the admiring words of the English merchant John Darell, a "Famous and Metropolitan City."[9]

The Courten Association's insistence on Asian colonization along Dutch lines promised a more aggressive approach to the region than the factory model employed by the East India Company. Trade factories were cheap to set up, requiring only a small population of traders in residence. Colonization was only one possible path to prosperity, and colonization itself took many different forms. It was expensive: it forced investors to part with their money with little expectation of a return on their investment for years. New settlers depended on supplies from England or elsewhere—costly both to purchase and to ship—until they could support themselves. They also required regular infusions of newcomers to replace those who might die of disease or who might abandon the enterprise. So investors who sought to profit from overseas enterprises did not automatically envision colonization as a suitable risk or a viable undertaking. It had a notoriously slow rate of return.

Madagascar's first promoters envisioned a new kind of English settlement in the Indian Ocean, one that would bolster English power in the region. By 1636 a circle of men that included Thomas Howard, the Earl of Arundel, Prince Rupert, and several courtiers pondered with excitement the possibility of settling Madagascar with English men and women. Rupert was Charles I's nephew, the son of his sister Elizabeth, the Queen of Bohemia, and Frederick V, the Elector Palatine. During the Thirty Years' War, his family had fled Prague in 1620 and landed in exile in The Hague. Following his older brother, Prince Rupert came to visit England in February of 1636. This first plan for Madagascar placed Prince Rupert at the center, and his royal presence was important in shaping promoters' visions for the settlement.

It is difficult to discern now the origins of this colonial scheme, not least since many contemporary explanations came from critics. One such opponent was Powle Waldegrave, who barely survived his time on Madagascar. He suggested in an account written almost fourteen years after the plan first emerged that Arundel and a courtier named Endymion Porter were motivated by piracy (not, of course, an uncommon motive for overseas exploits, but employed by Waldegrave to discredit Arundel and Porter).[10] Arundel's long acquaintance with Courten and other East Indies traders likely joined a long-standing interest in colonization, dating back to his childhood admiration for Sir Walter Ralegh. In a grisly father-son outing, Arundel had even taken his oldest son to see Ralegh's execution in 1617.[11] He had supported one aborted settlement along the Amazon in 1618, and he loaned his enthusiasm and prestige to the proposed colonization of Madagascar.[12]

Rupert's mother, Elizabeth, greeted the proposal with dismay and derision. She referred to it dismissively as a "romance," with Endymion Porter playing the squire to Rupert's Don Quixote. She pleaded with her old friend Thomas Roe in the spring of 1636 to put the "windmills" out of her son's head.[13] Elizabeth raged at her weak position, unable to curb her son's enthusiasm or, in exile as she was, a queen with no kingdom, to provide him with an alternative outlet for his energies. She found this vision of Rupert's reign on Madagascar to be utterly fanciful, "but beggars must be no choosers."[14]

A year later the plan still circulated, although Roe was as critical as Elizabeth. In March and April of 1637, advocates seemed energized, according to the Venetian ambassador, Anzolo Correr. The Privy Council labored over the matter, he wrote, and Arundel himself "has maintained the propriety of the enterprise more vigorously than any one else." Rupert would rule, while courtiers "aspire to the greatest advantages and very fat profits." More reasonable people thought of these plans as "light fancies" and assumed they would go nowhere, because of the challenge of supplying such a large fleet and the looming problem of defeating the bellicose people of the island.[15] The English had already experienced some of the variability of the island's hospitality. Richard Rowles stopped with his ship at Augustine Bay in 1609, and lost two of his crew to the inhabitants there, while a merchant was captured. Rowles fled to the northwest coast, but along with several other sailors was captured and killed.[16] Despite England's own inauspicious history at Augustine Bay, conquest and occupation there captured the enthusiasm of the royal court.

No one was more extravagant in his praise of the proposed venture than the playwright and poet William Davenant, who had found a steadfast patron in one of Madagascar's great advocates, Endymion Porter. After his previous patron, Lord Brooke, was murdered by his valet in 1628, Davenant transferred his loyalties to Porter, whose patronage was valuable both personally and professionally. As Davenant struggled with syphilis (which cost him his nose) and the deadly mercury cure, Porter continued to support him, and it was Porter's patronage that helped Davenant establish himself as a playwright. When Porter caught the Madagascar fever, Davenant demonstrated his gratitude in verse.[17]

His poem, *Madagascar*, was published in 1638, by which time coloniza-tion had lost its momentum, but it was presumably written sometime in 1637. In 21 pages, *Madagascar* tells the reader of a fantastic dream Davenant had of Madagascar. In it, Davenant was transported to Madagascar, and there he witnessed Prince Rupert's conquest. This invasion (seaborne, not airborne), in fact, was the real plan for Madagascar. Rupert was to lead a fleet of thirty-six ships. He would seize the island in a bloodless conquest over the island's native inhabitants before he then took on England's European rivals. Davenant described the military campaign and the riches to be found there, including gold and such abundant stores of ambergris, a substance derived from whales and used in making perfume, that it piled in mounds of "Black Sudds."[18] This was a conquest that would yield multiple riches, not only in mineral wealth but in political dominance and the displacement of European rivals.

In securing the interest of Davenant, the Madagascar promoters accom-plished what we might now consider a public relations coup. But the strategy of launching a colony in fanciful verse—in what a poet frankly described as an out-of-body experience in which his soul traveled at night while his body slept in bed—might be a dubious method to persuade people to take a personal and financial risk. Who would be so reckless as to stake one's life on a poet's dream?

Davenant's poetic conquest, which crowned Rupert "the first true Mon-arch of the Golden Isle," proved far easier than England's subsequent efforts to settle the island. Poetry, indeed, could accomplish what men could not.[19] And, in fact, plans for the venture fizzled quickly, despite Arundel's hard work to make the conquest happen, proposing himself as a replacement for Rupert if the prince could not be convinced to take part.[20] To Elizabeth's certain relief, Thomas Roe was able to confirm the Venetian ambassador's growing skepticism and reported by May of 1637 that the plan had evapo-rated. Rupert was safe. "A blunt merchant called to deliver his opinion, said it was a gallant design, but such as wherein he would be loth to venture his younger son."[21]

The envisioned Madagascar conquest receded for two years but was revived in 1639 by the Earl of Arundel, who at the time was suffering rever-sals of political and financial fortune. He had been appointed to the head of the Scottish campaign in 1639, part of an ongoing effort by Charles I to bring his Scottish kingdom under closer ecclesiastical control, and returned home in the wake of a humiliating treaty. His personal fortunes, moreover, were also at a low ebb. Soon after his return from Scotland, he turned his attention once again to Madagascar.

Arundel approached the reinvigoration of the scheme in several different ways. He took concrete action, readying a fleet of five ships with the promise of one more from the king. He gathered supporters. Giovanni Giustinian, the Venetian ambassador, reported that Arundel had persuaded "many of the gentry" to join him.[22] That Arundel himself intended to move to Madagascar was highly unusual. George Calvert, Lord Baltimore, was the most illustrious man to undertake colonization personally in this period, motivated largely by his outsider position as a Catholic. After he converted in the 1620s, Calvert lost access to the public offices that had previously made him so powerful in England (Calvert had been secretary of state), and he came to regard colonization as his sanctuary and salvation. He spent some time in Newfoundland, but after a difficult winter in 1628–1629 he resolved to establish himself and his colony of Maryland in the Chesapeake region in 1630s. In the same decade the members of the Providence Company, a London-based consortium with the patent to three islands in the Caribbean, proposed their own relocation to their Caribbean investment but changed their minds. Like Calvert in the 1620s, many of these men languished outside court life and political power as puritans in the 1630s in a decade when Parliament did not meet. For a political *insider* to harbor such a vision of colonial relocation was remarkable. No one of Arundel's quality or stature had ever contemplated such a transplantation. It reflected both an imaginative ambition and his response to a series of personal and professional disappointments.

While most colonial promoters published broadsides to attract attention to their enterprise, Arundel also commissioned a painting from Anthony Van Dyck (figure 6.3). Van Dyck followed close instructions from Arundel about the composition of this work.[23] The painting depicted Lord and Lady Arundel seated in sumptuous robes of silk and ermine. Between them was a globe, positioned to reveal Madagascar to the viewer, and Lady Arundel held in her hand a compass to point to the island's location.[24] A bust known as the Arundel Homer stands in the right side of the painting, evoking the classical world and its heroic epics.[25] The painting itself might have been intended to be distributed to further the colony's promotion, since several versions exist.[26] Colonies were generally launched by a paper trail: a royal charter; formal legal agreements among investors; broadsides and pamphlets to recruit settlers; bills of credit and exchange to arrange provisions; maps that contained the most accurate geographic information possible. But were there any other colonies that were launched so dramatically in a painting of such spectacular quality? The artist embedded the paper detritus of colonial promotion within the painting by dangling a document on the side of the globe.

The painting might have been intended to help secure support from men of the highest rank in society, but Arundel's multifaceted efforts to promote his colony suggested that he sought to draw in people of all sorts. Arundel produced a document for public circulation and display to alert

Figure 6.3. Anthony Van Dyck's Madagascar portrait depicts Thomas Howard, the Earl of Arundel, with his wife, Countess Aletheia, pointing toward Madagascar on the globe (reproduced by kind permission of His Grace the Duke of Norfolk, Arundel Castle).

interested parties to his proposed colonization. Written in September of 1639 and posted on the pillars of the Royal Exchange and elsewhere, his *Declaration Concerning Madagascar* identified his reasons for engaging in the enterprise.[27] In addition to following the platitudes of predecessors and contemporaries who justified colonization by asserting that they sought to advance Christianity and revive trade, Arundel also deplored the loss to England if Madagascar were settled by others. Unspoken was the lament about missed opportunities of the sixteenth century, when central and south America were left to the Spanish, with tremendous consequences for English power in Europe. If England had missed its chance for regional and hemispheric dominance in America, another prospect beckoned in the east. The merchant Richard Boothby shared this sentiment: "he that is Lord of Madagascar may easily in good time be Emperour of all India."[28] Practical information accompanied these lofty aspirations. Those who wished to invest with Arundel were urged to do so by December 20 and to pay their money to Abraham Dawes. Those who could not afford to pay their own passage could travel as servants and could then secure the privileges of freeman, a status otherwise reserved for those who put in £20, for which their passage would be arranged. Fortunate men with desirable skills could earn wages on Madagascar.

Arundel's *Declaration* suggested that he worried about being taken seriously. The document starts by challenging those who might believe his plan to be "a vayne and ayrye undertaking," not least since he planned to go himself and to risk his own money. His reiteration of this theme at the end of the document, his hope that the world saw his venture as "serious and reall," indicated his anxiety about public perceptions.[29] Perhaps the plan would have conveyed greater gravitas with more than a painting to promote it and with more practical information at hand. Like previous efforts, Arundel's vision for Madagascar collapsed, for reasons including Lady Arundel's reluctance to move her household to Madagascar, Parliament's convening, insufficient financial support, and Arundel's poor health.[30]

After Arundel's withdrawal, interest in Madagascar received fitful support. An aborted effort in 1640 produced a short pamphlet by William Monson, an English admiral and the author of a series of naval tracts. In pushing for settlement in the Indian Ocean, Monson departed from earlier arguments for Madagascar. Previous advocates had pointed to Madagascar as a vehicle to enhance trade in the region. But Monson turned his attention away from India and toward America in his delineation of the colony's advantages. His is the first extant publication to make these comparisons so pointedly, and from an author who had considerable credibility when he cast about for comparative frames of reference. In his long career at sea beginning in the 1580s in privateering and other pursuits, Monson had traveled around the Atlantic and had a deep knowledge of English commercial, colonial, and other extractive activities. Monson believed the trip to Madagascar to be more reliable than that to Virginia, with Atlantic winds and weather so uncertain. He argued that it cost less to carry men to Madagascar. Ships to Virginia were specially fitted for that purpose, whereas any vessel bound to India could transport twenty men for the plantation. The country was likely to be more profitable than America. While all domestic animals had to be transported from England to North America, Madagascar already contained sheep, chickens, and cattle. Monson praised the people, preferring their "more civiller conversation and humane behaviour" over that of the Indians of America. Monson also identified advantages to trade. He envisioned Madagascar as a permanent trans-shipment point. East India ships could sail between Madagascar and India, while a separate fleet made the journey from Madagascar to England. Monson insisted that this settlement plan be compared to American enterprises "without partiality." He complained that American settlements were too scattered to be able to assist each other in defense. In his mind, Madagascar was a viable, even superior, option.[31]

Monson's pamphlet provided a crucial transition for Madagascar advocates. Previously their ambitions were shaped primarily by rivalry with the East India Company, but Monson took the idea of plantation, refracted it through American experiences, and used the comparison to illustrate the advantages of Madagascar. Although Madagascar proponents remained aware of the example of a place such as Batavia, American comparisons shaped these new colonial expectations in important ways. A year later, the scheme resurfaced, and this time, eight years after the idea first circulated at court in 1636, with a momentum that would lead to the actual transportation of settlers to the island. Parliament granted permission for settlement there, and the Venetian ambassador, Gerolamo Agostini, reported no difficulty recruiting settlers during the unsettled early years of the English Civil War, "since it is now impossible for the poor to live in this kingdom."[32]

Colonies were places ideally suited for utopian expectations: the prototypical utopia, given life by Thomas More, was itself located in an imagined world associated at the time with exploration. Colonial undertakings offered creative men the opportunity to devise a new kind of society. Even at the most pragmatic level, every colonial venture had utopian elements, made visible in a range of documents, from the joint-stock agreements that organized investments to the proposed sources of colonial wealth to the constitutions that aspired to orderly government. Broadsides published to recruit luxury craftsmen, the belief that crops dependent on heavy rains might grow in the desert or that crops that preferred a dry climate could thrive in the tropical wetlands: all revealed the lofty hopes of colonial investors and proprietors. Colonial leaders needed the ability to shepherd a shift from paper dreams to tangible practicality, to reconcile halcyon visions of silver mines with daily drudgery, to settle for corn, cotton, or wheat where once there had been dreams of silk and gold. Those colonies that failed often did so for a variety of reasons, but certainly the burden of lofty expectations was one factor as they forced inhabitants to deny the real circumstances in which they lived and instead to seek alternative realities.

If almost every colony had its unrealistic underpinnings, the Madagascar experiments had a deeper utopian theme at numerous levels—personal, political, commercial, national. The proposed 1644 venture was a product of its tumultuous time. In the 1640s, England was wracked by civil war. The war played itself out in a variety of ways in trading posts and colonies. Some colonies manifested their own civil wars, although usually nonviolent, and all colonies were eventually forced to take sides when confronted with rival leaders appointed by the crown or Parliament.[33] For William Courten and his associates, these political trials were particularly acute because their original charter was a royal concession, granted by Charles I in large part because of the advocacy of Endymion Porter.

Politics, however, complicated colonization schemes in the 1640s. Richard Boothby's promotional pamphlet for the settlement at Augustine Bay conveyed his frustration with politics at home. It is an unusually political pamphlet for a colonial enterprise reliant on fund-raising. He dedicated his book to Charles I—although he hedged his bets, invoking Charles as "His most Royall (and I trust in God (yet) Most Gracious Sovereign,"—and to Parliament. He suggested that war might even have been averted had Prince Rupert adhered to the original plans of 1636–1637 and undertaken a conquest of Madagascar. Boothby proposed a solution to the lingering political strife in England caused by the presence of bishops who had been dismissed from Parliament. If they continued in their challenges to king and parliament, Boothby recommended that they be sent to Madagascar to convert the people there. In Boothby's hands, Madagascar ultimately offered a place of refuge for those distraught by English upheavals.

> What an honour, accommodation and happinesse must it certainly be, to a pious Christian protestant Nation, unspotted and undefiled with Idolatry, Atheisme, Papisme, Anabaptimse, Brownisme, Antinomianisme, or otherwise heresie or errour, to be possessed with a quiet peaceable secure and wealthy habitation, in so excellent, pleasant and fruitfull a Country, a little world in it self.

Boothby conceded that this "little world" was much larger than England, but it was blessed by its distance from other countries, which would help defend it from "Idolatrous superstitious or Malignant Christians" who might seek to "hurt or annoy" those who settled there.[34] In 1636 Madagascar colonization had offered a kingdom for a prince whose father had lost his own; by 1639 it promised to salvage the personal honor of England's Earl Marshall after his failure in Scotland and to redeem his dwindling fortunes; and in 1644 it held out the possibility of national redemption at a time of violent division. And these ambitions persisted, following the colonists to the Indian Ocean, haunting them there.

THE SETTLEMENT AT AUGUSTINE BAY, 1644–1646

If there was an interest surrounding a Madagascar colony in the summer of 1636, when Prince Rupert visited England, it returned in the spring of 1644 in the form of "great talke and rumour" about a settlement there.[35] This venture was to be based at Augustine Bay, located at the southwestern part of Madagascar, at the mouth of the Onilahy River, near the modern city of Toliara. The location was chosen largely for strategic and political reasons: the English had stayed at the Bay before, had traded successfully for cattle, and had made alliances with local rulers.[36] Based on their prior knowledge, they thought they would be welcome to take up residence there.

Madagascar was the phoenix of colonial experiments, forever rising out of the flames when it should have been beyond resurrection. At this juncture, with colonization a real possibility, access to good information was crucial. But this was Madagascar, a colony launched earlier in a poem and a painting. It would be equally poorly served by the promotional works designed to publicize it, however abundant accurate information was from merchants and mariners who had tarried there on their way to and from India.[37] Instead, these promotional works contained flat and simplistic depictions of the people at the Bay as innocent inhabitants of an Edenic paradise. In this vein, promoters followed a time-honored strategy. Powle Waldegrave created verbs out of this inclination, complaining of one Madagascar promoter's tendency toward "Canaanizing and Paradising" the place.[38]

Walter Hamond's 1640 promotional pamphlet, *A Paradox. Prooving, That the Inhabitants of the Isle called Madagascar, or St. Lawrence… are the happiest People in the World* first announced the proposed Madagascar venture in prose and did so in an exuberantly utopian fashion, which subsequently earned Hamond the bitter enmity of the Madagascar settlement's unfortunate governor. Hamond had spent four months at Augustine Bay a decade earlier, between July and October of 1630. He envisioned an island conquest by the English in which the natives would not be "betray[ed] … to servitude," but rather instructed in "Religion and the Arts." Hamond was not sure of the religious beliefs of the people, but he suspected them to be Muslim.[39] There had been Muslim intrusion in the region by around 1600, although Islam did not dominate the region. Richard Boothby picked up a religious book in exchange for six cows when he visited the Bay in 1630, likely an Anteimoro *Sorabe*, or Sacred Book, which contained cabbalistic and religious materials understood only by highly specialized religious practitioners.[40]

Hamond's pamphlets were full of information that might lead prospective colonists to think their settlement would be easy. Food was abundant, not just the plants of the woods but goats and wild hogs as well. The people themselves were agreeable, "affable, courteous, and just"; the English lived among them "as if we had beene all of one Nation, and their Countrey had beene our owne."[41] They were, moreover, scrupulously honest, punishing theft with death, a point Hamond illustrated with the story of a father who killed his own daughter for stealing a few beads. For all his invocation of Eden, however, Hamond thought little of the country's people. "If any where, the proverbe, *terra bona, gens mala*, may be here applied," he wrote critically, complaining that the inhabitants were "a sluggish and slothfull people" who needed neither to plant nor sow, "yet live plentifully by the fat of the Soyle," a phenomenon of which Hamond clearly disapproved.[42] While people in other parts of God's creation must struggle to cultivate food, on Madagascar, food grew "naturally." All was in abundance, and as for the people, they resembled in their dress "Adams in his innocency" and maintained a form of government that Hamond understood to be communal, in which all except wives—who were guarded jealously—were held in common.[43] Repeated comparisons to Adam and Eve populate Hamond's pamphlet, and for those who were yet unconvinced, Hamond wrote a second pamphlet three years later titled *Madagascar, The Richest and most Fruitfull Island in the World*, where he laid the comparison out still more bluntly.[44] Even the beasts of the field and forest there were "as humble, and serviceable to man as they were before his transgression."[45]

These two promotional works were followed by a third, Richard Boothby's *A Breife Discovery or Description of the most Famous Island of Madagascar*, published in London in 1646. Boothby's book was long in planning: Endymion Porter and John Bond had solicited him to write about his experiences several years before his tract appeared.[46] This was a considerably more substantial work, seventy-two pages to forty-five for Hamond's two pamphlets combined. Like many of the men who were employed by the Courten Association, Boothby had prior experience with the East India Company. The East India Company, bitterly opposed to the crown's attack on their monopoly by opening the trade to competitors, referred to the Courten Association as the Interlopers Association, and although the employees of both consortiums assisted each other in the Indian Ocean at times of need, there was considerable mutual animosity.[47]

Boothby was a merchant with a profound sense of injury against the Company and his hostility permeated his pamphlet. He had been imprisoned by the East India Company in 1629, when he had been the principal merchant at the factory at Brodera (Vadodara in western India). The charges included private trade (which everyone engaged in, despite prohibitions, but discretion was important) and even having an objectionable personality at a dinner party. Boothby, of course, maintained he had been condemned unjustly, but found inspiration in the writings of Samuel Purchas, whose *Pilgrims* contained the story of Captain John Smith. Famous for his adventures in Virginia, Smith's success (in Boothby's mind) attracted the envy of the Virginia council and led to false accusations.[48] Boothby identified with Smith, and, with equal modesty, with Walter Ralegh as well. His venom— and his sense of himself as a successor to the global exploits of Smith and Ralegh—fueled his promotional text.

The pamphlet's publication had been planned for August of 1644, to precede the fleet that sailed two months later and to be of practical value to the colonists themselves and of promotional value to those who hoped to secure funds for the undertaking. Illness and other impediments hindered publication. An East India Company merchant, Francis Lloyd, a friend of Boothby who had been to Madagascar five times, wanted to read the manuscript. Since Boothby had been to India only once, and spent much of that time imprisoned, he wanted to take advantage of Lloyd's expertise.[49] Although Boothby's pamphlet did not appear until after the plantation had failed, it was conceptualized and drafted at the same time and for the same purpose as Hamond's pamphlets.

Hamond's and Boothby's pamphlets suggested a variety of economic opportunities for the English, particularly the abundant provisions with which the English could supply ships, but also the slave trade. The English expected to engage in the carrying trade in the region, while they hoped to enjoy the cheap labor and low maintenance their own slaves might provide. They even aspired to attach themselves and the Indian Ocean to the growing transatlantic slave trade by taking captives and rice to Bahia in Brazil, where a sugar boom fueled the need for laborers and food.[50] Moreover, Hamond was certain of England's destiny to occupy the island. If "Nature" trapped the English on an island, "Art revengeth the injury," for shipping gave the English access to the world. "The Sun doth neither set nor rise, but where we are admitted, or make our selves free denizens."[51] The English, Hamond proclaimed, had become the masters of the seas.

Hamond's optimism was paired with a dim understanding of circumstances on Madagascar. Hamond reassured his reader of the charitable impulses the English had toward these future subjects. Yet his own pamphlet suggested one reason for the people's acquiescence to the English presence, and Boothby concurred: the desire for alliances. During their visit the English met some of the men who subsequently played an important role in the colony itself, including one leader, Andria Pela, whom they described as a "king" and who promised land to the English if they wished to live there. The unspoken but clear *quid pro quo* was the expectation of English military allegiance against Andria Pela's enemies, whether the Portuguese or other Malagasy.[52]

The people persuaded the English that they needed their help to liberate them from the Portuguese friars who sought to convert them to Catholicism, although at the time the Portuguese were no longer active in the region and one disillusioned priest, Luis Mariano, wrote in 1617 that he thought conversion efforts anywhere on the island—and he had traveled all the way around looking for likely converts—were hopeless.[53] So Hamond misrepresented the people of Madagascar when he claimed they were living "under the Tyranny of Satan" and eager for English rescue.[54] But obviously Andria Pela exploited and encouraged this confusion. Andria Pela told Boothby, in his attempt to entice the English to join them as allies, that the Portuguese had been very cruel to his people, especially by capturing them (presumably for the slave trade).[55] Andria Pela also hoped for English alliance against local enemies, the "Massagoces, with whom they have mortall wars."[56] Various European accounts attest to the political fragmentation of the region.[57] The divisions and rivalries the English described and hoped to exploit were part of the expansion of the Sakalava, whose political dominance spread north over the course of the seventeenth century. These internal rivalries might explain the reception the English received north of Augustine Bay, when they sailed up a river where they were jubilantly welcomed by as many as 100 people who ushered their visitors to the town, a modest settlement of huts.[58]

So much for the harmony of Eden. This was obviously a bellicose society, much like that the English knew at home. Richard Boothby gave some souvenirs to Endymion Porter in 1637, including weapons—darts, a long knife, and a bow and arrow—whose existence might have suggested the likely response of the region's inhabitants. Hamond even witnessed mock battles put on for the entertainment (and perhaps edification) of the English.[59] He described the practice of warfare as "continuall."[60] But despite the visible evidence of war, as far as Hamond was concerned, only two impediments stood in the way of settlement, the people of Madagascar and the passage: he dismissed the former concern because of the thirty or forty years of English trade with them, and as for the latter, he simply urged a prudent choice of season.

In Madagascar's case, the gap between promoter's dream and colonist's reality was wide indeed. Most colonies were launched and accompanied by promotional literature, whether pamphlets or broadsides, prose or verse.

What makes Hamond's pamphlets important, and more than merely the fanciful and formulaic conjecture of an adventurous London merchant, was their impact. For we know that they were read, and we know that Hamond's depiction of the people and of their willingness to trade with the English was believed by the man whose judgment mattered most, the colony's governor, John Smart, who railed at the misrepresentations of the promotional pamphlets. He singled out Walter Hamond's erroneous depiction of the people, writing that "Mr. Hamond must excuse me, if I tel him he lyeth in mainetayneing their equety & fidelitie, there not being a more perfidious theevish people liveing upon the earth."[61] All the advice he had received about trade from another source, M. Goubard, he dismissed with disgust as "ribble, rabble...meere chimeras." By the end of his time on Madagascar, the governor had come to see the colony, so far from Eden, as a "more then miserable prison."[62]

After his Madagascar ordeal, John Smart died in Acheh, and so never made it home to correct the misinformation that bedeviled his settlement effort. Powle Waldegrave, one of the surviving settlers, did manage to return to England. He discovered there Boothby's promotional pamphlet, which so enraged him that he set to work refuting every point. On the "treachery" of the people Waldegrave could barely restrain himself. He harbored a separate, fiercer, anger for the deception of Boothby and Hamond. Rather than forgive Hamond and Boothby for mistakes, Waldegrave accused them of deliberate and malicious deceit. He wrote on his return that if either Hamond or Boothby had been at the settlement at Augustine Bay, "the rage of starving men would have torn them in pieces."[63] Of Hamond's lies, Waldegrave melodramatically reported that they were "seal'd with the blood of divers Englishmen."[64] Survivors placed the blame for death firmly in the hands of the promoters. Waldegrave was so determined that no subsequent colonists be duped by Boothby's vision that he took on each chapter, item by item.[65]

The three promotional works of the 1640s, like Monson's 1640 tract, made explicit references to American colonies. Boothby recommended, for example, avoiding the adversarial relations with indigenous people that characterized Virginia, particularly in the wake of another major Indian attack, yet again led by an aged Opechancanough, on the English in 1644.[66] He prodded colonial investors to entice settlers overseas with promises of headrights, or free land for every person who was transported.[67] Caribbean enterprises also provided models. Trinidad, only recently open to the English for trade, offered its inhabitants "freedome of customes," which Boothby advocated to encourage settlement on Madagascar. Boothby also invoked Trinidad to inspire timorous readers, who might have been daunted at the power of the Malagasy or by other European nations. As the adventurers of Trinidad overcame their fears of the Spanish presence, so too should the English who journeyed to the Indian Ocean.[68]

The English brought with them to the Indian Ocean in the 1640s several decades of experience trading there, in addition to their familiarity with trade and settlement in other parts of the world, particularly the Caribbean and Atlantic. The Indian Ocean in the seventeenth century shared important features with the Caribbean, so perhaps it seemed plausible to the English that they might apply skills from one basin to another. Both ocean basins were characterized by the presence of several competing European nations, particularly the Spanish, French, Dutch, Portuguese, and English. Yet within each region European powers conducted themselves differently. Europeans ventured to the Indian Ocean primarily as traders. Successful trade required insinuation into local networks and accommodation to local mores. While Europeans fought with each other, they had to be more careful in their dealings with indigenous people, whose alliances and support promised the wealth that initially attracted European merchants. In the Caribbean, Europeans jostled for territory, primacy, and goods. They turned the region into their own battleground, and by the middle of the seventeenth century these endemic rivalries could be carried out without inconvenient concerns about the political interests of dwindling indigenous populations. But the English, French, and Dutch had also learned to tread carefully as latecomers to a region claimed by Spain. Walter Hamond was surely thinking of this constraint when he remarked that the English who settled on Madagascar would not have to worry about the opposition of the king of Spain, "who hath too many Irons in the fire already" to be bothered with the English there.[69]

When Europeans traveled from one place to another, they had to adapt to different cultures. Their inability or reluctance to do so could spell disaster for colonial settlements: Hamond's comment about the Spanish crown's indifference to English settlement in the Indian Ocean signals both the awareness of international rivalries and a tacit permission for the English to bully their way into places unclaimed by European rivals. Hamond's insight boded ill for English settlement in a region where Europeans were generally accommodating of local mores. The conduct of these settlers, which was at odds with other English interactions in the region, suggests that these colonial models inspired a combative style of interaction that accelerated the failure of Indian Ocean plantations.

The colony on Madagascar suffered from a number of impediments: an adverse disease environment would likely have dictated the colony's demise regardless of other circumstances. But the evidence of the colony's records also points to the problematic intersection of Atlantic colonization models and Indian Ocean schemes. Investors envisioned the settlement as a supply colony and a place of permanent habitation.[70] The English were particularly dependent on landing spots for resupplying their ships on their long voyage to the Indies. English ships in the seventeenth century were smaller than those of European competitors: with these vessels the English gained speed but sacrificed space for provisions, forcing the English to leapfrog in their travels and call regularly for supplies along the way.[71] A supply colony on Madagascar could generate considerable profit if it could offer much-needed food and equipment to European mariners. But the success of the colony depended not only on the survival of the settlers but also on the ability of these settlers to procure necessary goods. Both proved insurmountable challenges, the first because of disease and the second because of bungled relations with the Malagasy that were prompted by adherence to models of settlement better suited for the Atlantic and Caribbean.

The settlement effort commenced in October of 1644, when a convoy of three ships, the *Hester*, the *Sun*, and the *James*, containing some 140 passengers, departed England for Augustine Bay. Aspirations for settlement were signaled in the population of men, women, and children who journeyed to Madagascar: four babies, all boys, were born on the long voyage to the Indian Ocean. Plantation entailed a more diverse population than would be true of a male-dominated trade factory. These adventurers possessed a range of skills. Some were capable of locating and identifying mines for minerals, including gold, silver, tin, or iron.[72] The people on board and the equipment they transported conveyed the intentions of the organizers. Powle Waldegrave detailed the supplies the settlers brought along: "Iron, Steel, Tackling for small Vessels, Carpenters tools, Ordnance, Arms and Ammunition, and every thing for Trade and Commerce, that our information did judg requisit."[73]

A starting population of 140 in the first voyage to an unestablished settlement was typical for English ventures in this period. The first fleet to Jamestown in 1607 carried 144 passengers and sailors; approximately 120 people sailed to Maryland in 1633; and the *Mayflower* fleet to Plymouth carried about 102. For an initial foray, the Madagascar-bound population of 140 was substantial. But disease and death characterized the venture from its inception, as was the case for any voyage from western Europe around the Cape of Good Hope.[74]

The first indication of real distress for the Courten Association's Madagascar fleet came when the ships stopped at the Cape at Saldanha Bay in January, three months after their departure, where they planned to regroup before the final trip to Madagascar. Until then the *Sun* had enjoyed a relatively salubrious voyage from England. The ships had stopped at Maio, a small island in the Cape Verdes used by Europeans in this period for salt and provisioning. There the fleet acquired goats, pumpkins, salt, and fresh fish. If the *Sun*'s human passengers fared well, however, the dogs on board did not; Smart requested a fresh supply of mastiffs, greyhounds, and hunting dogs.[75] But by the time the *Sun* reached Saldanha Bay, the *Hester* and *James* had already arrived. The *James* had been there for nine days with many sick people, both passengers bound for the plantation and mariners, and no refreshment at hand, only one sheep and one calf extracted from the people there. After considerable deliberation and deference to the advice of mariners, the *James* and *Hester* went to Coney Island (now Dassen Island) in search of conies, or dassie rats (after whom Europeans had named the island), penguins and seals. When the *James* finally reached Madagascar after her five-month voyage, "most of their people [were] sicke, and had she contynued at sea but one weeke longer (without Gods great mercy they had all perished)."[76] The sick were carried on shore to recover.

The starvation on board might have derived from a lack of supplies, but could also reflect the physical consequences of scurvy, which results from nutritional deficiencies, and particularly of vitamin C. Scurvy was common during long sea voyages, for example, when passengers and mariners could not get access to fruit, meat, or vegetables. Those unfortunate souls who suffer from scurvy initially experience joint pain, malaise, and shortness of breath. Gradually, their teeth loosen making it difficult to eat; they suffer from internal hemorrhages; their hair cannot grow and lesions appear. Jaundice, convulsions, and death can occur in patients who endure the deficiency for an extended period. Scurvy was a staple of India voyages, and by the time mariners reached Madagascar, the symptoms revealed themselves with vigor. It was precisely because of scurvy that a supply station on Madagascar was so crucial to facilitate recovery with fresh provisions.

Once safely on land, however, the Madagascar settlement's inhabitants shared the health problems of most new colonists. Illness was a defining feature of young settlements. Even regions later distinguished by the relative salubriousness of the climate witnessed high mortality rates in the first years of colonization. Although New England was distinguished among most places of settlement in the seventeenth century for the longevity of its inhabitants, one-half of the new arrivals died during the first winter at Plymouth. They joined a long list of colonists who perished in northern climates during the winter. During their one winter on St. Croix Island in 1604–1605 off the northeastern coast of Maine, thirty-five or thirty-six of the seventy-nine French residents died. So alarmed were the survivors at the repeated deaths of their comrades that they violated any number of religious and cultural taboos to perform an autopsy on one corpse, slicing his skull open to examine his brain. Their skeletons, excavated in recent years, show the ravages of scurvy.[77]

However much these colonists suffered in the cold misery of a North American winter, warm climates offered no respite from mortality, although death there often took other forms. Repeated English failures to establish colonies in the region of the Amazon point to the problems of a hostile disease environment. At least five major English colonial efforts there failed. In Surinam, the number of men able to bear arms dropped from 1,500 to 500 in the space of a single year.[78] Some regions of the tropics were hosts to disease-bearing mosquitoes. The fevers that troubled settlers were often manifestations of malaria and the more virulent yellow or dengue fevers. The eagerness of Europeans to settle on rivers could increase exposure to disease when those rivers were tidal with poor water quality at the mouth.[79]

The colonists (called "planters" in contemporary terminology) at Augustine Bay were quickly plagued by disease, by "tedious & violent burning Agues…others with fluxes."[80] Although the settlement was in the dry southwest, it was nonetheless affected by malaria. European visitors remarked on the fevers that swept their crews during even the shortest stay on the island.[81] Today Madagascar is unusual in that all four species of malaria exist there. The miseries of the English settlers attest to the likely presence of malaria among them, although it is always risky to read back from modern data. The Malagasy who lived in the southwest would likely have suffered from malaria themselves, but not as much as the newly arrived Europeans, who settled at the mouth of the river.[82] Powle Waldegrave, who survived the settlement at Augustine Bay, characterized the differential health of the inhabitants there succinctly. A place was not salubrious for all, he remarked, simply because the permanent inhabitants lived there in health. Newcomers might not fare so well.[83]

The "fluxes" colonists suffered generally indicated dysentery, a dangerously dehydrating intestinal condition caused by bacteria in contaminated water or food, and usually a result of unsanitary settlements. In the first two months at Augustine Bay, the governor reported, only he and about fifteen others stayed healthy. Only forty men were able to bear arms, the rest "soe old ignorant weak fellowes that they are not able to performe the parte of men." Within nine months, no medicine was left and all the important craftsmen, smiths, house and ship carpenters, sawyers, and the bricklayer, were either dead or "dangerously sicke."[84]

The settlement's governor and his colleagues clearly agitated over the illnesses and discussed likely causes. In August they shared their analysis in a letter to their employers in England. "Wee impute" this sickness, Smart wrote, "to ye eating of fresh Beefe" with neither salt nor bread, and also to bad water.[85] Smart was a great believer in the curative power of surgeons. He repeatedly requested more medicine, and of good quality, and claimed that the high mortality in the first months of 1646 was caused in large part by "want of a knowing chirurgeon and medicine." Men, Smart fumed, should "not perish like beasts for want of looking after."[86] The mortality rate of this venture was staggering. By December of 1645 only 100 people (sixty-six percent) of the original contingent of 140 were alive after nine months in residence, and when the governor left in that month on a trip around the island, he returned to find only sixty-three still alive. Sixty survived to be evacuated in May of 1646. However incompetent the English proved in their dealings with indigenous people, high mortality—in this case a sixty percent mortality in fourteen months—predicted the failure of the colony.

This sickness on Madagascar was accompanied by hunger.[87] Despite the predictions of the colony's promoters, colonists did not find cheap "necessaries both for back and belly...out of India," and they were instead wholly dependent on supplies from England.[88] Their own vessels arrived depleted. In 1645, two India-bound ships reached Augustine Bay in the early fall, and "had they remained at sea but tyn dayes longer, they had all beene starved."[89] Although outbound ships stopped along the way to replace exhausted and rotten provisions and to give travelers and sailors the opportunity to recover their health, the lengthy voyage landed passengers in conditions of great weakness. A report from the East India Company agent Francis Breton to the Company in January of 1646 noted that some East India Company ships had stopped in Augustine Bay in July, where they found "Capt. Smart with divers poor people on shore...and indeed if supplies arrived not sudainely like to be in a deplorable condition."[90] When in December of 1645 outbound ships reached the small colony at Augustine Bay carrying neither trade supplies nor passengers beyond a gardener and some vines, Governor Smart wrote his cousin Thomas Kynnaston that the inhabitants "were utterly dismayed."[91]

One significant problem was that crops did not thrive. The west coast of Madagascar is generally dry; the moisture that comes with the trade winds from the east is blocked by the mountain range that dissects the island. Summers there (the northern hemisphere's winter) are the dampest season, when tropical storms bring rainfall, but the winter months are arid, so dry that baobabs are tapped for their water.[92] The English planted crops as soon as they arrived in March, but the parched plants withered in the dry winter months. The colony's governor characterized the place as "altogether unfitting for our residence, as not affording any thing for or subsistence, the earth being barren [of] Salt, and not produceing any thing of seede, plantes, or rootes that have beene sowne."[93] Waldegrave, who arrived with the fleet at the Bay in the fall, said later that there was no fertile ground for 150 miles to the south, and that even the plain nearby was not suitable for agriculture.[94]

Because the colony was envisioned as a supply colony, self-sufficient and able to secure needed commodities through local trade, outbound ships from England were not prepared with enough goods to provision the settlement (despite the lesson the English learned at Jamestown about the extensive supplies new settlements required). Initial indications had suggested that the English could rely on the people of the Bay to aid them. They had greeted the English as allies, and indeed Waldegrave described one fight that involved twenty of the English alongside the Malagasy, and that impressed him with how adept the people were with their lances and darts.[95] But relations deteriorated, and the English were unable to secure the cattle they required.

The colony's records convey the colonists' low morale. The mortality among their company was bad enough. But they also dreaded attack by the Malagasy and endured daily anxieties about food. The governor and his advisors characterized the mood as one of "continuall feare."[96] Illness led to social disorganization, at least in the eyes of colony leaders: other inhabitants might have characterized their greater liberty differently. But the governor observed that the starving men at Augustine Bay, allotted only a bit of salt beef a day, took to eating the hides from cattle. Waldegrave reported that they ate their dogs as well.[97] Smart criticized these men for wasting the hides because his lieutenant was too sick to direct them. The men grew "insolent and unruly saying what they thought fitt themselves, no man daring to controle them."[98]

The Malagasy supply of cattle was all that stood between the settlers' survival and starvation, and the colony's records reveal a steady preoccupation with procuring cattle both for personal consumption and to have available to supply English ships (figure 6.4). Unfortunately, the cattle the English purchased died of hunger from poor grazing as soon as they reached the English settlement. Moreover, a cultural practice in which sellers reclaimed (or stole, as the English put it) their own cattle after the English believed they had purchased them outright made it very hard for the settlers to hang on to their livestock. The diplomatic relations that guaranteed food were particularly problematic for the English. The promotional literature had encouraged them to expect the Malagasy to provide for their wants, unlike the sufferings of the English in New England and Virginia who endured "the treachery of the Salvages." Boothby promised that the inhabitants of Madagascar were "affable and curteous."[99] When the Malagasy instead proved reluctant and thwarted English expectations, the settlers reacted violently.

This English inclination toward violence proved disastrous at Augustine Bay, where the inhabitants were long accustomed to dealing with European visitors and where local political alliances were themselves in considerable flux. References in the colony's surviving records suggest the political complexity of the region. John Smart's final letter from Augustine Bay in May of 1646 detailed the various leaders of the region: to the north were Andria Brindah, Andria Massara, and "one Malory." At the Bay the English traded with Andria Pela and Andria Soris. At the river—perhaps the Onilahy River—was Andria Pison and Andria Copuck.[100] The English sought to pursue alliances with all of these men. Madagascar's seventeenth century was a

Figure 6.4. The people and animals of Augustine Bay are carefully delineated in this 1598 image, which shows the weapons that English commentators described, the cattle which the English hoped would sustain them, abundant fruit lying on the ground, and what is likely a ring-tailed lemur perched in the tree at right. Willem Lodewycksz, *Premier livre de l'histoire de la navigation aux Indes Orientales, par les Hollondois* (Amsterdam, 1598). This item is reproduced by permission of The Henry E. Huntington Library, San Marino, California.

period of political transformation especially for those people who lived in regions popular with European traders, invaders, and pirates. They gathered in larger communities, both to fend off outsiders and to fend off each other, as has been documented for the region of French settlement at Fort Dauphin.[101] European traders brought guns and goods prized for their role in display, and traded these goods in return for the cattle they needed to sustain themselves and the slaves by which they hoped to profit. Competition for these new trade goods encouraged the rise of short-term martial alliances.[102]

In many respects, the responses of the people of Madagascar to outside visitors, whether traders or more predatory invaders, resemble those found in the Americas. The Pequots of southeastern New England, for example, built palisaded villages in the seventeenth century in response to the violent commercial culture of the region as Dutch, English, and indigenous traders competed for wares. But the people of Madagascar had one advantage that Americans lacked in their efforts to fend off or to engage outsiders, and it made all the difference in the world: the disease environment. In the 1850s, the last queen of Madagascar, Ranavalona III, identified precisely the fevers of malaria as one of the two best defenses of her kingdom, the other being the forests.[103] Their relative immunity to the diseases that weakened and killed Europeans meant that those who lived in regions of European incursion could decide whether or not to pursue trade and whether or not to tolerate a European presence. The Malagasy at the Bay might have initially encouraged the English to settle there, but they could easily remove their support and leave them to die, as the Powhatans could have done to the English in Virginia.

The English slashed their way into this politically volatile world, with various rulers who controlled separate groups of people, different territories, and different herds of cattle. What might have worked in North America where Europeans often benefited from the cultural and political dislocations caused by the epidemics that preceded or accompanied occupation proved reckless and self-destructive on Madagascar. In a final desperate effort to recover some stolen cattle the English thought were already their own, a party of Englishmen traveled north. After devising an elaborate and theatrical scheme complete with a bottle of wine and "strong waters" to distract their hosts, the governor in disguise, and a secret password (King Charlie), the colonists employed a time-honored strategy from Atlantic endeavors and kidnapped a neighboring chief, Andria Brindah (a man his neighbors called "Capt King"), and his son for a ransom of cattle in October of 1645.[104] The English made peace with Andria Brindah after his men offered 200 head of cattle to the English, and Andria Brindah and his son were released from their imprisonment aboard the *Friendship* after the cattle were delivered on November 24.

But the English troubles with local leaders continued. In December, Smart set out on a voyage to the north to Assada in search of supplies, and in his absence, relations deteriorated. In January of 1646 two Englishmen were sent to get some cattle from "Dynero Black" and were murdered on their way home by men associated with Andria Pela. The English retaliated by executing two men in their custody who were subjects of Andria Pela, "considering," they solemnly recorded, "of the insufferable wrong that wee have sustained by the loss of two of our people which are of more vallew to us then all the Blackes of this Island."[105] This act they ominously referred to as "the beginning of their Revenge."[106] Five Englishmen altogether were killed during this period of conflict. Their holdings were also attacked: a barge was burned, a skiff set adrift, the forge burned. Finally in May, after fourteen dismal months on Madagascar, the surviving colonists—thirty men, eleven women, and nineteen boys—abandoned the plantation and evacuated to the Courten factory at Acheh on Sumatra, leaving behind letters naming the four chiefs who had damaged English expectations, justifying their flight, and pleading with subsequent visitors for revenge on their behalf.[107]

Such violent dealings with the Malagasy were particularly problematic in light of the population's long experience with European traders, and, of course, their even longer experience with Indian Ocean trade. They possessed crucial goods, most especially cattle and their skill tending them, for the survival of Europeans outbound to India. Scattered trading posts gave Europeans and Malagasy experience dealing with each other. When, for example, the English colony at Augustine Bay dispatched the *Sun* to the other side of the island to trade, the captain found the French already settled there and in control of local trade.[108] They discovered, moreover, that the Dutch were "settled and fortified" elsewhere on the island, at Antongil, on the island's northeast coast.[109] In those instances when the Dutch or French proved shrewder trading partners, the indigenous people were reluctant to trade with or supply the English. It was particularly important to have the correct trade goods on hand. When the first colonization party reached the Bay in 1645, the English governor reported indignantly that "the Rogues" refused to trade unless the English gave them an orange rolled small India bead, called vacca. But a month later, Governor Smart fumed that only brass wire, used for personal adornment, would satisfy them.[110] Moreover, local traders knew the price the market could bear. When Smart sought cattle on one provisioning foray, the sellers demanded "great rates knowing our necessitie."[111] Confronted with these savvy traders and their own inadequate preparation, English planters turned to combative styles of interaction more commonly associated with Atlantic invasions.

This style earned the stern criticism of those Englishmen more familiar with the mores of the region, the traders of the East India Company. The

East India Company greatly resented the presence of Courten's men and ships in their territory. Although Courten never made a fortune through his Indian exploits, every piece of trade transacted by his men, every ship seized as prize by his small fleet, was money out of the East India Company's pocket. So the men of the East India Company were loathe to support Courten's colonization efforts, and recorded with a grim satisfaction the debacle of the first colony. Francis Breton, the East India Company's agent at Surat, reported that two of the three Courten ships languished at Rajapur (on the Malabar coast), "in a deplorable if not desperate condition, expecting lading for England where appered neither goods, nor meanes to purchase any."[112]

Courten's men lamented their embarrassing position; their agent at Rajapur, John Farren, wrote John Smart complaining about the lack of stock and the associated mountain of debts. He reported dejectedly that he had written Courten himself and "humbly besought him to consider how himselfe (as wee his servants) in want of Imploymt were exposed to ye laughter of our Ennemies (whose gaine consists of or ruine)."[113] The East India Company's factors even accused Courten's men of making counterfeit coins at their settlement and passing the coins off in their trade activities.[114]

When the East India Company heard of the acrimonious relations between Smart's company and the Malagasy, they placed interests of trade above any alliance with other Englishmen and blamed Courten's men for their "inhumane" treatment of the people and for their almost irreparable damage to trade. As one merchant put it, he required of the people "rather their Bulls then themselves in sacrifice," in response to Smart's written plea for all future English traders to retaliate against the four local leaders for him.[115] One trader found in July of 1646 that he could not trade because the people at the Bay were afraid of the English, and once trade was finally secured, they remained mistrustful. The East India Company labored to reestablish old alliances. John Duisson, an East India Company employee, was an old friend of Andria May, one of the leaders at Augustine Bay, and Duisson entertained Andria May and Andria Pela on board his ship in August of 1646. He offered them beads for presents and shared his hospitality, but worried that the people at the Bay would still not trust the English.[116] Only when the failure of Courten's men threatened trade for the East India Company did the Company intervene. Such was the case in 1646 when the East India Company factor at Surat complained to his employers that Courten's factory at Goa was in such a deplorable state that the result would be "an extrordinary dishonor to our Nacon, & prejudice to your trade."[117] Trade required amicable relations; provisions for English ships similarly depended on the support of local merchants and leaders. Settlement modeled on colonial ventures in the Atlantic undermined the careful harmony English traders secured in a volatile and competitive marketplace.

What of those people who were evacuated from Augustine Bay? They met a variety of fates: only twelve out of the original 140 are known with certainty to have made it home to England. When the evacuees disembarked at Johanna (Anjouan, in the Comoro Islands), they refused to reboard Smart's ship. Smart issued a warrant requiring the people to get on board, but they mutinied, saying that from Johanna they had expectations of being able to get to England, so they did not want to go on to nearby Mayotte, where they feared that no ship would come to rescue them and they would instead be "kept there slaves all theyre life tyme." This, Smart reported, was the decision of all of the women and most of the men, who agreed they would rather be hanged then forced on board again. Smart could do nothing to persuade them otherwise, "for from heare they will not stirr except for ye coast of India with hopes to get home."[118]

The survivors dispersed from Johanna. Smart tried to arrange passage especially for "the widdowes and maydes that are unmarried for India, where they may get home ye first ship for England."[119] Some ventured to Goa, hoping to find work with the Portuguese. Others went to Surat, and sought work with the East India Company. Two of the married people and two widows sailed on the *Dolphin* to Rajapur. Mr. Barrett and his wife, "appearing to be people of better quality," and unwilling to sail to England because Mrs. Barrett was pregnant, stayed on until the following year.[120]

As for poor John Smart, who had already been forced to abandon his colony, he went to Acheh only to discover upon his arrival that his cousin, Arthur Kynnaston, had died three days before. The merchant selected to replace him, Walter Atkins, died three days after Smart's arrival. Both men suffered from pain in their stomachs, vomiting, and convulsions. Kynnaston endured convulsions for nine days, and experienced memory loss as well.[121] Smart himself died after writing home about the flux he was suffering (likely dysentery), at the same time that his wife in London petitioned the East India Company for their help in giving her husband passage home from Mayotte.[122] If the main theme of their time at Augustine Bay was death, that dolorous tune continued with little variation for the survivors after their evacuation.

ASSADA: THE BARBADOS OF THE INDIAN OCEAN, 1649–1650

One of the twelve men who made it home was Powle Waldegrave. And, incredibly, he tried again. Waldegrave was part of a second English effort to settle a colony on Madagascar, near Nosy Be, the island the English called Assada. The first plantation effort drew on Caribbean and North American colonial models derived from Virginia, New England, and Trinidad. In the second initiative, Caribbean models came to the fore, providing the impetus for settlement, shaping recruitment, and revealing the fusion of East and West Indian enterprises. The second effort to plant an English colony in this part of the world proved even less auspicious, although the colony seemed to possess advantages not present in the colony at Augustine Bay. Three challenges to successful colonization—competition with other English merchants, the absence of supplies, and the menace of unwelcoming residents combined with English diplomatic gaffes—could be circumvented with adequate planning and trained personnel. While the first colony was organized by men vehemently opposed by the East India Company, the second effort, initially organized by a group called the Assada Adventurers, was absorbed into the Company in December of 1649.[123]

The colony was carefully modeled on Barbados, the great success story of the 1640s. Barbados was first claimed and settled by the English in the 1620s. It presented a number of advantages to aspiring planters, particularly the fact that it was uninhabited. Sustained by the labor of English indentured servants, the planters there raised corn, cotton, and tobacco, seeking a crop suitable for export and profit. Tobacco had saved the Virginia colony, but there were always problems of oversupply and of competition with tobacco of better quality, particularly the fine Trinidad tobacco which set the standard. Barbados's sugar revolution of the 1640s secured the prosperity of planters and investors. Land prices soared and planters switched from indentured laborers to enslaved Africans. Barbados offered England its first direct access to sugar for consumption and export. The extent to which Barbados would dominate the value of total imports from American holdings was not yet apparent in the 1640s, but the trend must have been clear to informed observers.

Robert Hunt seized on the Barbados model to promote and shape his proposed venture. He had gained valuable colonial experience in the West Indies when he was governor of Providence Island from 1636–1637. He wrote a promotional pamphlet for this new venture, and included a small note to his "Deare Friends," which explained why one with a "comfortable provision" in England and a wife "so deare unto me" should consider leading an uncertain colonial enterprise thousands of miles away. He sought to proselytize, "to make knowne God in the World." And the advantages to England of trade in the region permitted Hunt, an ardent puritan, to make double his contribution to the commonwealth. With Hunt, the different forces prompting interest in colonization united.[124]

In his short promotional pamphlet, Hunt optimistically detailed the commodities he hoped to raise on Assada: sugar, indigo, ginger, cotton, rice, pepper, and tobacco to export; for their own consumption, corn, cattle, hogs, poultry, rice, and citrus fruits. His sojourn on Providence had given him familiarity with some of these commodities, but sugar offers the real clue to Hunt's aspirations to recreate Barbados in the Indian Ocean. A mill to grind cane even accompanied the first planters.[125] Hunt explicitly compared Assada with Barbados in his promotional pamphlet. Drawing on contemporary climate theories that maintained that similar latitudes should contain similar climates, Hunt explained that the latitude of the two islands was the same, and that the same crops grew in each place. Nosy Be lies at thirteen degrees south of the equator, while Barbados is at thirteen degrees north. He even provided a chart that helped potential planters evaluate expenses (see table 6.1).

Several assumptions undergirded Hunt's chart. Hunt anticipated that cattle could be acquired easily and cheaply, although in this respect the English were always at the mercy of good diplomatic relations with local merchants and of access to desirable trading commodities, as the experience at Augustine Bay revealed. Slaves, he thought, would be similarly cheap (the English themselves engaged in the coastal slave trade in the Indian Ocean), and while costs would certainly have been lower than in Barbados, he was perhaps overly optimistic about the bargains awaiting English planters. The other great saving was in land, which the Assada Merchants planned to offer planters at a cheap rent. While Barbados's shift to sugar caused arable land to skyrocket in value, land on Assada was artificially regulated by the Company's scheme to purchase the whole island and to dole out land to planters.[126] Hunt anticipated that provisions were cheaper to transport to Madagascar than to the Caribbean: in this he was certainly incorrect, as voyages to Madagascar were long and debilitating, and only the death of people in transit would have the possible consequence of deflating the prices of their provisions for

Table 6.1. Hunt's Comparison of Costs

Item	Barbados	Assada
300 Acres	£2,000	£15 (12d/acre)
20 English servants, transported and provisioned	£300	£300
100 "Negroes"	£2,700 (£25–30 each)	£100 (20s each)
Tools, clothing	£300	£200
20 cattle	£700	£25
Total	£6,000	£640

Source: Robert Hunt, *The Island of Assada* (London, 1650), 3–4.

survivors on arrival. Daily expenses were lower as well, Hunt reported, since he anticipated that it cost less to raise crops there, while the island's location promised a thriving local trade. Like Lord Arundel before him, he made his pitch to the wealthy and even to the impoverished, assuring potential servants that after four years of service they would be given as much land to cultivate as they could use, with provisions for six months and three laborers described as "Negro servants."[127] Hunt's goal was to attract men who might otherwise have ventured to Barbados.

Barbados guided other considerations as well, especially in terms of regulating laborers. The small island the English sought permission to inhabit was, like Barbados, an "empty" land awaiting English settlement. Hunt planned to populate it quickly, anticipating an enormous population of 100,000 people, with room for 200 sugar mills.[128] He was not insensitive to the potential problems of slave labor and slave regulation. Although he anticipated that some English people might venture to Assada as servants, he imagined a laboring population drawn from Arabia, Africa, India, and Madagascar. He proposed a ratio of one Englishman for every ten of these other people, which he believed reflected the English capacity to regulate subordinate laborers. In contrast to Barbadian planters' indifference for their slaves' spiritual lives, Hunt insisted that those living under English domination on Assada would be educated in Christianity.[129] No English colony, however, experienced a 10:1 ratio of non-European laborers to planters in this period, and in fact Barbados still contained more Europeans than Africans. Batavia probably inspired his comparison: as Hunt put it, he imagined Assada to be to the English "As Batavia is to the Dutch, and Goa to the Portingalls."[130]

The English were familiar with Assada, located in Ampasindava Bay, which was the site of the old Islamic port of Mahilaka. John Smart had sailed there for supplies during his months at Augustine Bay. Over the course of the seventeenth century, the region came under the political control of the Sakalava, who had established their dominance over most of the western portion of Madagascar by the end of the period. Although the west coast of Madagascar is generally arid, the one exception is the Sambirano region in the northwest, where Nosy Be is. This equatorial zone was favorable for human settlement: fresh water was abundant, and it was a fertile agricultural land.[131] Here, perhaps, was finally a promising area for English habitation. In fact, John Smart had considered relocating the Augustine Bay settlement there in 1645.[132] The East India Company's support for this project, and their large-scale aspirations to constitute a colonial society there, reflect the Company's diverse interests in projects beyond trading posts and illustrate its willingness to constitute civil societies overseas. Had Assada succeeded, the settlement would have been pivotal in reshaping East India Company activities and in broadcasting the Company's state-building ambitions.[133]

It was a densely settled area. One East India Company employee saw forty towns on the coast alone.[134] Hunt's account included a description of a prior visit by some English merchants, who spent eight months there and went to a coastal town on the mainland they called Antasta, a port where the people exchanged commodities from India and "Cullivers" (calivers, or light muskets) and knives for rice. Twenty miles further on, past two more villages, was the town where the ruler resided in a large palace and governed over an area Hunt believed stretched 200 miles. The land in between was well inhabited, with fields of rice and sugar and abundant cattle. The ruler gave the English permission to trade, and invited them to return. Hunt's description made it clear that the English perceived this ruler as a man of prestige and wealth. He displayed his treasure, pieces of eight, silk, and satin, to the English visitors, and ruled his people as if they were his slaves.[135]

The Assada Adventurers sought to secure amicable relations with the King of Assada (Sultan Assad), thus preventing the miseries of the southern experiment and drawing on the extensive diplomatic expertise of the East India Company. After he ventured to Assada in the winter of 1649–1650, Hunt delivered a letter to the king from the East India Company pledging their service and assistance and alerting the king to their plans to cultivate sugar on the island.[136] The Company also took pains to secure gifts that they hoped would insinuate themselves into the king's affections. At a meeting in London in January of 1650, triumphant bargain hunters reported that they had discovered an old chariot of Queen Anne that they could purchase for £16–17, although it had originally cost £100. They hoped to accompany this treasure, a suitable gesture of respect for a distant king, with a sword worth forty shillings and a looking glass, procured for twenty shillings.[137] The planters in Nosy Be requested that the king give them an island to settle, singling out Nasara (also called Goat's Island) but ready to settle for some other convenient place.[138] As part of the religious connection he sought to secure, Hunt planned to leave "three Godly men" with the king at the north end of Madagscar as agents, who were to educate the ruler and his people about Christianity and to live in peace among them.

After Hunt's voyage, more planters, 210 altogether, were organized and equipped by the East India Company over the course of the next year.[139] These English adventurers consisted only of men: not for Assada the family settlement of Augustine Bay. Indeed, the prominence of men echoed migration patterns to Barbados in the island's first decade of settlement.[140] Several were craftsmen. The organizers took care to send several gardeners, a glover, butcher, baker, cook, weaver, cooper, falconer, and bricklayer, along with husbandmen and two gentlemen.[141] These adventurers were well supplied.[142] And they were enticed overseas with a device familiar to planters of America, headrights. Although the East India Company had not secured any legitimate claim to land, for each servant he sent, a planter could receive thirty acres.[143]

Yet these efforts did not secure success. What precisely led to the failure of the plantation is not clear, but an early massacre that killed Governor Hunt and nine other men prompted survivors to flee to safety and suggests that, as in the case of the Augustine Bay settlement, careless relations with indigenous inhabitants destroyed the colony. There would be no Barbados in the Indian Ocean.

The colony's demise was discovered first by the many East India Company supply ships that traveled to the island.[144] As early as June of 1650, as the ship *Bonito* reached Assada to deposit planters, the ship's purser Charles Wilde recorded in his journal a report from the men of the *Assada Merchant* that the colony's governor had been killed with nine others only days before the *Assada Merchant* arrived. They had allegedly been lured by the king who offered them a big piece of ambergris, but he killed them. Thoughts of settlement were not yet abandoned. Wilde's party included four ships, with many planters, and some of the men ventured on shore.[145] Wilde himself drew a map, carefully labeling Assada, "where wee went to In Habbitt."[146] A new governor, Major Hartley, was appointed to replace Colonel Hunt. In July the planters went on shore with the carpenters to fortify a new settlement, but this second effort did not succeed, either.

In October, yet another East India Company ship, the *Supply*, searched for the settlement on Nosy Be and on the islands nearby. The distant sight of a small sail at first caused the agitation of a false alarm. Finally an armed expedition was sent to march on shore under a white flag to search for the colony, but to no avail: the only people the English spied were indigenous people who prudently eluded the English. Discouraged, the English ship sailed to a larger town and port of Antisia, where the mariners found the town "ruinated, and the most parte burnte." Scattered homes and the skulls of dead men offered the only evidence of habitation: the piece of a feather bed tick, a scrap of a blanket, and some abandoned shoes and slippers suggested to the English party that the remains belonged to the missing English planters. In the river they found a Company sword, exactly like the ones for the plantation. The men from the ship continued to probe the island, provoking small skirmishes from the inhabitants mistakenly perceived as timorous by their uninvited guests but described by one English captain as "blacke long shagge haird villaines." They sailed on to Nosy Be, still looking for signs of the plantation, but finding only violent attacks from the island's inhabitants. Finally the captain gave up and sailed on, abandoning the colony as its survivors had earlier abandoned their deceased comrades.

The only report the English had of their colleagues' fate came later from the king of Johanna, who reported that all of the men who had gone to settle

Assada were "cutte of," and that the king there would allow none to settle his territory. Twenty altogether had been murdered. These men had abandoned the plantation by August 20, and sailed off in the *Assada Merchant*. The East India Company head merchant at Surat who interviewed the survivors offered a slightly different version of the story from the one heard by James Berblock, an East India Company employee who traveled on the *Supply*. Seven men had been killed since the *Bonita* and *Lioness* left the plantation in June, and the murders happened after they left in a party to rob a town three to four miles away from the settlement. Berblock trusted no one: he reported that the people of Johanna professed public outrage at the king of Assada's attack on the English, but he suspected that they privately approved his actions. "I know their feare, and treacherie," he wrote.[147] It is also possible that the English settlement became entangled in European rivalries in the region. A Portuguese account reported that the English had appropriated an island not given them, and that the Portuguese encouraged Sultan Assad to attack the English settlement.[148] The entire effort was abandoned and the refugees hired instead by the East India Company at various trading posts abroad.[149]

Sixty-six men survived to be evacuated to Swally Marine (near Surat). Some died of the diseases of the region, as Major Hartley, the governor of the plantation, did at Gambroone (as the English called Bandar Abbas) on his way to Madras. Other Assada planters loitered at Surat, running up debts and occasionally dropping by Sunday services at the English trading post.[150] Because of the time lag that characterized the transmission of news in this period, the East India Company was still involved in recruiting men for the plantation effort after the colony itself had been abandoned. Hunt's promotional pamphlet appeared posthumously.

The loss of Assada was a failure that infuriated another man who had traversed the island in search of the lost colony. Dismayed by the desertion of the colony "upon such slender grounds," Captain Blackman, bound for Surat as the new East India Company factor, fumed that it was the planters' own folly that destroyed the colony, not "the Peoples treachery." He raged at the recklessness of the planters, who had been warned "the day before" by the "Arabians" of the treachery against them, but took no precautions. What people, he queried, would in "meere madness...carelessly goe ramble up into the country," despite knowing the anger of the people toward them? As for the deadly diseases that also reduced the settlement's population, Blackman had a plan. Adapting to regional customs would secure greater health: the English should emulate the local habit of sleeping a foot off the ground with a fire under them to protect them from those "Contadious vap[or]s yt assend from the Earth, and infest their bodyes wth pestilentiall diseases."[151] Certainly the smoke would have kept mosquitoes at bay. Blackman proposed solutions to the two main hazards of

Indian Ocean settlements: high mortality from disease, and adversarial relations with powerful indigenous people. In ordering would-be planters to embrace local habits, he urged planters to follow the commercial model of adaptation and accommodation in circumstances in which the English had neither political, military, nor epidemiological advantages over the region's indigenous inhabitants. Blackman was determined that a third effort was not only possible but desirable. His inspiration came from other English adventurers. "Had those who are to bee honoured for planting, Virginia, & S. Christopher, deserted them upon such slender grounds, I believe wee had not had at this Day a Plantation in America." And he knew what the plantation would need: 600 to 800 men, with two or three ships to stay permanently with them.

Nobody listened to Captain Blackman, and Assada was abandoned for good. But he understood the lessons of previous colonies, not only the recent failures on Assada and Madagascar, but also the distant successes on Virginia and St. Christopher. And he believed ardently that a sugar colony on Assada, modeled after Barbados, would benefit the East India Company as fully as did its trade factories along the coastline of the Indian Ocean. On Assada, Blackman hoped to see the intersection of trade and settlement, of an Indian Ocean plantation on a West Indian model. Blackman, however, was precocious in his aspirations. Abundant manpower in the first decades of the seventeenth century might have secured English plantations in the Atlantic, but personnel alone would not resolve challenges in the Indian Ocean, where disease staked a claim and where acumen, experience, and relative resistance to malaria characterized the indigenous inhabitants. Atlantic and Caribbean experiences and models only complicated and imperiled settlement efforts elsewhere in the 1640s.

A lost colony, high mortality, repeated rebuffs from indigenous inhabitants—these did not deter European colonization efforts in the Caribbean and North Atlantic. The English overcame the abandoned settlement of Roanoke and the deadly and debilitating years at Jamestown to establish a profitable enterprise; the French settled Quebec in 1608 after the miserable winter of 1605 at St. Croix Island; the English established themselves in New England in 1620 after the deadly winter at Sagadahoc in Maine in 1607–1608; and the lethal tropical settlements of the "wild coast" of South America did not deter repeated English, Dutch, and French efforts there over the course of the seventeenth century. Yet the English declined to try again on Madagascar, a decision probably embedded in transformations within the region. Madagascar had proved repeatedly to be an inhospitable place for Europeans. By the time the English attempted their settlement at Augustine Bay, the Portuguese and Dutch, deterred by the disease environment, had already given up interest in long-term settlement in the same region. The Bay even contained distinct burial grounds marking the demise of Dutch and French visitors. Instead, Augustine Bay, like Nosy Be to the north, ultimately became a haven for pirates and a center of the slave trade.[152] Only the French succeeded (between 1642 and 1674), on the other side of Madagascar, and remarkably so, for their colony at Fort Dauphin was in fact their first settlement in the Indian Ocean. But regional transformations also made an English settlement on Madagascar no longer so necessary. The urgent need for a supply colony was reduced once the Dutch established just such a station at the Cape of Good Hope (in 1652), and later when the English East India Company created its own supply station at St. Helena in the south Atlantic in 1673. The French had also established themselves at Bourbon in the 1660s. English aspirations to recreate Barbados, moreover, were obviated in the Indian Ocean by the rise of sugar production in other islands of the West Indies.

But all of that lay in the future: the English present in 1646 and 1650 contained ruined dreams, murdered friends, scattered remnants of clothing and bedding, and lost colonies. If the colonization of Madagascar began with ambitious optimism, launched in verse, on canvas, and in exuberant prose pamphlets, it ended, in Governor Smart's angry words, as a "chimera." The venture so enraged survivors that they ranted about the deceit of promotional works, and they carried their fury home with them. Dreams too easily became deadly nightmares for those forced to enact them. The thwarted settlements on Madagascar were products of trade aspirations by the Courten Assocation, which, in contrast to the East India Company factory model, sought to establish permanent settlements in order to improve trade. These ventures were born in a world of trade. But they were shaped as well by a world of colonization, albeit a pattern defined thousands of miles away in circumstances that could not be reproduced in or transferred to the Indian Ocean.

The English who ventured to Madagascar could not be faulted for poor preparation. They came equipped with men who could find mines, should the promised mines appear.[153] They loaded their ships with supplies to launch a new settlement, with desirable trade goods, and in the first effort with the women and children whose presence promised demographic stability. They carefully read the available literature. They approached these ventures as if their lives depended on their success, as indeed they did. These planters and their supporters in England likewise brought the accumulated experience of decades of trade and settlement with them. The English were relatively successful by the 1640s in many of their colonial enterprises in America. The rate of failed experiments had diminished considerably. Past results in the Atlantic might have predicted future accomplishments elsewhere. But this growing American expertise proved not to be portable, at least not to the Indian Ocean in the mid-seventeenth century, at a time and in a place where the English still struggled with basic survival and could not match the political power of indigenous states and kingdoms. Trade factories, however ephemeral any single one might be, and the culture of accommodation that sustained them, proved to be the most enduring approach to the region.

7

THE COSMOPOLITAN CLERGY, 1620–1660

As the East India Company ship the *Royal James* rounded the Cape of Good Hope in 1621, the thoughts of the travel-weary merchants and mariners on board likely turned with the vessel toward England. Their actions, however, revealed a competing interest, thanks to the initiative of Patrick Copland, an East India Company chaplain who was heading home from his second stint in the Company's service. The Scottish cleric galvanized his fellow travelers to donate just over £70 to establish a free school in the young colony of Virginia, several thousand miles away in North America. The contributors directed the institution to be named after their employer, and all East India Company employees whose children hoped to attend the school were ensured preference. The Earl of Southampton received the funds on behalf of the Virginia Company in November of 1621, and the Company in turn granted land for the institution.[1]

This scene aboard the *Royal James* displayed in tangible form some of the main themes of this book: the overlapping and intersecting worlds of commercial and colonial enterprises and the transoceanic global perspective that men derived through their travels from one ocean basin to another, in this instance, quite literally, as the vessel navigated the turbulent waters where two oceans meet. The donors communicated a sense of kinship with the remote and precarious Virginia experiment. They even imagined that their own children—England's next generation—could benefit from the distant Virginia school. Linking families in England, a tiny colony in America, and vital trade in the East Indies, this philanthropic moment was an expression of optimism as much as it was an act of charity.

The man responsible for this initiative was a minister. Governors, ambassadors, soldiers, consuls, mariners, merchants, and colonists might be the most historically visible officials, agents, and employees who circulated around the world, but ministers did the same. They were a crucial part of all overseas ventures, on board ships as chaplains and in residence at both trade factories and colonies. A close look at English trading posts, colonies, and the ships that transported men to them reveals that ministers were everywhere, yet we know little about the relationship between the clergy and English overseas activity before 1660.

This neglect stands in vivid contrast to the history of Iberian expansion in the sixteenth and seventeenth centuries. At a time of Protestant challenge, the Roman Catholic church presented a comparatively uniform face to the world. Although Catholicism always had local variations in Europe, the Americas, Asia, and Africa, as the faith absorbed however reluctantly and unwittingly elements of pre-Christian religious practices, it was nonetheless a universal religion. Some kingdoms such as Spain defined themselves through their Catholicism, and for them, evangelical mission became a central component of commercial or colonial expansion. In the wake of the Reconquest, the protracted victory by the Catholics of the Iberian peninsula over the Muslims who had lived there for centuries, to be Spanish was to be Catholic. The forced conversions of Muslims and Jews in the fifteenth century, as well as their subsequent expulsion, signaled the urgency of religious conformity for Spanish identity. The crown's commitment to conversion in the Americas represented not only acquiescence to papal decree (the 1493 Papal Bull, *Inter Caetera*) but also an important strategy for absorbing conquered people as Christian subjects. Portuguese traders were similarly accompanied by priests, who introduced Catholicism with varying degrees of success in places as diverse as the kingdom of Kongo and Japan. Particularly in the age of Catholic Reformation, which coincided with England's entrance into a world of overseas trade, the Catholic church and its educational orders articulated a doctrinal uniformity that gave Iberian commercial and colonial enterprises religious coherence and evangelical vigor.

Protestant monarchs in Europe similarly took to heart the association of faith and nation in a time of bitter and bloody rivalries. Divergent confessional traditions offered a language of both identity and opposition that gave voice to national rivalries that manifested themselves wherever disputants met around the globe. Nonetheless, from country to country, from kingdom to empire, religious settlements varied. England was a Protestant nation, unusual among many of its European rivals in its national church, but there was little agreement beyond separation from Rome on what Protestantism in England entailed. Moreover, there were still Catholics in England. The latitudinarian policies of Elizabeth I permitted a range of practices that enabled worshippers to contest the association of any single doctrine or practice with the nation. Ministers at home could not provide the cultural, national, or social glue that Catholic priests transported around the world.

If religion resides awkwardly in the narrative of an English nation regularly wracked by religious dispute and with overt conflict in the 1640s and 1650s, religion sits even less comfortably in a history of English expansion in these early decades. In the sixteenth and seventeenth centuries, English engagement in a wider world was evident in the growth of long-distance trade companies and parasitic settlements and colonial ventures. With the notable exception of historians of early New England, who have rarely questioned the centrality of religion to that region's settlement, and the smaller number of scholars of English Protestant missionaries (a statistically insignificant population in the early seventeenth century), historians have generally suggested if only through their silence that religious considerations were subservient to secular, strategic, and pecuniary motives. Perhaps that is the correct order of things. But in fact religion had been a centerpiece for some of the earliest justifications for colonization, especially in the context of the bitter English and Spanish rivalries of the late sixteenth century. Richard Hakluyt's "Discourse on Western Planting" advocated colonization in part as a way to spread Protestantism to the western hemisphere as early as 1584, and evangelization always occupied a prominent place in his later writings. In America, Hakluyt believed, the inhabitants "crye oute unto us their nexte neighboures to comme and helpe them."[2] Colonial charters often required companies to promote Christianity, as the Virginia Company patent did in 1606.

These early visions of Protestant mission to thwart Spanish expansion, however, proved unrealistic. But if ultimately England's track record in American missionary work was weak (and in fact trading companies were explicitly barred from proselytizing), religion was nonetheless important enough to overseas companies and to the men who worked for them that ministers accompanied every phase of English expansion. English companies hired hundreds of ministers, both to tend to the spiritual needs of merchants and settlers in foreign cities and settlements and to serve as ship chaplains during long voyages. Many of the men who ventured once overseas took subsequent trips. Their circuits often intersected those of the displaced clerics of these tumultuous decades, men whose religious inclinations drove them from official favor and gainful employment, forcing them into hegiras to the continent and across the Atlantic. As important as their voyages from one trading post to another, or from colony to colony, was their journey home. Factory chaplains served short tours and, if they survived, went back to England. Colonial clerics—even those who moved to America with their families—returned home in high percentages in the 1640s and 1650s, bringing innovative practices with them to affect England's ecclesiastical settlement during the years of the Civil War and Commonwealth.

In their commitment to Protestantism, ministers provided the most visible and visceral symbol of England that the English overseas might identify. English traders operated in an international marketplace and worked to accommodate local cultural norms. What set them apart almost everywhere they went was the performance of their faith, privately in trade factories, publicly in colonies. The mandatory rituals of daily prayer, the possibility of a Sunday service, the distinct liturgy of the Church of England, the service in English—all these features demarcated the English. When clerics and their congregations were in accord, ministers overseas enhanced cultural cohesion. Yet religious expression often provided a focal point of conflict, not only in colonies but also in trading posts, in a period when the liturgy was deeply controversial. Every sermon was an opportunity to give offense; every sacrament, offered or withheld, provided another occasion to chasten rivals. Ministers brought these disputes overseas and at times exacerbated them, particularly in the tiny populations of distant settlements, where a single man could be profoundly divisive. Even in trading posts and European capitals a minister could provoke international conflicts by performing Protestant ceremonies indiscreetly or by giving the appearance of proselytizing.

In these turbulent times, religion was no cohesive force at home and could not provide cohesion abroad. Ministers overseas illustrated a welter of motives, experiences, opinions, preferences, interests, and ambitions. Amid this heterogeneity, the clergy bring into focus how overseas experiences transformed men and enabled them to have a profound impact on individual colonies and trading posts and on England. If clerics who ventured abroad were predisposed to intellectual curiosity and doctrinal innovation, chaplaincies and colonial posts exaggerated these qualities. Moreover, as these individuals ranged into new intellectual and doctrinal positions in settings often remote from the ecclesiastical discipline of the Church of England, they found themselves at odds with the established church. The colonies offered ministers an opportunity to crystallize doctrinal sentiments safely outside the jurisdiction of the Archbishop of Canterbury, and ministers and the radical laity were able to re-export their changed views to England. In this respect, the dissenting clergy had their greatest political and religious effect on England in the 1640s and 1650s, while the cultural impact of the scholar-chaplains and their translated texts and collected manuscripts continued into the 1660s and beyond. But that impact, like the multiple incompatible doctrinal positions of the clergy themselves, was often fragmented and inconsistent. That, indeed, was the crucial contribution of English forms of Protestant expression to the early British Empire: religious practices contributed to the heterogeneity and localism of English life overseas even as traveling ministers themselves linked discrete places and transported new religious practices with them.

The church occupied a complex position in colonization and commerce. Ministers (acting as individuals) were also promoters, investors, and participants. They joined colonial enterprises with their families, risking their lives and goods on uncertain ventures. They often served aggressively as promoters, both for trading companies and for colonial settlements. With their education and social stature, ministers gave enterprises a veneer of respectability. Trading companies placed their employees within societies with cultural and religious practices at odds with England's, risking the fidelity and morality of merchants vulnerable to the lure of new faiths. The stamp of clerical approval could mitigate this collective peril. The East India Company agreed in 1614 to give some poor preachers in London funds and to have them pray for the prosperity of their impending voyage.[3] The Company thereby linked public charity, good will, and divine intercession to their hopes for a profitable voyage. Ministers often delivered formal sermons at the request of overseas companies, as John Donne did for the Virginia Company in 1622.[4] Some ministers played active roles in colonial ventures, going overseas and recruiting others to join them, a pattern of migration that contributed to the distinctive settlements and ecclesiastical structure of numerous New England towns. Even those clerics with no direct involvement in colonial enterprises supported overseas ventures. Ministers, for example, circulated news about the world to parishioners. They read aloud letters from the pulpit, and they were occasionally directed to promote specific undertakings. In an age with no formal press, clerics served as public mouthpieces for private companies.

Ministers were of such consequence to overseas endeavors that their selection was undertaken with as much attention as was devoted to the employment of company and colonial officers and merchants. Chaplains ministered to the souls of factors and merchants, but they also helped to regulate the behavior of these men. The East India Company's minutes record how ministers came to the Company's attention and how they secured employment and negotiated the circumstances of their residence overseas. The East India Company hired ministers to serve as ship's chaplains, and they also retained ministers for different trade factories, including Bombay, Madras, Ajmer, Bantam, and Surat.[5] As one Mr. Johnson put it at a Court meeting in 1613, "as they had beene carefull for p[ro]vision of thinges necessary for the bodies of their men," the Company must also arrange "for the releife of their soules."[6] Although its charter made no such requirement, the Levant Company had similar arrangements, hiring ship's chaplains and also ministers for their factories at Aleppo, Smyrna, and Istanbul.[7] Companies backing larger settlements similarly devoted time and energy to satisfying their employees' spiritual needs. The Virginia Company lamented the paucity of ministers in 1620, with only five ministers for the colony's eleven boroughs, and hoped to send "one sufficient Devine" to each of these settlements, "for the Comfort of the soules of the inhabitants, by preachinge and expoundinge the word of God unto them."[8] Most populations of English overseas, whether small trade factories, colonies, or embassies, had chaplains. As a result the number of ministers who worked abroad in any single year, either at sea or on dry land, was quite high. Once the New England colonies were established in the 1630s, the number of English ministers overseas would likely exceed 300.

The presence of Jesuits in trade factories abroad, from Europe to Japan, presented a special challenge for the English, who feared the Jesuits above all other religious orders. Jesuits had been at the center of real and imagined plots against English sovereigns since the 1580s. In a sermon promoting the Virginia plantation and urging the Company to be more attentive to religion in the colony, Patrick Copland invoked precisely this fear about the Jesuits. He singled out their "double diligence" and their success at "poysoning with the Coloquintida of Popery" thousands of people in the East Indies and Japan.[9] (*Coloquintida* comes from colocynth, a bitter apple of the gourd family that produces a purgative from its pulp.) Yet the English also respected their erudition, tenacity, and missionary accomplishments. East India Company minutes noted the special need for a minister "of learninge and couradge to oppose the Jesuists (sic)."[10] The Company specifically noted the Jesuits' skills in disputation, and sought a man of "learninge and gravitie able to contest wth and hould argument wth the Jesuits that are buysie at Suratt."[11] Ministers who worked where Catholicism was strong also had to safeguard the Protestant beliefs of English residents in the face of these concerted challenges, and so John Sanford, the chaplain to the English embassy in Spain in 1611, reported at length on the activities of different Catholic orders, particularly the Jesuits.[12]

A minister's skills, therefore, influenced his placement. While some East India Company members thought Mr. Leake belonged at Surat to combat the Jesuits, others thought he should be at Bantam, "that place beeinge the Rendezvous for or people from all places, where they shall have most neede of soe sufficient a teacher."[13] At Bantam the priority was the English population, not disputation with rivals. The Company believed that a good minister might make employees more tractable or, as one Company member put it, a minister might "reduce them to a conscionable and dutyfull respect, both to God and their Masters," and rejected applicants who were too young to gain the respect of traders at Bantam.[14]

The East India Company quickly developed a regular routine for screening candidates. Once employers identified candidates, the members scheduled a sermon, with the text occasionally set by the Company, and all Company members were invited to attend the sermon and give their opinion to the membership at the next meeting. "Rehersall sermons," as they were styled by the Virginia Company, could take a lot of time: one busy Sunday as the East India Company was trying to equip the fleet and thus especially pressed to hire new preachers, members attended two different sermons.[15] The Levant Company scheduled as many as four or five talks by different candidates before filling a position.[16] The required texts do not demonstrate any clear connection to the unique trials of ministering overseas; one applicant was told, for example, to preach on Matthew 5:5, "blessed are the poor in spirit."[17] The Virginia Company gave one candidate, Mr. Leat, several texts to choose from, but he told the Company he preferred one of their choosing, so they set Isaiah 9:2, "the people that walked in darkness have seen a great light: they that dwell in the land of the shadow of death, upon them hath the light shined."[18] John Luke's trial sermon in 1664 was so impressive that the Levant Company requested that it be printed, and so it was, with 500 copies made and given to the governor for his distribution.[19] Ministers could also enhance their employment prospects by their ability to support other aspects of overseas enterprises. Mr. Burdett sought a position with the Providence Company and suggested that he would help sway some colonists bound for New England to venture to the Caribbean instead.[20]

As talks were scheduled, delivered, and evaluated, companies gathered further information about applicants' characters. One well-prepared candidate, Mr. Staples, presented a certificate to the Virginia Company in 1621 "from many Divines" in London who attested that he was "of honest converation and a good Scholler."[21] The East India Company rejected one candidate in 1614 because of rumors that he "delighteth in tobacco, and wyne, wch they conceyveinge to be unfit pts, for one of his pfession."[22] Mr. Williams Evans, who was a minister in Barking, seemed an ideal candidate, with travels in Spain and the West Indies and experience practicing physick in England and France. Moreover, with an MA and his studies in divinity, his intellectual qualifications were assured. Yet the East India Company heard reports "by some that have enquirde of his conversation, that he hath bene a gentleman abroad, who hath spente his tyme yill, an hath noe greate good reporte give of him." Such a characterization gave the Company pause. Further reports muddied the waters, since people heard both good and ill. He was finally hired in 1614 at £60 per year, but no sooner was the deal struck than a creditor presented himself with claims on Evans's wages. It is unclear if Evans ever actually went abroad.[23]

The East India Company occasionally settled on a candidate only to have another more likely man come to light. In January of 1607, the East India Company governor was in the process of finalizing plans with one candidate when one Mr. Foxe, "a man of more gravitie," presented himself for the voyage, and the Company deferred their final decision.[24] Other attributes that might work against a candidate included marital status; for that reason the Levant Company did not hire two married men, Mr. Whetstone in 1615 or Mr. Pindar in 1647.[25] Yet there seems to have been no firm policy in this regard.

For all of these careful efforts, however, companies often erred in their selection and Patrick Copland complained from India in 1618 about both a fellow minister and the East India Company's recruitment methods. Copland criticized the minister who accompanied him, Mr. Golding, who abandoned the English at Surat, preferring to chase "after the women," disguised, incredibly, especially given his occupation, as a "moor." Copland used Golding's peculiar deportment to condemn the whole manner of East India Company recruitment, relying as they did on letters from noblemen. Better, he urged, to send no preachers than to send such men, "for how can they work faithfully in the factories when they are dissolute themselves?"[26] Indeed, just the previous year the Company sent home an English preacher who visited brothels in Surat.[27] Reports of insufficiently sober ministers, like Mr. Rous, who taught songs on board ship during his voyage to Providence in 1634, and sang these tunes even on Sundays, troubled employers.[28] The Levant Company learned in 1607 that Mr. Biddulph was combative, and told him that if he could not behave himself, he would have to come home.[29]

Finally, after sermons had been delivered and assessed, and recommendations received and evaluated, companies voted on their candidates, using balls in the case of the Levant Company.[30] Once the selection was formalized, protracted negotiations commenced. Ministers bargained for their salaries, and especially for funds to equip themselves for their voyages. The East India Company acknowledged their status by providing ministers with boys to serve them, and all employers arranged for separate funds for buying books. Salaries ranged in the first decades of the seventeenth century from £50 to £100 per annum, with as much as £50 for supplies. These wages compared favorably to those earned by ministers who stayed in England: Ralph Josselin, the vicar of Earls Colne, Essex, had a living valued at £24 in 1650, although he had expectations of earning as much as £80 per annum through other financial benefits and incentives.[31] Pestered by a cleric's creditors, companies occasionally had to settle debts. Overseas employment, in fact, could help relieve a minister of financial strain. John Walker, who embarked in 1582 as a minister on a voyage in search of the northwest passage, hoped that his debts would be relieved by the profit he intended to reap from his journey.[32] John Covel similarly expected to benefit from his position as chaplain in Istanbul, and negotiated for the right to his own trade in cloths.[33] This was a perk often made available to those clergy who asked. Mr. Egerton, bound for India, was permitted to venture £200 in trade.[34] The privileges of office varied with what a particular destination might offer. The Virginia Company made three ministers freemen before their voyage to Virginia in 1622.[35] Ministers in Virginia had tenants who came with the position as well as a small salary.

All East India Company ministers received funds ranging from £30 to £50 to equip themselves for their journey. With this advance, they purchased clothes and especially books: in their need for printed matter, the ministers required special equipment for their new positions. In 1621, the cost-conscious Virginia Company sent off one minister, Thomas White, with accompanying instructions to the governor and council to provide him with books out of the libraries of the many people who had died.[36] But ministers often required specialized texts not easily found in the motley collections of the recently deceased. The Levant Company arranged for several such books to be shipped to Smyrna in 1672: Matthew Poole's *Synopsis*, to join a polyglot Bible that had been sent previously, and the *Lexicon Heptaglotton*, an enormous two-volume work that was to be secured in chains there as part of the Company's property.[37] Two years later, the widow of the Levant Company's governor donated more works, including volume two of Poole's *Synopsis*; Seaman's New Testament in Turkish (William Seaman had been a minister in Turkey, and undertook a translation there); and a Turkish grammar (likely also Seaman's grammar). Finally, four years later, the Company responded to a request from their Smyrna chaplain John Luke and procured the three remaining volumes of Poole's *Synopsis* (published in 1673, 1674, and 1676) to join the earlier volumes, all chained in the Company's library.[38] From his distant post, Luke had obviously been following the publication of these works and the Company seemed eager to please the chaplain. All texts would help a Levant minister to master new languages and would provide him with intellectual stimulation. These were not works designed for the recreational reader, but weighty, erudite tomes, indicative of the scholarly bent of these men.

The willingness and availability of clerics to travel overseas was an outgrowth of the migratory nature of clerical education and employment in England. Clergy were among the best traveled in an already-mobile nation. Young men moved for their educations to Oxford or Cambridge, and then tended to move on as they sought positions. Professional specialization required this willingness to migrate: all ministers moved for either education or employment, and usually for both. Within this peripatetic population were the even more mobile dissenters. Employment in the church was deeply political in this age of divided loyalties and sensibilities, and disputes prompted migration. Three cycles of clerical migration occurred between 1620 and 1660, first in the 1620s and 1630s involving dissenters, a second cycle in the 1640s and 1650s involving both dissenters flocking to England and orthodox Anglicans departing the realm, and the third beginning with the Restoration of Charles II in 1660. These cycles were linked to the political turmoil of the time. The crown dictated England's religious settlements, and with the death of each monarch a newly vigilant or indifferent sovereign came to the throne.

Take, for example, the career of the puritan Thomas Shepard. He was born in Northamptonshire in 1605, educated at Cambridge, employed in Essex, then far to the north at Yorkshire, where he married. He settled briefly in Northumberland and was forced into hiding in London for his religious views. Shepard ultimately fled to New England.[39] Other puritans exiled themselves on the continent. Such was the case for Hugh Peter, originally of Cornwall, and later educated at Cambridge. After he received his degree, he preached and worked in London and Essex. After a falling out with the Bishop of London for his criticism of the queen, Peter migrated to Rotterdam and served the English congregation there before he sneaked back to England and boarded a ship for New England in 1635.[40]

Peter and Shepard were joined in their flights by hundreds of other clerics during the 1620s, 1630s, and 1640s. Ecclesiastical visitations throughout England in the 1620s and 1630s scrutinized the behavior and conformity of ministers and many, like Shepard, were fired for their conduct. These formal reviews also prompted ministers to travel to Europe, America, and Asia in search of more palatable conditions of employment. But the Civil War of the 1640s and the era of the Commonwealth in the 1650s brought some of these men home again. 114 ministers traveled to New England in the 1620s and 1630s. Thirty-five of these men (thirty percent) returned from their colonial retreats to England in the 1640s and 1650s, when the ecclesiastical polity seemed more sympathetic to their position and when they believed that they might influence events.[41] Religion and politics were inseparable.

Previously conforming Anglican ministers were turned into dissenters when their supporters were out of power. Such was the case for ministers in the 1640s and especially the 1650s. No one was immune from the political turmoil of the period, but ministers were particularly susceptible. Edward Pocock's return from Turkey in 1641 was blighted by the fact that his patron, Archbishop Laud, was imprisoned in the Tower of London and was later executed. Pocock's hostility to the nonconformity of the Parliamentary side lost him his position at Oxford. Not until after 1660 did Pocock experience a scholarly rehabilitation. Another orthodox Anglican, Robert Frampton, received his BA from Christ Church, Oxford, in 1641, but he put off obtaining his MA because he disliked the Covenant of 1643, which promoted Presbyterianism. During the Commonwealth, he worked as a chaplain to the Earl of Elgin, and in 1655 he secured the position at Aleppo, removing himself altogether from the religious uncertainty of home.[42]

A final cycle of clerical migrations commenced again in the first years of the 1660s, when the restoration of Charles II to the throne resulted in the displacement of hundreds of nonconformists from their pulpits.[43] Edmund Calamy's hagiographic compilation, *The Nonconformist's Memorial*, traced these migrations, although that was not the author's purpose. He studied the careers of ministers who were fired in 1662 in the wake of the Act of Uniformity. His biographies reveal that many of these men were migratory before their eviction from their positions with the Restoration: the 1630s had been an equally difficult decade for them. Of the men he profiled (who were only Presbyterians, not the Independents, or Congregationalists, whom he hated) thirty-five left England at different points in their careers for European destinations, including especially English congregations in the Netherlands but also churches in Ireland. Forty-five left England for colonies or trading posts, mostly New England but also occasional journeys to Turkey, India, and the Caribbean. One served as a ship's chaplain. The clergy in general were migratory, while dissenters (in any period) were particularly prone to migration.

In this political climate, some overseas outposts promised relative sanctuary, although with the exception of the Levant chaplaincies they all technically fell under the jurisdiction of the Bishop of London.[44] Ministers were not free agents, and of course no one could travel freely in this period. Their ordination bound them to the dictates of the Church of England. The church (represented by the Archbishop of Canterbury) occasionally intervened in the selection of overseas ministers. Official concerns about the fidelity and orthodoxy of clerics manifested themselves most vividly in the 1630s, a period of enhanced enforcement of ecclesiastical policies under William Laud and a simultaneous time of vigorous colonial settlement in North America. The first challenge for dissenting ministers was to secure permission to depart England, and because so few were able to do so, they had to sneak aboard ships to effect their migration.[45]

Ministers referred frankly to the political circumstances that made so many of them available for overseas enterprises. John Oxenbridge was an experienced colonial preacher, himself a product of the first wave of dissenting migration. After his strict puritan habits got him fired from a position at Oxford, Oxenbridge left England for Bermuda in 1635. In 1641 he returned to England to lobby Parliament on behalf of the colony and was waylaid there by the possibilities of new ecclesiastical organization with the war that commenced the following year. After Charles II returned to the throne in 1660, Oxenbridge looked anew at colonial opportunities. He was an advocate of English settlement efforts in Surinam, a region of intermittent English activity and the site of renewed interest in 1652. Oxenbridge joined the colony in 1662 and later wrote a pamphlet promoting the centrality of religion in that enterprise. He proposed eight categories of likely candidates for migration from England, including "reall preachers as are taken off their work." Oxenbridge was clearly thinking of those many now dissenting—and, consequently, unemployed—ministers who had been displaced from their pulpits. Such ministers, Oxenbridge insisted, would fare better converting the people of America (or Columba, as he styled it) than laboring at home.[46]

The politics of religion focused employers' attention on a candidate's stance on several contested issues, from the sacraments (which ones, and how to perform them) to the very structure of a church. Men who invested in overseas companies and sought to instill religious sensibilities of which they approved in trading posts and colonies overseas were careful to hire men of sympathetic religious opinions. The puritan companies—that is, those overseas companies dominated by puritans—looked for puritan ministers for the colonies of Bermuda, New England, and Providence Island, although in smaller colonies such as Providence where the settlers themselves were not all of puritan sensibilities investors had to temper the zeal of island ministers lest they antagonize valued inhabitants. Those alert to the subtleties of divisions within reformed Protestantism hoped the choice of colonial ministers would be made with care. Roger Wood, the governor of Bermuda, wrote to a friend in England in 1634 for ministers and asked specifically for Englishmen, "for I like not to have a scottish presbiterie amongst us."[47]

One way to ensure like-minded clerics was through patronage networks. Extant records reveal the word of mouth that preceded and accompanied appointments, whether recommendations from professors at Oxford or Cambridge, other clerics, highly placed religious figures, or company men. Elias Harvey (related to the Levant Company ambassador, Sir Daniel Harvey) put the matter succinctly when he wrote John Covel in March of 1670 telling him "this afternoon I have gott you chosen to goe chapline for Constantinople," with only a sermon to be preached on a text of Covel's choosing to secure the position.[48]

The correlation between university education and jobs in specific locations hints at the informal connections that led to employment. Most of the chaplains at Istanbul and Smyrna had attended Cambridge; most of the chaplains at Aleppo in the same period were Oxford men.[49] Similar patterns prevailed in some colonial settings. New England, for example, attracted many men with Cambridge educations. Seventy-one percent of the ministers who reached the region in the 1620s and 1630s had studied at Cambridge, and only twenty-three percent at Oxford.[50]

These patterns were not mere coincidence. Ministers recommended colleagues and classmates for positions. Thomas Curtis, for example, with a degree from Cambridge, was first recommended by a minister at London, Mr. [Richard] Holdsworth, also a Cambridge man and later master of Emmanuel College. When Curtis left his position in Smyrna without warning, he recommended as his successor Jeremiah Burroughs of Emmanuel.[51] An old boys' network thrived among men of the cloth. A second factor explains the preponderance of any single institution. Universities, and particularly individual colleges, reflected doctrinal inclinations. Some colleges were associated with puritanism, particularly Trinity College Dublin and Emmanuel in Cambridge.

Political exigencies drove many clerics out of England, but equally enticing, and balancing the pain of exile, was the attraction of opportunities overseas; when Oxenbridge looked for a new position outside of England, he surely had options other than a place as deadly and remote as Surinam. Different types of men seem to have been attracted to different posts. The minister's library at Smyrna—full of its scholarly works and translations, weighty tomes so valuable they were secured with chains—suggests the intellectual interest that attracted John Luke to his position there. In this cerebral penchant Luke was not alone. Although any such characterization is crude at best, the Levant Company attracted the most intellectually inclined of the company chaplains.

Several of the men who served as Levant Company chaplains went on to have distinguished careers as scholars who specialized in Semitic languages or sacred texts. Of the thirty-four ministers appointed before 1670, seven taught at Oxford or Cambridge or engaged in major works of translation or scholarship (excluding travel accounts or published sermons, which ministers commonly produced). John Luke, who was in Smyrna from 1664 to 1669 and again from 1674 to 1683, became a professor of Arabic at Cambridge. Henry Denton (in Istanbul in 1664) published a translation in 1678 of a description of Mt. Athos.[52] Thomas Smith (in Istanbul in 1668) was one of the great scholars of the Company, author of some sixteen different works. Robert Huntington (at Aleppo from 1670 to 1681) collected oriental manuscripts.

Among these scholar-chaplains, Edward Pocock was one of the most distinguished, and with his early sojourn in Turkey he established the pattern of Levant Company intellectuals. Pocock served at Aleppo in the 1630s, and he subsequently held the first position as lecturer in Arabic at Oxford. Pocock started studying Semitic languages while he was a student at Oxford, and after he earned his MA in March of 1626, he continued his linguistic and religious studies in London with a distinguished Arabic scholar, William Bedwell. The culmination of his interest in Semitic languages came with his translation of a Syriac New Testament, complete with commentary. Pocock was appointed by the Levant Company to the chaplain's position in Aleppo in 1629, and before he went, was ordained as a minister.

Pocock was a reluctant voyager. He wrote his friend Thomas Greaves complaining about his residence among "the barbarous people of this country."[53]

Yet his sojourn in Aleppo enabled him to continue the language studies he loved. He studied Hebrew, until he concluded that he could not learn the language fruitfully there. He worked on Syriac; and he especially studied Arabic, hiring a doctor or sheikh to teach him and attended by a servant with whom he conversed. Pocock drew on his surroundings to improve old translations of scriptures. His time in the Ottoman Empire introduced him to the Turkish jackal, which persuaded him that the Syriac word should be translated as jackal, and not as dragon (thus correcting his own translation). He had similar insight into the description of threshing corn in Turkey, which was a far more onerous undertaking than was the case in England. During his time in Aleppo he worked hard on translating texts, particularly one large collection of 6,000 proverbs, which he rendered in Latin. He purchased books and manuscripts and motivated friends to do the same for him, and when he could not purchase the books he coveted, he copied them on the spot. Pocock was also commissioned by his patron, Archbishop Laud, to find items for him, including ancient coins and manuscripts that would be appropriate for a university library.

After three years, Pocock returned to England, where he was soon presented with another opportunity to travel. John Greaves, the mathematician, had returned from Italy with commissions for more travel (he was collecting for the Earl of Arundel) and wanted Pocock to go with him. For all his profession to be a reluctant traveler, Pocock agreed. He returned to the Ottoman Empire, but this time he settled with the English merchants at Istanbul and renewed his language studies. He obtained a job in Istanbul as a chaplain for the ambassador Peter Wyche, whose chaplain had recently returned to England. In Istanbul, Pocock studied Hebrew with greater success than he had at Aleppo. He befriended some Greek Orthodox Christians, including the patriarch, Cyril Lucar, who was a favorite among the English (Peter Wyche named his son after him), in addition to other Greeks with valuable libraries, and a Syrian Christian, Abdel Messiah. He was so immersed in his studies in Istanbul that his friends had to urge him to come home, reminding him to launch his career while his patron was still able to assist him. When he returned home, Pocock resumed his lectures in Arabic at Oxford.[54]

Nothing similar to this aggressive intellectual engagement appears among the chaplains of the East India Company, the other major trade company with a regular commitment to staffing chaplaincies at factories abroad. These Asian-bound ministers all had formal university educations, but they did not pursue the same intellectual endeavors as their counterparts in Turkey and Syria. Of course, their lifespans tended to be shorter and perhaps their ambitions were curtailed by death. Nine out of forty-five (twenty percent) chaplains who held East India Company posts before 1666 died on the voyage out and back or in India. Given the absence of complete information for many of these men, it is likely that the mortality rate was considerably higher, and some of the forty-five might never have sailed to India at all. Of these forty-five, a few had multiple visits, including Arthur Hatch, who signed up for three voyages between 1618 and 1633.[55] Not one of these men pursued an academic career, but instead the survivors tended to settle down as parish ministers. The East India Company chaplain Edward Terry wrote a long book about his ministry there in the 1610s, and is the closest this cohort comes to an intellectual bent. The Levant Company seems to have been uniquely attractive in the seventeenth century to those with scholarly inclinations, especially men with linguistic facility and an interest in the early church.

The colonial ministers, particularly those who were puritans, occupied a middle range between the intellectual, polyglot, publishing powerhouses of the Levant Company and the adventurers of the East India Company. While their counterparts in Aleppo, Smyrna, and Istanbul occupied themselves in language and religious study, and in the location, analysis, and translation of manuscripts, the colonial clergy focused their energies in two main areas. Foremost was their effort to decide the shape of colonial churches. Second was their evangelical efforts targeting indigenous Americans. The first enterprise particularly occupied ministers in puritan colonies who believed that their colonial residence gave them an opportunity to rebuild their religious world. If the Levant scholars generated erudite commentaries from the authentic site of the primitive church, these colonial ministers drew on the same original texts as they sought to *restore* the true church thousands of miles away. Their evangelical enterprises, especially in the Chesapeake around 1620, or in New England in the 1650s, focused their attention on learning indigenous beliefs and languages. In this respect, they emulated the translation efforts of Levant chaplains but in reverse, rendering as John Eliot did the English Bible into Algonquin in 1663.[56] They also published books and pamphlets to chart their evangelical progress.

From the vantage of Europe, where conversion of foreign people was an abstraction and understanding of the legitimacy and depth of indigenous religious practices incomplete, the Americas offered fertile soil for those with missionary interests. Patrick Copland was an advocate of evangelization, and his enthusiasm derived from being given an East Indian boy during one of his East India Company voyages. By communicating through signs, Copland taught the child to speak, read, and write (in both the Roman and secretarial hand) English in less than a year, and within three years had educated the boy in Christian doctrine so that he was publicly baptized before the East India Company.[57] After his baptism, he learned Latin. Copland drew on stories of comparable success in Virginia, singling out Opechancanough's interest in Christianity to promote evangelization there.[58] But Copland's individual labors reveal how protracted the process of communication and education could be: first the acquisition and mastery of language, and then a lengthy period of religious instruction. At Copland's rate of three years per convert, the conversion of the 15,000 people of Virginia alone would take 4.5 centuries if 100 ministers worked full-time. Moreover, Copland's first colonial home was in Bermuda, which contained no indigenous people who might be targets of his enthusiasm. John Oxbenbridge (a former resident of Bermuda) explicitly rebuked ministers who settled in places without Indian inhabitants in his promotional work for Surinam.[59]

At the same time that Copland was immersed in educating his captive Indian boy, Alexander Whitaker worked on the other side of the world to convert another Indian, the Powhatan Pocahontas. Whitaker was drawn to Virginia in its first years because of his evangelical energies. He conceptualized the people and bounty of Virginia in terms of his missionary impulse. The English were sent to Virginia to seek out the "riches and bewty of Nature." In their search, they had the opportunity of sharing with the Indians their own "most excellent merchandize," the Gospel.[60] Whitaker's model of the marketplace suggested that religion was an optional trade good: in Virginia, Opechancanough, who feigned interest in Christianity in order to mislead the English before he launched his attack in 1622, revealed that it was also a way to dupe the English into false illusions of indigenous acquiescence to English rules and ways. If Christianity suggested to the English a means of drawing Indians into a cooperative stance with colonization, to Indians it often offered other possibilities.[61]

Because trade privileges banned missionary activity, any minister with a real commitment to evangelization went to colonial settlements. There were some exceptions. While a Christian could not proselytize among Muslims in the Ottoman Empire, Jews apparently were fair game. Mr. May, the preacher at the Aleppo factory, seized the opportunity afforded him there in 1600. He "was permitted to dispute in the chefest sinagog" in Istanbul. The merchant John Sanderson thought little of "that troblesom May" and his efforts, for he "was derided and confuted (as they say) by a Jewe that had ben a Christian; and that his disputation (as som Jewes say) rather confermed the[n] revoked them from ther Jueismie."[62]

By their individual inclinations and abilities, ministers represented different points in a spectrum of clerical erudition and scholarship, but all of the overseas clergy shared a general curiosity about the world outside England, whether the wealth of religious practices it contained or its natural wonders. Richard Madox, appointed along with a second minister, John Walker, for a fleet embarked in a search for the northwest passage in 1582, described the plants, birds, fish, people, and animals he saw, recorded vocabulary lists for Java and Labrador, and even illustrated his diary with some remarkable and historically important images, including a sketch of a woman in Sierra Leone with carefully marked tattoos.[63]

Overseas ministries also satisfied cerebral goals. Samuel Johnson served as a chaplain to the English ambassador at Denmark, and savored the access he found there to great theologians and their libraries.[64] The intellectual enthusiasm that defined some of these men appears in their passion for books and manuscripts. The clergy launched their journeys with the acquisition of books to sustain them in their homes far from libraries. But they added to those collections quickly. In Japan Copland acquired a cherished Japanese language catechism, so dear to him that he mentioned it in a letter to John Winthrop twenty years later.[65] A minister's collections could also be emphatically pragmatic, offering important reminders that ministers were deeply embroiled in the economic ambitions of their employers and companions. John Sanford, who was a chaplain at the English embassy in Spain in 1611, sent a Spanish grammar before he left to Sir Thomas Edmondes, "wch I have lately printed for our company that ar bound for spaine." That is, he not only procured (or perhaps even compiled) the grammar; he arranged for its printing.[66] Their level of education and their knowledge of languages put ministers in a strong position to lend such linguistic aid to facilitate commercial relations. Some ministers tended to souls and pocketbooks with almost equal energy.

Collecting materials and visiting libraries necessitated and invited intimate contact with men of different faiths. In Istanbul, John Covel went to the library maintained there by the patriarch of Jerusalem, where he was disappointed not to find ancient manuscripts as he had expected.[67] As ministers collected manuscripts, they also collected friends and information. For many clerics, these manuscript hunts were linked to genuine interest about other faiths. Thomas Smith, who was in Istanbul in the 1660s, described this trait as "an inbred curiosity."[68] Covel shared this intellectual posture. "It was my design when I first left England," Covel explained to a colleague, "to see and understand and take an account with mine own eyes (and not to be beholden to ye fallible relations of others) of what was acted and believed by all people abroad where I went in my travailes." And he relayed some of those places he saw—mosques during prayer; all sorts of devotions; prayers in Arabic and Greek; synagogues. He went to services of Greeks ("a hundred times," he reported later), Armenians, Georgians, and Russians.[69] Covel attended a Greek service on the Feast of the Assumption in Turkey, and described the mass in detail, including the size of the Host and how it was broken. He witnessed the consecration of the new patriarch in November.[70] Not only did he visit services, but he also spoke with religious leaders and he read their books. He interrogated strangers. He marveled at the array of "superstitions" he encountered among Muslims, Greeks, Jews, and Armenians.[71] He tried to learn what he could of their customs and included in his journal the fruits of his knowledge, such as one discussion about the different beliefs about the dead held by Armenians and Greeks.[72] When the Ragusan ambassador came to visit, Covel befriended him, too, and learned from him of a Jewish woman who was believed to be a witch. The ambassador summoned her so that Covel could interview her.[73] There was no limit to his enthusiasms.

Covel's travels and his interrogation of the priests and laity he met led him to some remarkable conclusions. He believed that in "outward practice and profession" all religions were the same, with saints and learned leaders whom people followed. "They all have strange fancyes and human conceits of ye stations in eternity. they all have factions and furiously persecute, censure, damn one ye other . . . they all stricktly persist in their own way." He admitted that he preferred the "inner practice" of his own variant of worship, but believed that Christianity was much degraded from Christ's vision.[74]

Covel's experiences suggest that some ministers might acquire an ecumenical vision in their travels, although in his own case he seemed deeply predisposed to one. Edward Terry took a similarly open-minded approach to his study of the religions of India during his stay between 1616 and 1619. He especially admired the dedication of the Muslim imams he saw there and the piety of the people, and he applauded the freedom of religion that all enjoyed. In a time-honored tradition of travelers, Terry employed these attributes of Indian society to critique the negligence of English Christians, particularly their lack of piety and the poor treatment of underpaid ministers.[75] But travel by no means encouraged or persuaded a cleric to embrace alien religions: to do so would have been to subvert their own careers and identities. Edward Pocock, for example, dedicated himself to demonstrating the errors of Islam.[76]

The English understood travel to be a perilous enterprise, shaking a man's fidelity to his faith and his nation. Ministers were supposed to be a bulwark of Protestant faith—however bitterly contested—and thus of English nationality. So the clergy ideally helped wandering Englishmen resist the attractions of other customs. Yet their distraction from their obligations to the English alone and their voracious interest in the worlds they encountered made them vulnerable to criticism. After his stint in Istanbul, John Covel went to Rome to serve the English community there. He was as passionate about sightseeing in Italy as he had been everywhere else he traveled. Covel's ecumenism is the clerical version of the merchant's cosmopolitanism, and it got Covel in trouble. In Rome, Covel heard rumors being spread by Jesuits that he had converted to Catholicism. Covel deployed his interests in Catholic sites to defend himself. At the location of a miracle in Naples, for example, he was banned entry because he refused to say he was Catholic. Thus how could he have converted? The evidence against him, he speculated, was his attendance at several functions of the Pope and cardinals in Rome, events that were also attended by other English gentleman. He believed, as a minister, that it was particularly urgent that he defend himself against such charges. The accusations made him irate and indignant. They suggested that a man should not read and view the religious practices of others, lest he invite such criticism. Covel insisted that he was no more Catholic than he was Greek or Jewish or Muslim or Armenian.[77] In his defense Covel articulated a cosmopolitan posture: he could not be any one thing without being equally another. And yet he knew with certainty that he was Protestant—so he signed his letter quite clearly, as "a true son of ye protestant church." The indomitable Covel's career was not over after this misfortune in Italy: he was a chaplain to the English community at the Hague in 1681.[78]

For all the excitement they promised, these posts overseas were also quite clearly jobs, sources of income and, for many, anticipated avenues for advancement. In answering a patron's call, ministers immersed themselves in webs (and sometimes snares) of obligation. John Sanford, the chaplain to the English ambassador in Madrid, was reluctant to leave his post at Brussels for his new job in Spain. Once there, he wrote chatty and gossipy letters that revealed his fascination with the affairs (political and amorous) of people at court. But he had not been eager to move to Spain. "My opinion of Spaine," he wrote in 1611 as he prepared for his departure, "as also mine affection towards it, is the same that ever it hath bin." He knew that Catholics who came from there spoke highly of the country, but Sanford was skeptical, and he dreaded his voyage. He referred obliquely to the circumstances ("there was cause") of his departure from a job he preferred, but "god out of his love towards me, hath allwaies crossed me in that wch I most desired, & taken me from that wherein I most delighted."[79] Sanford's letters communicate his sense of obligation to his patron. For all the excitement of a remote posting, for all of the challenges that chaplains might be eager to meet, a chaplaincy was first and foremost a source of financial support. The ministry was, at its best, a vocation, a calling by God, and the men who selected themselves for it were dedicated to the spiritual and pastoral obligations of their position. For others, it was a way to get access to offices, the best occupation in which to employ other skills and interests. But whatever brought them to their employment, all ministers faced hard work in their new jobs.

The education of the clergy offered them a mixed preparation for the day to day challenges and obligations of ministering in these unusual parishes around the world. Their university training was rigorous and classical. Immersed in the languages and texts of the scriptures, they were uniquely well-informed about the history of the places they saw, particularly in regions such as the Mediterranean. With adequate Latin and Greek, their linguistic training meant that they could communicate with other educated Europeans and particularly with religious figures of other Christian traditions. While merchants employed the languages of trade, ministers used the languages of the ancient world. On his journey to Istanbul in 1670, John Covel paused at Malaga, where he saw the sights in the company of Robert Huntington, who was making his own way to the chaplain's post at Aleppo, and some men, presumably priests, described as "the good Fathers." The religious men communicated in Latin.[80] But languages change over time, as Charles Robson discovered. Bound for his new position as chaplain at the Aleppo factory in the 1620s, Robson passed through the Greek islands and visited a church at Mykonos. He read from the Bible, a feat that greatly amazed an old man who was there. The two men attempted to communicate, Robson in his "learned" Greek and the man in his modern variant ("degenerate," to Robson's ears), but the gulf between the two languages was so vast that Robson could not be understood.[81]

But for all the utility of their linguistic educations, Oxford and Cambridge did not offer practical training in how to minister to the individuals who made up a parish. Services and sermons on Sundays; morning and evening prayer; comfort to the sick; spiritual guidance to the young; communion, baptism, marriage, burial: these were the rituals that shaped a minister's life. The new job began on the ocean journey, for clergy were expected to deliver sermons, perform appropriate services (shipboard deaths were frequent), and to lead daily prayers. Life on board ship reminded clerics that they might live at sea in a well-ordered community, but it was one governed by the rigors of travel and structured by the demands and preferences of a sea captain. The minister himself was under the authority of the captain. His desires could be only requests, his urging that of a supplicant, if circumstances were not to his liking.

Ministers helped to instill or inspire good conduct aboard ship, or so captains hoped. But mariners had their own culture, and a minister could not expect to alter customary practices with any dispatch or permanence. If, for example, Patrick Copland objected when Captain Thomas Best gave his man Nathaniel Fenn to the ambassador of Siam in 1613 rather than put him to death, thus placing him permanently outside a Christian world, there is no evidence in Best's journal.[82] It was an important lesson for ministers to learn on their way to trading posts, where merchants enjoyed sexual and social latitude. The journey itself was crucial in preparing ministers for some of the different pastoral and doctrinal challenges awaiting them, taking them through a transition from orthodoxy (however contested) in the Church of England to the complex and often morally ambiguous worlds of trade factories and colonies.

Preaching and pastoring on board ship occupied as much time as similar responsibilities on land. John Walker reported in 1582 his shipboard round of daily morning and evening prayers, "besyde other several prayers at other tymes of the daye," preaching on Sundays, and reading from Scripture after dinner. The mariners on board, he remarked, had never experienced such piety, and their lives were, in his estimation, "marvelouslye delyghted."[83] When chaplains led services on board ships, they did so in challenging circumstances. The architecture of the sacred space on land reinforced the minister's elevated position to his congregants and privileged his words and actions. From the pulpit he could survey his domain, with the hierarchies of the church reflected in his physical displacement from the congregation. On board ship the minister spoke to a crowd of easily distracted men. He had to project his voice, speaking over creaking timbers and the roar of the wind. If most sea travelers dreaded a calm that stranded a ship, a minister must have had mixed feelings when the calm fell on a Sunday.

Distractions often presented themselves during worship. On many Sundays during his two East India Company stints, Copland delivered two sermons a day, and never in easy circumstances. During his first voyage, his ship had endured bad weather as it rounded the cape in May and June of 1612, "extreme fowle wether," one experienced mariner reported. The men were sick with scurvy, eager for fresh supplies. The fleet rested at Saldanha Bay for three weeks for the men to recover. Copland delivered there a sermon that was attended by the inhabitants of the area, who behaved "peaceably" during the service although he thought they were "of little or no religion."[84] While the fleet recovered, the minister prepared to offer communion, so he must have been occupied before the service organizing the bread and wine, and after several weeks at sea the bread was likely in miserable condition. Moreover, communion was always preceded by a lengthy period of examination and introspection, as communicants and the minister determined who was worthy of the sacrament. For Copland, these intimate exchanges must have been opportunities to get to know the mariners and merchants in a new light. The men were refreshed, thanks to "fresh salletts, fresh aire, fresh watter" on shore. They had perhaps begun to steel themselves for the long voyage that still remained. Maybe some hoped to find some guidance, some wisdom, in the minister's words, something to give meaning to the great discomfort and danger of the voyage thus far. But if a gathering of mariners promised souls likely to be in great need of a cleric's intervention, the distractions of this particular day introduced too much competition. During the sermon, the minister faced unusual rivalry in the form of a whale that was fighting with a swordfish and a thresher. "The whale," reported the captain, "did so roare that he did much intteruptt the preacher in his sermon, that most of his audience did more regard the whalle and the fishes then they did his instructions."[85] On other occasions Copland had to contend with men who were drunk during the sermon and forbear those who skipped services to swim to shore and drink with prostitutes.[86]

Ministers were certainly not alone in finding their long sea journeys to be a trial, but they extracted providential meaning from these ordeals and educated their companions on God's will in the tempest, whether man-made or natural. Covel almost experienced a battle at sea on his way to Istanbul. As the crew prepared the ship, the captain told Covel that he could go below with the surgeon and wait in safety, but Covel announced that he could pray as well from the deck as from the hold. The captain thanked Covel for this encouragement to the men, and Covel stayed on board, with the other passengers gathered around him. The alarm proved false, but Covel's actions impressed the men.[87] But a minister had to be careful to strike the right tone. Copland delivered a sermon in the Indies before the English fought the Dutch. He had to defend himself before the East India Company on his return home in 1621 against reports that his sermon "disanimat[ed]" the mariners rather than sparking their courage. Copland insisted that the charges were unjust, and was ready to defend himself with the journal he had maintained.[88] He had, apparently, reproved the commanders—a fair criticism, according to one witness, who found the leaders more eager to feast than to fight.[89]

Every passenger was grateful to reach land when a ship finally anchored, but the ministers faced special challenges as the designated bulwark of their faith in a land dominated by another. Perhaps the Levant Company minister Charles Robson described the feeling best. He set out for Aleppo from London in 1625 or 1626, at the age of twenty-seven or twenty-eight. When he reached Aleppo, he was so diverted by "the novelty of the place," that, as he later explained, it "made mee forget almost my selfe."[90] And, in his distracted state, he missed the departure of the first ship, failing to meet the obligation of all travelers to write home to their anxious friends reporting their safe arrival.

Ministers went overseas to minister to English flocks, to guard against their conversion to other faiths, to police their behavior, to comfort them far from home, to bolster a trade company's authority, to offer sacraments, and to provide a visible symbol of English institutional life in distant outposts. In trade factories outside western Europe, merchants often traveled outside of the English residence in local garb, blending in as much as possible. Trade consuls and ambassadors labored under more constraints, because of a need for them to maintain appearances commensurate with the status they sought. Edward Terry explained in his account of his time in India that Sir Thomas Roe and his "company," presumably that small coterie of servants and companions who traveled with him, wore English-style garb but employed lighter fabrics to help contend with the great heat of the climate. Terry, in contrast, must have stood out considerably in the long black cassock he wore whenever he went out. It is no surprise that everyone who saw him and the other English gawked at these strangely dressed creatures.[91] But for the English in India, Terry's customary garb, however exotic in its new setting, provided visible evidence of an English presence (see figure 7.1).

Ministers helped fragile communities define and, through the sacraments of marriage and baptism, reproduce and sustain themselves. Unlike parish priests in England or in the New England colonies, clergy in trade factories and most new colonies ministered to an odd demographic flock composed primarily of men. Some of the regular routines of parish life—baptisms and marriages—were largely replaced by the frequent performance of funeral rites amid adverse disease environments. The sacrament that most occupied chaplains on their sea voyages was burial. A minister would have to adapt the burial service from the Book of Common Prayer, which in this period contained no variation for a burial at sea.[92] On land, as epidemics of typhoid or dysentery or bouts of malaria or yellow fever spread among the men around them, the ministers shared the fear that gripped all who watched the daily ritual of burial. The Book of Common Prayer offered a guide for many of these circumstances for even the most panicked cleric: the order for the visitation of the sick ushered a minister through the rituals and prayers that would be appropriate, with abridgements for those too sick to hear the entire text. Even in the most perilous setting, a minister's duties continued with the regular rhythm of prayer and worship and the episodic demands of the sacraments. After the *Sea Venture* wrecked on Bermuda in 1609, Richard Buck performed the sacraments of marriage and communion (twice). Two children, both named after their island home, were christened. Five unfortunate souls were buried.[93] Buck's career performing sacraments in an altered world was doubtless epitomized by the marriage he consecrated a few years later in Virginia between John Rolfe and Pocahontas.

If overseas ministers spent a disproportionate amount of time praying over the sick and burying the dead, some sacraments and rituals were not as commonly performed, especially for those ministering in trading posts. The thanksgiving for women after childbirth, for example, would be infrequently heard in a trading post and even in many young colonies with their predominantly male populations. Without a bishop present, confirmation lapsed into disuse, and likewise the words of baptism, which provided the valuable renewal of Christian commitment for all witnesses of the sacrament. In those rare instances when it was performed, baptism might test a minister's ingenuity or require him to overlook the circumstances of a child's birth. In Hirado, Arthur Hatch, the chaplain for the East India Company ship the *Palsgrove*, baptized the illegitimate son of Henry Smith, the

Figure 7.1. Depicting a compass and a globe, the frontispiece of the minister Edward Terry's account of his time in India, written some forty years after his time there, shows the author's continued definition of himself as a traveler. *Voyage to East India* (London, 1655). This item is reproduced by permission of The Henry E. Huntington Library, San Marino, California.

purser of the *Royal James*, and a Japanese woman.[94] Hatch was obviously undeterred by this unusual challenge, and signed on for two more East India Company voyages. Overseas baptisms might also involve adult converts. In Tangier, the minister performed a christening for a man described simply as "an Indian."[95] Ministers likely found themselves counseling men inclined to convert either from or to Christianity. One adamant convert to Islam, an English soldier at Tangier, was executed for desertion in 1671. Before his execution, as was customary, the minister tried to speak to him to prepare him and his soul for the ordeal ahead, but the soldier refused to talk to him either before or at the execution.[96]

Sermons were the mainstay of a chaplain's regular duties and occasionally revealed a minister's personal commitment to the success of commercial and colonial undertakings, at every stage, from the launch of an expedition to a castaway fleet's survival. Richard Madox delivered a sermon to the 1582 northwest passage fleet specially designed on the spot. Before the fleet sailed, the commander invited people from shore to join the whole fleet on board the galleon for a farewell dinner. Edward Fenton asked Madox to preach, "and to handle such matter as [he] thought meetest for ye tyme." Madox rose admirably to the occasion. From Psalms 24.1 (the earth is the Lord's, and the fullness thereof; the world, and they that dwell therein), Madox preached on three questions, all marvelously self-serving: "first shewying how lawful a thing was travel and merchandyce, and yt wee had best ryght to ye indyes"; second, he proved how the English might in good conscience trade with "infidels" despite accusations that they transported necessities to them; and finally he demonstrated that a man's life cannot be curtailed.[97] Madox "exhorted every man of religion and manhood," demanding not only their zeal but their masculinity in pursuit of these remote riches. God's plan apparently included a northwest passage for the English and the direct access to Asian goods such a route promised, and Madox's sermon indicated his own fervent commitment to the venture.

Sermons in adverse settings might be fruitfully shaped to lift the spirits of a demoralized congregation. Richard Buck, shipwrecked on Bermuda, dutifully delivered two sermons each Sunday, and led public prayer each morning and evening at the ringing of a bell. As for his sermons, reported William Strachey, "the contents (for the most part)…were especially of thankfulness and unity, etc.," perhaps welcome messages for this island-trapped population wracked by division and mutiny.[98] In 1616, William Ford preached the funeral sermon for Lady Anne Glover, the wife of the Levant Company ambassador Thomas Glover. She died in Istanbul, like Sarah, a stranger in a foreign country, after five years there with her husband, and Ford, only newly arrived, led the service. Little of the lengthy sermon was about Glover herself. Instead, Ford focused on how important it was for Christians to learn how to die. But he realized the particularity of his audience. Printed marginalia referred to the varied assemblage present for the service. "Most Nations under the Sunne" were in attendance, including, as he categorized the mourners, English, French, Dutch, German, Italian, Hungarian, Transylvanian, Russian, Greek, Armenian, Bedouin, Turk, Jew, "Popish," "Molda," and "Wallachian" (Romanian). In consideration of his audience of merchants and diplomats, Ford illustrated his sermon with the story of a merchant "(like your selves)" and his conversation with a hermit. To demonstrate how one should not mourn the dead, he referred his Istanbul audience to the familiar example of the Greeks and their conduct at funerals, condemning their excessive emotion, which they with their "owne eies witnes...at everie solemne funerall." To help the mourners understand how they must submit as slaves to God's will, he conjured the image of "the greatest Basha," who yielded to the orders of his king. As Abraham was sent to wander the earth, so were these merchants allowed to enjoy the pleasures of the world, but all must be ready to be called home by God.[99] Even Ford, newly arrived in Istanbul, knew how to draw on his new environment—its customs, its ruler, its cosmopolitan, polyglot, multireligious population—to give his sermon resonance for mourners.

These diverse sermons reveal a minister's perception of his own association with the success of a venture and with its personnel. If a minister and worshippers occupied the same position on a doctrinal spectrum, then both might find the rituals of worship highly satisfying and each service might reaffirm a community's cohesion. Given the fragility of trade factories and new colonies, both of which were undertakings characterized by high mortality and by the likelihood of failure, church services provided an opportunity for public affirmation of an enterprise's survival. William Strachey described the ritual of church services in Virginia in the deadly and precarious first years of the colony's settlement. Two sermons were preached on Sunday, and another sermon on Thursdays, in addition to regular morning and evening prayer. Sunday services gave the small community the opportunity to display the hierarchy of the settlement. "Every Sunday," reported Strachey, "when the lord governor and captain general goeth to church, he is accompanied with all the councilors, captains, other officers, and all the gentlemen, and with a guard of halberdiers in His Lordship's livery, fair red cloaks, to the number of fifty, both on each side and behind him." Once inside the church the display continued. The governor had a special seat in the choir. It was covered in green velvet, and he kneeled on a velvet cushion placed on a table in front of him, so that his knees would have a soft landing as he made his obeisance before God. He was framed in his seat by the councilors and officers, who sat on either side of him, "each in their place," and at the end of services when the governor returned home, the procession reversed itself, and he was "waited on to his house in the same manner." The lush fabric, the elaborate hierarchy, the procession, the place of the governor in the church's choir, all rendered in a visible form the hierarchies of colonial life, reinforcing the importance of authority in a place thousands of miles from England, and all carefully presided over by the minister who guided the congregation through worship. To appreciate fully the importance this ritual had for the inhabitants of Virginia, consider John Smith's description of worship just two or three years earlier: "our walls were rales of wood, our seats unhewed trees...our Pulpit a bar of wood nailed to two neighbouring trees." Amid the unrelenting trials of survival, the colony's residents labored to construct a church that replicated the rituals and hierarchies and architecture of home.[100]

In New England, Bermuda, or Providence, or anywhere a gathered church might organize itself, a different kind of church order played a similar cultural role. The gathered church, a congregation composed of men and women who had affirmed their own right to membership without relying on a hierarchy of church authorities or the automatic entrance provided by baptism, was one of puritanism's greatest innovations. Participation in Sabbath worship (required by law in some jurisdictions) or attendance at the weekly lecture reminded church members and the rest of the community of the special mission of their own colonial experiments. They followed a different liturgy; their ministers abandoned the garb of English pastors; and they adhered to a more rigid order. All of these acts signaled that these were different communities, defined in opposition to the Church of England in its current form.

Accompanying ministers' pastoral and symbolic duties were a range of other social, political, and diplomatic activities. Nathaniel Butler's arrival as the new governor in Bermuda in 1619 was bolstered by the worship service that was held after Butler's inaugural speech, in which he declared his rule to the populace. The minister, Lewis Hughes, preached a sermon "wherein was briefly touched the necessitye of the magistracye, the submission due unto it, the hopes and expectations of the future in particular, with some other pointes fitt and proper for that day and action."[101]

Because clerics could bolster secular authority in a range of important ways, those ambassadors, consuls, and governors who lived and worked intimately with ministers sought to dictate their selection, as Thomas Roe did when the East India Company hired him as their ambassador to Surat and he demanded his own choice of minister.[102] These ministers served as companions, offering counsel and friendship. Roe's record of his embassy in India rarely mentions his chaplain, John Hall, but when Hall died in 1616, Roe wrote despondently of his "great greife and discomfort" at the loss of "a man of a most gentle and mild Nature." Hall's death prompted a litany of laments from Roe, who named the inconveniences he suffered without his chaplain. His complaints suggested the role Hall had filled in his life in India, since his death left Roe with "noe Comfort, no conversation...no such entertaynment as my qualetye required nor which might have appeased and made other inconveniences tollerable," and no one to perform the sacraments, abandoning Roe to "live the life of an Atheist" until a replacement could be found.[103]

As Roe's comments indicate, ministers provided companionship for merchants, ambassadors, and high ranking colonial officers in overseas outposts, providing not just erudition and religious support as "qualetye required" but also educated and diverting distraction. When ambassadors went to speak to foreign rulers, they often brought their ministers along in the entourage that accompanied them. Like consuls and highly placed company officers, ministers met most of the celebrities who passed through their posts. John Sanford met the infamous traveler Thomas Coryate in Madrid in 1612, while Edward Terry shared a tent with him four years later in India.[104] And like company officers, they were provided with good accommodation. The English in Tangier built a house for their minister, Mr. Turner, "which when finished will bee one of the prettyest in Towne and is capable of greate additions," John Luke observed in 1670.[105]

Company officials who sometimes worried about talking freely to each other trusted clerics. The vice-admiral of the 1582 northwest passage fleet sought out John Walker's counsel while Walker was lying in bed one night. Walker ultimately intervened in the personality conflicts on the fleet "& all concluded frendes."[106] Patrick Copland obviously played a similar role mitigating conflicts on board ship, and described himself as a peacemaker in reference to one quarrel on his East India Company voyage.[107] But such trust was often misplaced. Ministers could be important allies for their employers and patrons in England, and thus at times played the role of a spy. Such was the case with Richard Madox. Madox and his fellow chaplain John Walker deeply mistrusted one of the ship commanders, and exchanged missives secretly in Latin. Madox even maintained a shipboard journal in English, Greek, and Latin, to preserve his privacy from less linguistically skilled snoops. And both Walker and Madox reported on the activities of the ships' officers to their patrons in England.

As privileged members of a ship's company, clergy took part in all sorts of negotiations. When the East India Company fleet reached Surat in January of 1613, Copland went ashore with several of the merchants "to dispatch bussiness."[108] Madox and Walker were deeply involved in strategic decisions about their journey, arguing about routes and debating what to do with captives. But ministers sometimes interjected an inconvenient morality into the deliberations that guided voyages and colonies, particularly in regard to the

rights of people—including Spaniards and American Indians—who lay outside of the English nation. John Walker worried about the morally correct
solution to the problem of Spanish captives, taken in a bark the English had
captured in December of 1582. Walker tried to point out what "chrystyan
charitye" might entail in this situation, arguing that if the captives (which
included two women and a child) were simply abandoned on shore to the
hazards of "indyans or wylde beastes," then the English were as guilty as if
they had killed them. The captives were ultimately set loose in their bark.[109]

Those English who were most agitated about the justice of English claims
to land tended to have religious training: Roger Williams posed the issue in
New England in the 1630s, and John Oxenbridge did the same in Surinam
in the 1660s. Although powerfully motivated by his goals of conversion of
the people of Surinam, John Oxenbridge revealed an unusual sensitivity to
English claims to the place. He observed that the land he eyed was not occupied by the Spanish, so there were no international rivalries to concern the
English, and "not yet filled by the Natives," which led him to conclude that
English occupation there would to no "reall wrong to any."[110] Clerics also
infused a religious justification into more general social criticism. In India,
Edward Terry was troubled by the habit of men being carried around on
the shoulders of others, turning men into packhorses. He found it demeaning for men to behave in such a way, when all would do well to remember
that everyone had a "Master in Heaven, with whom there is no respect of
persons."[111]

When ministers elected to act on their consciences, to correct civil officials for their conduct, the results could be polarizing and tumultuous.
In this contentious age, it was always likely that clerics would further, not
dampen, conflict. They could do so through the simple observance of the
sacraments and liturgy as they believed them to be rightly performed. John
Sanford learned this lesson in Madrid in 1611, where he was the chaplain
to the English ambassador and where he almost sparked a diplomatic incident with his first sermon. English Protestants in Spain were allowed to perform religious ceremonies privately in the ambassador's residence. Upon his
arrival, Sanford alerted the household that there would be a communion at
a future service. News of this plan reached the Cardinal of Toledo, head of
the Inquisition. The Cardinal sent a message to the ambassador asking him
not to allow the communion, concerned both for the scandal of permitting
communion "after calvins fashion" and for the risk that "strangers" (Catholics) might attend the service. The Cardinal also warned the ambassador that
he possessed forbidden books, which were to be burned. The ambassador
defended his books on the grounds that he had them only for his own and
his family's reference and education, and he denied that strangers attended
the English services. The ambassador tenaciously adhered to his right to

worship freely in private, and especially to the right to communion. For Sanford, it was a rapid introduction to the political perils of Protestant worship
in Spain.[112]

Other ministers found themselves in trouble among the English for the
type of Protestant worship they practiced. Hope Sherrard, a minister on the
island of Providence, tried in the 1630s to organize a gathered church there.
He refused to permit some people to take communion, and he excommunicated others. Island residents were trapped: they had no other minister to go
to for the sacraments. They complained to the Providence Company in London, and the Company, loathe to antagonize the cleric because it was so hard
to hire pious personnel, urged Sherrard to employ "Christian moderacon"
in his actions. A new governor, Robert Hunt, who shared his ardent puritan
stance gave Sherrard some much needed support, and he stopped performing the sacraments altogether by the end of the decade. He refused to baptize
children, to the great distress of those island residents who desired the sacrament for their children. In 1639, a new minister reached the island and the
sacraments were finally performed. Yet church affairs continued to trouble
Nathaniel Butler, who had replaced Hunt as governor. Butler lamented the
"uncharitabel and dangerous suggestions out of ye pulpitt," which he had
heard one Sunday, and finally he stopped attending church altogether—a
remarkable public rebuke of the minister. He returned only to find the sermons little more than "malicious Invectives."[113]

This incident was not Butler's first conflict with a colonial minister. On
Bermuda in 1620 the governor had lost his patience with the loquacious
minister Samuel Lang. Even by the period's conventions of lengthy services,
Lang apparently outdid himself. Butler complained that Lang spent too long
in sermons and prayers in his Sunday services, "which," reported the island's
other minister, "doth tire the people, and cause some to change his name,
calling him Mr Long."[114] Butler also resolved fights over the liturgy between
the island's two ministers, a conflict that reminded him of the old proverb,
"'so many men, so many minds,'" an apt characterization of English ministers and the religious disputes they engendered at home and abroad.[115] When
differences between secular and religious leaders moved from personal irri-
tation to doctrinal conflict, the consequences were severe. On Providence,
with an English population outnumbered by slaves, Sherrard's religious
energies challenged and subverted political authority, alienating the governor and other island leaders.[116] It is impossible to overstate the importance
of such religious disputes in this period: a religious conflict such as the Antinomian controversy in New England in 1637 almost brought Massachusetts
to civil war, while governors lost valuable allies and gained dangerous enemies when ministers abandoned them for religious principles that they did
not share.

A company chaplain or colonial minister could prove deeply divisive precisely because of the closed nature of English society overseas. In England worshippers were expected to attend services at their own parish, but evidence from ecclesiastical visitations in the 1630s reveals that people walked to adjacent parishes if they objected to a minister's observance (or nonobservance) of the Book of Common Prayer. Similarly, there was a choice of ministers available within England. An unsatisfactory cleric might be fired and a more palatable minister secured. Far from England, in company towns and small English enclaves, worshippers were dependent on what was available, unable to baptize their children or to take communion if such was the whim of their minister. John Luke, an English official in Tangier, objected to the minister there, Mr. Turner. He complained about a service he attended in December of 1670. Mr. Turner selected the text, "sabbaoth was made for man and not man for the sabbaoth," but offered what Luke regarded as "a most unseasonable discourse against strict sabbatarians." In Luke's eyes, Turner showed little sensitivity to the particular context of his congregation, "this place without doubt being inclined rather to too much liberty then an over sincere strictnesse."[117] Yet Luke was a captive audience. Christmas Day brought "a scholastique sermon but the most insignificant one that I have at any time heard," but it also offered the opportunity to take communion, and since Turner administered it in accordance with Church of England practice, Luke stayed with a small group of communicants to receive the sacrament.[118]

All the irritations and disruptions of a Turner or a Sherrard, however, paled next to the challenges posed to civil authorities by the self-proclaimed ministers of the gospel who inserted themselves in overseas communities during the religious upheavals of the 1650s. The Quakers, fearless in their adherence to the light within and determined to spread the word around the world, appeared in colonies and trade factories alike, and always refused to defer to secular authorities. Officials responded harshly, particularly in puritan colonies: Massachusetts banished, whipped, mutilated, and hanged Quakers. After enduring punishment in Massachusetts in 1655, Mary Fisher took her ministry to the Mediterranean, where she was "moved of the Lord to go and deliver his Word to the Great Turk." Her route took her to Smyrna, where the English consul tried to ship her back to Venice, to no avail. She traveled by land until she encountered the Ottoman army, and she talked to the Sultan himself. He was, Quaker hagiographies reported, touched by her conviction, and by the tenacity of "One as should take so much pains to come to them so far as from England with a Message from the Lord." Offered a guard, Fisher declined, putting her faith in her god instead, and reached Istanbul unscathed, from which city she obtained passage home.[119]

Residing even further outside the national church's parameters of appropriate conduct than Quakers such as Mary Fisher were Catholics. While there were many English priests outside of England—and Protestants believed them to be constantly plotting against the English—they existed apart from and often hostile to English state church structures. Overseas companies did not hire Catholic priests to minister to their employees overseas. The single exception was the colony of Maryland, established by a Catholic proprietor, Cecil Calvert, in 1632. The colony permitted Catholics to worship publicly, although they were still outnumbered by Protestants, and two Jesuit priests accompanied the first fleet to the colony in 1633. Like some of their Protestant counterparts, these priests pursued missionary work; like their Protestant rivals, they fared poorly in North America. If priests were absent from most English settlements overseas, the Catholic laity were not. Like the many Catholics who lived privately in England, Catholics were dispersed around the Atlantic and in trading posts, concentrated in some places, such as Montserrat, and in small numbers elsewhere. Father Andrew White remarked on the English and Irish Catholics he met in Barbados on his way to Maryland in 1634.[120] But unlike Protestants, who could enjoy communal worship even as they bickered and fought over its correct expression, outside of Maryland, Catholics found few opportunities for services and for the sacraments that defined their faith.

Ministers in colonies and factories alike could foment antagonisms and challenge civil structures. But they could also shape affairs in England. Their collections and their linguistic training affected the intellectual life of English universities, but the wandering clergy also affected politics more dramatically than did any other globetrotting constituency. Their impact is most effectively seen through the single example of puritanism and politics in the 1640s and 1650s. In England in the 1630s, puritans enjoyed the unity of victims, and particularly that of victims unable to enact their own ecclesiastical vision once Laud's visitations enforced orthodox Church of England practices, dictating the use of the Book of the Common Prayer, wearing surplices, and the location of the altar and communion railing. But once they ventured overseas, puritans, both laity and clergy, often found themselves in stark and unexpected disagreement on core principles of church organization and practice, and their old unity, born of oppression, unexpectedly and dramatically dissipated.

In the 1630s and 1640s, colonies functioned as religious laboratories. Ministers were able to experiment with a range of forms, many profoundly rigid and uncompromising. Each New England town contained a gathered church, which was free to devise its own interpretation of scripture, and on Providence and Bermuda ministers followed the New England example and sought to implement their own gathered churches. The opinions ranged considerably. Should women be veiled in church? The people of Salem,

Massachusetts, thought so, while other congregations did not. Which of the three methods for baptism was suitable, sprinkling, pouring, or immersion? The people of Scituate in the Plymouth Colony were unable to agree and split their church in two in 1643.[121] How should a church be gathered? In fact, *should* a church be gathered? How should a minister be selected? Who should receive sacraments, and how often? Liberation from orthodoxy (as it was defined in England in the 1630s) generated astonishing and unexpected heterodoxy, with numerous schisms within both churches and civil polities. The founding of new towns and colonies in regions dominated by puritan inhabitants can be understood in many cases as outgrowths of religious disputes, as in the case of the settlement of Eleuthera (in the Bahamas) by exiles from Bermuda who had tried to create their own gathered church.

These colonial experiments affected events in England in the 1640s and 1650s. Controversies erupted in colonies—and came right back to England on ships that carried their participants and their writings. The London press published many of these texts, and the pamphlets sailed all around the Atlantic. Men at the center of some of the most disruptive religious controversies in the colonies, such as the Antinomian controversy in Massachusetts or the church divisions in Bermuda, found their way to England, as Henry Vane did. As Protestants sought to work out a new church order in England in the turbulent years of war and commonwealth, they looked to the colonies for inspiration or cautionary tales. Presbyterians at the Westminster Assembly, a gathering of ministers appointed by the Long Parliament to reorganize the Church of England, drew heavily on New England's experiences in the 1630s to make their case against religious toleration. John Ball, a minister in England, found nothing to admire in New England. He detailed nine positions, which once in England all had shared. But now, Ball wrote, the English ministers learned that their New English counterparts had embraced "certaine vain opinions such as [they] disliked formerly," including methods of baptism, access to communion, excommunication procedures, church membership, and ordination.[122] Ball was joined by others who deployed New England church schisms as evidence for a campaign to discourage state religious toleration in England. They looked to the events that wracked New England to demonstrate their view of the folly of such a stance.[123] In response, New England's religious radicals lobbied on their own behalf. The church settlement that emerged in England was shaped by former New Englanders and also by the evidence that New England provided for men in different factions.

The process Ball identified was one of dangerous fission: these issues were divisive enough contained within colonies where people of relatively similar dispositions dwelled, but transported to England at a crucial moment of church reorganization and political turmoil, the impact was explosive. Moreover, these doctrinal shifts did not engage only the clergy. The laity as well, particularly those who had elected to go to New England in part to escape religious tribulations at home or to follow a favorite puritan pastor, embraced these discussions. Because churches in New England were gathered, laymen had considerable power over religious affairs. Thus a sojourn in the colonies empowered laity to take control over ecclesiastical polities and encouraged clerics to experiment aggressively in pursuit of a newly revealed scriptural purity. When Civil War broke out in England, many of these most zealous puritans, particularly ministers, felt the call to return, to carry out God's vision in old England and for some to implement Cromwell's vision for Ireland in parishes there. They brought with them solutions to ecclesiastical and political problems that had been worked out individually in overseas settings.[124] The migration of clerics helped ideas and experiences circulate around the globe in the era's distinctive English style of empire and nation building, from the periphery to the center.

The ministers who fomented deep and agonizing political and social divisions through their ecclesiastical actions and the men who were so consumed by curiosity about the world around them might seem at first glance to belong to separate worlds, yet these were the same individuals. Patrick Copland illustrates these trends, revealing how ideas and people changed over time. He made a career overseas, taking two voyages with the East India Company, appointed to run a proposed college in Virginia but deterred by the attack by Indians there in 1622 that killed one-third of the colonists, moving to Bermuda in the 1620s, before a final migration to Eleuthera because of religious conflicts on Bermuda. He embraced the prospect of conversion, believing while he was in India that all Christians should get along, that all could be included in the world of Christendom. He even wrote a Dutch minister from Bantam in 1619, lamenting the disputes that divided Christians.[125] In Bermuda, however, he insisted that the only legitimate ecclesiastical structure was a gathered church of the elect. Copland ended his career amid a tiny congregation of like-minded worshippers on Eleuthera (although the colony itself promoted religious toleration), while another cosmopolitan cleric, John Covel, ended his first overseas stint defending himself against accusations of conversion by insisting adamantly on his right to immerse himself in the religions of others.[126]

The paired examples of Copland and Covel illustrate that the cosmopolitan clergy as a whole provide no monolithic lesson about the meaning of experiences overseas either for individuals or for civil polities. English Protestantism was not a coherent faith that could function as a uniform and consistent arm of conquest. No population more thoroughly mirrored the political vicissitudes that characterized England in these decades than did the wandering clerics who brought an infinite variety of Anglicanisms with

them overseas. The familiar figure of an English minister, ga
gown like Edward Terry in India, might lead an observer t
man communicated a regular belief system, enacted in uni
nothing could be further from the truth. Moreover, there
ture of the religious traveler, but as many different styles (
there were personalities and religious opinions in a tumult___
could both broaden one's horizons and solidify doctrinal rigidity. Ministers
facilitated the creation of some of the most intolerant colonial regimes the
English established, participating actively in the disenfranchisement and
destruction of indigenous people in Ireland in the sixteenth and seventeenth
centuries and in parts of the Americas. Faith there was a crucial arm of conquest. Yet elsewhere, ministers turned a blind eye to some of the egregious
excesses of English flocks and initiated personal and professional friendships with religious leaders of different faiths, eagerly engaging in intellectual
exchanges that occasionally became lifelong friendships. Back in England,
their collections of books, manuscripts, artifacts, and other detritus about
foreign religions and cultures enriched English libraries and collections and
introduced to a Protestant nation a variety of information about other faiths,
particularly Islam and the branches of the orthodox church.

The irony is rich. In a world where overseas investment was entirely in
private hands, the character of settlements and factories was fragmented. The
only national institution that English companies consistently transported
overseas was the church. Yet the clergy were themselves deeply fragmented,
and so could provide no uniformity to overseas ventures, which continued
to be shaped by indigenous constraints and economies and by the varied
and shifting English personnel who inhabited them. The English state in
these turbulent years was unable to express, impose, or sustain any single
religious settlement, and so religious expression overseas defined English
ventures through heterogeneity and dispute and experimentation and, often,
toleration. These characteristics proved as important at shaping England's
style of overseas expansion as a uniform Anglican settlement might have
been. The English Empire did indeed have religious origins—but they lay in
the schismatic, innovative, and dispersed nature of religious settlement during decades of instability at home.

8

IRELAND, 1649–1660

Come over and help us.
     —The Dublin Commissioners to Comfort Starr, 1653

All the English language I can recollect is, transport, transplant, shoot
him, kill him.
     —Éamonn an Dúna, "Mo lá leóin go deó go n-éagad," 1650s

In the conventional story of English territorial expansion, Ireland occupies
pride of place at the beginning. In the wake of the Irish uprising of 1565,
Sir Henry Sidney proposed a scheme to bring the kingdom under firmer
control, and thus launched England's first major attempt at colonization. But
as this study has illustrated, English adventurers brought a wide range of
models with them from the different places they traveled, colonized, and
traded around the globe, and enterprises in North America and elsewhere
reflected this breadth of knowledge and experience. Moreover, Irish colonization could hardly be considered a success worthy of emulation. Ireland
remained a fractious and problematic site of intermittent warfare for a long
time. Uprisings in 1603 and again in 1641 revealed the forceful rejection
by many in Ireland of the settlement envisioned by Protestant English and
Scots invaders.

As a parallel and simultaneous colonial experiment, Ireland occasionally provided a model but often existed in its own separate world, its demographic, strategic, political, diplomatic, and religious contexts too singular to
have universal or replicable relevance. In the Americas, indigenous people
succumbed to Eurasian diseases, facilitating conquest and prompting European views of indigenous weakness, but the Irish population shared the same
epidemiological history as the invader. Everywhere European conquerors
identified important cultural differences between themselves and indigenous
people, and the English in Ireland did the same, but they found their cultural dichotomies complicated by the presence of long-time inhabitants of

Anglo-Norman descent (the Old English) and the intermarriage and bilingualism of English and Irish. Finally, an emphasis on Ireland as a starting point for English expansion overlooks the continued relationship between Ireland and other sites of English trade and settlement. The Irish themselves were active in English and other European enterprises overseas. There were Irish men and women, often in significant numbers, in the failed settlements along the Amazon, in the more successful ventures in the islands of the Caribbean, in Newfoundland, and in Virginia.[1]

Rather than an inspiration for English colonization efforts, Ireland in the 1650s was a culmination of prior experiences. Under Oliver Cromwell, new colonists were enticed to relocate to Ireland from established settlements and the Irish were scattered within and out of Ireland in all directions. Cromwell's conquest of Ireland that began in 1649 is legendary for its brutality, although it was certainly consistent with other state conquests in this period. Sir William Petty, who conducted land surveys of Ireland in the 1650s, estimated that the kingdom lost some 600,000 people through violence, starvation, and disease out of a population of 1.5 million. He detailed the causes of this terrible decline: 112,000 Protestants between 1641–1652, and some 37,000 of those during the first year of the rebellion; 167,000 Irish Catholics during the war; another 275,000 during the plague that ravaged the beleaguered kingdom from 1649–1652; and 40,000 Irish Catholics forcibly transported to the continent.[2] Lost amid this appalling legacy of violence, death, and depredation is the centrality of migration in Cromwell's conquest and his envisioned reconstitution of the kingdom. Plans for the resettlement of Ireland were dependent on migration, both forced and voluntary. During the 1650s, the English state manifested a new commitment to overseas enterprises and new strategies, one of which emphasized migration and a hemispheric reshuffling of population to establish new territories and to pacify the old.

Migration was crucial to the success of all overseas ventures, of course, but until the 1640s and 1650s these were typically private ventures, joint-stock companies organized to profit from overseas trade or settlement. As the English attempted increasing numbers of settlements, colonists (called planters in the terminology of the time) joined other travelers, generally in much larger numbers. The growth of England's population with little expanded economic opportunity at home generated tens of thousands of able-bodied young men for overseas ventures. Only the continued migration of these young men enabled colonies to withstand the high mortality of early years of settlement and to endure. They flooded into the islands of the Caribbean and onto the North American mainland. As increasing numbers of ventures were tried (and abandoned) by the English, the pool of experienced colonists for new ventures expanded. Their availability shaped how new schemes were planned. To settle Tobago in 1640, for example, the Earl of Warwick sought to recruit men from Bermuda and St. Lucia, and he enticed them with free transportation, arms, and "great freedomes" to "incourage them to stay and perfect that plantacon."[3]

These were voluntary migrations orchestrated by merchants and investors and planters themselves. State-sponsored and state-enforced migration in order to ensure national security and the viability of multiple overseas enterprises emerged as a coherent policy under Oliver Cromwell. The English government obviously regulated migration throughout this period. Laws that spanned the social scale governed movement within and outside of England, penalizing unregulated travelers as vagrants, and requiring licenses for foreign travel. Early promotional literature dating to Richard Hakluyt had advocated state-sponsored migration of paupers and vagrants. The state also compelled the migration of felons. Although transportation of convicts remained a large-scale venture for the future, small cohorts of prisoners in Newgate were exiled to the colonies.[4] These state-sponsored schemes, however, remained small-scale, linked to single colonies and, aside from early promotional writings that advocated relieving England's poor through settlement overseas, not part of a coherent vision of domestic stability and overseas viability. As he cast about for ways to secure his occupation of Ireland, Cromwell embraced the forced migration of thousands of Irish within Ireland and overseas to the continent and the colonies, and he sought to persuade selected men from American colonies to join his renewed colonization in Ireland. The state asserted itself forcefully in its aggressive pursuit of displacement, replacement, transportation, transplantation, and migration.

As a result of these commitments, migration moved to the center of imperial activity. This new English empire was conceptualized in terms of migration, forced and voluntary, required and encouraged by the state's highest officials. The eagerness of the English state in the 1650s to orchestrate the mass migration of its subjects reveals a new sensibility in which populations could be relocated across large swathes of territory for the benefit of the constituent parts of an empire. A state can claim an empire if it is capable of enforcing its will on distant people: in the English case, those people were English, Scots, and Irish (the Welsh having been long since absorbed), not foreign subjects, and the most dramatic expression of the state's control lay in its willingness to forcibly relocate individuals for state purposes. These new ideas took shape in Ireland in the wake of the 1641 rebellion. They peaked in the 1650s with forced and voluntary migration across and around the Atlantic, and with the simultaneous pursuit of Spanish territories in the Caribbean, the campaign known as the Western Design. This forcible relocation of subjects was part of a larger trend in the period not only toward centralization by a strong and expanding state, but also toward the intense use of subjects in state expansion—in an enlarged army and navy and in the demand for their bodies and lives in overseas undertakings. The military campaigns in Ireland and the West Indies required a massive and often coercive mobilization of people.[5] Ireland's ordeal in the 1650s was emblematic of a transformation underway, and the intertwined processes there of military conquest and migration (both forced transplantation and voluntary recruitment) illuminate a crucial shift in the 1650s toward a centralized state capable of imposing its will on subjects well outside of its domestic borders—and thus well on its way to becoming an empire.

1641 AND ITS AFTERMATH

During the wave of aggressive colonial expansion in Ireland, the Caribbean, and North America from 1580 to 1642, Ireland emerged as one of England's most prosperous colonial regions, but also one of its most problematic and the site of frequent rebellion and endemic opposition to English occupation.[6] The rebellion raised by the Irish in 1641 surpassed in length any comparable indigenous revolt in English America and left as many as one-seventh of the English colonists dead.[7] The goals of the uprising were embedded in the kingdom's complex political and religious history, its long-standing relationship with England, and the different interests of its varied populations. In the twelfth century, Anglo-Norman conquerors of Ireland left behind men to govern the kingdom. These Old English (as they were called) remained Catholic even as the kingdom of England became Protestant in the sixteenth century. They developed close relations, moreover, with the Irish they were sent to govern. In contrast, the New English were Protestants, men and their families sent to subdue and occupy Ireland under the reigns of Elizabeth I and James I. Vastly outnumbering these small English constituencies were the Irish themselves, who were Catholic. The 1641 uprising was an effort to expunge the Protestant presence in Ireland.

The rebels did not reject royal authority over Ireland—indeed, many rebels claimed they fought with Charles I's sanction—but they hoped to rid themselves of the authoritarian policies promulgated by his agent, Thomas Wentworth, later the Earl of Strafford (equally disliked by New English religious dissenters, who tended to be puritans), and they especially feared an increase in anti-Catholic policies. Depositions generated in the wake of the 1641 uprising intimate a Catholic perception that their moment in Ireland had finally come: a Catholic kingdom was at hand. The protracted division in England between king and parliament and the Bishops' Wars in Scotland in 1639 and 1640 distracted royal authorities and occupied English soldiers and thus created conditions that made uprising in Ireland possible, although the particular tensions in Irish society were unique to the island.[8]

Catholics launched attacks beginning in Ulster, but the violence spread throughout the regions of Protestant settlement, into Leinster and Munster (see figure 8.1). As in all religious wars of the period, civilians were stripped, beaten, tortured, and murdered. Colonists found their property destroyed, their houses and crops burned, their livestock slaughtered, and the clothes ripped from off their backs. The fortunate fled toward Dublin and the garrisoned towns equipped with tales of woe and the meager possessions they salvaged, although many arrived virtually naked and suffering from exposure and hunger, having made their flights in the winter months after mob attacks. A much smaller number suffered in the massacres that accompanied the uprising, but like most mass slaughters of civilians these deaths had an impact far out of proportion to the number killed.[9] Tales of atrocities (some real, some invented) from the upheavals of the winter of 1641–1642, of Catholics murdering Protestants without regard to age or sex, further hardened attitudes on the Protestant side and led to vengeful murders.

The insurrection prompted England to renew an aggressive settlement of Ireland, a scheme that put migration at the center of conquest and occupation. In the immediate aftermath of the rebellion, the English government was unable to respond effectively, constrained as it was by seven years of full-scale civil war at home, culminating in the execution of Charles I in 1649. It was not until that year that the forces of the New Model Army (as the Parliamentary forces were called after their reorganization in 1645 into a professional fighting force) moved across the Irish Sea to subdue the kingdom. But even in the first years as Parliament assimilated the horror of the insurrection, authorities envisioned the reclamation of the kingdom in terms of colonization. The same strategy was apparent once Cromwell's forces marched into the field. As early as 1642, a scheme that granted English investors land forfeited from Ireland's rebels funded the English army. The investors, called the Adventurers for Ireland, provided money up front to fund Ireland's subjugation, but could not claim their land until the rebellion was put down. Zealous puritan investors were quick to combine the welcome possibility of profit with the opportunity to ensure the violent destruction of a Catholic foe. Once these men had made their investments, however, colonization and displacement became inescapable outcomes. The adventurers were committed to confiscation in order to recover their money, and negotiation and compromise were impossible, although actual implementation and returns on investments lay some years in the future.[10] Had the state been interested in negotiation, it would have been thwarted or at least challenged by these private investors.

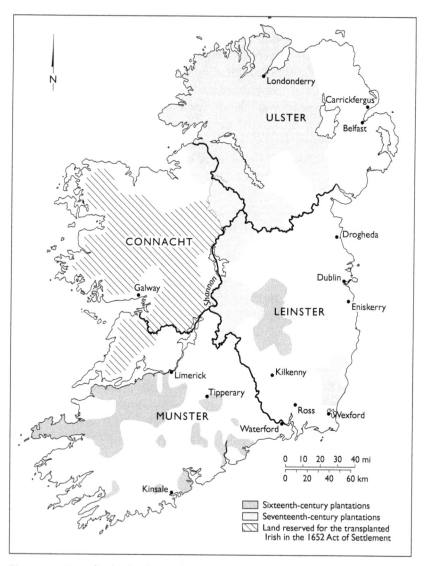

Figure 8.1. Map of Ireland. Adapted from Nicholas Canny, ed., *The Origins of Empire* (Oxford: Oxford University Press, 1988), map 6.2.

The 1641 insurrection's accompanying massacres suggested to Cromwell and others in charge of the subsequent pacification of Ireland that the country needed to be reconstituted in such a way as to confine the dangerous Catholic element permanently and to open the rest of the land to reliably pious Protestant settlers. The first step was conquest. As Cromwell led his forces through Ireland between 1649 and 1652, a time marked by violent victories for the English and utter dislocation for the Irish, he published letter after letter relating his successes and frankly describing his merciless treatment of the rebels. These epistles minimized the tenacity of Irish opposition and cast English suppression of the Irish as just punishment of a stubborn and blasphemous people. In Drogheda, about 2,000 people were put to the sword. One group of Irish soldiers who had fled to a church steeple perished when the steeple was set on fire. Of those Irish who had defended themselves in a tower, all officers were executed, "knockt on the head." One out of every ten soldiers was killed, while the rest were shipped to Barbados. The English killed all priests as well. Justifying his savage reprisals, Cromwell simply referred to the tales of atrocity during the 1641 rising. "I am persuaded," he explained, "that this is a righteous Judgement of God upon these Barbarous wretches, who have imbrued their hands in so much innocent blood." He hoped, furthermore, that the horrors of Drogheda would inspire rebels elsewhere to lay down their arms.[11]

Subsequent reports highlighted the intersection of conquest and a new colonization. Parliament ordered that Cromwell's account of the defeat of Wexford in 1649 be read by all ministers in London and the nearby parishes to their congregations on the following Thursday. Cromwell explicitly paired his tale of slaughter with a pitch for colonization. Cromwell regretted the great damage to the town, which he thought would have proved useful to the army, but believed Wexford's destruction revealed God's own plans for that town and its inhabitants. It was, Cromwell reported righteously, a just punishment indeed on a place whose inhabitants had allegedly committed two massacres of Protestants. According to English sources, more than one hundred Protestants had been drowned in an old vessel in the harbor, while others were starved to death when they were confined in a chapel.[12]

The worshippers who listened to their ministers' recital of Cromwell's actions had no need to wonder what role they might play in God's plan for Ireland, for once the Irish were removed, Wexford needed only some better inhabitants to settle it. "The Town," Cromwell wrote in this public epistle, "is now so in your power, that the former inhabitants I believe scarce one in twenty can challenge any propriety in their houses, most of them are run away, and many of them killed in this service; and it were to be wished, that an honest people would come and plant here, where are very good houses, and other Accommodations fitted to their hands, and may by your favor be made of encouragement to them." Wexford was a town "pleasantly seated, and strong," and well-suited to a new Protestant population.[13]

A Parliamentary proposal for recruiting and raising troops in England for Ireland in 1651 likewise revealed the connection between conquest and colonization. Although ostensibly about raising and transporting a regiment for towns including Waterford and Ross, the proposal focused on housing these men, with the unspoken expectation of lengthy stays. The men were to receive three-year leases for their houses, and had the right to sell their interest. They were entitled to the land of the former residents and guaranteed freedom from impressment into military service. Their goods could be transported free of custom, with their servants similarly unencumbered by military obligations as long as they held a contract. Those who could not afford their own transportation could travel to Ireland if they were willing to assume the responsibility of guard duty, for which they would receive a regular allowance.[14] The provisions are reminiscent of prior attempts to recruit settlers for colonies, whether Madagascar or Virginia, with similarly favorable terms and guarantees of rights to lease and sell land. Military conquest and colonial occupation were inextricably linked.

By 1652, after three years of violent suppression, the ultimate pacification of Ireland seemed assured, and, not coincidentally, the planned colonization of Ireland took a more sinister twist. To inspire potential colonists from England and elsewhere and to help frame the Parliamentary debate on the fate of Ireland and the Irish, the English Commissioners in Dublin gathered tales of the 1641 rebellion and Irish attacks on Protestant colonists. Concerned by perceptions of lenity toward the Irish (especially the vicious rebels described in Cromwell's accounts), and troubled by talk of Parliament making peace with the rebels, the commissioners provided Parliament with stories of the "barbarous cruel murthers." It was particularly urgent, they believed, to record these stories because so few of the old colonists "were left undestroyed especially who had any particular knowledge of the massacres."[15] Six folio pages of atrocities followed this epistle, offering a county by county reckoning of the sufferings of the English colonists: horrific stories of English shut in buildings to starve to death or to be burned alive, of Protestants executed, men, women, and children; of people buried alive; of one family murdered, even though the father had "turned to mass" (presumably in hopes of saving his family). A Mr. Hayward was murdered and his wife hanged with two children, "a Dog and a Cat" joining the Haywards in their fate.[16] One puritan minister in Ireland, James Stevenson, reported "that he saw one take the child of his sister, and dash its brains against a tree."[17] Another Englishman, newly arrived in Ireland with the army, warned of the peril of these "skulking Tories."[18] These grim tales of atrocities, so carefully gathered in Dublin, were solemnly read before Parliament in May of 1652, and they shaped that body's deliberations on the type of settlement deemed suitable for Ireland.

Oral and published tales of the 1641 civilian slaughters proved inflammatory both in the immediate aftermath of the uprising and for a long time thereafter. These stories sanctioned brutal treatment by English soldiers in the field of battle. Even before the final Parliamentary invasion of Ireland commenced in 1649, English soldiers dealt harshly with Irish soldiers wherever they found them in retaliation for the violence of the 1641 rising. In David Leslie's report of his army's activities in Scotland in 1647, for example, he seized holdings that were defended by the Irish. Leslie particularly noted that all the Irish soldiers taken were put to the sword.[19] Refugees brought their stories of horror with them to England and Scotland. The publication of their miseries spread the word effectively. In England, people contributed small sums of money to support the settlement of Ireland, and donated food and money to the refugees. In Scotland, men responded by volunteering for military service in Ulster.[20] The attack on co-religionists struck Protestants outside of Ireland as viscerally as if their kingdoms had been attacked by foreign rivals.

The tales, moreover, circulated around the Atlantic. One letter from Massachusetts in 1650 referred to the delight of New Englanders at the news of Cromwell's "execution of his just vengeance upon those bloody monsters of mankinde."[21] The stories haunted Irish refugees who had been relocated to Protestant strongholds. In Bermuda in 1661, the governor and council heard reports from some Irish servants that others were conspiring along with some slaves to rise up against the English. If the Irish could not have their freedom, according to the informants, then they would cut the throats of the Englishmen on the island. A full twenty years after the 1641 uprising, the governor issued a proclamation in response to this threat. "Not being willing to have them destroyed by these bloody people who did use most horrible cruelties to our English Protestants in Ireland, which like hath not bin heard of in any nation," the governor ordered strict regulation of the Irish. They were to be disarmed, and any Irish and slaves who gathered in groups of two or three were to be punished.[22] The memories of 1641 and the fear of Catholic violence shaped Bermuda's response to these alleged conspirators.

The news that circulated about the hardships Protestants experienced during the Irish insurrection and the efforts of the English government to ensure the formal dissemination of these stories helped produce the Act of Settlement, passed by Parliament in August of 1652. This sweeping act made into official policy what had been happening already in Ireland: the forced removal of the Gaelic Irish and some of the Catholic Old English and their replacement by the English. Formalizing decisions taken by Parliament as early as 1642, the act divided the higher ranks of the Irish population into different categories depending on their involvement in the uprising and in the attacks on Protestants. Some were excluded from any possibility of pardon, while others were pardoned but had to forfeit two-thirds of their estates.[23] Those Irish who had any remaining claim to property could take land only where Parliament permitted, and what Parliament devised was a large Irish reservation in the province of Connacht. This region could be guarded with relative ease because most of it was divided from the rest of Ireland by rivers, leaving only a short segment of land to be garrisoned. Once they relocated, all Irish landowners would receive the equivalent of the land they owned elsewhere. Successive revisions brought increasing numbers of Irish into the category of those required to move.[24] The Act exempted certain people from the forced migration: Protestants; women who had married Protestants before December 2, 1650, provided they renounced Catholicism; and boys under the age of fourteen and girls under the age of twelve who could remain as servants. Everyone else was supposed to move west of the Shannon River by May 1, 1654, under penalty of death. Exceptions aside, the intent of the legislation was to preserve the rest of the country for new English Protestant settlement.[25] The Act also imposed penalties on the Old English, who if they had not supported the rebellion itself displayed a disquieting loyalty to the Stuarts and Catholicism.

Although these visions for mass migration within and out of Ireland focused particularly on the Catholic Irish, the Presbyterian Scots who were thickly settled in the province of Ulster also threatened English settlement. In the early seventeenth century, Ulster settlement had appealed to Scots for a variety of reasons. Long accustomed to emigration because of adverse economic circumstances at home, Scots found in Ulster a new option aside from continental military service or trade in places such as Poland.[26] They had poured into the region in the first decades of the seventeenth century. Dominant in Ulster, where they outnumbered the English colonists by as much as fifteen to one, they posed a threat to English hegemony. A scheme to relocate the Scots who had settled in Ulster to an area farther away from Scotland, however, was never pursued.[27]

This separation of the English and Irish populations, officials hoped, would both speed the new settlement of Ireland by encouraging the English to relocate and protect Protestants and their property from repeats of the 1641 attacks. Segregation might redress perceived deficiencies of earlier English settlements, which tended to be scattered about the kingdom despite efforts to create coherent and large plantations. And once word reached England and Ireland in 1655 about the attack on the Protestants of the Piedmont by Catholic forces (including, it was rumored, one group of Irish mercenaries), the transplantation of Irish Catholics gained a fresh urgency. (This incident sparked harsh condemnation throughout Europe, and so inflamed

Cromwell that he threatened to send forces to the region.) The Catholics in Ireland, the Lord Deputy of Ireland (and son-in-law of Oliver Cromwell) Charles Fleetwood believed, possessed "as bad, if not a worse spiritt" than those who had committed the sectarian murders on the continent.[28]

The Act of Settlement was not without its opponents, both English and Irish. A verbal skirmish ensued when Vincent Gookin, a Protestant English planter in Munster (Ireland's southwestern province), published a pamphlet objecting to the plan. He thought the English might convert the Irish to Protestantism more successfully if the two populations lived together. With this argument he confronted fears of cultural degeneracy head-on. The Protestant English, as they pursued their conquest of Ireland in the sixteenth century, had been shocked by what they perceived to be the degradation of the Old English population. These old settlers had been unable or unwilling to maintain a cultural separation from the Irish. Instead, they intermarried, spoke Irish, employed Irish wetnurses, and in many ways assimilated to the dominant culture around them. All subsequent English plantation schemes took this lesson as a cautionary tale: it demonstrated the fragility and mutability of culture and pointed to the importance of working to maintain cultural distinction. The contrast with the goals of a trade factory (where accommodation was prized) is stark, and illustrates the special challenges people faced who circulated among these different ventures and were obliged to draw on radically different approaches to cultural interaction in order to satisfy different strategic goals.

Gookin's pamphlet redirected this fear of amalgamation and instead proposed cultural proximity to elevate the Irish. Isolating the Irish in Connacht, he argued, simply ensured the endurance of Catholic rebels. Permitting the Irish to stay among the English, especially with a reinvigorated English population, would encourage the Irish to emulate the English. Failure of prior efforts to create exemplary English settlements did not dissuade Gookin, who conceded that earlier English settlers had adapted themselves to the Irish, but he found circumstances in Ireland in the 1650s sufficiently different to suggest a new malleability in *Irish* culture, not that of the English colonists. Before the uprising an English resident in Ireland might be a tenant to a wealthier Irishman, and thus encouraged to adapt himself to a dominant Irish culture, but that situation was now reversed. Previously the Irish held high offices as lawyers, judges, and members of parliament, but now the English would be paramount. The Irish language was once employed in commercial affairs, and the English had been bilingual, but now the main language would be English, and the Irish would learn it. Irish parents would put their children into the care of the English, in order for them to learn English customs and to secure the many advantages that would come from familiarity with the occupiers' ways.[29]

Everything suggested to Gookin that the Irish would confront incentives to acculturate themselves to a newly dominant English polity, but his vision of acculturation depended on the ability of the Irish to maintain their residence among the English. He cautioned against those expecting a hasty transformation. In a "few centuries," he speculated, no one would be able to distinguish the English from the Irish, who would be "swallowed up." Moreover, he thought the scheme of forced removal through transplantation was impracticable: it was not possible to bring over enough English people to replace the Irish labor shipped to Connacht. Especially after years of war, famine, and plague, Ireland had been terribly depopulated.[30] English planters, both those already resident and those newly enticed to Ireland, needed Irish labor for their farms to thrive. Indeed, by making strenuous efforts to expel the Irish who lived in provincial centers, English officials deprived the towns of competent craftsmen and laborers. Finally, signaling the period's crucial shift from private to state-sponsored colonization, Gookin believed that old colonization schemes had failed because of the absence of public (government) support; too much power had been left in the hands of the Irish. The state's renewed commitment to Ireland made a successful colonization possible.[31]

In his second pamphlet on the subject, Gookin justified his opposition to the proposed mass transplantation by drawing on the prior colonial experiences of other Europeans.[32] First, he rejected as ill-founded his opponent Richard Lawrence's attempt to compare the Irish forced west across the Shannon with other European colonists. Those Dutch and French who crossed the Atlantic to America may have taken a longer journey, but Gookin pointed out that they were *voluntary* migrants, whereas the Irish were *forced* out of their homes in the envisioned transplantation. European colonists in America, moreover, found support from the crown and from private investors, while the Irish—reduced to "beggars, an undone people"—were prohibited from taking the most fundamental steps to support themselves and build homes, even banned from cutting wood without licenses.[33] His second critique derived from historical precedent. While he studied the ancient Romans, he also cast his eyes west across the Atlantic to Spanish America, and looked similarly close to home at the English settlement in the Pale (the region around Dublin). In all cases, he argued, colonizers subdued the people they invaded, but they also settled among them, for indeed it was the indigenous people of the Indies who made the place profitable for the Spanish.[34] American models suggested examples that might be followed in Ireland.

However much it was embedded in contemporary precedent around the Atlantic, Gookin's plea for proximity failed. Parliament's plan, even after it was tempered from its original vision of complete relocation of all Irish, was a scheme even the most ambitious American colonist could not have

realistically hoped for in the 1650s: the complete removal of an indigenous population, to be replaced by an English population. While this turn
of events may have been achieved as a result of the epidemics and wars
unleashed on North America's indigenous populations, original colonization schemes in the early seventeenth century did not envision removing
these populations by force before colonization itself commenced. Indeed, as
Gookin observed, many American colonization plans had initially placed
an indigenous presence at the center of their success—indigenous traders, consumers, and laborers promised prosperity to new colonies, and the
evangelization that legitimized colonial endeavors likewise required proximity. But by 1652 Ireland had been a target of renewed English colonization for almost a century, and frustration prodded a vengeful and ardently
Protestant Parliament to move toward expulsion of the Irish from Ireland,
proposed but not implemented in the aftermath of the Nine Years' War.[35] Its
renewal in the 1650s reflected decades of colonial experience and a commitment to draw on that experience and on the availability of skilled colonists for the state's benefit.

The most fervent opponents of resettlement were the Irish themselves,
who struggled to remain in their homes. Appeals for exceptions and dispen-
sations flooded local courts from the Gaelic Irish and the Old English alike.
The effort proceeded gradually, reported Charles Fleetwood in May of 1655,
in part because those required to transplant lingered at home, hoping for a
reprieve from England. The commissioners in Dublin were forced to move
the deadlines for transplantation repeatedly because of both the logistical
difficulties such a massive relocation required and the petitions that burdened local courts. Finally officials set a firm deadline and performed some
exemplary executions.[36]

In 1656, Oliver Cromwell's son Henry, then acting Lord Deputy in the
absence of Fleetwood, took advantage of the refusal of some men to move
west to arrest "the most considerable, active, and dangerous persons reside-
inge within the provinces of Munster, Leinster, and Ulster, whoe may legally
be disposed of...to forreign service or otherwise."[37] His forcible removal
of the Irish resisters points to another important element in these new
state-sponsored migration schemes: the *mandatory* resettlement of subjects in new colonies or military ventures. If the Irish refused to move west
across the Shannon, then the English would compel them further west across
the Atlantic. An earlier hint of this plan was clear in Cromwell's conquest,
when he shipped defeated soldiers from Drogheda to work as bound laborers in Barbados, an island with such acute labor shortages in this period of
intense sugar cultivation that English soldiers who were impressed to serve
in Cromwell's forces worried that the Caribbean campaigns were entirely
made up, and that they would in fact be sold as mercenaries or as slaves.[38]

Labor needs, especially in the West Indies, made this forced Irish migration a convenient solution, and this cohort from Drogheda was part of as many as 10,000 Irish (joined as well by thousands of Scots) who were shipped to the Caribbean in the 1650s.[39]

Ireland was not the only place in need of a makeover. The transplantation of the Irish coincided with the English acquisition of Jamaica, another venture requiring a massive infusion of soldiers and settlers. Hard-won from the Spanish as part of Cromwell's Western Design, the West Indian island required a complete settlement of laborers and planters. One scheme to populate that island was to round up a supply of men and girls in Ireland and to ship them overseas. Scots were destined for Jamaica as well. Henry Cromwell, who was in charge of Irish recruitment for Jamaica, further suggested that John Thurloe, the secretary of state, might consider sending almost 2,000 boys there. "We could well spare them," he explained, "and they would be of use to you; and who knows, but that it may be a meanes to make them english-men, I meane rather Christianes."[40] Here Cromwell offered an interesting insight into the difference between the two colonization plans. Ireland was so fragile a Protestant polity that all landholding Irish were to be banished west of the Shannon River. The Irish who remained in the English-occupied areas would become a permanent servile class. The Irish who went to Jamaica, on the other hand, might benefit from the experience in the minds of contemporaries. Indeed, precisely as Vincent Gookin had suggested would be the case for a new Ireland, it was possible that the Irish in Jamaica could become proper Christians (meaning Protestants) and even English. In a cultural hierarchy that prized English ethnicity and Protestant belief, the colonial scheme for Ireland offered permanent degradation for debased Irish laborers living in or near English settlements; the plan for Jamaica promised cultural elevation through amalgamation overseas.

The forced migrations of the 1650s offered a new and insidious twist on a long-standing "culture of emigration" in Ireland among the Catholic population in the period before 1641. As many as 33,000 Irish journeyed to the continent as mercenaries between 1603 and 1641, and they were part of a cohort as large as 100,000 (out of a population of approximately 1 million in 1603 and 1.5 million in 1641), which left Ireland altogether for England, Wales, and the continent.[41] Emigration was a long-standing response to invasion, conquest, and colonial rule, exaggerated in the 1650s by the massive exodus the English anticipated and by the link between migration and social transformation. The English hoped that Ireland and the Irish, wherever they might be sent, would be made anew through the successful implementation of migration policies that linked different parts of England's overseas holdings.

SEEKING GODLY PLANTERS

To assist Irish exiles in their forced anglicization in Jamaica, Oliver Cromwell turned to established colonial planters on the American mainland and in the Caribbean. In the early years of English colonial experimentation, employers had turned to soldiers to lead ventures, but in later years they were able to draw on men with relevant and appropriate colonial experience, after some twenty colonies had been attempted in the Atlantic. In 1656 Cromwell extended a formal invitation to the people of Massachusetts to move to Jamaica. The General Court of Massachusetts wrote Cromwell in response, grateful, they explained, for the confidence his invitation suggested but disturbed by the high mortality they had heard reported (accurately) from Jamaica. The Massachusetts agent John Leveret presented the letter to Cromwell and reported on their conversation at greater length. Cromwell maintained that God might call his people to Jamaica in the same way that he had called them to New England, and that they could profit there as well as they did in North America. Nonetheless, Leveret raised several concerns. Leveret pointed to the general prosperity of New Englanders in their colonial homes; they did not enjoy the great wealth of men in other colonies, but they were able to live "more comfortably like Englishmen than any of the rest of the country." They worried about the unhealthiness of Jamaica, and Leveret singled out the fear of pious New Englanders that their "spirits, principles, manners, and customs" would put them at odds with the less devout people there. Cromwell hoped that if enough New Englanders relocated, then they would be able to control the government and could regulate the behavior of others. Very few New Englanders accepted this invitation.[42]

In his effort to populate Jamaica, Cromwell turned to the people of Nevis, far more convenient for a trip to Jamaica, and inhabited by colonists already familiar with the geopolitical and environmental perils of the region. He secured the assistance of the governor, Luke Stokes, who reported that he could not persuade prosperous planters to transplant themselves. Only the poorer inhabitants were inclined to migrate, and their transportation costs needed to be paid. Stokes, a veteran of numerous colonial experiments, was part of this planned migration. He relocated to Jamaica with his family, but in less than two months, confirming the suspicions of New Englanders about Jamaica's disease environment, Stokes and his wife had died.[43]

The settlement of Jamaica and the reorganization of Ireland were simultaneous enterprises, and both were equally urgent. Both, moreover, revealed the new way in which the state regarded the obligations of English subjects to English holdings, wherever they might be. Despite Irish and some English opposition to transplantation, the Commissioners of Ireland, first through their own commission and later under the direction of the two Lord Deputies who represented the English ruler (crown or protector) in Ireland, first Charles Fleetwood, then Henry Cromwell, put the plan into action. But the successful implementation of the scheme, as the Act itself made clear, hinged on migration, not simply the *emigration* of the Irish but also the *immigration* of a viable replacement population. One possibility was soldiers: their salaries in arrears, soldiers in Ireland and others who had fought with Parliament's forces during the Civil War were promised land in Ireland in lieu of their salaries. Land was distributed to these soldiers in twenty-two different counties.[44] Henry Cromwell had little faith in the soldiers' suitability as planters, however, and he urged John Thurloe instead to "find out some employment for them abroad."[45]

The selective relocation of carefully identified planters was particularly important for Oliver Cromwell because his new regime had almost no support within Ireland.[46] Cromwell himself was only in Ireland briefly, leaving the completion of military occupation to Charles Fleetwood and Henry Cromwell. But Oliver Cromwell took seriously his hopes of securing Ireland with a religious settlement consistent with his own congregational vision, one that rejected both the conventional rule of the Church of England through bishops and also free of the radical elements pervasive in the army and emerging among the civilian population in England at a time of unprecedented religious experimentation. His task was not only to subdue the kingdom but then to reconstitute it with loyal supporters. Thomas Harrison, who was Henry Cromwell's chaplain in Dublin and also a New England migrant, articulated this popular perception of the malleability of Ireland and the importance of shaping the kingdom with the religious zeal of the new invaders. "Ireland was 'clay upon the wheele, ready to receive what forme authority shall please to give it.'" Repopulating Ireland with pious settlers who were also prosperous, ready to assume control of local government, and able to assist in the reinvigoration of trade was the biggest challenge confronting the regime in the 1650s—and it proved its biggest failure.[47]

Cromwell's plan depended on the successful recruitment of men well-suited to the task at hand, not just investors, nor soldiers, whose work was supposed to be ended as colonization commenced, but men who passed litmus tests of faith and fealty and whose puritan commitment was beyond question. Moreover, Irish towns and trading centers were devastated after a decade of warfare and disruption. Recruitment efforts targeted Dutch merchants from Rotterdam, as well as Dutch and Huguenot artisans.[48] The quest for continental dissenters who might bolster Ireland's economic fortunes and its religious character echoed the recruiting efforts of puritan companies and investors in the 1630s and anticipated the aggressive continental recruitment of European pietists by William Penn for his colony of Pennsylvania in the 1680s.

The plea for people became a refrain in letters that Charles Fleetwood wrote to the English Secretary of State John Thurloe in 1655. On his tour through the country, Fleetwood remarked on the good order of the people and the "fruitfullnes and pleasantnes of this countrey…though it be very wast at present…The greatest want this nation hath," continued Fleetwood, "is a better people." Were the population improved, he thought "there would be but little difference betwixt it and England."[49] Fleetwood was particularly engaged in the work of transplantation, "which I have chiefelye in my eye," he wrote Thurloe.[50] The minister Nathaniel Brewster (another New England transplant) agreed after a six-week "long progresse" around the country a year later with Henry Cromwell. His tour prompted Brewster to write Thurloe of the condition of the principal ports and towns, which were, he wrote, "sadly decayed and unpeopled, being likely to continue so till better encouragement be offered to planters, especially merchants."[51] Henry Cromwell was particularly concerned that Galway, which he had "cleared" of Irish inhabitants, be "well planted" with English, since there were only six families in the town as of January 1656. He urged Thurloe to find some London merchants to take on this project, by which he intended that a syndicate of investors would fund the transportation and settlement of new inhabitants.[52] When that proposal evoked no action, the Council of Ireland wrote to Thurloe in April 1657 and proposed that Galway be "disposed of" to the English city of Gloucester, which had suffered greatly during the wars and had been ordered by Parliament to receive some forfeited lands. This, the council wrote, was the perfect solution. Such efforts were better undertaken by "society," not "private interests" (an obvious departure from older approaches, and part of a larger shift underway in the period). If Galway were "well planted," it might secure peace in Connacht and "subdue the spirits more than ever to be taken care of, seeing so many proprietors, sword-men, and other dangerous and disaffected persons are transplanted thither from all other parts of this nation."[53]

REFORMING IRELAND

In the search for proven Protestants with colonial experience and a commitment to Cromwell's vision of good order, where better to turn than to those inhabitants of England's most religiously orthodox colonial region, New England? Cromwell looked particularly to New England to replenish the wasted towns, including places such as Waterford and Galway that were of economic and strategic importance.[54] The New England men who were specifically recruited for Irish settlement brought a special style of puritan conquest with them that state officials hoped would enable them to reform Ireland. New Englanders had an ideology to export—their innovative ecclesiastical polity of independent congregations established by the laity themselves, not by an external church hierarchy—and they were, moreover, adept at quelling internal dissent. In the tumultuous decade of the 1630s, when puritans in America who were unleashed from oppression pursued religious ideas in all directions, Massachusetts had banished religious dissidents, including Anne Hutchinson and Roger Williams, and thus put in place mechanisms for enforcing conformity. These were precisely the challenges facing Cromwell and other orthodox puritans in England and Ireland in the 1650s. When his cherished New Englanders were criticized by one interloper on a conversation for their "rigidness and persecution," Cromwell leapt to their defense, revealing his preference for their style of church discipline.[55] Cromwell sought experienced colonists—but not cosmopolitans. These were, instead, men who preferred stark separations in their worlds, between Christian and heathen, English and Irish, circumspect and profligate, saved (they hoped) and damned. Unlike other travelers, these transplanted puritans from southern New England were not men eager to appreciate the diversity of humanity.

Ultimately these New England transplants failed to reproduce their orthodoxy in Ireland. The experiment there was cut short by the restoration of Charles II to the throne in 1660, but even before then it was clear that an insufficient number of people in Ireland had the stomach for the strict church settlement of Massachusetts in the 1630s or even England in the 1650s. Ireland, like England and New England before it, experienced the eruption of religious dissent characteristic of English Protestantism in this period, and a firm congregational settlement proved impossible. There was no uniformity among the score of New Englanders known to have ended up in Ireland. Some were exemplary planters, the types of men Cromwell had hoped to recruit. But others were precisely the loose cannons who challenged orthodoxy in New England and similarly thwarted a settled church order in Ireland. The orthodox puritans who left New England were joined by religious radicals, men who joined the Parliamentary side against the crown in the 1640s but who in the 1650s sought their own vision of God's plan for England and Ireland. Oliver Cromwell wanted to draw on only one model of religious settlement in the Protestant Atlantic. Unfortunately for him, it was the form that was in the process of becoming the most marginalized. Cromwell sought to replicate the intolerant regime of Massachusetts or New Haven at a time when the English Atlantic had moved toward a commitment to tolerance (as it was defined in this period).[56]

New Englanders were accustomed to calls from old England and to recruiting efforts from proprietors of other colonies who hoped that New Englanders would transport not only themselves and their goods but also some of the admirable elements of their region's culture.[57] The outbreak of the Civil War and especially the execution of Charles I signaled to devout puritans opportunities to build God's kingdom not in a remote American setting but rather in a newly restored England. In this charged atmosphere, many New Englanders, as many as fifteen percent of the 21,000 people who had ventured to the region between 1630 and 1642, returned to England.[58] New Englanders in England found their services as soldiers, ministers, and godly magistrates in great demand. Many returned to the parishes and counties from which they had first emigrated and reintegrated themselves into networks of cousins and friends.

The call to Ireland combined the lure to serve God in England with the enticements offered by colonial proprietors and investors to persuade experienced colonial residents to try new ventures. It is possible to trace the careers of a few of those New Englanders who answered Cromwell's appeal for help, although the loss of the Commonwealth records in the fire and explosion at the Four Courts in Dublin in 1922 makes it very difficult to sketch these lives in full. The richness of New England's local records in some way compensates for the dearth of comparable sources in Ireland, enabling us to surmise what circumstances in America might have prompted some men to leave for Ireland or might have made them appear to be desirable colonists for Ireland.

The first invitations to New Englanders accompanied Cromwell's victories in Ireland, and Cromwell made his appeal to orthodox ministers and stalwart civil leaders. Independent (congregational) ministers were especially important in Cromwell's vision of a newly planted Ireland, a place that by 1650 was greatly depleted of puritan clerics. Trinity College in Dublin had been a puritan stronghold—the Massachusetts founder John Winthrop had sent John Jr. from England to study there in the 1620s—but under the stern rule of Thomas Wentworth, dissenters in Ireland had been penalized. So effective was Wentworth's discouragement of the puritans that the Archbishop of Canterbury William Laud remarked to a friend on Wentworth's inability to procure men to settle the Munster plantation, "and that the while, there should be here such an universal running to New England."[59] As a result of that pressure, by the 1640s, many of the New English colonists in Ireland had become conforming members of the Church of England.[60]

When Cromwell arrived in Dublin in 1649, he, joined later by Parliament, moved quickly against Anglican practices, forbidding, for example, the use of the Book of Common Prayer, removing many clerics from their offices, restoring Trinity College to its puritan origins, and paying puritan ministers out of public funds.[61] The most severe problem, however, was that few ministers were still in Ireland by 1650. During the 1641 uprising, English

Protestant ministers were prime targets, and consequently many fled Ireland. While puritan chaplains traveled to Ireland with English army regiments, these men could not easily assume the responsibility of tending to parishes in addition to their official military duties. Recruitment, then, became a central concern. And the ministers required for new settlements had to be orthodox puritans: not the egalitarians known as Levellers, not Fifth Monarchists (who anticipated that Jesus would intervene directly in the morass of English politics), not Anabaptists (who rejected infant baptism), not even (although the opposition was less stringent here) Presbyterians. In theory, the Irish Commissioners hoped *not* to transplant the sectarian disarray that characterized England to Ireland, where it might imperil the firm settlement they envisioned. The problem for them lay in the army, which bred these radical religious and political sentiments. Already by 1650 the army had brought with it radical ministers, including one prominent Anabaptist, Thomas Patient, who had lived in New England.[62]

The need for ministers launched the recruitment efforts that brought New England to the forefront of Irish affairs. Sometime in 1650 Oliver Cromwell wrote several luminaries in Massachusetts, including the ministers Peter Bulkeley of Concord, Samuel Whiting and Thomas Cobbett of Lynn, and John Knowles of Watertown, and the Ipswich colonists Daniel Denyson and John Tuttle. In their response of December 1650, they observed that in seeking to plant the rule of Christ in Ireland, Cromwell looked not only to "godly people and ministers in England," but also "upon such like in America also." On behalf of themselves "and some others" the correspondents resolved to determine if God, who had called them to New England, called them again to serve him in Ireland.

The tone of the letter was polite yet suggested that the writers were uncertain that God's will lay in Ireland. Nonetheless, it concluded with a series of conditions that these six men proposed for their settlement in Ireland. They required several guarantees: church government as they enjoyed it in New England; land set aside for a school and college; their own choice of a military governor of the garrison where they would settle; funding for poor but godly people to join them; and freedom from public assessments. Two other requests seem derived from their experience in New England. "That in regard we come from a pure Ayre," these men demanded, "we may have a place in the more healthfull part of the Country." And they were adamant, perhaps in light of their own unhappiness dwelling among the Indians of southeastern New England, "that noe Irish may inhabite amongst us, but such as we shall like of."[63] Given the separation they demanded it is clear that these New England saints envisioned no evangelical mission in their call to Ireland but intended to bolster English settlement and to set an example to the other colonists around them. A year later the prominent Boston minister

John Cotton received an equally unsuccessful invitation for ministers in New England to move to Ireland. But these solicitations were in many respects premature, as the English army was engaged in suppressing the rebellion until 1652. Of the six men who replied to Cromwell, only one, John Tuttle, ultimately accepted the invitation. Altogether I have identified seventeen New England men who ventured to Ireland between approximately 1648 and 1659. Table 8.1 lists these men, their occupations, their first appearance in Ireland, and, when known, their place of death.

Several New Englanders who responded to their recruitment for Ireland had already demonstrated their success as planters and community leaders in godly commonwealths. Others were experienced ministers, and six men had just completed their college training but already had sterling puritan pedigrees. At least four of these men were accompanied by their wives, and at least two brought their children along to Ireland. These men reflected different patterns in their migrations to Ireland. Some (Weld, Ludlow, Tuttle, Hobart, and Millard) went directly to Ireland from New England in response to invitations. Others (Cooke, Brewster, Samuel Mather, Aspinwall, Patient, and Harrison) went first to England during the 1640s or 1650s and then migrated to Ireland. A handful of these men (Increase and Nathaniel Mather, Brewster, and Hobart) made only short visits to Ireland in the 1650s. All were born in England: ten had been adults when they reached New England during the so-called "Great Migration" of the 1630s, whereas the other seven had been children or teenagers. Perhaps the most striking characteristic is that twelve were ministers. Their presence reflected the arduous recruitment efforts by Oliver Cromwell and the deputy and commissioners of Ireland.

If it is apparent why Ireland's English occupiers wished to entice puritan planters from New England to join their colonial venture, it is less clear why established New Englanders would take such a risk, involving another dangerous and uncomfortable sea voyage followed by settlement in a land laid waste by war. A glimpse at the four men of New England's first generation who were not ministers suggests some common characteristics. George Cooke, Samuel Shepard, Roger Ludlow, and John Tuttle were well-suited to the new settlement of Ireland. All were distinguished friends of orthodoxy in Massachusetts and Connecticut. They had relevant experience in office holding, church membership, and military affairs. Ludlow had ventured to New England with the Winthrop fleet in 1630 aboard the *Mary and John*, while Cooke, Shepard, and Tuttle had traveled to New England in 1635. Cooke and Shepard were men of such well-known puritan beliefs that they were only allowed to leave England because they disguised themselves as servants, following a strategy common among America's early illegal immigrants.[64]

All four men reached New England in a relatively privileged position: Ludlow was already a Massachusetts Bay Company officer; Cooke and

Table 8.1 New England Residents Who Ended Up in Ireland, 1648–1659

Name	Occupation	First in Ireland (and where)	Died
Thomas Akers	soldier	1649?	Ireland?
William Aspinwall	minister	1659, via England (Kildare) (Antinomian in N.E.)	
Nathaniel Brewster*	minister	1655, via England m. Ludlow's daughter in Ireland	L.I., 1690
George Cooke and family	soldier	1648, via England (Wexford)	Ireland, 1652
Thomas Harrison	minister	1655, via England (Tandragee, Dublin)	England?
Joshua Hobart*	minister	1656 (New Ross, brief stay)	N.E., 1717
Roger Ludlow and family	civil official	1654	Ireland, by 1666
Increase Mather*	minister	1657 (at brother Samuel's request)	N. E., 1723
Nathaniel Mather*	minister	165? visit 1671 (took over Samuel's church)	London, 1690
Samuel Mather*	minister	1655, via England (Dublin)	Dublin, 1671
John Millard	minister	1655 (Waterford)	
Thomas Patient	minister	1650 (Kilkenny, Water- ford, Dublin) Anabaptist	
Samuel Shepard and wife	planter	1658	
Zephaniah Smith	minister	1656 (Roscrea; Corkaree)	
Thomas (or Robert) Thornton	minister	1654 (Clare, Limerick)	
John Tuttle and wife	planter	1652? (Carrickfergus)	Ireland, 1656
Edmund Weld*	minister	1654 (Kinsale; St. Finbarr's)	Ireland, 1668

*Harvard graduate

Sources: St. John D. Seymour, *The Puritans in Ireland 1647–1661* (Oxford: Clarendon Press, 1912), especially appendix 1; James Savage, *A Genealogical Dictionary of the First Settlers of New England,* four volumes (Boston, 1860–1862, repr. 1965); John Langdon Sibley, *Biographical Sketches of Graduates of Harvard University* (Cambridge, Mass.: Charles William Sever, 1873), vol. 1; Robert Charles Anderson, *The Great Migration Begins: Immigrants to New England, 1620–1633,* three volumes (Boston: New England Historic Genealogical Society, 1995); Frederick Lewis Weis, *The Colonial Clergy and the Colonial Churches of New England* (Lancaster, Mass.: Society of the Descendants of the Colonial Clergy, 1936).

Shepard traveled with a wealthy patron, and Tuttle brought wealth and relations with him to ease his adjustment to a new life in New England. As men who had joined New England in its first few years and who had moved to the helm of this fragile colonial society with its contested religious order, they had invaluable experience that recommended them for a second puritan conquest. They had been colony leaders during the twin ordeals of the Pequot War and the Antinomian controversy in the 1630s. All four were church members. If you were looking for men trained in governing colonists and conquering indigenous people, Cooke, Tuttle, Shepard, and Ludlow were safe bets.

Ludlow served as a deputy governor and a colony assistant in Massachusetts, and he held the same offices in Connecticut after he moved there in 1635. Building a new colony required a range of skills, and Ludlow made special use of his English legal training, with which he wrote the 1650 code of laws for Connecticut, and his martial inclinations. He built Castle William, the fortified island in Boston harbor. He had intimate acquaintance with the tribes of southern New England in war and peace and owned at least one Indian servant or slave, a man called Adam.[65] The invitation to Ireland offered Ludlow a fresh start when he was most in need of it. Ludlow's bellicose sensibilities against the Dutch peaked during the first Anglo-Dutch War (1652–1654), and Ludlow hoped for war with New Netherland. Ludlow's martial ambitions had been undermined in New England by a timely peace with the Dutch and contemporary writers thought he was humiliated by the experience. Perhaps like the Earl of Arundel, similarly humiliated in his thwarted campaign against Scotland in 1639, he sought redemption overseas. If so, Ludlow found ample opportunity in Ireland. In November of 1654 he served on a commission to determine claims to forfeited land in Ireland, an enormously important job, since the settlement of Ireland depended on the fair and peaceful allocation of lands.[66] He was subsequently appointed to administer justice in Dublin.[67] Moreover, Ludlow's cousin Edmund was prominent in Irish affairs. He was Commander-in-Chief there for almost a year in 1651 and 1652 and received a large estate near Dublin to compensate him for his unpaid salary. A chance meeting of the two cousins at Holyhead (the Welsh port of departure for passage to Ireland) suggests that Edmund Ludlow did not pave the way for his cousin Roger, but it is possible that Roger was drawn to Ireland not just because of the possibilities this new colony offered but also because of the potential patronage of a powerful relative.[68]

George Cooke similarly seems to have found in England and Ireland a larger arena in which to display his talents than New England permitted. In Massachusetts Cooke served as a captain in the militia and was a deputy in the General Court. He had distinguished himself as a soldier in

New England but his theater there was modest. Cooke's greatest blow on behalf of orthodoxy came when he was sent to Rhode Island in September of 1643 with forty soldiers to arrest the Gortonists, followers of Samuel Gorton, who had been thrown out of Massachusetts and Plymouth for his religious beliefs. Cooke and his party returned with the nine prisoners in "military order": Cooke had his soldiers walk in two files, "and after every five or six soldiers a prisoner," an elaborate arrangement hardly necessary for these nonviolent religious dissenters.[69] Here was suitable training for Ireland.

Cooke went first to England in the 1640s and to Ireland probably in 1648, by which time he was a lieutenant colonel in Colonel Needham's regiment.[70] In the wake of Cromwell's seizure of Wexford, Cook was appointed governor.[71] In 1650, he took Enniscorthy and put the entire garrison to the sword.[72] The bishop of the diocese of Wexford, Nicholas French, remembered Cooke as "especially remarkable for his brutality." French held Cooke responsible for a massacre that left 4,000 people "atrociously butchered." He also accused Cooke of shutting 300 people into a house and burning the house down with the people in it.[73] Wexford did suffer terribly when Cromwell's forces attacked it. Approximately 1,500 soldiers and townspeople were killed in the town square, and hundreds more drowned as they tried to escape across the Slaney River. There is, however, no other corroborating evidence of the type of attack French described, nor of a population so large.[74] It would not be surprising that a massacre of a similar sort took place: its close resemblance to the alleged attacks on puritans in 1641 at a time when stories of the 1641 massacres were receiving fresh press makes such retaliatory gestures ring true. And Cooke was a professional soldier who likely shared his commander Oliver Cromwell's strategy of devastation. Less reliable is French's report that Cooke personally relegated a small boy to the flames when one of his officers hid the child. If the story is untrue, however, its telling suggests the type of reputation Cooke made for himself in Ireland as one eager to inflict the most grisly and painful death on the smallest and most vulnerable child.

Cooke's tenacity in his punishment of the Irish led to further professional opportunities. In 1651 he went to Kilkenny and Tipperary to chase after a leader of the Irish insurgents.[75] By 1652, the English had declared that any people found within a newly constructed pale in Wicklow were to be regarded as enemies, and Cooke also pursued these men.[76] Cooke's soldiers took part in forays into bogs and woods, chasing down the guerrilla soldiers whose tenacity made the English conquest so protracted. Cooke and the other New England soldiers might even have brought the practice of scalp-taking to Ireland, which was more efficient than the custom of taking entire heads to prove the defeat of the enemy.[77] Cooke's men fired all the houses, cabins, and crops they found, "burning and destroying," he reported in March of 1652, "for four daies." So abundant was the food that even though the men burned their own quarters every day there was still plenty to eat, and only the most "idle soldier" could not find "a fat lamb, veale, pig, poultry, or all of them, every night to his supper."[78] Cooke died two weeks later on his way from Wexford to Dublin when his convoy was attacked by Captain Nash, "a very active enemy." Cooke was shot "with a Brace of Bullets whereof he immediately died." The Dublin commissioners praised Colonel Cooke in a letter to the Speaker of Parliament: "the merit of the Gentleman was very great in his zeal to God, and ye service, and in his activity and valeur against the Common Enemy—in which he hath been sundry times successfull."[79]

As for Samuel Shepard and John Tuttle, their motives for leaving New England remain more obscure, as indeed does the timing. Tuttle had been singled out by Oliver Cromwell as early as 1650 for residence in Ireland and was perhaps flattered by the attention of so distinguished a man. Tuttle was in Ireland by 1654, when he was appointed a commissioner to examine and report the accounts of the army. Tuttle had moved from England to Ireland "at great expense," and petitioned Cromwell as Lord Protector for a satisfactory salary in 1655. He was granted £300 a year.[80] But by 1656, Tuttle had died in Carrickfergus, a location that shows the intention of the English to settle Ulster with English congregationalists, not Scottish Presbyterians. Of the Scots in the north of Ireland Henry Cromwell reported in 1655 that they were "a packe of knaves."[81] Samuel Shepard's Irish career is particularly opaque. Shepard was in Ireland with his wife by 1658 but the Shepards left their daughter with friends in Cambridge (Massachusetts), perhaps waiting until conditions were more settled in Ireland before bringing her to join them.[82]

These four planters together show the important New England characteristics—church membership, colonial leadership, martial experience, and in at least one case intimate acquaintance with New England's indigenous people—that could serve colonists in a second venture in an equally unsettled land. All four were men of New England's first generation. All had weathered the various crises of the first decade of settlement, including Indian wars and a religious schism, and their proven willingness to suppress their foes recommended them for Irish service.

The younger generation was comprised of six preachers and one soldier, Thomas Akers, who went to Ireland about 1649 to fight and was never heard of again.[83] The migration of the six ministers, all Harvard-educated, echoed a pattern for this first generation of Harvard men. As early as 1645, the colony's governor, John Winthrop, remarked on the inability of Harvard graduates to obtain positions, since ministers trained at Harvard soon outnumbered the attractive posts available in New England. The tumult of the

Civil War and Commonwealth, moreover, prodded Harvard-trained ministers versed in congregationalism to take the place of episcopal ministers expelled from their English pulpits. Altogether over one-third of the graduates in the College's first seventeen classes sought employment in Europe.[84]

But if the New England colonists revealed Cromwell's aspirations for a stable and orthodox Irish settlement, the presence of these six New England ministers, and the recruitment efforts of others, demonstrated a more complicated element in Cromwell's aspirations for Ireland's religious settlement. The laity proved suitably ardent in enforcing orthodoxy, but the ministers flagged; the first generation clerics (Patient and Aspinwall) had already been proven theological misfits in orthodox Massachusetts, while the second generation did not embrace the intolerance of their fathers.

Ireland offered these pious puritans of New England's younger generation a chance to serve God in the same momentous way their parents had in their flight to New England. For some of these young men, such as Increase Mather, Nathaniel Brewster, and Joshua Hobart, who paused in Ireland on his way from England to Barbados, preaching in Ireland was a brief stop on what sounds like the New England equivalent of a clerical grand tour. While English-trained ministers ventured to Europe and the Mediterranean, these New Englanders preached their way through Britain and Ireland. John Millard, Edmund Weld, Thomas or Robert Thornton, Thomas Harrison, Samuel Mather, and William Aspinwall served longer terms as Irish preachers. But these ministers, both transient and sedentary, were ultimately unable to transplant the parts of New English culture, especially orthodox puritanism, that Cromwell most desired for his reconfigured Ireland.

The connection here between New England and Ireland is tenuous, a connection more of expectation than of achievement. Too few New Englanders answered the call to go to Ireland, and the records in Ireland are too problematic to delineate their impact. The failed Cromwellian vision for Ireland had many sources, but viewed in the light of New England migration, it reveals the limits of what one colonial region could export to another. The clerical migration to Ireland offered the colony of Massachusetts an opportunity to transfer its most distinctive commodity—the gathered church. Indeed, this ecclesiastical innovation was exactly what Ireland's new leaders sought from New Englanders. In Ireland, however, the ecclesiastical transplantation did not fully take, as, indeed, the complete transformation of Ireland failed. A number of measures indicate that orthodoxy in its Massachusetts or New Haven versions was not planted in Ireland. The mixed Protestant polity in Ireland made rigidity difficult, if not impossible, and the relative toleration of the two Lord Deputies, Charles Fleetwood and Henry Cromwell, likewise impeded a firm puritan settlement.

The shifting church settlement in Ireland is evident partly through the colonial residence of men who were recruited from New England. Altogether twelve ministers went to Ireland, but at least fifteen others were invited.[85] St. John Seymour, who examined the Commonwealth records before they were destroyed, compiled a list of ministers who were invited from New England who *declined* the invitation. This list of luminaries reveals a significant shift in the geographic origins of the men whom Irish authorities courted. Over time, as expectations for an orthodox settlement in Ireland diminished, New Englanders from the most unorthodox colonies came to the attention of recruiters. It is easy to depict New England as a uniform region, but in fact the area contained several different jurisdictions with unique ecclesiastical settlements, each with a different idea about the connection between church membership and civil participation and with varied methods of church organization. In 1651 Cromwell sent a general invitation to several people in Massachusetts inviting them to go to Ireland. These seem to have been invitations broadly distributed, for the General Court of Massachusetts referred to "the great noise and general report of so many invited." In his invitations, Cromwell explained that he believed such a mass migration would be for "the glorie of God and the welfare of this people." The people of Massachusetts disagreed, and the General Court sent a polite letter outlining six objections that focused on the advantages of their settlement in North America. The Court also lamented the "discouragement and weakening to the whole bodie of the colonie" occasioned by these invitations, and the poor reputation that the interest in Ireland brought to Massachusetts, by making it seem deficient by comparison. Although the Court made it clear that none would be prevented from moving there if they were so inclined, it hoped to alert Cromwell to the bounties they enjoyed at home.[86]

Some evidence survives of the specific targets of these invitations. Five Massachusetts ministers were invited by 1651 (Whiting, Cobbett, Knowles, and Bulkeley in 1650, John Cotton in 1651); Comfort Starr, formerly of Massachusetts, was called by the Dublin Commissioners who wrote him in 1653, pleading "Come over and help us."[87] The Commissioners might not have appreciated the phrase's resonance to Starr, who certainly would have recognized the language of the plea; it appears on the seal of the Massachusetts Bay Company, uttered by the Indian contained in the circle. But Starr resisted the appeal and preached in England instead.[88]

When efforts to lure Massachusetts luminaries failed, Cromwell and his commissioners turned their attention to New Haven. John Davenport got the call in 1654. He was promised a "comfortable subsistence and help towards the expense of removing," but declined the opportunity.[89] According to the eighteenth-century historian Thomas Hutchinson, the appeal to New Haven planters received the same solemn consideration that the 1650 invitation to Bulkeley, Cobbett, Whiting, Knowles, Tuttle, and Denyson had merited. The New Haven inhabitants "had serious thoughts of removing but did not carry their design into execution."[90] In the religious geography of the English Atlantic, the recruitment of ministers from these colonies was significant. New Haven and Massachusetts were the most orthodox of puritan polities, the only two colonies where citizenship and full political participation were determined by church membership. Men recognized with civil office in these colonies could be entrusted with the challenges of building a puritan polity in Ireland. Also in 1654 William Courbett, Peter Bulkeley (again), and Samuel Stone of Hartford were solicited to come to Ireland.[91]

By 1656, however, either desperation or a commitment to the religious toleration more characteristic of the English Atlantic as a whole dictated a shift in interest. Henry Dunster, the former president of Harvard, was solicited by Henry Cromwell, then Deputy for Ireland, and his council to come to Ireland but he too declined the opportunity. Dunster was an Anabaptist.[92] In 1656, the commissioners' attention also turned to Plymouth, a New England colony characterized by its greater latitude in church discipline. Edward Bulkeley (Peter's son and at the time a minister in Marshfield), a Mr. Witherell (presumably William Wetherell of Scituate), a Mr. Raynell (probably John Rayner, the minister at Plymouth), and two younger men, Jeremiah Hobart (Harvard graduate, class of 1650, and the younger brother of Joshua Hobart, who did go to Ireland briefly), and John Hubbard or Hobart were invited to Ireland. In that same year an order was passed by the Council that governed Ireland "for encouraging N. E. ministers to come to Ireland."[93] The commissioners broadened their interests and relaxed the requirement for orthodox ministers alone. As a result of the difficulty recruiting orthodox puritans, a variety of puritanisms permeated Ireland from New England and elsewhere, replicating not the orthodoxy of Massachusetts but rather the sectarianism of Rhode Island or England.

Anabaptists were tolerated in Ireland, not only under Fleetwood, who was himself an Anabaptist, but also under Henry Cromwell. As one critic lamented, "the horrid schismes of the Anabaptists, the madnesse of the quakers," joined with "the crueltyes and insolencies of the romane beast" to promise a difficult religious settlement in Ireland.[94] Henry Cromwell reported with some satisfaction that he had managed to bring the Anabaptists "and others" under control, but significantly did not want "to crush them quite, lest through despair they attempt things dangerous." Moreover, Henry Cromwell did not have the stomach for repression; he explained that it was "against his conscience to bear hard upon any, merely upon the account of a different judgment, or to do any thing, that might make them think so."[95]

The conditions in which first Fleetwood and later Cromwell labored in Ireland, a land laid desolate by war and that still required a military presence to regulate a disadvantaged and penalized indigenous population, rendered a firm church settlement more difficult. A variety of indicators point to the failed strict settlement of puritanism in Ireland. The success of an Anabaptist such as Thomas Patient—who was one of only seven ministers appointed in Dublin to determine how to recruit suitable clergy for Ireland—shows that Ireland's Protestant settlement was as broad as England's had become under the Commonwealth. Indeed, on the civil list of 376 ministers were 65 episcopalians.[96] By 1659, William Aspinwall, a Fifth Monarchist, had found his way to an Irish parish in Kilcullen; he had taken part in Massachusetts's great religious upheaval in 1637 during the Antinomian crisis and had moved to Rhode Island.[97] New England's religious radicals had found a new home in Ireland, and even conforming puritans were loathe to take action against them. Samuel Mather himself, whose orthodox puritan credentials in terms of education and parentage were sterling, refused to enforce requirements that episcopal ministers be displaced.[98] Two other measures point to the failed settlement. Quakers suffered persecution in Ireland but not the death sentences meted out in Massachusetts. And another occasional indicator of a strict puritan regime and godly reformation in behavior, witch accusations, shows the relative leniency of the Irish church settlement: St. John Seymour's search through Irish records yielded one trial ending in an acquittal.[99] So New England's greatest potential contribution to Atlantic religious and political affairs, the gathered church and the association of civic participation with church membership, failed to take root in Ireland. But in fact if we can see that the Massachusetts and New Haven ecclesiastical structures failed to take hold, the relatively latitidinarian policies of Rhode Island and Plymouth colonies and of England itself did. Those same men and women who left Massachusetts for England and other destinations to seek greater freedom in worship found their way to Ireland.

If a religious settlement along congregational lines faltered, dependent as it was on failed recruitment of enough experienced colonists and the context of a land laid waste by war, the English military occupation of the island did not. Although the envisioned mass expulsion did not come to pass, the English nonetheless displaced and demeaned the Irish in order to strengthen English dominion. Ireland's Catholic population suffered terribly in what Jane H. Ohlmeyer has characterized as an "all-encompassing calamity." Estimates suggest that Catholic landholding declined from fifty-nine percent in 1641 to twenty-two percent in 1688.[100]

The Irish Catholics who were the targets of the military campaign and subsequent forced relocation within Ireland and across the Atlantic cast their own memories and responses in terms of migration. The political poems of the 1650s barely touch on the ordeal of the war itself. They focus instead on defeat and on the subsequent penalties imposed on the Irish, and they particularly emphasize the forced migration that accompanied English conquest. Irish soldiers were transported to serve in Spanish and other continental armies; thousands of other Irish Catholics were transported to American colonies overseas; and thousands more were subjected to the forcible transplantation of the Act of Settlement. In some of these poems, English phrases appear amid the Irish: "*All the English language I can recollect is,* transport, transplant, shoot him, kill him."[101] The intimate pairing of the violent murderous assault of English armies with the consequence of that conflict, forced transplantation, highlights the migratory ordeal. Other poems Hibernicized English words: in one poem that similarly linked the appropriation ("he ordered their lands to be measured with ropes"), replacement and confiscation ("he replaced the pure Irish with Saxons"), and displacement ("and transplanted them all") of conquest, transplantation appears as *transplantátion*.[102]

The experience New Englanders brought with them made them in some respects model planters, civil magistrates, ministers, and military officials, but at the same time the gathering of colonial clerics in Dublin prompted the Lord Deputy Henry Cromwell to scrutinize how colonial environments altered men's behavior. The accumulated wisdom of various colonial enterprises ultimately resulted not in this instance in a successfully transplanted religious orthodoxy but rather in a fresh assessment of colonization as an enterprise that molded men's characters, and not for the better. Although men from one colony might prove valuable and experienced additions to a second, Cromwell, who was a thoughtful observer of political and social dynamics in Ireland, worried that these experienced settlers brought problems unique to colonial circumstances. He reported to John Thurloe that several ministers from all over Ireland had recently met in Dublin in 1658 and had assured him that religious affairs were in order. Cromwell believed that the ministers might be right, but then again observed that "Something is indeed to be abated for the flattering genius, which usually reigns in colonies, such as Ireland is."[103] He elaborated on this point in a letter the same day to his brother-in-law. " 'Tis true," Cromwell explained, "we are but a kind of colony, the inhabitants of which places are commonly more compliant with their present governours, more flexible to change, more dextrous in the practise of flattery than other men; for their being indigent and continual suitors for some advantage or other, pensioners to the publick, *such as have tryed their fortunes in many places before*, used to the little tyranny of country governours, and always in expectation of changes in their superiours, makes them such; begetting in them a genius, more ingenious indeed, but less ingenuous than those have, who reside nearer the seat of empire."[104]

Cromwell's observations reflect one of the contributions New England made not just to Ireland but to an evolving imperial conceptualization. Cromwell was able to generalize on the basis of his Irish experience both because of the number of colonies England had successfully established by the 1650s and because of the relocated colonists he encountered in Ireland. His depiction of the synod of sycophants who assured him of the solid state of religious affairs in Ireland is particularly interesting because four of the most important figures in religious life in Dublin were the former New Englanders Thomas Patient, William Harrison, Nathaniel Brewster, and Samuel Mather. Harrison and Brewster were Cromwell's particular confidants and travel companions, although Brewster had left by 1658.

Cromwell paired the practice of migration and the unique culture of colonies in his critique. Colonies required their own special asymmetries of power, and men with experience in different places under different leaders were particularly adept at negotiating these dynamics to their own advantage. Transplanted colonists permitted him to assess the nature of colonial societies. He learned to distrust his most intimate religious advisors because of how the colonial setting shaped their character. In this regard, we come full circle, back to an environmental model of character formation. In sixteenth-century Ireland the English devised models of cultural degeneracy to explain the failings of the Old English, men who identified too strongly with the Irish they were supposed to govern. In seventeenth-century Ireland another English ruler could see in the men around him the weakening impact of a colonial setting far from "the seat of empire" where men strived to curry favor. But in the sixteenth century, it was the deleterious influence of the Irish that corrupted the English. By the 1650s, Cromwell suspected, it was colonization itself and the migration it required that undermined men's characters. Familiarity with the exigencies of colonial life and the practical need for men to migrate to new settlements induced a pessimistic view of colonial planters among colonial leaders.

All new undertakings were logically planned and envisioned in light of prior experiments. The investors at Jamestown cast about and hired men with experience in military, maritime, and commercial ventures for their Chesapeake undertaking. The proprietors of Madagascar fused East and West Indian experiences and looked especially at Atlantic models in their aspirations for success in the Indian Ocean. They even found an experienced Caribbean governor to lead their envisioned sugar colony. In their renewed effort to subdue Ireland, English conquerors did the same. But by the time

Henry Cromwell considered the fate of his Irish experiment, the English had almost a century of experience as colonizers in Ireland, a period long enough to accommodate four generations of invaders and their progeny. The consequence was a pessimistic assessment of what such experience might offer. If all proprietors and investors adhered to the wisdom of hiring experienced men, Cromwell suggested the limitations of such individuals— too much identification with their new home, too much malleability, too willing to please rulers one served under temporarily. As their contemporaries understood, colonists, too, were travelers, people who might be easily molded or wholly transformed by external circumstances, like the aspiring traders whose loyalty the East India Company mistrusted, or the ministers whose visits to Catholic sites raised concerns about conversion, or the tourist whose change of clothing suggested a new identity.

The English colonists who moved from New England to Ireland, especially those men such as Ludlow or Cooke, were hardly interested in altering their identity nor in expressing an appreciation for the culture or customs of Irish around them. They were committed puritans, unable to imagine any value in Irish ways of life. But Henry Cromwell's comment about the malleability of colonists points to another kind of cosmopolitanism, this one well within their reach: this was their ability to adapt to the demands and wishes of different colonial governors, to please those in command if it served their advantage, to adapt not to those beneath them in a colonial hierarchy, one that in Ireland was shaped by religion and ethnicity, but rather to those above them whose favor could advance their own interests.

Whatever malleability led officials to mistrust colonists, the state displayed a new commitment in the 1650s to colonization as an important path toward geopolitical dominion. If colonies were not always profitable, they were often essential to fend off rival claimants to territory, to regulate unwilling subjects, and to protect England's vulnerable coastlines. These imperatives united in the 1650s, as Oliver Cromwell sought simultaneously to secure Ireland by enticing new colonists there and by isolating the Irish, and to absorb new territory in the West Indies with the help of subjects. Experiences in Ireland crystallized the need for coercion. Success in Ireland hinged on the forced participation of British subjects—English, Welsh, Scots, and Irish. The dramatic growth of the army and navy heralded the change. An army once based around decentralized militia service swelled by 1653 to a permanent force of some 30,000 men. A navy fleet that had contained only some 4,000 men during the major English assault on the Île de Rhé in 1628 grew to almost 20,000 in 1653. Previously the navy had been a mixture of private and government ships, but after 1653 the state made a commitment to funding both the navy and the army. And these forces became permanent fixtures. This shift took place largely between 1649 and 1660, and Ireland exemplified the transition.[105] A new pattern, violent, coercive, and state-orchestrated, was established in Ireland in the 1650s and it shaped English overseas activities in the centuries to come. This new pattern paralleled, rivaled—and over time came to eclipse—the cosmopolitan accommodation essential to trade relations that had its origins in the Mediterranean and that had sustained English expansion since the 1570s.

CONCLUSION

By the middle of the seventeenth century, England had transformed itself from a weak kingdom on the margins of Europe, one struggling to participate in the major overseas opportunities of the period, to a nation able to vie with and sometimes to defeat Dutch, French, Portuguese, and Spanish rivals in their competition for new territory and coveted commodities. At the accession of Elizabeth in 1558, the English traded in western Europe and fished in the North Atlantic but elsewhere were a negligible presence, not even in firm control of Ireland. Charles II came to the throne in 1660 to an altered world characterized by vigorous English engagement in colonization and commerce. A tour of the globe at the restoration reveals small and sometimes lucrative pockets of English settlement and enterprise. The English had acquired considerable strongholds in the Atlantic, where colonies in the West Indies and on the North American mainland signaled the viability of English settlement schemes. English trade was secured in the Mediterranean and the Indies, although individual trade factories flourished or failed with the volatility common to all new undertakings in a developing economy.

The English had claimed, acquired, and built this collection of overseas territories and trading ventures in a distinctive style derived from their position of weakness in the sixteenth century. Several core ingredients defined their approach: private companies with loose royal oversight, multiple styles of engagement with an emphasis on accommodation, the circulation of men among different ocean basins, the knowledge and experience they carried, and the impact of events in overseas ventures both on newly imagined enterprises and on affairs at home. At its inception, this had been a highly decentralized system. The impoverished Elizabethan state, eager to participate in global enterprises but unable to fund expensive and risky undertakings, turned to private companies with royal monopolies. Late and often last among Atlantic Europeans to reach remote ports, the English by necessity learned from others and sought to accommodate foreign customs and people. Their accumulation of overseas territories and opportunities was facilitated by the people who staffed every enterprise, the traders, mariners, ministers, soldiers, governors, consuls, and colonists who populated trading factories, fisheries, colonies, and other extractive ventures. These individuals brought knowledge and experience from one venture to the next, and they similarly circulated their painfully acquired wisdom in hundreds of manuscripts and printed texts, reaching well beyond their immediate circle and shaping English and company policies. These men lay at the heart of English expansion.

To assert the centrality of cosmopolitanism in England's transition from a weak kingdom to an emerging power is not to deny the reality and importance of its opposite: xenophobia. Not all English who traveled abroad embraced the unfamiliarity of new surroundings, and many English overseas enterprises were predicated on the displacement of indigenous people and foreign rivals, not a cultural embrace. The son of the English trader William Eaton and the Japanese woman Kamezō, like Thomas Rolfe, the son of the planter John Rolfe and Pocahontas, represented one possible English response to a world beyond its shores, but these offspring (who lived simultaneously in England) were also part of a world of vicious loathing of foreigners, both within Europe and far from home. Cosmopolitanism in this context was not a coherent system of behavior or a uniform worldview. Rather, it emerged organically and by necessity from a willingness (for some, a predisposition) to learn how to respond to new circumstances. And this willingness, with each individual who sailed from England, embedded England in a transformed global world.

This cosmopolitan sensibility was an approach the English had forged first and most urgently in the Mediterranean, and they deployed it around the world in Asia and America as they sought to establish themselves during the first decades of English expansion. Two other trends, however, accompanied this process of expansion; they had emerged by the 1650s and challenged the relevance and necessity of an accommodating demeanor. One trend was toward centralization; the second was toward the use of coercion and force. Both were linked. If cosmopolitanism had first made the British empire, it ultimately became less relevant.

The most pronounced shift in the period lay in the government's eagerness to take direct control over its overseas holdings. Oliver Cromwell had signaled this commitment, linking labor, coercion, and empire, in his dual conquests of Jamaica and Ireland. Cromwell's hope to exile Scots and Irish to Jamaica and to persuade colonists from the North American mainland and colonies such as Nevis to migrate to new and fragile settlements points to a hemispheric vision of English territories. The planned relocations of the 1650s drew on the entire British population, conceptualizing new undertakings both in terms of the people available within the kingdoms at home and the populations likely to move from established settlements across the Atlantic. These migrations tightened the Atlantic world, enabling dreams of exploitation, appropriation, and profit to flourish and yoking far-flung territories together. The convergence of events in the 1650s was crucial in clarifying new imperial strategies. There were four key ingredients: several decades of English experience establishing colonies, an available pool of skilled settlers ready to relocate, an uprising in Ireland that demanded an inventive and coherent response to the challenges of pacification, and, finally, Cromwell's aspiration for English power in the Caribbean, with its own requirements for soldiers and settlers.

All these variables were united in the hands of a state that took charge of people for its own imperial purposes. And in the hands of a stronger state, with a large army and navy, the government could impose its will, not only over its own subjects but over its rivals, seizing territory from the Spanish in Jamaica in 1655 or from the Dutch in New York in 1664. New capability, new confidence, and the weakness of some old rivals enabled the English to adopt a new demeanor in overseas ventures, replacing accommodation with brute force.

One of the most vivid symbols of a state's authority over its subjects is the regulation of their persons. Capital punishment takes that physical control to its most extreme form, but forced migration is part of the same spectrum of violence and coercion. By the 1650s, state regulation over people in England and its colonies coincided with state aspirations to regulate territory: the two were intertwined, and without the former the latter would fail. If "Empire," as David Armitage has written, "was always a language of power," it was also about the tangible implementation of that power, and the state's coercive authority took intimate, bodily, and geographic dimensions by the middle of the seventeenth century.[1] The coerced and voluntary relocations of this period orchestrated by English leaders anticipated some of the large-scale labor migrations of later periods that were designed to benefit the global British empire: forced African migration across the Atlantic, banished dissidents and criminals turned into bound laborers, and Indian contract labor. All of these came to define the British empire, and they had their origins in the 1650s. First chartered in 1660 as the Company of Royal Adventurers Trading to Africa, and rechartered in 1672, the Royal African Company's monopoly on the slave trade highlighted the state's growing commitment to coerced labor. It signaled, moreover, a shift in English connections to slavery and the slave trade. This book has highlighted the many different experiences the English had with slavery: they worked as pirates and slavers in the Mediterranean, sought to enter the Indian Ocean slave trade from their Madagascar base, bought and sold people when they had opportunity to do so, embraced slavery in Barbados in the 1640s, were served and accompanied and rowed by slaves, and also found themselves enslaved. After 1650, however, the more common English experience was not as the victim of slavery, but rather as the perpetrator.

None of this interest in mobilizing the bodies of subjects, whether in the army, the navy, bound in the hold of a ship, or part of a colonial enterprise, would have been possible without a shift in the state's conception of its role in overseas affairs. State centralization slowly began to erode an old style of piecemeal expansion governed by the large overseas companies. Trading companies that had once carried out their own diplomacy, funded their own armies, fortified their trading posts, and equipped their merchant ships with heavy guns for protection found some of these functions reclaimed by the state. The trend accelerated in the 1640s and became more pronounced in the 1650s. The Navigation Acts of 1660 and 1663 (originally passed by Cromwell in 1651 and confirmed by Charles II) were part of this process. Although these acts were oriented toward enhancing revenue and control, they also reflected a new attitude toward overseas holdings, one that joined different enterprises together in a coherent mercantile system and that codified through law the networks and linkages previously forged by individual adventurers and trading companies. The Council of Trade was established in 1650 to help administer territory, and by the 1670s, the Privy Council acquired responsibility for the regulation of plantations in the Americas and the West Indies. Both bodies centralized available information in order to inform crown policy. The crown also assumed direct control for diplomacy. The old trading companies in Europe, responsible for negotiating their own trade privileges with foreign rulers, largely disbanded by the end of the seventeenth century as the state sent its own diplomats to conduct negotiations. With the rise of a state-funded navy after 1650, the Eastland Company, whose trade focused on the Baltic and its naval stores, also faded away.[2]

The new king accelerated this trend toward centralization. Charles II embraced the global opportunities he inherited along with the crown. Although he sought in some ways to distance himself from the international accomplishments of his predecessor, the larger theme of his reign from the perspective of imperial aspirations was one of continuity and of new coherence to previously discrete endeavors. Charles faced considerable challenges when he came to the throne and overseas holdings were an integral part of both the problem and the solution. After two decades of intense political upheaval in the English Atlantic, the loyalty of English people who lived in North America and the Caribbean was uncertain, and he had to secure their fidelity. He also confronted the continued financial constraints that had so plagued his father, and he envisioned overseas holdings as potential sources of liquid revenue. His reign witnessed the aggressive extension of English territorial ambitions in North America: New York (acquired from the Dutch), the Jerseys, the Carolinas, Pennsylvania—these new ventures, organized as proprietary colonies under favored courtiers and supporters, were launched under Charles's reign. Charles II brought existing ventures under tighter control, requiring new charters for some existing colonies (especially those in New England) and seeking new methods to enhance revenue from overseas sources.

Yet this move toward centralization was a trend, not a universal policy shift, and the English continued to pursue multiple strategies. The Royal African Company may have signaled the state's support of trade in people, yet the Company's traders relied on an accommodating demeanor in order to secure trading privileges from coastal rulers in Africa. Another new trading company established at Hudson's Bay (1670) in order to pursue the fur trade similarly relied on commercial policies geared toward cooperation. Moreover, expansion and the imposition of order on acquired territories and people continued to challenge the English. If the events of the 1650s in Ireland and the Caribbean revealed a new understanding of how the state might benefit from a systematic assertion of dominion over people and places, old patterns continued. Colonization and commercial schemes continued to overlap and intersect, never moving on parallel tracts but always intertwined, generating peculiar and misplaced plans for exploitation. Indigenous people continued to assert their own will against invaders and occupiers, often forcing the English to comply with local customs, to conform to regional styles of interaction, or to abandon new ventures altogether. The aborted English occupation of Tangier, which was a state-sponsored venture, illustrates the continuation of these multiple and sometimes incompatible patterns.

Tangier, acquired by the English in 1661, came at a moment when, thanks to activities in the Indian and Atlantic Oceans, the English had a range of experiences in their arsenal of commercial and colonial expansion. Until the 1660s, English engagement in the Mediterranean was characterized by a pragmatic style of accommodation and dissimulation. Both qualities facilitated travel and especially trade, the main reason that the English entered the region in the first place. Decked in local garb, adept in indigenous languages, scrupulously adhering to local sumptuary laws, prepared to deny both nationality and religion, the prudent and accommodating English travelers in the region proved walking advertisements for Fynes

Moryson's injunction: "he that cannot dissemble, cannot live."[3] The English had exported this style of interaction to trading posts around the world and even to new colonial settlements such as Virginia in the first decades of the seventeenth century.

In 1661, however, England's relationship with the Mediterranean changed. With the marriage of Charles II to Catherine of Braganza, the English restored dynastic ties with the Catholic monarchs of southwestern Europe. And with Catherine's dowry, Charles acquired the fortified North African city of Tangier. Tangier gave the English both a first tenuous toehold in a Muslim stronghold and a strategically and financially advantageous port. Demonstrating their eagerness to embrace the emphasis on force that had emerged as a hemispheric strategy under Oliver Cromwell, the English attempted to apply coercive habits of colonization and commerce learned elsewhere to the region where the English previously had to travel so gently and carefully. Yet the example of Tangier demonstrates both the continued tenacity of Mediterranean patterns and, as witnessed in the failed settlements on Madagascar, the difficulty of transplanting more aggressive models of colonization in this period. Even at the end of the seventeenth century, the Mediterranean remained a region outside of English control and dominion, one where English success depended on accommodation to local mores. It was a lesson the English learned again, in a refresher course of earlier discoveries.

English ambitions for Tangier reveal expectations about colonization and trade on a global scale. By the 1660s, the English had learned a great deal about the world and how to interact with foreigners. If Mediterranean styles of accommodation were once exported with English traders around the globe, patterns of bellicose interaction developed and deployed elsewhere in North America could similarly be transported back to the Mediterranean. It was soon clear in Tangier that, when it was possible, the English were eager to embrace a more rigid and exclusionary style of domination: they promptly banished decades of timorous and tactful interactions in the region for an impractical and unrealized colonization scheme and the fortification of the town. In their efforts to turn Tangier into a profitable port, however, the English recreated the cosmopolitan commercial communities that characterized the Ottoman Mediterranean. Inexperience at governing such a cosmopolitan world and the necessity for constant military vigilance undermined the viability of the Tangier experiment.

Where the English had previously traveled gently in the Mediterranean as a vulnerable minority, in Tangier they signaled their arrival with expensive fortification schemes that reflected their apprehension about likely attacks by the Moroccans they both disdained and rightly feared and whom they banned from the city except between "sun & sun."[4] Tangier ultimately became an important naval base (another indicator of the new era of state centralization) and commercial port for the English, its value embodied in the large pier whose construction and maintenance proved a steady English preoccupation.[5] But before English officials determined the city's strategic and economic role, one enthusiastic supporter of Tangier, an Englishman named James Wilson, proposed an elaborate colonization scheme for the city and its hinterland.[6] Wilson readily conceded the commercial opportunities the city afforded, but his ambition was more broadly strategic and colonial, and in that respect consistent with the coherent vision that had begun to emerge under Cromwell in the 1650s. Wilson believed that English settlement of Tangier offered two benefits: first, it could thwart Spanish power, and, second, it could prevent the Portuguese and the Dutch from defeating the English in trade with Europe or the East Indies, serving in this respect as a crucial linchpin in English global strategies. But to secure the status of the town, Wilson advocated not only the construction of fortifications and an enormous pier, a point on which most agreed. He also insisted on the necessity of colonization, by which he meant the aggressive recruitment of men and women to settle there in a model that by 1661 had become increasingly common in the Atlantic, as the forced recruitments associated with the Western Design and the occupation of Ireland revealed. Like all colonization schemes, his drew directly on prior efforts, wherever they might be found, and on contemporary religious and political concerns in England. He readily integrated the global and the national, just as predecessors had done in planning Virginia and Madagascar.

The scale of Wilson's ambitions was considerable. He set his plan in the specific context of Britain's complex and multiple kingdoms, proposing that if one-third of the population of Scotland ventured to Tangier, it would be no loss for the king, who derived little benefit from that kingdom, but a great gain for Tangier. Drawing on previous plans for recruitment, Wilson suggested that all English ministers be required to tell their parishioners how they could improve themselves and promote England's trade by resettling in Tangier. Moreover, he hoped that English circuit judges would become engaged in recruitment, while schoolmasters should "aplaud out the poets such as passed seas & land to setle new collonis," which would, he was sure, "so worke with younger fry that theire would be found in a short time more then sufficent." Such historical figures as Walter Ralegh and John Smith had inspired other English colonial ventures, including the two settlements on Madagascar, so Wilson correctly assessed the value of historical guides in launching new undertakings. He likewise drew on the religious rivalries that continued to characterize European geopolitics. Zealous Protestants, particularly those who "are of a homor to pull downe the pope," would be particularly engaged in the enterprise because of the closer proximity of their target, although he also conceded more pedestrian motivations for those lured by the gold of Barbary. The recruitment of Protestants from the continent, facilitated by royal agents established for that purpose, would further bolster the town's prospects, and Wilson envisioned assimilation of these foreigners into "good english men" in the space of one generation, just as Henry Cromwell had hoped in 1655 that the Irish might be turned into good English subjects in Jamaica.[7] Murderers might well be banished to Tangier, where they would "become honest people," but he drew the line at drunkards. Wilson was adamant on the need to include women, whom he regarded as important for cultural reasons, their presence rendering English men more tractable and preventing their unnecessary and scandalous recourse to "women of the country," a social practice that was a defining feature of English commercial culture overseas and which he emphatically rejected.

Proximity, a familiar climate: all boded well for this venture, making it, Wilson argued, more profitable than either the East or West Indies. He even assured the king of a silver mine to rival Potosí. He imagined the creation of the free port as part of a process of "perfecting the worke of making our nation masters when not of all yet of the greates parte of the comerce of the world." Wilson envisioned a line of English settlement that stretched to Tripoli: in other words, he pictured a European settlement on the model of the North American coast, mirrored directly across the Atlantic on the African coast, characterized by loosely contiguous pockets of English settlement.

This plan explicitly emulated Atlantic models, and if decades earlier the Mediterranean had inspired Virginia, in the 1660s, North America inspired the Mediterranean. In fact, Tangier ended up as a fortified commercial town. It contained a large garrison, a city council, and a cosmopolitan merchant community. Surviving documents indicate considerable tension between these different constituencies. The success of the city as a free port depended on the ability of the English to recruit an international commercial community there and to guarantee them the legal protections necessary to transact business. Although Tangier's profits derived from its commercial enterprises, the English remained preoccupied by issues of security and were similarly ambivalent about the composition of the commercial community. Tangier's population, like that of nearby Ottoman and North African ports, was polyglot and multinational, with English merchants, Dutch, Portuguese, French, Italians, and Jews all in residence.[8] The English in Tangier even had a galley that was fueled by slave labor.[9]

The English, however, were less adept at reproducing the complex legal privileges that permitted these groups in the Ottoman world to function legally and economically and to worship freely. A city council complete with alderman replicated the structures of an English urban government, but the merchants, both freemen and denizens, worried about safeguarding their financial interests. When one merchant, the Genoese Benita Moroone, was ordered to pay forty-eight percent interest for a debt that he said was not his to pay, and then imprisoned, a number of foreign merchants petitioned the authorities for redress. They had settled in Tangier, they asserted, assured of justice and equity, and had generally found them, but they worried in 1668 or 1669 that changes in the civil government would damage their privileges. They were excluded from the common council and therefore unable to speak for themselves.[10] There was even a population of "African Jewes" in Tangier, but they were expelled in October of 1672, rejecting the model of Ottoman pluralism of the region.[11]

For all the centrality of commerce, Tangier was overshadowed by its military presence and intense fortifications: the large garrison manifested the new importance of the army in England's international ambitions. The martial tone was pronounced, with soldiers and the military justice that governed them visible. The company of soldiers contributed to the quirky cultural milieu of the port: one evening in February of 1670 the soldiers of the garrison performed John Dryden's *The Indian Emperor*, "where some of them did very well."[12] The play, written in 1667, was a sequel to *The Indian Queen* and was set during the Spanish conquest of Mexico. If the ambitious James Wilson could not replicate Potosí and Spanish successes in Tangier, the garrison's entertainment could make the link for him.

English claims to Tangier added a new level of diplomatic disturbance to an already volatile region, but the English presence in North Africa also enhanced English safety.[13] English travelers and merchants, for example, could enjoy the protection of the English navy on its way to Tangier rather than experience the usual perilous journey through the Straits and into the Mediterranean, protected only by the guns that merchants were willing to buy for their fleets.[14] From Tangier, moreover, the English could labor more efficiently for the redemption of English captives. Scores of Englishmen were redeemed from captivity in Algiers in 1672 and embarked from there to Tangier in several English ships.[15]

If, however, Tangier altered English interaction in the region, giving the English a feeling of military security that rendered unnecessary the timorous conduct that had earlier characterized English engagement in the Mediterranean, the change proved short-lived. The Moroccans had other plans for Tangier. Despite English efforts to ban them from the city, their persistent attacks on the city made it too expensive to fortify and defend. The English evacuated in 1683–1684, ending English claims in the region and returning the English to the old accommodating style of travel and trade in the Mediterranean. At the end of their occupation, English engineers set to work blasting the pier and fortifications into rubble, an overt symbol of their failed tenure in the region. English designs for mastery in the Mediterranean were thwarted until 1704, when the English took Gibraltar, and prudent English travelers and traders resumed their older style of interaction in the region. Tangier, then, proved a false cadence. Great expectations to remedy the financial plight of the monarchy, to infuse energy into global colonization schemes, and to gain a perch in the Mediterranean remained unfulfilled. The English reverted for a little while longer to the dominant Mediterranean style, in which persuasion and dissimulation promised more success than force and violence.

The Tangier case exemplifies the continued existence of multiple English paths toward imperial rule. It revealed a new commitment to force and displacement, one made possible by the army and navy who occupied the town. But this settlement continued to be conceptualized as so many new ventures were, in light of what had gone before. In this instance, Wilson looked west across the Atlantic to America in order to imagine how a settlement in North Africa might emerge.

While the clear trend in the middle of the seventeenth century, seen even in the failure at Tangier but more readily in the many simultaneous efforts elsewhere, was toward a centralized imperial state, one interested more in displacing and regulating foreign people than on accommodating their mores, the assimilationist style endured. It appeared wherever small cadres of English sought to trade in places ranging from Hudson Bay to West Africa. It manifested itself in places where the English occupied a weak diplomatic or strategic position, whether against other Europeans or indigenous people, and prudence compelled them to charm rivals and to woo allies. As had been true in 1580 or 1620, the English always had multiple ways of interacting with the world beyond their shores. Their ability to impose their will through force did not obviate the importance of reaching out in less coercive ways. They turned when possible to violence and coercion, and especially by the second quarter of the seventeenth century violence emerged as a dominant style in the Atlantic. But in a period when prosperity still came primarily from commercial ventures in Asia and the Middle East, the English relied on the accommodating style of the trading factory. Only slowly, in fits and starts, did the English learn how to subordinate people around the world and they discovered repeatedly, in a succession of new and unfamiliar places, the many constraints that hindered their goals.

The British Empire ultimately spanned the world—but first the world made the empire, through the weight of history and experience that shaped ventures in new places and that individuals linked in their travels. Single voyages created initial ties between England and distant places, but the repeated movement of people wove a dense web with London at the center, and thickening linkages of personnel and knowledge continued to inform all subsequent ventures. Migration of people and of expertise created its own distinctive geography and culture of empire. Those interested in securing new territory or opening new trade reached out, both to the past and all around the world, seeking the experience of those who had tried their hand at other ventures. The English had learned during their first tentative forays between 1560 and 1660 that innovation helped secure success. Individuals—their adaptability, their knowledge, their expertise—anchored that process. A willingness to learn from rivals, from precedent, from simultaneous efforts elsewhere, all formed an English style of expansion. As numerous experiments indicated, including in places as diverse as Madagascar and Tangier, there was no single colonial template in place, no clear sense yet that people around the world could be lumped together as subjects to be governed in a uniform style under British administrators and governors. This sensibility was characteristic of a later style of British rule, and perhaps the logical consequence of the trends evident in the seventeenth century toward centralization and force. But even as the assimilationist model waned, replaced by racist ideas that called for rigid hierarchies, displacement, separation, and exclusion, and even as cosmopolitanism no longer defined how the English would encounter the world, the larger lessons cosmopolitans had imparted—the necessity of knowing and understanding the world beyond England's shores—shaped the empire that came in their wake.

ABBREVIATIONS

Add.	Additional Manuscripts
BL	The British Library, London, England
Bodleian	The Bodleian Library, Oxford, England
CSPC CD-ROM	*The Calendar of State Papers, Colonial: North America and the West Indies, 1574–1739*, version 1.0 (Routledge, 2000) CD-Rom
CSPC-East Indies	W. Noel Sainsbury, ed. *Calendar of State Papers, Colonial Series, East Indies, China and Japan* (London: Her Majesty's Stationery Office, 1870)
CSPD	*Calendar of State Papers, Domestic Series 1547–1704* (London: Green, Longmans and Roberts, 1856–1872)
Folger	The Folger Shakespeare Library, Washington, D.C.
Games, *Migration*	Alison Games, *Migration and the Origins of the English Atlantic World* (Cambridge, Mass.: Harvard University Press, 1999)
Huntington	The Henry E. Huntington Library, San Marino, Calif.
IOR	India Office Records, The British Library
NAS	National Archives of Scotland, Edinburgh
NLS	National Library of Scotland, Edinburgh
PRO	The Public Record Office, TNA

Records of the Virginia Company	Susan Myra Kingsbury, ed., *The Records of the Virginia Company of London*, four volumes (Washington, 1906–1935)
TNA	The National Archives of the United Kingdom, Kew

NOTES

INTRODUCTION 1

1. Patrick Copland, *Virginia's God be Thanked* (London, 1622), 6–7. This was possibly his third voyage. See S. J. McNally, "The Chaplains of the East India Company" (1971, 1976), 26, typescript in the Oriental and India Office Collections Reading Room, BL.
2. Dale was dead by the time of this 1620 storm; although Copland remembered that he met Dale in Japan, either they met a year earlier or Copland simply intended Japan to refer to the whole East Indies (May 7, 1623, *Records of the Virginia Company*, vol. 2, 400).
3. Thomas Dale to the East India Company, March 1, 1619, Jacatra, *CSPC-East Indies, 1617–1621*, vol. 3, item 609, 254; Dale to Sir William Throckmorton, Jacatra, 15 March 1618/19, L.b.667, Folger.
4. See especially Kenneth R. Andrews, *Trade, Plunder, and Settlement: Maritime Enterprise and the Genesis of the British Empire, 1480–1630* (New York: Cambridge University Press, 1984).
5. The Scots did not form a unified cohort within English enterprises, in contrast to the Portuguese within the Spanish world. See Daviken Studnicki-Gizbert, *A Nation Upon the Ocean Sea: Portugal's Atlantic Diaspora and the Crisis of the Spanish Empire, 1492–1640* (New York: Oxford University Press, 2007).
6. Thomas Smith, *An Account of the Greek Church* (London, 1680), A2recto; James Spens to his parents, 23 February 1632 (new style), RH 9/2/242, NAS.
7. Tony Ballantyne employs the metaphor of the webs of empire for a later period in *Orientalism and Race: Aryanism in the British Empire* (New York: Palgrave, 2002). For cosmopolitanism in this period, see Margaret C. Jacob, *Strangers Nowhere in the World: The Rise of Cosmopolitanism in Early Modern Europe* (Philadelphia: University of Pennsylvania Press, 2006). David J. Hancock profiles a group of

eighteenth-century Scottish cosmopolitans in *Citizens of the World: London Merchants and the Integration of the British Atlantic Community, 1735–1785* (New York: Cambridge University Press, 1995).

8. For examples of new approaches to imperial history, see Nicholas Canny, ed., *The Oxford History of the British Empire*, vol. 1, *The Origins of Empire* (Oxford: Oxford University Press, 1999), which emphasizes the accidental nature of English imperial expansion; and Kathleen Wilson, *A New Imperial History: Culture, Identity, and Modernity in Britain and the Empire, 1660–1840* (Cambridge: Cambridge University Press, 2004).

9. Nathaniel Butler, *The Historye of the Bermudaes or Summer Islands* (London: Hakluyt Society, 1882), 1.

10. Dutch report of Thomas King's activities, in Joyce Lorimer, *English and Irish Settlements on the River Amazon, 1550–1646* (London: Hakluyt Society, 1989), 159.

11. Nathaniel Butler, *Colloquia Maritima: or Sea-Dialogues* (London, 1688), 88.

12. Richard Boothby, *A Briefe Discovery or Description of the most Famous Island of Madagascar, or St. Lawrence in Asia neare unto East-India* (London, 1646), 1; Mr. James Wilson to (?), 5 October 1661, Add. 4191, fols. 11–14, BL.

13. H. V. Bowen, *Elites, Enterprise, and the Making of the British Overseas Empire, 1688–1775* (New York: St. Martin's, 1996), 5.

CHAPTER 1

1. James Spens to his parents, 23 February 1632 (new style), RH 9/2/242, NAS. Spens's letters can be found in RH 9/2/231–242.

2. As many as twenty percent of young men emigrated from Scotland in this period. On the migration of Scots to the continent, see T. C. Smout, Ned Landsman, and T. M. Devine, "Scottish Emigration in the Seventeenth and Eighteenth Centuries," in Nicholas Canny, ed., *Europeans on the Move: Studies on European Migration, 1500–1800* (Oxford: Oxford University Press, 1994), 85. The Scots traveler William Lithgow remarked on the many Scots he encountered in Poland. He believed the wealth from Poland to be the origin of the wealth of the best Scots merchants. Lithgow estimated 30,000 Scots families there. He may not have been as far off as that number suggests since between 30,000 and 40,000 Scots migrated to Poland between 1600 and 1650. William Lithgow, *The Totall Discourse, of the Rare Adventures, and Painfull Peregrinations of Long nineteene Years Travayles* (London, 1632), 422.

3. James Spens to his wife, Riga, 1628, RH 9/2/237, NAS.

4. James Spens to his parents, Riga, 1 October 1630, RH 9/2/240, NAS.

5. James Spens to his parents, Amsterdam, 12 November 1631, RH 9/2/241, NAS.

6. James Spens to his mother, Riga, 24 May [no year], RH 9/2/238, NAS.

7. Court minutes for the East India Company, 4 December 1607, B/3, fol. 64recto, IOR, BL. Palmer's book was apparently based on Theodor Zwinger, *Methodus apodemica* (Basel, 1577).

8. Sara Warneke has explored this subject in *Images of the Educational Traveller in Early Modern England* (New York: Brill, 1995), 6–8, 14.

9. Anthony Parr's analysis of the genre of travel plays in this period suggests that English interest in travel was paired with "anxiety about the moral and physical danger posed by foreign places." Theater was one venue in which a growing public curiosity about travel and about the larger world more generally might be satisfied. Plays dramatized events around the world, including colonial affairs and famous travel accounts. Anthony Parr, ed., *Three Renaissance Travel Plays* (Manchester, UK: Manchester University Press, 1995), introduction, quotation from p. 2.

10. Joseph Hall, *Quo Vadis: A Just Censure of Travell* (London, 1617), A3verso–A4recto, A5recto, 1–6, 35, 36, 65–66, 87–88. Those who pursued Hall's advice and resolved to stay home could take comfort in Samuel Lewkenor's guide for the anti-traveler, *A Discourse not altogether unprofitable, nor unpleasant for such as are desirous to know the situation and customs of forraine Cities without travelling to see them* (London, 1600). Lewkenor surveyed the universities in Europe. He noted which subjects were taught particularly well, and where, although his homebound readers could hardly avail themselves of this knowledge. Another traveler, Robert Southwell, offered a more balanced assessment during his time in Rome in 1660. He pondered whether travel was better than study at home, and he remarked that not all could benefit from one or the other, because people themselves differed (Robert Southwell commonplace book, 1660–1661, Egerton 1632, fol. 16recto, BL).

11. Edward Arber, ed., James Howell, *Instructions for Forreine Travell (London, 1642, 1650)* (London, 1869), 11 (quotation), 13.

12. Clare Howard, *English Travellers of the Renaissance* (New York: B. Franklin, 1968, 1914), xi. It would have been more accurate to give the Scots such a title.

13. Peter Mancall, *Hakluyt's Promise: An Elizabethan's Obsession for an English America* (New Haven: Yale University Press, 2007), 74, 86–87. For a thoughtful introduction to travel, see the introduction by Jaś Elsner and Joan-Pau Rubiés, eds., *Voyages and Visions: Towards a Cultural History of Travel* (London: Reaktion Books Ltd., 1999), 1–56. For early modern European travel, see Peter C. Mancall, ed., *Bringing the World to Early Modern Europe: Travel Accounts and Their Audiences* (Leiden: Brill, 2007).

14. Richard Hakluyt, *Diuers voyages touching the discouerie of America, and the ilands adiacent vnto the same made first of all by our Englishmen* (London, 1582), *The principal navigations, voiages, traffiques and discoueries of the English nation* (London, 1589), and then the three-volume revised edition, *The Principal Navigations, Voyages, Traffiques and Discoveries of the English Nation* (London, 1598–1600). Samuel Purchas published travel accounts (rewritten in his own words) beginning in 1613 with *Purchas his Pilgrimage. Or Relations of the World and the Religions Observed in All Ages and Places Discovered, from the Creation unto this Present* (London, 1613) and with subsequent revisions. Hakluyt passed his unpublished manuscripts to Purchas by 1625 and Purchas adopted Hakluyt's style

of publishing accounts as their authors wrote them. Mancall, *Hakluyt's Promise*, 274–275.

15. Andrew Hadfield, *Literature, Travel, and Colonial Writing in the English Renaissance 1545–1625* (Oxford: Clarendon Press, 1998), 17–33.

16. Christopher Hibbert, *The Grand Tour* (New York: G. P. Putnam's Sons, 1969), 11.

17. David Beers Quinn, *The Elizabethans and the Irish* (Ithaca, NY: Cornell University Press for The Folger Shakespeare Library, 1966), 106.

18. John Stoye, *English Travellers Abroad, 1604–1667: Their Influence in English Society and Politics* (New Haven: Yale University Press, 1952, 1989), xi.

19. Palmer, *Essay*, A4recto.

20. Palmer, *Essay*, 18–19. See Thomas Herbert, *A Relation of Some Yeares Travaile* (London, 1634), n.p., on this point about the age of travelers.

21. Fynes Moryson, *An Itinerary Written by Fynes Moryson gent. First in the Latine Tongue, and then translated by him into the English* (London, 1617), Part 3, 1.

22. Howell, *Instructions*, 63.

23. For one such extension in 1615, both to extend travel and to provide specific permission to go to Rome, see MS 1879, fol. 80verso, NLS.

24. GD 40/7/48, NAS. During the political upheavals of the 1640s people sought passports from a variety of authorities. One Scot who had served in Charles I's armies under Montrose had a French passport from Henrietta Maria for a voyage to Italy. See Draft of a passport, 4 March 1649 (1650?), GD 220/3/193, NAS.

25. Moryson, *Itinerary*, Part 1, 198–199.

26. Charles Hughes, ed., *Shakespeare's Europe; unpublished chapters of Fynes Moryson's Itinerary, being a survey of the condition of Europe at the end of the 16th century* (London, 1903), xiv–xv, explains this peculiar but apparently not uncommon practice. See Geoffrey Wilson Clark, *Betting on Lives: the Culture of Life Insurance in England, 1695–1775* (Manchester: Manchester University Press, 1999).

27. Palmer, *Essay*, 35.

28. Moryson, *Itinerary*, Part 1, 197.

29. Palmer, *Essay*, 35–41; quotation from 41.

30. Sir John Wray, The Pilgrims Journall, Huntington MS 1574, Huntington. Wray wrote his account for his father, which might explain his somewhat preachy tone.

31. Moryson, *Itinerary*, Part 3, 19. Moryson's 27 precepts are found on 11–36.

32. Moryson, *Itinerary*, Part 3, 85; Howell, *Instructions*, 28 (clothes), 18 (map).

33. Diary of Sir John Lauder, travels in France 1665–1667, La.III.270, n.p., Edinburgh University Library Special Collections. Lauder's journal has also been published: see Donald Crawford, ed., *Journals of Sir John Lauder Lord Fountainhall, Publications of the Scottish Historical Society* 36 (Edinburgh: University Press for the Scottish Historical Society, 1900).

34. J. B., *The Merchants Avizo. Verie necessarie for their sons and servants, when they first send them beyond the seas, as to Spaine and Portingale, or other Countries* (London, 1607), 5.

35. Southwell Commonplace Book, fols. 20recto, 29recto.

36. "Instructions for my sone going abroad," 1663, MS 3234, Yule Collection, n. 118, NLS.

37. Moryson, *Itinerary*, Part 3, 17.

38. William Biddulph, *Travels of Certaine Englishmen* (London, 1609), 100–101.

39. The Earl of Tarras to Gideon Scott, Paris, January 24/February 3, 1670, GD 157/2100/36, NAS.

40. Somerset went to France and Italy two years after his marriage in 1609. Michael G. Brennan, ed., *The Travel Diary (1611–1612) of an English Catholic Sir Charles Somerset* (Leeds: The Leeds Philosophical and Literary Society, 1993), 15.

41. Moryson, *Itinerary*, Part 1, 40–41.

42. Ibid., Part 1, 197, 271.

43. See Wes Williams, "'Rubbing up against others': Montaigne on Pilgrimage," in Elsner and Rubiés, 101–123, for an interesting discussion of this universal fear of the traveler's altered identity.

44. Brennan, ed., *Travel Diary*.

45. Howell, *Instructions*, 72–73.

46. Moryson, *Itinerary*, Part 3, 12–13.

47. Palmer, *Essay*, 85, 128.

48. Antoni Maczak, *Travel in Early Modern Europe*, trans. Ursula Phillips (Cambridge: Polity Press, 1995), 136.

49. See their letters, all dated 1645, in GD 18/2467, NAS.

50. Howell, *Instructions*, 40.

51. I have surveyed about thirty published and manuscript accounts for the period. The travelers who left records were predominantly male, single, English, Protestant, and well-off, although numerous accounts exist of Catholic travelers (I have included three, including one woman), and of non-English travelers (I have included one Anglo-Irishman and nine Scots.) The accounts are primarily by those who undertook travel specifically for their pleasure, education, or recreation, not those whose employment overseas required them to travel to reach their new positions.

52. Journal of Thomas Abdie, Rawlinson D1285, Bodleian (hereafter cited as Abdie Journal).

53. Diary of a person in the entourage of the earl of Peterborough, 1661–1662, V.a.184, Folger (hereafter cited as Peterborough Entourage).

54. Journal of travels through Egypt by a Scotsman, 1655–1656, Sloane 3228, BL (hereafter cited as Egypt Journal).

55. Howell, *Instructions*, 20.

56. Egypt Journal, fols. 1–8.

57. May 29, 1661, Tour to Naples, Add. 42096, fol. 1, BL.

58. Peterborough Entourage, n.p.

59. Brennan, ed., *Travel Diary*, 51.

60. A Breife Depsription (sic) of my traveils taken by my selfe anno domini 1648, Rawlinson D120, fols. 23–26recto, Bodleian (hereafter cited as Breife Description).

61. Peterborough Entourage, n.p.

62. Howell, *Instructions*, 27.

63. Walter Scott, Earl of Tarras, to Gideon Scott, Loudun, December 20/10, 1667, GD 157/2100/4, NAS.

64. Lauder Diary, n.p.

65. Diary of travels by Sir J. North (1575), MS Add. C 193, Bodleian. Every travel venture, whether royal or humble, required these records. Prince Charles's visit to Spain in 1623, for example, had its own account book (MS 1879, NLS).

66. The Latin certification reads "*et omnia alia sancta ut pia loctam* (sic) *intra, quam extra, sanctam civitatem visitari solita vistasse.*" GD 90/2/69, NAS.

67. Lithgow, *Discourse*, 351.

68. Howell, *Instructions*, 18; Moryson, *Itinerary,* Part 3, 15.

69. Abdie's switch occurred on 29 April 1634, on his departure from Blois. Abdie Journal, fol. 75recto. He started his language study on November 15, at the cost of a demi-pistol per month.

70. Howell, *Instructions*, 41.

71. Ibid., 21.

72. Henry Erskine to the Earl of Mar, Saumur, 22 December 1617, GD 124/15/34/5, NAS.

73. Breife Description, fol. 3recto.

74. Moryson, *Itinerary,* Part 3, 17–18.

75. Ibid., 15.

76. Howell, *Instructions*, 21.

77. Lauder Diary, n.p.

78. Thomas Penson's Short-Progresse into holland, Flanders, and France with remarques, 1690, MS 3003, 97–99, quotation from 99, NLS.

79. Howell, *Instructions*, 26, detailed this schedule.

80. Palmer, *Essay*, 46–59.

81. John Schaw to the Earl of Mar, Burge[Bourges], 26 December 1617, GD 124/15/32/1, NAS.

82. John Schaw to the Earl of Mar, Saumur, 21 April 1618, GD 124/15/32/9, NAS.

83. June 1633–December 1633, Abdie Journal, fol. 157verso.

84. November 9/19, 1669, Paris, GD 157/2100/32, NAS.

85. John Schaw to the Earl of Mar, Saumur, 22 December 1617, GD 124/15/32/8, NAS.

86. Protestant German-speaking kingdoms and principalities did not adopt the switch until 1700.

87. Breife Description, fol. 1recto.

88. Anonymous voyage to Tripoli, 1650, Sloane 3494, fols. 4verso, 5recto, BL.

89. See the correspondence in GD 157/2100/1-59 and GD 157/2072/1-14, NAS.

90. Lauder Diary, n.p.

91. Ibid. Joan had not yet been canonized.

92. Tour to Naples, fol. 4.

93. Warneke, *Images,* 163.

94. Hugh Lee to Secretary of State, 12 July 1607, 26 November 1608, 1 April 1617, SP 89/3, fols. 85verso, 112recto, 190verso, TNA: PRO.

95. James Brown to John Clark, Bordeaux, 23 October 1645, GD 18/2467, NAS. Brown was a Scottish merchant, and explained the arrangements of one Scots traveler to have his letters of credit sent to the Scots college in Rome. Samuel Lewkenor remarked in a guide for the anti-traveler that the English seminary at Rome educated a great number of English youths (Lewkenor, *A Discourse,* 27). In 1662 a traveler to Lisbon remarked on the English college and nunnery there. Peterborough Entourage, n.p.

96. On the paired themes of exile and escape, see Michael G. Brennan, *English Civil War Travellers and the Origins of the Western European Grand Tour* (London: The Hakluyt Society, 2002), 7.

97. Lauder Diary, n.p.

98. Diary of Francis Mortost, Sloane 2142, September 17, 1658, fol. 4verso, BL.

99. Mortost Diary, fols. 12verso–13recto.

100. Brennan, ed., *Travel Diary,* 73–78, 84.

101. John Schaw to the Earl of Mar, Paris, 7 October 1619, GD 124/15/32/18, NAS.

102. Lithgow, *Discourse,* 344–345.

103. Wray, Pilgrims Journall, fols. 10recto, 11recto.

104. December 27, 1658, Mortost Diary, fol. 30.

105. Brennan, ed., *Travel Diary,* 221.

106. Holy week rituals in Rome, described in a Tour to Naples, fols. 40–41.

107. Journal of Lady Whetenall, Add. 4217, fol. 23verso, BL.

108. December, 1624, Sir William Karr's journey to Italy, c. 1625. MS 5785, fol. 8recto, NLS.

109. Journal of Lady Whetenall, fol. 32recto.

110. Ibid., fol. 36verso.

111. Wray, Pilgrims Journall, fol. 2verso.

112. Biddulph, *Travels,* 123, 130.

113. Moryson, *Itinerary,* Part 3, 23.

114. See for example Henry Erskine to the Earl of Mar, Saumur, 22 December 1617, GD 124/15/34/5, NAS, with news of Thomas Murray and of two Scottish lords who had just "endit ther voyage." The Earl of Mar was at the time Lord Treasurer of Scotland.

115. Henry Erskine to the Earl of Mar, Bourges, 16 July 1617, GD 124/15/34/2, NAS.

116. John Schaw to the Earl of Mar, Saumur, 11 August 1618, GD 124/15/32/12, NAS.

117. Lithgow, *Discourse,* 330.

118. Ibid., 396–397, quotation from 397.

119. Henry Blount, *A Voyage into the Levant* (London, 1636), 32–33.

120. Edinburgh, 1607/8, petition to lords for redress, GD 1/1126/1, NAS.

121. Stoye, *Travelers*, 289.

122. Breife Description, fol. 2recto.

123. Journal of Lady Whetenall, fol. 31recto–verso.

124. Breife Description, fol. 2recto.

125. October 3–10, 1658, Mortost Diary, fol. 7verso.

126. Journal of Lady Whetenall, fol. 3recto.

127. Such was how he described the sights of Milan in Journal of Lady Whetenall, fol. 18recto, and Florence, fol. 19verso.

128. Journal of Lady Whetenall, fol. 22verso.

129. See references for Antwerp, Gand, Bruges, Nieuport, etc., Journal of Lady Whetenall, fols. 9–10.

130. Journal of Lady Whetenall, fol. 10verso.

131. Ibid., fol. 42verso.

132. Ibid., fols. 35recto, 45recto.

133. Thomas Birch, ed., *Miscellaneous works of Mr. John Greaves, professor of Astronomy in the University of Oxford*, four volumes (London, 1737), vol. 2, 479.

134. Ibid., 497–498.

135. Dr. Edward Browne, travels, 1668–1669, Sloane 1905, fols. 11verso–12verso, BL. Browne also published two versions of his travels, *An account of several travels through a great part of Germany* (London, 1677) and *A brief account of some travels in Hungaria* (London, 1673; expanded in 1685, and 1687).

136. Brennan, ed., *Travel Diary*, 143.

137. Browne Travels, fol. 2recto.

138. Ibid., fol. 7verso.

139. Journal of Lady Whetenall, fol. 28verso.

140. Howell, *Instructions*, 29.

141. Brennan, ed., *Travel Diary*, 110, 163 (on widows and marital separations in France), 173 (illegitimate children).

142. Kathleen M. Brown explores these English critiques of Irish and Indian women's apparent ease in childbirth in *Good Wives, Nasty Wenches, and Anxious Patriarchs: Gender, Race, and Power in Colonial Virginia* (Chapel Hill: The University of North Carolina Press, 1996), 35, 58; Jennifer L. Morgan analyzes European ideas about African women's childbirth practices in *Laboring Women: Reproduction and Gender in New World Slavery* (Philadelphia: University of Pennsylvania Press, 2004), chapter 1.

143. Lithgow, *Discourse*, 294.

144. Palmer, *Essay*, 63.

145. John Keymer, "Observations Regarding Trade," La.II.52, Edinburgh University Library Special Collections.

146. Palmer, *Essay*, 53.

147. Quotation from John Greaves, *A Discourse on the Roman Foot and Denarius*, in Birch, ed., *Works of John Greaves*, vol. 1, 178.

148. Moryson, *Itinerary*, Part 2, 1.
149. Hadfield, *Literature, Travel, and Colonial Writing*, 4–5.
150. Thomas Herbert, *A Relation of Some Yeares Travaile* (London, 1634), 1.
151. For an account of Sierra Leone and its inhabitants, see Herbert, *Relation*, 6.
152. *Coryats Crudities* (London, 1611), n.p.
153. Wray, Pilgrims Journal, fol. 3recto.
154. Tour to Naples, fol. 3; December, 1624, Sir William Karr's journey, fol. 11verso.
155. (May), Lauder Diary, n.p.
156. Moryson, *Itinerary*, Part 1, 216.
157. Blount, *Voyage*, 13. William Lithgow started his third round of travels in Ireland, and compared the Irish with "the Barbarian Moore, the Moorish Spaniard, the Turke," as the "least industrious, and most sluggish livers under the Sunne" (Lithgow, *Discourse*, 429). Thomas Herbert likened the clothes of the people of the Caucasus to those of "the Irish Troopes" (Herbert, *Relation*, 95).
158. Brennan, ed., *Travel Diary*, 54.
159. Thomas Coryate, *Coryats Crudities* (London, 1611), dedication.
160. Moryson apologized for boring readers with these practical notes. See *Itinerary*, Part 1, note to reader, n.p.
161. Moryson, *Itinerary*, Part 3, 8.
162. Blount, *Voyage*, 1, 3.
163. Howell, 3–4.
164. Letters from Alexander Erskine to his father, August–September, 1623, GD 124/15/35/12-16, NAS.
165. Howell, *Instructions*, 80.
166. Moryson, *Itinerary*, Part 3, 10.
167. Blount, *Voyage*, pp. 1, 3.
168. Hall, *Quo Vadis*, 21–22.
169. Parr, *Travel Plays*, 6.
170. Ibid., 34.
171. Lithgow, *Discourse*, 369.
172. Penson's Short-Progresse, MS 3003, fol. 4verso, NLS.
173. Wray, Pilgrims Journall, fol. 7verso. The *grotto del cane* was a regular stopping point: see also Breife Description, fol. 21recto; Sandys, *Relation,* 267; Moryson, *Itinerary*, Part 1, 114. Tourism seemed to place dogs in danger generally in this period. Outside Geneva along the Rhone, one English traveler remarked in his diary that at the place where the river went under ground, whatever you throw in never comes out again, "as hath been tryed by severall doggs, throwne in on purpose to satisfie the curiositie of some persons" (Tour to Naples, fol. 8). Little surprise, then, that the dogs "at sight of a stranger will quicklie get theme to the hills" (Sir William Karr's journey, fol. 12recto). Tommaso Astarita discusses the *grotto del cane* in the context of travel in southern Italy in *Between Salt Water and Holy Water: A History of Southern Italy* (New York: Norton, 2005), 224–225.

174. Sloane 2496 (1601), fol. 63recto, BL; Birch's notes on Greaves's tour in Egypt (1630s), Add. 4243, fol. 85verso, BL; Egypt Journal, fol. 100recto (1650s).

175. In *Philosophical Transactions* 137 (January 1677/78).

176. Add. 22,912, fols. 95–102, BL, contains this pamphlet.

177. January 30 (1663/4?), "Instructions for my sone going abroad."

178. Warneke, *Images*, 49. See also Maczak, *Travel*, on how travel diaries by the seventeenth century "had already lost their immediacy and originality," with travel diarists directly copying into their diaries the writings of others (185).

179. Bruce Redford offers a four-part definition of the Grand Tour to distinguish it from general continental travels: to qualify, there must be a young man of the gentry or aristocracy, a tutor, a fixed route with Rome as its goal, and a tour of two to three years. See Bruce Redford, *Venice and the Grand Tour* (New Haven: Yale University Press, 1996), 14.

Chapter 2

1. Tour to Naples, 1661–1662, Add. 42,096, fol. 16, BL.

2. S. A. Skilliter, *William Harborne and the Trade with Turkey 1578–1582* (Oxford: Oxford University Press for the British Academy, 1977), 23.

3. M. Epstein, *The Early History of the Levant Company* (London, 1908; New York: A. M. Kelley, 1968), 17–19.

4. See the succinct account in Fernand Braudel, *The Mediterranean and the Mediterranean World in the Age of Philip II*, translated from the French by Siân Reynolds (Berkeley: University of California Press, 1995), 612–627; and Daniel Goffman, *The Ottoman Empire and Early Modern Europe* (Cambridge: Cambridge University Press, 2002).

5. Reference to consul at Messina in John Smith, Account of a voyage to Smyrna, 1664–1665, Sloane 1700, fol. 22recto, BL. The consul at Patras was murdered. See William Lithgow, *The Totall Discourse, of the Rare Adventures, and Painfull Peregrinations of Long nineteene Years Travayles* (London, 1632), 66–67. Dr. Edward Browne referred to the English consul in Negroponte, Dr. E. Browne, travels, 1668–1669, Sloane 1905, fol. 19recto, BL. For a discussion of these Levant Company consuls, see Alfred C. Wood, *A History of the Levant Company* (Oxford, 1935; New York: Barnes and Noble, 1964), chapter 4.

6. G. D. Ramsay, *English Overseas Trade During the Centuries of Emergence* (London: Macmillan, 1957), 60; Ralph Davis, "England and the Mediterranean, 1570–1670," in F. J. Fisher, ed., *Essays in the Economic and Social History of Tudor and Stuart England* (Cambridge: Cambridge University Press, 1961), 117–137.

7. P. J. Marshall, "The English in Asia," in Nicholas Canny, ed., *The Origins of Empire* (Oxford: Oxford University Press, 1998), 267.

8. Directions to Richard Forster, 1 September 1583, Richard Hakluyt, *The principal navigations, voyages, traffiques & discoveries of the English nation made by sea or*

over-land to the remote and farthest distant quarters of the earth at any time within the compass of these 1600 yeeres (Glasgow: J. MacLehose and sons, 1903–05), vol. 5, 262.

9. On the importance of re-reading early encounters through this prism of assimilation, not conquest, see, for example, Nicholas Canny, "England's New World and the Old, 1480s–1630s," in Canny, ed., *The Origins of Empire*, 148–169; Karen Ordahl Kupperman, *English and Indians: Facing Off in Early America* (Ithaca: Cornell University Press, 2000); and Braudel, *Mediterranean*, 629. See also Kenneth Parker, *Early Modern Tales of Orient: A Critical Anthology* (London: Routledge, 1999), 28–29.

10. D. W. Waters, *The Art of Navigation in England in Elizabethan and Early Stuart Times* (New Haven: Yale University Press, 1958), 83–84.

11. William Biddulph, *Travels of Certaine Englishmen* (London, 1609), 5.

12. Sir John Wray, The Pilgrims Journall, Huntington MS 1574, Huntington. Wray was unusual in his early visit to southern Italy (in 1605–1606).

13. Dr. E. Browne was atypical in his land route, but he never reached the eastern Mediterranean or North Africa. Browne Travels, Sloane 1905, BL.

14. Henry Blount, *A Voyage into the Levant* (London, 1636), 74.

15. Journey to Jerusalem by Henry Tymberley (Timberlake), Sloane 2496, fol. 69recto, BL (hereafter Tymberley Journal).

16. Journal of travels through Egypt by a Scotsman, 1655–1656, Sloane 3228, fol. 132recto, BL (hereafter cited as Egypt Journal).

17. Egypt Journal, fol. 130recto.

18. Fynes Moryson, *An Itinerary Written by Fynes Moryson gent. First in the Latine Tongue, and then translated by him into the English* (London, 1617), Part 1, 210.

19. Braudel, *Mediterranean*, 345, 348; Blount, *Voyage*, 43; Roger Finlay and Beatrice Shearer, "Population growth and suburban expansion," in A. L. Beier and Roger Finlay, eds., *London 1500–1700: The Making of the Metropolis* (London: Longman, 1986), 39; David Harris Sacks, *The Widening Gate: Bristol and the Atlantic Economy 1450–1700* (Berkeley, CA: University of California Press, 1991), 353.

20. Biddulph, *Travels*, 45.

21. Charles Robson, *Newes from Aleppo* (London, 1628), 14–15.

22. George Sandys, *A Relation of a Journey Begun in An. Dom 1610* (London, 1615), 122–123.

23. Goffman, *Ottoman Empire*, chapter 3.

24. Lee to Wilson, 26 March 1609, new style; Lee to Wilson, 16 April 1609, SP 89/3, fols. 118verso, 122recto, TNA: PRO.

25. Hugh Lee to Thomas Wilson, 16 July 1609, new style, SP 89/3, fol. 130recto, TNA: PRO.

26. The first voyage of Master Laurence Aldersey, 1581, in Hakluyt, *Principal Navigations*, vol. 5, 204.

27. Diary of Francis Mortost, Sloane 2142, fols. 14recto–verso, BL; see also Tour to Naples, fol. 10.

28. Sandys, *Relation*, 146.

29. "A description of the Grand Seignor's seraglio," in Thomas Birch, ed., *Miscellaneous works of Mr. John Greaves, professor of Astronomy in the University of Oxford*, four volumes (London, 1737), vol. 2, 751.

30. Egypt Journal, fols. 135verso, 139recto, 143verso. This traveler was acutely aware of his own vulnerability in the region. He worried about how to get to Aleppo. The land route was dangerous because of thieves and because of taxes on Christians. "Frank christians," of which he was one, were vulnerable to all predators, who could "tak yt they plase." He ended up planning to travel in company with some Armenian Christians (fols. 160–161).

31. Sandys, *Relation*, 146–147; see Biddulph, *Travels*, 72–75, for a similar assessment of Jews in Turkey. For other accounts of worship, see Add. 42,096, n.p., BL; and the Journal of Lady Whetenall in her trip to Italy, 1650, Add. 4217, fol. 24verso, BL.

32. "A description of the Grand Seignor's seraglio," in Birch, ed., *Works of John Greaves*, vol. 2, 650–651.

33. 5 February 1621/2, SP 105/102, fol. 14, TNA: PRO.

34. 2 July 1622, SP 105/102, fol. 46verso, TNA: PRO.

35. Court, 1 February 1622/3, 30 June 1623, SP 105/102, fols. 71recto, 112recto, TNA: PRO.

36. Parker, *Early Modern Tales of Orient*, 25.

37. Charles Hughes, ed., *Shakespeare's Europe; unpublished chapters of Fynes Moryson's Itinerary, being a survey of the condition of Europe at the end of the 16th century* (London, 1903), 61.

38. Lithgow, *Discourse*, 126.

39. "Observations made by Mr. Greaves in his Travels; extracted from his Manuscripts in the Savilian Library at Oxford," Birch, ed., *Works of John Greaves*, vol. 2, 500.

40. See Tymberly's description of waiting at the gate, 1602, Tymberly Journal, fol. 63verso.

41. Sandys, *Relation*, 125.

42. Browne Travels, fol. 19recto.

43. Egypt Journal, fol. 155recto; Biddulph, *Travels*, 36. The patriarch spoke no Latin, so they could not talk about religion.

44. Biddulph, *Travels*, 38–39, at the Monastery of St. Mary.

45. Sandys, *Relation*, 110, 125, 136.

46. Ibid., 171.

47. William Lithgow, *The Totall Discourse, of the Rare Adventures, and painefull Peregrinations of long nineteene Yeares Travayles* (London, 1632), 103, Folger, STC 15713 copy 2.

48. April 13, 1662, Diary of a person in the entourage of Earl of Peterborough, V. a.184, Folger.

49. May, 1655, John Weale, Journal of a voyage to Tunis, Sloane 1431, fol. 29recto, BL.

50. Lithgow, *Discourse*, 155.

51. "A description of the Grand Seignor's seraglio," vol. 2, 652. Likely written by Robert Wither, this account was given to Greaves during his time in Istanbul.

52. "A description of the Grand Seignor's seraglio," vol. 2, 800.

53. Sandys, *Relation*, 69.

54. Blount, *Voyage*, 82.

55. Tour to Naples, fols. 17, 22.

56. Tymberly Journal, fol. 68verso.

57. Egypt Journal, fol. 124verso.

58. Blount, *Voyage*, 14.

59. Sandys, *Relation*, 73.

60. Lithgow, *Discourse*, 384; see also Lithgow's remarks on sodomy and prostitution in Fez, 369.

61. Blount, *Voyage*, 113.

62. "A description of the Grand Seignor's seraglio," vol. 2, 696.

63. Hughes ed., *Shakespeare's Europe*, 20.

64. One Scots voyager devoted long pages in his diary to an account of the Knights of Malta. Egypt Journal, fols. 56–65.

65. Sandys, *Relation*, 69.

66. "A description of the Grand Seignor's seraglio," vol. 2, 759.

67. Edwyn Sandys, *Europae Speculum, or a View or Survey of the State of Religion in the Westerne Parts of the World* (The Hague, 1629), 19, 38–39, 60. This work was first published in 1605.

68. John Greaves to William Laud, 1638, Add. 34,727, fol. 64recto, BL.

69. Petition of Roger Howe, 7 September 1649, Records of the Chancery of the Ambassador at Constantinople, SP 105/174, 282, TNA: PRO. See also the passes Sir Thomas Roe wrote for people going from the Ottoman empire to "Christendom," including the pass for Zacharia of Zante, 18 October 1649, SP 105/174, 323–324, TNA: PRO.

70. Robson, *Newes from Aleppo*, 12.

71. On Mary Magdalene's cave, see, for example, Egypt Journal, fol. 51verso.

72. Lithgow, *Discourse*, 234. See also Moryson on the meaning of Jerusalem, *Itinerary*, Part 1, 217.

73. Sandys, *Relation*, 3–4.

74. Lithgow, *Discourse*, 127–128.

75. Tour to Naples, fol. 25.

76. For Milan, see Tour to Naples, n.p. (this portion of the journal works backward after fol. 48, and has no meaningful pagination), BL; for Carthage, see Weale, Journal, fol. 21verso; Lithgow, *Discourse*, 355–356; Biddulph, *Travels*, 2.

77. George Sandys equipped himself for a voyage from Smyrna to Istanbul with a Greek interpreter. Sandys, *Relation*, 15.

78. Blount, *Voyage*, 48–49, 55.

79. Robson, *Newes from Aleppo*, 12.

80. 28 August, 1–3 September, 1628, John Bruce, ed., *Journal of a Voyage into the Mediterranean by Sir Kenelm Digby, 1628* (London: Camden Society, 1868, vol. 96), 55–57. Although the published journal reads "Delphos," the context establishes this island as Delos.

81. Edward Arber, ed., James Howell, *Instructions for Forreine Travell (London, 1642, 1650)* (London, 1869), 83; see also William Biddulph, *Travels*, 10.

82. Lithgow, *Discourse*, 118.

83. Robson, *Newes from Aleppo*, 9.

84. Egypt Journal, fols. 68recto–69recto.

85. Ibid., fol. 139verso.

86. Robson, *Newes from Aleppo*, 10.

87. Ibid., 13.

88. Sandys, *Relation*, 47.

89. Blount, *Voyage*, 90. He remarked particularly on the ineffective quality of milder Roman justice.

90. Ibid., 51.

91. Sandys, *Relation*, 46.

92. Howell, *Instructions*, 82.

93. Moryson, *Itinerary*, Part 1, 198.

94. Clare Howard, *English Travellers of the Renaissance* (New York, 1968, 1914), 75–76.

95. Sara Warneke, *Images of the Educational Traveller in Early Modern England* (New York: E. J. Brill, 1995), 166–167.

96. Howell, *Instructions*, 38.

97. John Stoye, *English Travellers Abroad, 1604–1667: Their Influence in English Society and Politics* (New Haven: Yale University Press, 1952, 1989), 260–262.

98. Henry Kamen, *The Spanish Inquisition: A Historical Revision* (London: Weidenfeld and Nicolson, 1997), 277–279.

99. Mary Brearley, *Hugo Gurgeny: Prisoner of the Lisbon Inquisition* (New Haven: Yale University Press, 1948), 134.

100. Lithgow, *Discourse*, 20.

101. Thomas Maynard to [?], 19/29 July 1611, SP 89/5, fol. 27recto, TNA: PRO.

102. *Strange and Wonderful Things Happened to Richard Hasleton* (1595), in Daniel J. Vitkus, ed., *Piracy, Slavery, and Redemption: Barbary Captivity Narratives from Early Modern England* (New York: Columbia University Press, 2001), 80.

103. Thomas Palmer, *An Essay of the Meanes how to make our Travailes, into forraine Countries, the more profitable and honourable* (London, 1606), 44.

104. See surviving passes for 1615 (MS 1879, fol. 80verso) and 1633 (GD 40/7/48), in which Rome was specifically added on at the request of the traveler, NAS.

105. H. Lundres to M. le comte de Straherne, 16 February 1632, GD 22/3/595, NAS.

106. See, for example, *The Lamentable Cries of at least 1500 Christians* (1624) reprinted in Vitkus, ed., *Piracy, Slavery, and Redemption*, 344–346.

107. Tour to Naples, fol. 1.

108. 9 June 1628, 7 August 1628, Digby, *Voyage*, 37, 50.

109. Virginia West Lunsford, *Piracy and Privateering in the Golden Age Netherlands* (New York: Palgrave Macmillan, 2005), 121.

110. Andrew Barker, *A True and Certaine Report of Captaine Ward and Danseker, Pirates* (London, 1609). Ward converted in 1610.

111. Ramsay, *English Overseas Trade*, 42.

112. K. R. Andrews, "Sir Robert Cecil and Mediterranean Plunder," *The English Historical Review* 87 (July, 1972), 513–532.

113. Insurance rates listed in the Amsterdamse Pryscourant of 20 February 1634, Collectie Commerciele Couranten, AMS.1.01, Nederlands Economisch Historisch Archief, Amsterdam, The Netherlands. My thanks to Henriette de Bruyn Kops for sharing these archival findings with me.

114. Robert C. Davis, "Counting European Slaves on the Barbary Coast," *Past and Present* 172 (2001), 106, 118; Robert C. Davis, *Christian Slaves, Muslim Masters: White Slavery in the Mediterranean, the Barbary Coast, and Italy, 1500–1800* (New York: Palgrave Macmillan, 2003), 3

115. Davis, "Counting European Slaves," 90. See especially Ellen G. Friedman, *Spanish Captives in North Africa in the Early Modern Age* (Madison, 1983), chapter 3, for a discussion of life in captivity and the impact of captivity on Spanish society.

116. Blount, *Voyage*, 59.

117. Lithgow, *Discourse*, 60–62.

118. For instructions to emissaries, see, for example, *The Negotiations of Sir Thomas Roe, in his Embassy to the Ottoman Porte* (London, 1740); commission to Captain John Harrison to treat with the rulers of Barbary, 10 November and 5 December 1626, Add. 21,993, fols. 281–284, BL; Translation of a letter from Queen Elizabeth I to Mustafa Beg, 25 October 1579, in Skilliter, *Harborne*, 74; On proposed swaps, see Lee to the Secretary of State, 1 April 1617, new style, SP 89/3, fol. 189verso, TNA: PRO. On the difficulties of the always underfunded job, see Richard Forde to the king, Algiers, 24 February 1621/2, SP 71/1, fol. 40recto, TNA: PRO; Davis, *White Slaves*, 6; Lee to [Winwood], 6 September 1615, new style, SP 89/3, fol. 180verso, TNA: PRO; Richard Knolles, *The Generall Historie of the Turkes* (fifth ed., London, 1638), 1434–1435. Thomas Roe wrote this portion of Knolles' history. David Delison Hebb, *Piracy and the English Government, 1616–1642* (Brookfield, Vt: Ashgate Press, 1994), 140, 163. Wood, *Levant Company*, 60, provides an astonishing statistic: 466 English ships seized and their crews captured and enslaved between 1609 and 1616; Weale, Journal, fol. 28verso.

119. Will of Henry Thornton, 4 February 1639/40, Aleppo Minutebook, SP 110/54, fols. 219verso–220recto, TNA: PRO.

120. "A true relation of an escape made out of Argier," Sloane 3317, fol. 8recto, BL.

121. John Smith, *The True Travels, Adventures, and Observations of Captain John Smith* (London, 1630), in Philip L. Barbour, ed., *The Complete Works of Captain John Smith,*

1580–1631, three volumes (Chapel Hill: University of North Carolina Press, 1968), vol. 3, 186–203, quotations from 186, 189, 203.

122. Edward Webbe, *The Rare and most wonderfull things which Edw. Webbe an English-man borne hath seene* (London, 1590), quotations from B1verso. Galley service was universally deplored by those who endured it: see Samuel Harres's letter to his father, Tripoli, 16 July 1610, in Vitkus, ed., *Piracy, Slavery, and Redemption,* 347–348.

123. Letter to Sir Charles Cornwallis from English prisoners released from the galleys in Lisbon, 19 February 1607/8, Add. 39,853, fol. 126verso, BL.

124. For mussels, see Egypt Journal, fols. 74verso–75recto.

125. Egypt Journal, fols. 66recto, 78recto; *Pyramidographia* (London, 1736), in Birch, ed., *Works of John Greaves,* vol. 1, 136.

126. Moryson, *Itinerary,* Part 1, 265.

127. Blount, *Voyage,* 92.

128. Lithgow, *Discourse,* 361.

129. Biddulph, *Travels,* 27.

130. Egypt Journal, fol. 124verso–recto.

131. "A description of the Grand Seignor's seraglio," vol. 2, 760. See also Lithgow, *Discourse,* on the slave market, 136–138.

132. *A True Account of the Captivity of Thomas Phelps* (1685), in Vitkus, ed., *Piracy, Slavery, and Redemption,* 197. On this point see also G. E. Aylmer, "Slavery under Charles II: The Mediterranean and Tangier," *The English Historical Review* 114 (April 1999), 379.

133. Copy of a letter sent to Philip Bell, 20 April 1635, CO 124/1, fol. 76verso, TNA: PRO; John Donoghue, "Radical Republicanism in England, America, and the Imperial Atlantic, 1624–1661" (Ph.D. Dissertation, University of Pittsburgh, 2006), 156–161.

134. Blount, *Voyage,* 97.

135. Howell, *Travell,* 17. Howell believed fidelity in religion to be the foremost require-ment for the traveler.

136. Richard Ford to the king, Algiers, 3 November 1621, SP 71/1, fol. 38recto for quota-tion; see also fol. 30recto; Ford to King, 24 February 1621/2, SP 71/1, fol. 40recto, TNA: PRO.

137. An Anonymous voyage to Tripoli, 1650, Sloane 3494, fol. 23recto, BL.

138. Report on affairs at Algiers, 1620, SP 71/7, fol. 30recto, TNA: PRO.

139. "Laudian Rite for Returned Renegades (1637)," in Vitkus, ed., *Piracy, Slavery, and Redemption,* 361–366.

140. Adams to his father, Sally, 4 November 1625, in Vitkus, ed., *Piracy, Slavery, and Redemption,* 349.

141. Davis, "Counting European Slaves," 116.

142. Lithgow, *Discourse,* 397–398; Nabil Matar, "Verney, Sir Francis (1584–1615)," *Oxford Dictionary of National Biography* (Oxford: Oxford University Press, 2004).

143. Voyage to Tripoli, fols. 23recto, 25verso–27verso.

144. Blount, *Voyage,* 112.

145. Voyage to Tripoli, fol. 73recto.

146. Brearley, *Gurgeny*, 138.
147. 11 March 1649/50, Chancery Book, Constantinople, SP 105/174, 281, TNA: PRO.
148. Howell, *Instructions*, 29.
149. Biddulph, *Travels*, 61.
150. Moryson, *Itinerary*, Part 1, 144.
151. Ibid., 155.
152. Lithgow, *Discourse*, 20.
153. Robson, *Newes from Aleppo*, 4.
154. Moryson, *Itinerary*, Part 1, 168–169.
155. Blount, *Voyage*, 32–33.
156. Moryson, *Itinerary*, Part 1, 168.
157. Tymberly Journal, fol. 64verso.
158. Sandys, *Relation*, 249.
159. Hakluyt, *Principall Navigations*, vol. 5, 207.
160. Sandys, *Relation*, 64; Moryson, *Itinerary*, Part 1, 209–210; Lithgow, *Discourse*, 145; Biddulph, *Travels*, 64.
161. Moryson, *Itinerary*, Part 1, 208.
162. Blount, *Voyage*, 26.
163. Ibid., 31.
164. Sandys, *Relation*, 136; Tymberly Journal, fol. 63recto.
165. Hughes, ed., *Shakespeare's Europe*, 27.
166. Sandys, *Relation*, 120–121. Their original protector came again to their aid, stripped and beat their attacker, and hauled him off for formal punishment.
167. Moryson, *Itinerary*, Part 1, 27.
168. Biddulph, *Travels*, 100.
169. Moryson, *Itinerary*, Part 1, 217.
170. Blount, *Voyage*, 98.
171. Ibid., 33.
172. Moryson, *Itinerary*, Part 1, 236; Part 3, 8.
173. Biddulph, *Travels*, 117–119.
174. Blount, *Voyage*, 5.
175. Moryson, *Itinerary*, Part 3, 19.
176. Ibid., 29.

CHAPTER 3

1. *The Voyage of Captain John Saris to Japan, 1613*, ed. Ernest M. Satow (London: Hakluyt Society, 1900), 183.
2. Edward Maunde Thompson, ed., *The Diary of Richard Cocks* (London: Hakluyt Society, 2 volumes, 1883), vol. 1, 291.

3. W. E. Minchinton, ed., *The Growth of English Overseas Trade in the Seventeenth Centuries* (London: Methuen, 1969), 18–21; Nuala Zahediah, "Overseas Expansion and Trade in the Seventeenth Century," in Nicholas Canny, ed., *The Origins of Empire* (Oxford: Oxford University Press, 1998), 398–399 (quotation from 398).

4. T. K. Rabb, *Enterprise and Empire: Merchant and Gentry Investment in the Expansion of England, 1575–1630* (Cambridge, Mass.: Harvard University Press, 1967), 104.

5. Rabb, *Enterprise and Empire,* 104.

6. K. N. Chaudhuri, *The English East India Company: The Study of an Early Joint-Stock Company 1600–1640* (London: Frank Cass, 1965), 3.

7. Rabb, *Enterprise and Empire,* 108.

8. Ibid., 378.

9. The literature on merchants engaged in long-distance trade emphasizes the concept of merchant diasporas, first developed by Philip D. Curtin in *Cross Cultural Trade in World History* (Cambridge: Cambridge University Press, 1984). This chapter departs from a model that emphasizes the distinctive qualities of any single merchant or diasporic community by focusing instead on the mutability of factory culture in different settings. It emphasizes accommodation to local circumstances as opposed to the retention of English identity. See also Daniel Goffman's interpretation in *Britons in the Ottoman Empire, 1642–1660* (Seattle: University of Washington Press, 1998).

10. In his analysis of four European factories in the Ottoman Empire, Niels Steensgaard suggests that there was often a gap between the formal capitulations and actual practice. See "Consuls and Nations in the Levant from 1570 to 1650," *Scandanavian Economic History Review* 15 (1967), 54. Capitulations should probably be regarded as only suggestive.

11. J. B., *The Merchants Avizo. Verie necessarie for their sons and servants, when they first send them beyond the seas, as to Spaine and Portingale, or other Countries* (London, 1607), 3–7.

12. Instructions to Ph. Gyfford, 17 December 1639, Williams Letterbook, Stowe 759, BL.

13. October, 1613, *Voyage of Captain John Saris,* 160.

14. Letter from Saris to the East India Company, 17 October 1614, *Voyage of Captain John Saris,* appendix A, 204; "Advise for Goodes at Surratt, 1617"; journal entry for [February, 1617], William Foster, ed., *The Embassy of Sir Thomas Roe to the Court of the Great Mogul, 1615–1619* (London: Hakluyt Society, 1899), 486–487, 387.

15. September 12, 1613, "Relation of Master Richard Cockes, Cape Merchant, of what past in the Generals absence going to the Emperours Court," in *Voyage of Captain John Saris,* 149.

16. Richard Lakes to his mother, 25 November 1658, SP 110/11, fol. 13recto, TNA: PRO.

17. Remembrance to Mr. Richard Middleton when Williams left Istanbul for Livorno, 10 February 1639/40; P. Williams to brothers Williams and Rice, 30 March 1639; Williams to Mr. Gerrard Russell, 6 April 1639; Williams to uncle Watkin, 15 June 1639, Williams Letterbook.

18. Richard Lakes to Stephen Charlson, 22 October 1658, SP 110/11, fol. 3verso, TNA: PRO.

19. Richard Lakes to his brother, 22 October 1658, SP 110/11, fol. 3verso, TNA: PRO.

20. Richard Lakes to his brother, 22 October 1658, Lakes to Thomas Garron, 22 October 1658, SP 110/11, fols. 3verso–4recto, TNA: PRO.

21. Richard Lakes to Thomas Garron, 22 October 1658; letters sent around October 22, 1658, and November 25, 1658; Richard Lakes to Ralph Lee, 25 January 1658/9; Lakes to Ralph Lee, 6 June 1659, SP 110/11, fols. 4recto, 14recto, 31recto, TNA: PRO.

22. Richard Lakes to his mother, 3 September 1659, and to his sister, 7 September 1659, SP 110/11, fols. 39verso, 42recto, TNA: PRO.

23. Court, 6 February 1616/7, Minute Book for Aleppo Factors, SP 110/54, fol. 85verso, TNA: PRO.

24. Richard Lakes to his mother, 5 July 1659, SP 110/11, fol. 33recto, TNA: PRO.

25. Richard Lakes to Mr. Samuel Bernardister, 26 October 1660, SP 110/11, fol. 89recto, TNA: PRO.

26. Richard Lakes to Ralph Lee, 25 March 1660, SP 110/11, fol. 59verso, TNA: PRO.

27. Richard Lakes to Mr. William Hunt, 13 February 1659/60, SP 110/11, fol. 51verso, TNA: PRO.

28. P. Williams to cousin Humphrey Gyffard, 30 March 1639, Williams Letterbook.

29. Richard Lakes to Mr. Rich, May 8, 1659, SP 110/11, fol. 23recto; see also letter to Mr. Rich, 1 April 1659. fol. 15recto, TNA: PRO.

30. Richard Lakes to Mr. Thomas Rich, 1 April 1659, SP 110/11, fol. 15recto, TNA: PRO.

31. See P. Williams to Humphrey Gyfford, 14 September 1639; On his prior romantic entanglements, see P. Williams to William Williams, 13 September 1642, Livorno; P. Williams to Nich. Penning, 30 March 1639; P. Williams to William Williams, 22 December 1640, 26 December 1640, both from Livorno (italics added); P. Williams to brother Williams, 23 March 1640/41; P. Williams to Brother Williams, 26 October 1641, 13 December 1641; P. Williams to Wm. Williams, 5 July 1642, 19 July 1642, 13 September 1642, Williams Letterbook.

32. Richard Fursland, Thomas Brockedon, Augustine Spalding and Gabriel Towerson at Batavia to the East India Company, 10 December 1621, in Anthony Farrington, ed., *The English Factory in Japan, 1613–1623*, two volumes (London: The British Library, 1991), vol. 2, 867.

33. Court held 15 April 1618, Aleppo Minute Book, SP 110/54, fol. 15verso, TNA: PRO.

34. Chaudhuri, *East India Company,* chapters 1–2. See Derek Massarella, *A World Elsewhere: Europe's Encounter with Japan in the Sixteenth and Seventeenth Centuries* (New Haven: Yale University Press, 1990) for a detailed discussion of the Japanese trading venture.

35. The applicant in verse was John Wright, November 13, 1609, B/3, fol. 150recto, IOR, BL. He was sent as a steward's mate on the *Dragon*.

36. Court meetings, 16 December 1613; 20 December 1613, B/5, viii, xiv, IOR, BL.

37. Court meetings, 10 March 1613/14, 9 July 1614, 21 October 1614, 2 November 1614, 8 November 1614, 18 November 1614, B/5, 154, 250, 258, 265, 282, IOR, BL.

38. Court meetings, 9 September 1614, 4 November 1614, B/5, 215, n.p. for November meeting, IOR, BL.

39. Court meetings, 11 November 1614, 12 May 1615, B/5, 277, 422–423, IOR, BL.

40. Thomas Harod at Hirado to the East India Company in London, 14 December 1620, Farrington, vol. 2, 827.

41. Richard Cocks at Nagasaki to Sir Thomas Smythe and the East India Company, 10 March 1620, in Farrington, vol. 1, 792.

42. Massarella, *World Elsewhere*, 140.

43. 30 June 1617, *Diary of Richard Cocks*, vol. 1, 269.

44. William Adams at Hirado to his "unknown friends and countrymen, at Bantam," 23 October 1611, in Farrington, vol. 1, 65–72, quotation from 72.

45. John Saris, remembrance left with Richard Cocks at Hirado, 5 December 1613, in Farrington, vol. 1, 120.

46. Commission from Richard Cocks to Richard Wickham for voyage to Siam, 25 November 1614, in Farrington, vol. 1, 230.

47. Adams has featured in a number of literary and historical works, from James Clavell, *Shōgun: A Novel of Japan* (New York: Atheneum, 1975) to Giles Milton, *Samurai William: The Englishman Who Opened Japan* (New York: Farrar, Straus, Giroux, 2003).

48. Eiichi Kato, "Unification and Adaptation, the Early Shogunate and Dutch Trade Policies," in Leonard Blussé and Femme Gaastra, eds., *Companies and Trade* (The Hague: Martinus Nijhoff Publishers, 1981), 219.

49. Court, 8 September 1615, B/5, 473, IOR, BL.

50. Richard Cocks at Hirado to John Browne at Puttani [Patani], 16 December 1616, in Farrington, vol. 1, 531.

51. Court, 11 November 1614, B/5, 270, IOR, BL.

52. On John Portis, see Richard Cocks at Hirado to Sir Thomas Smythe and the East India Company, 14 November 1622, in Farrington, vol. 2, 908.

53. Mary Brearley, *Hugo Gurgeny: Prisoner of the Lisbon Inquisition* (New Haven: Yale University Press, 1948), 26; Hugh Lee to Thomas Wilson (Salisbury's secretary), 16 November 1609, SP 89/3, fol. 136verso, TNA: PRO.

54. August 9, 1613, "Cocks Relation," *Voyage of Captain John Saris*, 143–144. On Migell's alleged double-dealing, see 156.

55. See L. M. E. Shaw, *The Anglo-Portuguese Alliance and The English Merchants in Portugal 1654–1810* (Aldershot: Ashgate, 1998); and L. M. E. Shaw, *Trade, Inquisition and the English Nation in Portugal, 1650–1690* (Manchester: Carcanet, 1989), 20.

56. For licenses, see Shaw, *Trade, Inquisition*, 22.

57. Complaints by English merchants in Spain, 1584–1600, Add. 48,126, fols. 73–77, BL.

58. See a list of individual cases, including grievances of merchants, Add. 48,126, fol. 77 recto, BL.

59. See "Questions propounded by the comisures and familiars of the Inquisition," [1604], SP 94/10, fol. 219, TNA: PRO; for complaints by merchants trading with Portugal about the conduct of the Inquisition officers [undated], see SP 89/5, fols. 170–171, TNA: PRO. The Portuguese complaint addressed a wide range of trade grievances well beyond the scope of the Inquisition.

60. See the petition of Dorothy Cely to the Privy Council for the redemption of her husband Thomas from the Inquisition in Spain, n.d., SP 70/147, part 3, fol. 603, TNA: PRO.

61. Hugh Lee to Thomas Wilson, 3 August 1610, SP 89/3, fol. 140verso, TNA: PRO. By 1661, there were at least 33 traders in residence. In that year, 33 English merchants and factors signed a document from Lisbon. 19 February 1661, SP 89/5, fol. 171verso, TNA: PRO.

62. Brearley, *Gurgeny*, 23. Other nations, particularly the Dutch and the French, were less reliant on placing their own merchants in Lisbon, and were able to rely instead on commercial networks among Sephardic Jews and their New Christian relations.

63. Lee to Salisbury, 20 August 1607, SP 89/3, fol. 90, TNA: PRO.

64. See, for example, Lee to Salisbury, November 19, 1606; Lee to Salisbury, 16 April 1609, SP 89/3, fols. 74recto–verso, 122recto, TNA: PRO.

65. Lee to Salisbury, 4 February 1607, new style, SP 89/3, fol. 80recto, TNA: PRO.

66. See Brearley, *Gurgeny;* Hugh Lee, ambassador at Lisbon, to Salisbury, 8 September 1605 [1606?], SP 89/3, fol. 68, TNA: PRO.

67. Lee to (Salisbury), 7 September 1610, SP 89/3, fol. 142, TNA: PRO.

68. Will of William Gough, 4 August 1649, in Constantinople Chancery book, 1648–1651, SP 105/174, 163–166, TNA: PRO. See also Wood, *History of the Levant Company*, 72, for a discussion of the size of Levant factories: he estimated the factory in Istanbul, which was the largest English settlement, to be no more than 24–25 factors (plus dependents) in the first half of the seventeenth century.

69. Michael Cooper remarks on the oddity that the English produced so many documents in their brief ten-year stint in Japan, largely because of their dispersal pursuing trade opportunities in the region. Cooper, "The Brits in Japan," *Monumenta Nipponica* 47:2 (Summer, 1992), 265.

70. Court meeting, 8 November 1614, B/5, 268, IOR, BL.

71. Court meeting, 29 November 1614, B/5, 294, IOR, BL.

72. *Voyage of Captain John Saris*, 22.

73. Court meeting, 8 November 1614, B/5, 263. See also 15 November 1614; 16 December 1614, B/5, 277, 314, IOR, BL.

74. Letter from Keeling read at Court, 10 March 1615, B/5, 385, IOR, BL.

75. Captain Pring to the East India Company, March 18, 1618 on the *Royal James* at Swally, *CSPC-East Indies, 1617–1621*, vol. 3, item 302, 139. Pring's letter also reveals that there were some women along on this voyage.

76. William Foster, ed., *The Travels of John Sanderson in the Levant, 1584–1602* (London: Hakluyt Society, 1931), 10; Sanderson at Pera to Nicholas Leate in London [March 1600], in *Sanderson*, 197.

77. *The Voyage of Captain John Saris*, 83–84. Saris's voyage opened the factory.

78. See, for example, for Africa, George E. Brooks, *Eurafricans in Western Africa: Commerce, Social Status, Gender, and Religious Observance from the Sixteenth to the Eighteenth Century* (Athens: Ohio University Press, 2003); for North America, Sylvia Van Kirk, *Many Tender Ties: Women in Fur Trade Society, 1670–1870* (Norman: University of Oklahoma Press, 1983); for Batavia, Jean Gelman Taylor, *The Social World of Batavia: European and Eurasian in Dutch Asia* (Madison: University of Wisconsin Press, 1983); and for a wide-ranging and theoretically rich study, see Ann Laura Stoler, *Carnal Knowledge and Imperial Power: Race and the Intimate in Colonial Rule* (Berkeley: University of California Press, 2002).

79. Eaton at Osaka to Wickham at Hirado, 20 February 1616, in Farrington, vol. 1, 370.

80. See his letter to Richard Wickham, February 1614, in Farrington, vol. 1, 132.

81. Wickham at Edo to Nealson at Hirado, 25 May 1614, in Farrington, vol. 1, 164.

82. See Wickham to Nealson, 13 October 1615, in Farrington, vol. 1, 323.

83. Eaton at Kyoto to Wickham at Edo, 26 December 1615, mentions a chest delivered to Wickham's woman as per his instructions, in Farrington, vol. 1, 364.

84. See, for example, Wickham at Kyoto to Cocks at Hirado, 13 April 1616, in which he referred to bringing Eaton and "his wooman" as far as Fushimi, in Farrington, vol. 1, 398.

85. Will of William Adams, 16 May 1620, in Farrington, vol. 1, 795.

86. Eaton at Kyoto to Wickham at Edo, 26 December 1615, in Farrington, vol. 1, 365; *The Voyage of Captain John Saris*, 15. "Wife" also meant simply a woman, but paired as it was in these examples with a specific man, it seems to invoke the meaning of companionate status.

87. Wickham at Kyoto to Eaton at Osaka, 22 May 1616, in Farrington, vol. 1, 412.

88. October 31 and November 18, 1616, *Diary of Richard Cocks*, vol. 1, 199, 209.

89. Eaton at Hirado to Wickham at Kyoto or elsewhere, 22 June 1616, in Farrington, vol. 1, 438.

90. Cocks at Hirado to Edmund Sayers at Nagasaki, 2 October 1620, reported that Jno. Portis's woman Maddalina had given birth to a boy, but he died soon after birth and Maddalina herself was in poor health. He reported as well that Sayers's woman, Omaria, was sick. In Farrington, vol. 1, 802.

91. 6 July 1621, *Diary of Richard Cocks*, vol. 2, 174.

92. Michael Cooper, "The Second Englishman in Japan: The Trials and Travails of Richard Cocks, 1623–1624," *Transactions of the Asiatic Society of Japan* 17 (1982), 138–146; Massarella, *World Elsewhere*, 298–328.

93. Massarella, *World Elsewhere*, 321–322. Denization gave foreigners certain legal rights as English subjects, and it is interesting in this case that having an English father did not automatically give William Eaton, Jr., the rights of other English subjects.

94. Kamezō to Richard Cocks, 14 January 1624, in Farrington, vol. 2, 956.

95. Mateyasu to Edmund Sayers, 15 January 1624, in Farrington, vol. 2, 957; Massarella, *World Elsewhere*, 234.

96. On this important population of mixed-race children and their role in trading communities and diplomatic and cultural relations, see, for example, Margaret Connell Szasz, *Between Indian and White Worlds: the Cultural Broker* (Norman: University of Oklahoma Press, 1994).

97. Letters dated 23 May 1614, 20 September 1614, William Foster, ed., *Letters Received by the East India Company from its Servants in the East* (London: Sampson Low, Marston & Company, 1897), vol. 2, 36, 105.

98. Cocks at Hirado to John Saris in England, 10 December 1614, in Farrington, vol. 1, 254.

99. Cooper, "Second Englishman," 132–133.

100. William Eaton at Osaka to Richard Wickham at Hirado, 20 February 1616, in Farrington, vol. 1, 370.

101. William Nealson at Hirado to Richard Wickham at Edo, February 1614, in Farrington, vol. 1, 131; Richard Cocks at Hirado to Richard Wickham at Edo, Shizuoka, or elsewhere, 9 March 1614, in Farrington, vol. 1, 140.

102. Richard Watts at Hirado to Sir Thomas Smythe and the East India Company, 22 September 1621, in Farrington, vol. 2, 843.

103. August 12, 1616, Foster, ed., *Embassy of Sir Thomas Roe*, 238.

104. July 13, 1616, Foster, ed., *Embassy of Sir Thomas Roe*, 209.

105. 12 October 1613, "Relation of Richard Cocks," *Voyage of Captain John Saris*, 160.

106. William Adams to Thomas Best, 1 December 1613, Farrington, vol. 1, 111.

107. [February, 1617], Foster, ed., *Embassy*, 390.

108. July 13, 1616, Foster, ed., *Embassy*, 211.

109. Court, 26 August 1633, Aleppo Minute Book, SP 110/54, fols. 109verso–110recto, TNA: PRO.

110. See SP 9/209, fol. 135verso, TNA: PRO.

111. "Tonqueen, 1672 A Journal Register of all the Transactions in ye first settlemt of a factory there," Sloane 998, fol. 3recto, BL.

112. One letter in Arabic letters might be Ottoman Turkish; see Constantinople Order book, 1638–1643, SP 105/103, 467, TNA: PRO.

113. See, for example, Richard Wickham at Shizuoka to Hernando Ximenes at Bantam, 13 October 1615 (in Spanish), in Farrington, vol. 1, 318; Geronomo de Varreda at Nagasaki to Edmund Sayers at Hirado 2/12 July 1618 (in Spanish), in Farrington, vol. 1, 711–712; same to same, 17/27 July 1618, Farrington, vol. 1, 713 and 20/30 August 1618, 718. Cocks's record of letters received reflects this range of correspondence. On July 13, 1616, Cocks received letters from Bantam including one from the former captain of the Dutch factory and another from John de Lievana, a foreign merchant (*Diary of Richard Cocks*, vol. 1, 152).

114. 3 January 1616, *Diary of Richard Cocks*, vol. 1, 96.

115. 13 October 1613, "Relation of Richard Cocks," 161–162.

116. Cooper, "Second Englishman," 135, 155. Omitted from the Hakluyt Society edition of Cocks's diary, this detail about how the Dutch used the English flag can be found in *Diary Kept by the Head of the English Factory in Japan: Diary of Richard Cocks, 1615–1622* (Tokyo: The Historiographical Institute, 1979), vol. 2, 115.

117. *Newes out of East India: Of the cruell and bloody usage of our English Merchants and others at Amboyna, by the Netherlandish Governour and Councell there* (London, 1624?). In the retribution suitable for a ballad text, the Dutch instigator of the attack went mad when he saw the English graves. P. J. Marshall, "The English in Asia," in Canny, ed., *Origins of Empire*, 270–271; Holden Furber, *Rival Empires of Trade in the Orient 1600–1800* (Minneapolis: University of Minnesota Press, 1976), 48–49.

118. Copy of a letter to Mr. Philip Hertt, 27 December 1634; copy of letter to Mr. John Steavens, 27 December 1634; copy of letter to Mr. Richard Middleton, 1 January 1634/5, Aleppo Letters, SP 110/10, fols. 21verso, 22recto, 26verso, TNA: PRO.

119. For Christmas, see for example letters in December 1634, SP 110/10, fols. 21–26, passim, quotation from fol. 26verso, TNA: PRO.

120. 25 December 1615, *Diary of Richard Cocks*, vol. 1, 91.

121. 30 and 31 March 1616, *Diary of Richard Cocks*, vol. 1, 124.

122. 27 August 1615, *Diary of Richard Cocks*, vol. 1, 46.

123. 26 February 1617, *Diary of Richard Cocks*, vol. 1, 238.

124. "Relation of Richard Cocks," 160.

125. 2 October 1615, *Diary of Richard Cocks*, vol. 1, 65.

126. Kenneth Parker, *Early Modern Tales of Orient: A Critical Anthology* (London: Routledge, 1999), 15.

127. Massarella, *A World Elsewhere*, 96.

128. Inventory of John Kynnaston, 13 July 1638, Aleppo Minutebook, SP 110/54, fols. 205verso–206recto, TNA: PRO.

129. George Ball to Richard Cocks, 9 June 1617, in Farrington, vol. 1, 619.

130. 11 September 1615, *Diary of Richard Cocks*, vol. 1, 56. This Turkish history was likely Richard Knolles, *The Generall Historie of the Turkes*, a popular and enormous work that appeared in five editions between 1603 and 1638.

131. 9 March 1616, *Diary of Richard Cocks*, vol. 1, 118; Inventory of Wickham's goods at Bantam, November, 1618, in Farrington, vol. 1, 729–736.

132. "Relation of Richard Cocks," 153.

133. 26 October 1613, "Relation of Richard Cocks," 168.

134. 31 October 1613, "Relation of Richard Cocks," 170.

135. Cocks rented his garden on June 19, 1615. *Diary of Richard Cocks*, vol. 1, 11, 117, 334.

136. See volume 2 of *Diary of Richard Cocks*. There is a gap in the diary between January, 1619, and December of 1620. When the diary resumed, Cocks put the Japanese date in parentheses next to every English date.

137. 23 December 1615, *Diary of Richard Cocks,* vol. 1, 91.

138. 4 April 1616, *Diary of Richard Cocks*, vol. 1, 125.

139. 15 December 1618, *Diary of Richard Cocks*, vol. 2, 103.

140. October 28, 1615, *Diary of Richard Cocks*, vol. 1, 79.

CHAPTER 4

1. This percentage placed them somewhere in the middle of all overseas companies. One hundred percent of company members in six other companies, for example, held investments in other companies, down to a low of 35 percent for the Irish Company. At 40 percent, the Virginia Company was at a low end. T. K. Rabb, *Enterprise & Empire: Merchant and Gentry Investment in the Expansion of England, 1575–1630* (Cambridge, Mass.: Harvard University Press, 1967), table 12, p. 108. There are many excellent histories of Jamestown. For an interpretation that shares my emphasis on setting Jamestown in the context of English overseas ventures more generally, see Karen Ordahl Kupperman, *The Jamestown Project* (Cambridge, Mass.: Harvard University Press, 2007).

2. Philip L. Barbour, ed., *The Jamestown Voyages under the First Charter 1606–1609,* two volumes, Hakluyt Society, second series, vol. 136–137 (Cambridge, Mass.: Cambridge University Press for the Society, 1969), vol. 1, 14.

3. Barbour, ed., *Jamestown Voyages,* vol. 1, 17.

4. Instructions for the government, 20 November 1606, Barbour, ed., *Jamestown Voyages*, vol. 1, 41.

5. Ibid., 51.

6. Edward Maria Wingfield, *Discourse*, 1608, in Barbour, ed., *Jamestown Voyages*, vol. 1, 229.

7. Camilla Townsend, *Pocahontas and the Powhatan Dilemma* (New York: Hill and Wang, 2004), 43.

8. Townsend, *Pocahontas,* 81.

9. April Lee Hatfield, *Atlantic Virginia: Intercolonial Relations in the Seventeenth Century* (Philadelphia: University of Pennsylvania Press, 2004), 7.

10. Instructions to Gates, May 1609, *Records of the Virginia Company*, vol. 3, 22.

11. Edmund S. Morgan, *American Slavery, American Freedom: The Ordeal of Colonial Virginia* (New York: Norton, 1975), 45.

12. Richard Hakluyt, "Discourse of Western Planting," in Peter C. Mancall, ed., *Envisioning America: English Plans for the Colonization of North America, 1580–1640* (Boston: Bedford Books, 1995), 54.

13. Kenneth R. Andrews posed a similar question for the plantation colonies of St. Kitts, Nevis, and Barbados. Andrews, *Trade, Plunder, and Settlement: Maritime Enterprise and the Genesis of the British Empire, 1480–1630* (Cambridge: Cambridge University Press, 1984), 280.

14. Karen Ordahl Kupperman, *Indians and English: Facing Off in Early America* (Ithaca: Cornell University Press, 2000), 14.

15. Wesley Frank Craven, *The Dissolution of the Virginia Company* (New York: Oxford University Press, 1932), 26.

16. There was some disagreement on this legal position in England. Ken MacMillan, *Sovereignty and Possession in the English New World: The Legal Foundations of Empire, 1576–1640* (Cambridge: Cambridge University Press, 2006), 68–69.

17. On this mission, see Clifford M. Lewis and Albert J. Loomie, *The Spanish Jesuit Mission in Virginia 1570–1572* (Chapel Hill: University of North Carolina Press, 1953); Charlotte M. Gradie, "The Powhatans in the Context of the Spanish Empire," in Helen C. Rountree, ed., *Powhatan Foreign Relations, 1500–1722* (Charlottesville: University Press of Virginia, 1993), 154–172; and David J. Weber, *The Spanish Frontier in North America* (New Haven: Yale University Press, 1992), 71–72.

18. My thanks to Camilla Townsend for providing Paquiquineo's name.

19. On the six-year time frame, see Luis de Quirós and Juan Baptista de Segura to Juan de Hinistrosa, from Ajacán, 12 September 1570, in Lewis and Loomie, *Spanish Jesuit Mission*, 89. Frederic W. Gleach, *Powhatan's World and Colonial Virginia: A Conflict of Cultures* (Lincoln: University of Nebraska Press, 1997), 91.

20. "The Relation of Luis Geronimo de Oré" reports the efforts of Fr. Baptista to rebuke Don Luis's new habits. Lewis and Loomie, *Spanish Jesuit Mission*, 180–181.

21. Historians offer various interpretations for Don Luis's actions. Gradie, "Powhatans," suggests that he needed to prove himself as Indian when he settled back among his own people, and thus took several wives (169). His retaliation was part of that proof. Gleach, *Powhatan's World*, proposes that Don Luis felt no such conflicted loyalties, but rather was able to reconcile these different parts of his life. He interprets the attack as Don Luis's effort to give the Jesuits the martyrdom they always spoke of (95), reminding us yet again that it is important to be careful what you wish for. Some historians have believed that Don Luis was the same person as Opechancanough, the leader of the famous 1622 attack on the Virginia colony. But such a connection seems improbable and, moreover, unnecessary: the Spanish presence shaped Indian expectations without the particular linkage of one powerful individual. And had Don Luis been Opechancanough, the Powhatan confederation would likely have understood a great deal more about who the English were and what they wanted.

22. See Ralph Hamor, *A True Discourse of the Present Estate of Virginia* (London, 1615), 13; Townsend, *Pocahontas*, 10.

23. Helen C. Rountree, *Pocahontas's People: The Powhatan Indians of Virginia Through Four Centuries* (Norman: University of Oklahoma Press, 1990), 20.

24. Helen C. Rountree, *Pocahontas, Powhatan, Opechancanough: Three Indian Lives Changed by Jamestown* (Charlottesville: University Press of Virginia, 2005), 49.

25. On this population, see Alden T. Vaughan, "Powhatans Abroad: Virginia Indians in England," in Robert Appelbaum and John Wood Sweet, eds., *Envisioning an*

English Empire: Jamestown and the Making of the North Atlantic World (Philadelphia: University of Pennsylvania Press, 2005), 49–67; and on those who preceded them, see "Sir Walter Ralegh's Indian Interpreters, 1584–1618," *William and Mary Quarterly*, third series, 59 (April, 2002): 341–376; Louis B. Wright, ed., *A Voyage to Virginia in 1609; Two Narratives: Strachey's "True reportory" and Jourdain's Discovery of the Bermudas* (Charlottesville: University Press of Virginia, 1964), 92.

26. See especially David Quinn, *The Elizabethans and the Irish* (Ithaca: Cornell University Press, 1966); Nicholas Canny, "The Ideology of English Colonization: From Ireland to America," *William and Mary Quarterly*, third series, 30 (October, 1973): 575–598; and James Muldoon, "The Indian as Irishman," *Essex Institute Historical Collections* 111 (1975): 267–289.

27. Quinn, *Elizabethans*, 107.

28. On the Irish-American connection as a self-evident assertion, see for example Kathleen M. Brown, *Good Wives, Nasty Wenches, and Anxious Patriarchs: Gender, Race, and Power in Colonial Virginia* (Chapel Hill: University of North Carolina Press, 1996), 32–36; and Eric Hinderaker and Peter C. Mancall, *At the Edge of Empire: The Backcountry in British North America* (Baltimore: The Johns Hopkins University Press, 2003), 1.

29. David B. Quinn, *Ireland and America: Their Early Associations, 1500–1640* (Liverpool: Liverpool University Press, 1991), 17.

30. Andrew Hadfield, "Irish Colonies and the Americas," in Appelbaum and Sweet, 173–190.

31. William Strachey, *The Historie of Travell into Virginia Britania*, ed. Louis B. Wright and Virginia Freund (London: Hakluyt Society, 1953), 90.

32. Kupperman, *Indians and English*, 13.

33. Barbour, ed., *Jamestown Voyages*, vol. 1, 24–34, 41.

34. Quoted in Jeffrey Knapp, *An Empire Nowhere: England, America, and Literature from Utopia to The Tempest* (Berkeley: University of California Press, 1992), 231.

35. Philip D. Morgan, "Virginia's Other Prototype: The Caribbean," in Peter C. Mancall, ed., *The Atlantic World and Virginia, 1550–1624* (Chapel Hill: University of North Carolina Press, 2007), 349.

36. Samuel Purchas, *Hakluytus Posthumus, Or Purchas his Pilgrimes* (London, 1625), chapter 13, 1664.

37. Karen Ordahl Kupperman, *Roanoke: The Abandoned Colony* (New York: Rowman & Allanheld, 1984).

38. Rountree, *Pocahontas's People*, 24.

39. John Pory to Sir Dudley Carleton, Virginia, 30 September 1619, reproduced in William Stevens Powell, *John Pory, 1572–1636: The Life and Letters of a Man of Many Parts* (Chapel Hill: University of North Carolina Press, 1977), 106–107.

40. Darrett B. Rutman, "The Historian and the Marshal: A Note on the Background of Sir Thomas Dale," *Virginia Magazine of History and Biography* 68 (1960), 290–291.

41. Quoted in Alexander Brown, *The Genesis of the United States*, two volumes (Boston: Houghton Mifflin, 1891), vol. 2, 824.

42. Smith, *True Relation*, in Barbour, ed., *Jamestown Voyages*, vol. 1, 175.

43. Robert Appelbaum, "Hunger in Early Virginia," in Appelbaum and Sweet, 195–216.

44. Edmund S. Morgan called these mistakes a "formula for disaster." Morgan, *American Slavery*, 70.

45. Andrews faults the merchants who expected to run Virginia as if it were a trading company for the colony's failures (Andrews, *Trade, Plunder*, 339), but these were perfectly reasonable expectations from men with a direct hand in foreign trade and a conviction that lucrative commodities were awaiting their purchase in Virginia.

46. Edward Maria Wingfield, *Discourse*, 1608, in Barbour, ed., *Jamestown Voyages*, vol. 1, 231.

47. Alexander Whitaker, *Good Newes from Virginia* (London, 1613), 43.

48. James Horn, "The Conquest of Eden: Possession and Dominion in Early Virginia," in Appelbaum and Sweet, 31.

49. Strachey, *Historie*, 18.

50. Ibid., 22–23.

51. Ibid., 26.

52. Andrews, *Trade, Plunder*, 322; Andrew Fitzmaurice, *Humanism and America: An Intellectual History of English Colonisation, 1500–1625* (Cambridge: Cambridge University Press, 2003), 1–2; Craven, *Dissolution*, 24.

53. Gabriel Archer's *Relation*, in Barbour, ed., *Jamestown Voyages*, vol. 1, 101.

54. Instructions for the new government, 20 November 1606, Barbour, ed., *Jamestown Voyages*, vol. 1, 41; Craven, *Dissolution*, 51.

55. Perkin to a friend, 28 March 1608, in Barbour, ed., *Jamestown Voyages*, vol. 1, 159.

56. London Council's Instructions for the new government, written between 20 November and 20 December 1606, Barbour, ed., *Jamestown Voyages*, vol. 1, p. 53.

57. Smith, *Map of Virginia*, in Barbour, ed., *Jamestown Voyages*, vol. 2, 417.

58. Strachey, *True Reportory*, 72.

59. See, for example, Thomas Dale to the President and Council of Virginia, 25 May 1611, in Brown, *Genesis*, vol. 1, 493.

60. Morgan, *American Slavery*, p. 73.

61. James Horn, *A Land as God Made It: Jamestown and the Birth of America* (New York: Basic Books, 2005), 245.

62. Records of burgesses, as transmitted to Virginia Company and recorded there, Court meeting, August 4, 1619, *Records of the Virginia Company*, vol. 3, 175.

63. John Rolfe to Sir Edwyn Sandys, January 1619/20, *Records of the Virginia Company*, vol. 3, 242.

64. Company meeting, February 16, 1619/20, *Records of the Virginia Company*, vol. 1, 310. Similarly attracted to Indian cultures, and similarly dismissed as spoiled, was the Spanish child, Alonso, who had survived the Indian attack on the Jesuit mission

at Ajacán in 1571. He lived among the Indians until the Spanish reclaimed him in 1572. A priest named Juan Rogel thought little of the boy, claiming that "he has been quite spoiled after living alone with the Indians. He does not want to be one of us, he is not suitable." Juan Rogel to Francis Borgia, from the Bay of the Mother of God, August 28, 1572, in Lewis and Loomie, *Spanish Jesuit Mission*, 114.

65. Rountree, *Pocahontas, Powhatan, Opechancanough*, 99.

66. Donald E. Chipman, *Moctezuma's Children: Aztec Royalty Under Spanish Rule, 1520–1700* (Austin: University of Texas Press, 2005), chapter 2.

67. Smith, *Map of Virginia*, in Barbour, ed., *Jamestown Voyages*, vol. 2, 458–459; Rountree, *Pocahontas, Powhatan, Opechancanough*, 142.

68. Hamor, *True Discourse*, 40–42.

69. Strachey, *Historie*, 192.

70. Townsend, *Pocahontas*, 112; Pedro de Zúñiga to Philip III, London, 1 August 1612, in Brown, *Genesis*, vol. 2, 572–573. Letter to Captain Bell, 20 April 1635, CO 124/1, fol. 77 recto, TNA: PRO.

71. See Townsend, *Pocahontas*, and Rountree, *Pocahontas, Powhatan, Opechancanough*, for two good recent assessments of Pocahontas.

72. There is general skepticism of the veracity of the "rescue," with the exception of Gleach, 116–121. Of his Ottoman rescuer, Smith remembered that "all the hope he had ever to be delivered from this thraledome, was only the love of Tragabigzanda." John Smith, *The True Travels, Adventures, and Observations of Captain John Smith* (London, 1630), in Philip L. Barbour, ed., *The Complete Works of Captain John Smith, 1580–1631*, three volumes (Chapel Hill: University of North Carolina Press, 1986), vol. 3, 200.

73. See Barbara A. Mowat, "The Tempest: A Modern Perspective," in Mowat and Paul Werstine, eds., *The Tempest* (New York: Washington Square Press, 1999), 185–199; Wright, ed., *A Voyage to Virginia in 1609*.

74. "Letter of John Rolfe," in Lyon Gardiner Tyler, ed., *Narratives of Early Virginia, 1606–1625* (New York: Charles Scribner's Sons, 1907), 239–244.

75. Townsend, *Pocahontas*, 62; Rountree, "The Powhatans and the English: A Case of Multiple Conflicting Agendas," in Rountree, ed., *Powhatan Foreign Relations*, 178–179.

76. Gleach, 54–56.

77. Barbour, ed., *Jamestown Voyages*, vol. 1, 51.

78. Rountree, *Pocahontas's People*, 29.

79. Nicholas Canny, *Making Ireland British, 1580–1650* (Oxford: Oxford University Press, 2001), 45–47.

80. Rountree, ed., *Powhatan Foreign Relations*, 18–19.

81. Smith, *True Relation*, in Barbour, ed., *Jamestown Voyages*, vol. 1, 191.

82. John Smith, *Map of Virginia*, in Barbour, ed., *Jamestown Voyages*, vol. 2, 413–414.

83. Alden T. Vaughan, *American Genesis: Captain John Smith and the Founding of Virginia* (Boston: Little Brown, 1975), 46.

84. Barbour, ed., *Jamestown Voyages,* vol. 1, 52.

85. Hamor, *True Discourse,* 44.

86. Kupperman suggests that much of the English bad behavior can be explained by their fear. Kupperman, *Indians and English,* 214.

87. Hatfield, *Atlantic Virginia,* 9.

88. Capt. John Smith to Treasurer and Council of Virginia in London, between 10 September and early December, 1608, Barbour, ed., *Jamestown Voyages,* vol. 1, 243.

89. Horn, "Conquest," 42.

90. Pedro de Zúñiga to Philip III, 6/16 October 1607, in Barbour, ed., *Jamestown Voyages,* vol. 1, 121. On this Florida venture, see John T. McGrath, *The French in Early Florida: In the Eye of the Hurricane* (Gainesville: University Press of Florida, 2000).

91. Instructions to Sir Thomas Gates, May, 1609, *Records of the Virginia Company,* vol. 3, 17–18.

92. Thomas Dale to President and Council of Virginia, 25 May 1611, Brown, *Genesis,* vol. 1, 488–493; Gleach, 133.

93. Rountree, *Pocahontas, Powhatan, Openchancanough,* 138.

94. Horn, "Conquest," 43.

95. Strachey, *Historie,* Appendix A, 174–207

96. Thomas Weelkes, "Come, Sirrah Jack, Ho," Philip Ledger, ed., *The Oxford Book of English Madrigals* (Oxford: Oxford University Press, 1978), 70–71.

97. Peter C. Mancall, "Tales Tobacco Told in Sixteenth-Century Europe," *Environmental History* 9 (October 2004): 648–678.

98. John Rolfe, *A True Relation of the State of Virginia…in 1616* (Charlottesville: University Press of Virginia, 1971), 6.

99. Craven, *Dissolution,* 50.

100. Dale to President and Council of Virginia, 25 May 1611, in Brown, *Genesis,* vol. 1, 493.

101. Craven, *Dissolution,* 177–188.

102. Craven, *Dissolution,* chapter 6.

103. November 18, 1618, *Records of the Virginia Company,* vol. 3, 98.

104. John Pory to Sandys, January 14, 1619/20, *Records of the Virginia Company,* vol. 3, 254.

105. 31 May 1620, 23 June 1620, *Records of the Virginia Company,* vol. 1, 368, 372.

106. 13 June 1621, *Records of the Virginia Company,* vol. 1, 493.

107. July 3, 1622, *Records of the Virginia Company,* vol. 2, 74–75.

108. Whitaker, *Good Newes from Virginia,* 33, 37–39.

109. Strachey, *True Reportory,* 70–71.

110. Strachey's ambition was not accomplished in the seventeenth century. In 1686, English exports to the Chesapeake (Virginia and Maryland) totaled £35,107; imports of tobacco totaled £141,606. For the Levant Company some twenty years earlier in 1668, goods exported to Turkey totaled £466,703, and goods imported from Turkey totaled £191,458. See Nuala Zahediah, "Overseas Expansion and

Trade in the Seventeenth Century," in Nicholas Canny, ed., *The Origins of Empire* (New York: Oxford University Press, 1998), 410, 415; Alfred C. Wood, *A History of the Levant Company* (New York: Barnes and Noble, 1964), 102.

111. Smith, *True Relation*, in Barbour, ed., *Jamestown Voyages*, vol. 1, 185–186.

112. Desires to separate themselves from Indians were evident early on. Sir George Yeardley was instructed by the Council for Virginia to push the Chickahominy further away from English territoy "by all lawfull meanes" in the wake of violence. Letter to Sir George Yeardley, 21 June 1619, *Records of the Virginia Company*, vol. 3, 147.

113. Rountree, *Pocahontas's People*, 67.

114. Rountree, "The Powhatans and the English," in Rountree, ed., *Powhatan Foreign Relations*, p. 186.

115. Townsend, *Pocahontas*, 150.

116. Smith, *Map of Virginia*, in Barbour, ed., *Jamestown Voyages*, vol. 2, 332.

117. "A Declaration of the State of the Colony and Affaires in Virginia (1622)" in *Records of the Virginia Company*, vol. 3, 556–557, 558. The document drew at length on Spanish experiences and histories.

118. Thomas Harriot, *A Briefe and True Report of the New Found Land of Virginia* (Frankfurt, 1590), 13.

119. Strachey, *Historie*, 60, 71, 73, 81, 84, 85, 87. Strachey also made Irish comparisons. See, for example, *Historie*, 72.

120. *Records of the Virginia Company*, vol. 1, 348, 1620. For an exception, see George Thorpe and John Pory to Sir Edwyn Sandys, May 15–16, 1621, in which Thorpe wrote that he believed that the people of Virginia were not as serious as they should be about their conversion of the "heathen." *Records of the Virginia Company*, vol. 3, 446.

121. John Pory to Sir Dudley Carleton from Virginia, 30 September 1619, reprinted in Powell, *John Pory*, 109.

122. April 8, 1620, *Records of the Virginia Company*, vol. 1, 334–335.

123. Brief Declaration of the plantation of Virginia, July 1624, *CSPC* CD-ROM. "Slavery" appears in a similar context as an expression of government opposition in Bermuda, where five men fled the oppressive rule of Governor Tucker, resolving to escape than to endure such "slavery." Nathaniel Butler, *The Historye of the Bermudaes or Summer Islands* (London: Hakluyt Society, 1882), 83.

124. To be sure, not all Africans in Virginia in the seventeenth century were slaves, and a rich historiography exists on the issue of the status of Africans and people of African descent there, and the evolution of a legal code for enslavement. See especially T. H. Breen and Stephen Innes, *"Myne Owne Ground": Race and Freedom on Virginia's Eastern Shore, 1640–1676* (New York: Oxford University Press, 1980).

125. T. H. Breen, James H. Lewis, and Keith Schlesinger, "Motive for Murder: A Servant's Life in Virginia, 1678," *William and Mary Quarterly*, third series, 40 (1983), 120.

126. James Revel, "The Poor Unhappy Transported Felon's Sorrowful Account of his Fourteen Years Transportation at Virginia in America," in Warren M. Billings, ed.,

The Old Dominion in the Seventeenth Century: A Documentary History of Virginia, 1606–1689 (Chapel Hill: University of North Carolina Press, 1975), 137–142, quotation from 140.

CHAPTER 5

1. Nathaniel Butler, "A Discourse of the Miscarriages of or two late Expedicions and the Cares propounded for the Future," Add. 41,616, fol. 29recto, BL. This text dates from 1625 or 1626.

2. While it might seem obvious that colonial governors carried out state functions, it has seemed less apparent for the leaders of trading ventures. Indeed, one important debate about the early East India Company centers around the chronology of its status as a state, and its aspirations for governance. See Philip J. Stern, "Politics and Ideology in the Early East India Company-State: The Case of St. Helena, 1673–1709," *The Journal of Imperial and Commonwealth History* 35, no. 1 (March 2007): 2–3. Although in the first part of the seventeenth century the energies of trade ambassadors were directed primarily toward commercial concerns, the challenges consuls and ambassadors confronted meant that, when trading ventures did later seek to pursue territorial governance, crucial experience in doing so was already in place.

3. John Pory to Sir Dudley Carleton, Virginia, 30 September 1619, reproduced in William Stevens Powell, *John Pory, 1572–1636: The Life and Letters of a Man of Many Parts* (Chapel Hill: University of North Carolina Press, 1977), 106–107. Stephen Saunders Webb, *The Governors-General: The English Army and the Definition of Empire, 1569–1681* (Chapel Hill: University of North Carolina Press, 1979), 436–437.

4. On the lucrative opportunities, see David William Davies, *Elizabethans Errant: the Strange Fortunes of Sir Thomas Sherley and His Three Sons, as Well in the Dutch Wars as in Muscovy, Morocco, Persia, Spain, and the Indies* (Ithaca: Cornell University Press, 1967), 16.

5. John Smith, *The True Travels, Adventures, and Observations of Captain John Smith* (London, 1630), in Philip L. Barbour, ed., *The Complete Works of Captain John Smith, 1580–1631*, three volumes (Chapel Hill: University of North Carolina Press, 1986), vol. 3, 155–157, quotation from 155–156.

6. Richard Hakluyt, "Discourse of Western Planting," in Peter C. Mancall, ed., *Envisioning America: English Plans for the Colonization of North America, 1580–1640* (Boston: Bedford Books, 1995), 53.

7. Pedro de Zúñiga to Philip III, 16/26 June 1608, Philip L. Barbour, ed., *The Jamestown Voyages under the First Charter 1606–1609*, two volumes, Hakluyt Society, second series, vols. 136–137 (Cambridge: Cambridge University Press for the Society, 1969), vol. 1, 163.

8. Instructions to Captain Robert Hunt, 28 March 1636, CO 124/1, fol. 90recto, TNA: PRO.

9. Darrett B. Rutman, "A Militant New World 1607–1640" (Ph.D. Dissertation, University of Virginia, 1959; reprinted New York: Arno Press, 1979), 145–146. See the Lawes at http://etext.lib.virginia.edu/etcbin/jamestown-browse?id=J1056.

10. Richard S. Dunn, *Puritans and Yankees: The Winthrop Dynasty of New England, 1630–1717* (Princeton: Princeton University Press, 1962), 61–62.

11. Darrett B. Rutman, "The Historian and the Marshal: A Note on the Background of Sir Thomas Dale," *Virginia Magazine of History and Biography* 68 (1960), 291.

12. Letter to Captain Bell, 20 April 1635, CO 124/1, fol. 79recto, TNA: PRO.

13. Bell to Rich, March 1626/7, and March 1628/9, in Vernon A. Ives, ed., *The Rich Papers: Letters from Bermuda, 1615–1646: Eyewitness Accounts Sent by the Early Colonists to Sir Nathaniel Rich* (Toronto: University of Toronto Press, 1984), 283–291, 312–315.

14. Providence Committee, 17–18 April 1635, CO 124/2, 214, TNA: PRO.

15. Webb, *The Governors-General*. Although employers perceived these governor-captains as desirable colonial officers, Karen Ordahl Kupperman has suggested that these continentally trained military men often operated in a different mental world from some of the men they served and ruled, particularly puritans. Nathaniel Butler was at odds with the civilians he governed on Providence Island, and had little sympathy for the ecclesiastical organization of the island's separatist ministers. But there was no guarantee that a governor of like religious sympathies would succeed. Captain Robert Hunt had served on the continent, in the Netherlands and at La Rochelle. But he was a religious man, and he increased the island's conflicts when he reached Providence and allied himself with the minister. Moreover, the military model was a good strategy for launching and securing a new outpost, but it was not necessarily constructive for long-term settlement. Karen Ordahl Kupperman, *Providence Island, 1630–1641: The Other Puritan Colony* (Cambridge: Cambridge University Press, 1993), 190–192, 216–217, 267, 269; Karen Ordahl Kupperman, *Indians and English: Facing Off in Early America* (Ithaca: Cornell University Press, 2000), 13.

16. Janice E. Thomson, *Mercenaries, Pirates, and Sovereigns: State-building and Extraterritorial Violence in Early Modern Europe* (Princeton: Princeton University Press, 1994), 34–36.

17. Dale to Sir Ralph Winwood, 3 June 1616, *CSPC* CD-ROM; Rutman, "The Historian and the Marshal," 284–294.

18. Thomas Dale to Dudley Carleton, October 18, 1617, *CSPC* CD-ROM.

19. On the negotiations of Dale's absence and payment from the States General, see Sir Ralph Winwood to Lord Treasurer Salisbury, 6 February 1611, *CSPC* CD-ROM. On efforts to sort out Dale's payment, see Sir Ralphe Winwood to Sir Dudley Carleton, March 31, 1617; King James to Sir Dudley Carlton, Ambassador with the States General, November 11, 1617, *CSPC* CD-ROM.

20. East India Company court minutes, February 3, 1618, *CSPC-East Indies, 1617–1621,* vol. 3, item 262, 115–116.

21. Court for East India Company, February 14, 1620, *CSPC-East Indies, 1617–1621,* vol. 3, 350.

22. Sir Dudley Carleton at the Hague to secretary [Thomas Lake], 3 March 1618, *CSPC* CD-ROM.

23. Thomas Dale to the East India Company, March 1, 1619, Jacatra, *CSPC-East Indies, 1617–1621,* vol. 3, item 609, 253; Thomas Dale to Sir William Throckmorton, from Jacatra, 15 March 1618/19, L.b.667, Folger.

24. Aug. Spaldinge to East India Company, November 23 and December 9, on the *Unicorn,* Masulipatam road, 1619, *CSPC-East Indies, 1617–1621,* vol. 3, 325.

25. William Methwold to the East India Company, 7 December 1619, *CSPC-East Indies, 1617–1621,* vol. 3, 329. In the wake of their husbands' deaths, the governors' widows rallied as best they could. Thomas Dale's wife struggled to claim what was left of her husband's estate from the East India Company in the winter of 1621. After the Company announced on November 14 that no further funds were due her, she did not quit, arranging within the week to have an East India Company man arrested for money owed to her dead husband. She had greater success with the Virginia Company. She requested that the Virginia Company give her a patent for a plantation, which they did. East India Company Court minutes, October 19, November 14, November 23, 1621, *CSPC-East Indies, 1617–1621,* vol. 3, 471, 487, 489; Court, June 11, 1621, *Records of the Virginia Company,* vol. 1, 483.

26. Quoted in William Foster, ed., *The Embassy of Sir Thomas Roe to the Court of the Great Mogul, 1615–1619* (London: Hakluyt Society, 1899), iv. On the choice of Roe, see also Michael J. Brown, *Itinerant Ambassador: The Life of Sir Thomas Roe* (Lexington: University Press of Kentucky, 1970), chapter 2. Roe has been the subject of two book-length biographies: Brown, *Itinerant Ambassador,* and Michael Strachan, *Sir Thomas Roe 1581–1644: A Life* (Salisbury, Wilts: M. Russell, 1989).

27. Alfred Cecil Wood, *A History of the Levant Company* (New York: Barnes and Noble, 1964), 80–81.

28. Strachan, *Sir Thomas Roe,* 1–7.

29. Joyce Lorimer, *English and Irish Settlement on the River Amazon, 1550–1646* (London: Hakluyt Society, 1989), 36; the quotation is from Edmund Howes's *Annales* (London, 1631), quoted in Lorimer, 152.

30. Lorimer, 151–152.

31. Ibid., 41, 46; Sir Julius Caesar's notes on English activities in Guiana, in Lorimer, 151; and Howes's *Annales* in Lorimer, 151–152.

32. The best source for Roe's time in India is his journal, edited by William Foster in *The Embassy of Sir Thomas Roe.* Foster was able to work with the first part of Roe's original journal through the summer of 1617. At that point Foster had to switch

over to the mangled and heavily reduced version published by Samuel Purchas. And the original journals available to Purchas stopped in 1617, so Foster supplemented his collection with letters written to and from Roe.

33. Royal Commission to Thomas Roe, 29 December 1614, in Foster, ed., *Embassy*, 552.

34. September 25, 1615, Foster, ed., *Embassy*, 45.

35. September 26, 1615, Foster, ed., *Embassy*, 50.

36. October 15, 1615, Foster, ed., *Embassy*, 73.

37. See, for example, Roe's letter to Lord Carew, 17 January 1615/16, Foster, ed., *Embassy*, 110–115; August 17, 1616, Foster, ed., *Embassy*, 244. On the Prince's pride, see [October] 6, 1617, Foster, ed., *Embassy*, 424.

38. *Records of the Virginia Company*, vol. 1, 309–310.

39. Brown, *Itinerant Ambassador*, 112.

40. Shares and Transfers of Riches and Joseph Man ca. 1622, in Ives, ed., *Rich Papers*, 247. His share was in Harington Tribe (or Parish).

41. *Records of the Virginia Company*, vol. 1, 348, 397, 411, 416.

42. *Records of the Virginia Company*, vol. 1, 394–395, quotation from 394.

43. Reasons presented to the king by the Levant Company, 4 December 1625, SP 105/109, TNA: PRO.

44. Brown, *Itinerant Ambassador*, 119.

45. Thomas Smith, *An Account of the Greek Church* (London, 1680), 253.

46. John Ker at Scio to John Sanderson in London, 9 August 1603, in William Foster, ed., *The Travels of John Sanderson in the Levant, 1584–1602* (London: Hakluyt Society, 1931), 225.

47. Sanderson to John Kitely at Istanbul, 26 May 1604, in *Sanderson*, 227.

48. Item 53, Roe to the lords, 2 November 1625, SP 105/109, TNA: PRO.

49. Articles of Complaint Delivered to the Great Vizier, SP 105/102, fols. 126–127, TNA: PRO.

50. Richard Knolles, *The Generall Historie of the Turkes* (fifth edition, London, 1638), 1311.

51. Court, 12 August, 24 November 1628, 23 September 1629, SP 110/54, fols. 94recto, 96recto, 99recto, TNA: PRO. The problem was Sir Kenelm Digby's slaving in the region.

52. Roe to Secretary Sir Ralph Winwood (secretary of state), 30 November 1616, Foster, ed., *Embassy*, 358.

53. June 12, 1616, Foster, ed., *Embassy*, 191–192.

54. Wood, *History*, 39.

55. Reasons presented to the king, 4 December 1625, SP 105/109, TNA: PRO.

56. Court, 26 March 1622, SP 105/102, fol. 36recto, TNA: PRO.

57. SP 105/102, fol. 23verso, TNA: PRO.

58. Copy of the Capitulations made with Tunis and Algier, SP 105/102, fol. 87verso, TNA: PRO.

59. Court held December 21, 1622, SP 105/102, fol. 64recto–verso, TNA: PRO.

60. Court and Consultation held by Roe, Istanbul, January 1, 1621/2, SP 105/102, fol. 4recto, TNA: PRO.

61. Levant Company to Roe, 22 November 1622, SP 105/110, fol. 145recto, TNA: PRO.

62. Instructions to Governor Bell, 7 February 1630/1, CO 124/1, fols. 13–17, TNA: PRO.

63. Nathaniel Butler, *The Historye of the Bermudaes or Summer Islands* (London: Hakluyt Society, 1882), 231–232.

64. Hughes to Sir Nathaniel Rich, 12 January 1619/20 in Ives, ed., *Rich Papers*, 162.

65. Mr. John Schaw to the Earl of Mar, Venice, 29 February 1618/19, GD 124/15/32/16, NAS.

66. Christopher Hibbert, *The Grand Tour* (New York: G. Putnam's Sons, 1969), 13.

67. The ambassador at Valladolid reported several conversions. Clare Howard, *English Travellers of the Renaissance* (New York: B. Franklin, 1968, 1914), 84.

68. Hugh Lee to Secretary of State, 12 July 1607, fol. 85verso; 26 November 1608, fol. 112recto; 1 April 1617, SP 89/3, fol. 190verso, TNA: PRO.

69. Howard, *Travellers,* 47.

70. Fynes Moryson, *An Itinerary Written by Fynes Moryson gent. First in the Latine Tongue, and then translated by him into the English* (London, 1617), Part 1, 236.

71. Ibid., 245–249.

72. Butler, *Historye,* 15.

73. *Sanderson,* 85.

74. 30 August 1622, SP 105/102, fol. 41recto, TNA: PRO.

75. Butler, *Historye,* 284–285.

76. Butler's diary, pages of notes, Sloane 758, BL.

77. Butler, *Historye,* 172.

78. Dunn, *Puritans and Yankees,* 107.

79. Samuel Winthrop to John Winthrop, Jr., Antigua, 30 April 1671, Winthrop Papers, reel 10, Massachusetts Historical Society.

80. Butler, *Historye,* 76.

81. Ibid., 161–191.

82. Walter W. Woodward, "New England's *Other* Witch-hunt: The Hartford Witch-hunt of the 1660s and Changing Patterns in Witchcraft Prosecution," *OAH Magazine of History* 17 (July 2003), 16–20.

83. Butler, *Historye,* 75.

84. Ibid., 39–40.

85. Ibid., 78–79.

86. Ibid., 89.

87. Lewis Hughes to Sir Nathaniel Rich, March 1617/18, Ives, ed., *Rich Papers*, 106–107.

88. Butler, *Historye,* 280.

89. The other two-thirds went into the Company's coffers. Levant Company to Thomas Roe, 12 April 1622, SP 105/110, fol. 137recto, TNA: PRO.

90. The dragomans were Ottoman subjects but tended to come from minority groups within the empire. Dragomans could be Jews, Greeks, or Armenians. Daniel Goffman, *Britons in the Ottoman Empire, 1642–1660* (Seattle: University of Washington Press, 1998), 16.

91. 13 March 1648/9, Constantinople Chancery, 1648–1651, SP 105/174, 210–211, TNA: PRO.

92. Constantinople Chancery, 1648–1651, SP 105/174, 112, TNA: PRO.

93. Butler to Sir Nathaniel Rich, 23 October 1620, in Ives, ed., *Rich Papers*, 193–194.

94. Nathaniel Butler, "A Designe Upon the West Indies Fleet," Add. 41,616, fol. 30verso, BL.

95. Darrett B. Rutman, "The Virginia Company and Its Military Regime," in Rutman, ed., *The Old Dominion: Essays for Thomas Perkins Abernathy* (Charlottesville: University of Virginia Press, 1964), 1–10.

96. Butler, *Historye*, 47; Meeting, 23 November 1630, CO 124/2, 3, TNA: PRO.

97. Butler, *Historye*, 148.

98. Butler to Sir Nathaniel Rich, 12 January 1620/21, in Ives, ed., *Rich Papers*, 227; Lewis Hughes to Sir Nathaniel Rich, 12 February and 16 March, 1619/20, in Ives, ed., *Rich Papers*, 168.

99. Forster to the Company, 7 September 1650, J. H. Lefroy, *Memorials of the Discovery and Early Settlement of the Bermudas or Somers Islands 1511–1687*, two volumes (London, 1879), vol. 2, 8–9.

100. Edward Barton at Pera to John Sanderson (undated), in *Sanderson*, 148.

101. Ralph Fitch and others at Aleppo to George Dorrington, 4 August 1596, in *Sanderson*, 151–153.

102. George Dorrington at Aleppo to John Sanderson at Istanbul, 11 August 1596, in *Sanderson*, 154.

103. Court, 1 January 1621/2, SP 105/102, fol. 4recto, TNA: PRO.

104. Court, 1 January 1621/2, SP 105/102, fol. 4verso, TNA: PRO. Italics added.

105. Court, 12 March 1624/5, SP 105/102, fol. 204recto, TNA: PRO.

106. Court, 5 April 1625, SP 105/102, fol. 107recto, TNA: PRO. Perhaps Roe's difficulty working with the English merchants and factors in Istanbul contributed to his contemporaneous desire to leave the Levant Company's employment.

107. Lee to Wilson, 7 September 1610, SP 89/3, fol. 144, TNA: PRO.

108. Aleppo court, 3 April 1619, SP 110/54, fol. 25recto, TNA: PRO.

109. *Sanderson*, 10.

110. Shaw, *Anglo-Portuguese Alliance*, 48.

111. Lee to Secretary of State, 1 February 1615, SP 89/3, fol. 179recto, TNA: PRO.

112. Lee to Secretary of State, 25 April 1617, SP 89/3, fol. 192verso, TNA: PRO.

113. Letter from the Levant Company to Sir Thomas Roe, 12 April 1622, SP 105/110, fol. 137recto, TNA: PRO.

114. August 14, 1616, Foster, ed., *Embassy*, 243.

115. Constantinople Chancery, 1648–1651, SP 105/174, TNA: PRO.

116. *Sanderson*, 18.

117. Sanderson at Pera to Nicholas Leate in London [March 1600], in *Sanderson*, 197.

118. Williams to Mr. Jn. Lancelott, 1 August 1639, Williams Letterbook, Stowe 759, BL.

119. Journal of John Covel, October, 1670, Add. 22912, fol. 29recto, BL.

120. *Sir Thomas Smythes Voyage and Entertainment in Rushia* (London, 1605), B2recto, D1verso.

121. "Virginia Unmasked," *Records of the Virginia Company*, vol. 2, 375.

122. See Philip Bell's report to the Providence Company, General Court, 18 May 1637, CO 124/2, 298, TNA: PRO.

123. John Kitely at Istanbul to Sanderson in London, November 1607; Sanderson to Kitely, 20 February 1608; Sanderson to Glover, 7 February 1611; Sanderson to Glover, 22 February 1611, in *Sanderson*, 242, 246–248, 273, 274–275.

124. Sanderson to Glover, 24 May 1609, in *Sanderson*, 266.

125. Butler, *Historye*, 249–263.

126. Smith, *The True Travels*, in Barbour, ed., *Complete Works*, vol. 3, 157.

127. On the colorful history of the three brothers, see Davies, *Elizabethans Errant*.

128. On Sherley's role in the writing and publication of these texts, see Anthony Parr, ed., *Three Renaissance Travel Plays* (Manchester University Press: Manchester, 1995), 7–8.

129. Most of these histories remained in manuscript, although the governors published a range of items pertaining to their specific colonies and other overseas ventures during their lifetimes. Richard S. Dunn, Introduction, in Richard S. Dunn, James Savage, and Laetitia Yeandle, eds., *The Journal of John Winthrop 1630–1649* (Cambridge, Mass.: Harvard University Press, 1996), xi–xxxvii. See Butler, *Historye*; William Bradford, *Of Plymouth Plantation*, ed. Samuel Eliot Morrison (New York: Knopf, 1970); and Richard Knolles, *The Generall Historie of the Turkes* (fifth edition, London, 1638), in which Roe wrote the sections on the 1620s.

130. S. G. Culliford, *William Strachey, 1572–1621* (Charlottesville: University Press of Virginia, 1965), 61–65.

131. April 1646, A Relation of Sundry Voyages & Journey made by mee Robert Bargrave, MS Rawlinson C799, fol. 1recto, Bodleian. Bargrave's journals have been published in Michael G. Brennan, ed., *The Travel Diary of Robert Bargrave Levant Merchant (1647–1656)* (London: The Hakluyt Society, 1999).

132. Court, 3 December 1631, CO 124/2, 43, TNA: PRO.

133. Roe to Salisbury, in Lorimer, 153.

134. Thomas Roe to a friend [?], [1617?], Harl. 1576, fol. 225verso, BL.; Thomas Roe to Duke of Buckingham, Constantinople, 20/30 September 1624, Tanner 73, fol. 477recto, Bodleian.

135. Roe to friend, Harl. 1576, fol. 226 recto, BL.

136. August 20, 1616, Foster, ed., *Embassy*, 248.

137. Lee to Wilson, February 24, 1611(new style) SP 89/3, fol. 144recto, TNA: PRO.

138. Butler, *Historye*, 266.

139. 13–14 April 1639, Butler's Diary, Sloane 758, BL.

140. Butler, *Historye*, 275.

141. Knolles, *Historie of the Turkes*, 1325. See the later accounts of the death of Daniel Harvey in Istanbul in 1674: Journal of John Covel, Add. 22,912, fol. 153recto, BL. Journal of Charles Wilde on the *Centurion*, Sloane 2439, fol. 26verso, BL.

142. Knollys, *Historie*, 1375.

143. Roe to Salisbury, in Lorimer, 154.

144. Roe to the King, 29 January 1615/16, Foster, ed., *Embassy*, 121.

145. [March] 1615, Foster, ed., *Embassy*, 2.

146. Roe to Master Lescke, 27 April 1616, in Foster, ed., *Embassy*, 168.

147. August 12, 1616, Foster, ed., *Embassy*, 238.

148. Alison Games, "'The Sanctuarye of our Rebell Negroes': The Atlantic Context of Local Resistance on Providence Island, 1630–1641," *Slavery and Abolition* 19 (December, 1998): 1–21.

149. Kupperman, *Providence Island*, chapter 3, profiles Bell's time in office. For slavery in Bermuda, see Virginia Bernhard, *Slaves and Slaveholders in Bermuda 1616–1728* (Columbia: University of Missouri Press, 1999).

150. Letter from Company to Captain Bell, 20 April 1635 (copy of earlier letter dated February and March), CO 124/1, fol. 76recto, TNA: PRO.

151. Games, *Migration*, 97–98.

152. Report of Pedro Louis and his son Juan Pedro, 1615, in Lorimer, 159. See also George Carew to Roe, letter started January 1617/18, in *Letters from George lord Carew to Sir Thomas Roe, Ambassador to the Court of the Great Mogull, 1615–1617*, Royal Historical Society Publication no. 76 (Westminster, 1860), 98. Carew reported that Roe's men had sold £2,310 of tobacco in the Low Countries. Carew was skeptical of the rumors that they had also returned carrying ingots of gold.

153. See for example a letter he wrote to the Dutch ambassador at Constantinople, September 7/17, 1630, in SP 97/15, fols. 45–47, TNA: PRO.

154. Thomas Roe, Introduction, *A Discourse upon the Resolution* (London, 1628), 1.

155. James Horn, *A Land as God Made It: Jamestown and the Birth of America* (New York: Basic Books, 2005), 86. On the importance of Hakluyt's and Purchas's collections of voyages, see Peter Mancall, *Hakluyt's Promise: An Elizabethan's Obsession for an English America* (New Haven: Yale University Press, 2007), 237–245, 298–302.

CHAPTER 6

1. This chapter in English colonization has received little attention, neither from historians of the English overseas (who have focused on trade in the region) nor from historians of Madagascar (who have tended to look at the roots of French, not English, activities there). See W. Foster, "An English Settlement in Madagascar in 1645–6," *English Historical Review* 27 (1912): 239–250. Robert Brenner discusses the Madagascar experiment in *Merchants and Revolution: Commercial Change, Political Conflict, and London's Overseas Traders, 1550–1653* (Princeton: Princeton University Press, 1993), 171–181. Raymond K. Kent touches on the first effort and uses the published promotional pamphlets in *Early Kingdoms in Madagascar 1500–1700* (New York: Holt, Rinehart and Winston, 1970), 184–185. The settlement also suffers from the lack of historical interest that often characterizes lost colonies. See

Pier M. Larson, "Colonies Lost: God, Hunger, and Conflict in Anosy (Madagascar) to 1674," *Comparative Studies of South Asia, Africa and the Middle East* 27, no. 2 (2007), 45–46.

2. This was John Lancaster's voyage. See A. Grandidier, *Collection des Ouvrages anciens concernant Madagascar*, three volumes (Paris, 1903–1905), vol. 1. This compilation contains French translations of all extant material about the island.

3. Walter Hamond, *Madagascar, The Richest and most Fruitfull Island in the World* (London, 1643), 3. The Englishman William Finch, who stopped at the Onilahy River on an East India Company voyage in 1608, described an "ash-colored, white-and-black-tailed" animal that was certainly a ring-tailed lemur. F. Andriamial-isoa and O. Langrand, "The History of Zoological Exploration of Madagascar," in Steven M. Goodman and Jonathan Benstead, *The Natural History of Madagascar* (Chicago: University of Chicago Press, 2003), 1; and A. Jolly, "Lemur catta," in same, 1329.

4. Hamond, *Madagascar*, 1.

5. Those involved included the Earls of Southampton, Denbigh, and Arundel; Endymion Porter; and merchants, including Thomas (?) Kynnaston, Samuel Bonnell, and Paul Pindar. Mervyn Brown, *Madagascar Rediscovered: a History from Early Times to Independence* (Hamden, Conn.: Archon Books, 1979), 42.

6. Richard Boothby, *A Breife Discovery or Description of the most Famous Island of Madagascar or St. Lawrence in Asia neare unto East-India* (London, 1646), 48.

7. A copy of the original grant can be found in H39, fols. 91–141, IOR, BL; John Darell, *Strange News from th'Indies: or, East-India Passages further discovered* (London, 1652), 4.

8. Malay and Portuguese were the two lingua francas. Dutch ministers conducted their first services in Malay in 1613 (in Ambon) and in 1633 (in Batavia). By 1617, the VOC published school texts in Malay. Jean Gelman Taylor, *The Social World of Batavia: European and Eurasian in Dutch Asia* (Madison: University of Wisconsin Press, 1983), 18, 23, 25. For a more intimate glimpse at the complex domestic and colonial relations in Batavia, see Leonard Blussé, *Bitter Bonds: A Colonial Divorce Drama of the Seventeenth Century* (Princeton: Markus Wiener, 2002).

9. J. D., *A True and Compendious Narration...*(London, 1665), 2.

10. Powle Waldegrave, *An Answer to Mr Boothbies Book, of the Description of the Island of Madagascar. In Vindication of the Honorable Society of Merchants trading to East-India, from the many Aspersions laid upon them by the said Boothbie* (London, 1649), 5. Madagascar has had a long-standing association with piracy, most fully developed in the second half of the seventeenth century. A biographer of the Earl of Arundel, Mary Hervey, believed that Rupert himself came up with the idea of colonizing Madagascar, but the merchant and Courten (also spelled Courteen) employee Richard Boothby thought Arundel and others persuaded Rupert, not the other way around. Mary F. S. Hervey, *The Life, Correspondence & Collections of Thomas Howard Earl of Arundel* (Cambridge: Cambridge University Press, 1921), 416; Boothby, *Madagascar*, 2.

11. David Howarth, *Lord Arundel and His Circle* (New Haven: Yale University Press, 1985), 167.

12. Hervey, *Correspondence*, 147.

13. Elizabeth, Queen of Bohemia, to Thomas Roe, March 25/April 4, The Hague, 1636, in *CSPD 1635–1636*, 320–321.

14. Elizabeth to Roe, April 6/16, 1637, *CSPD 1636–1637*, 559.

15. Anzolo Correr to the Doge and Senate, April 19, 1637, *Calendar of state papers and manuscripts, relating to English affairs existing in the archives and collection of Venice, and in other libraries of northern Italy* (London: H.M. Stationery Offce, 1864–1923) (hereafter *CSP-Venetian*), 1636–1639, 184.

16. Brown, *Madagascar Rediscovered*, 37–38.

17. Gervas Huxley, *Endymion Porter: The Life of a Courtier 1587–1649* (London: Chatto and Windus, 1959), 169–173.

18. William Davenant, *Madagascar: with other poems* (London, 1638), 19.

19. Ibid., 16.

20. Correr to the Doge and Senate, April 17, 1637, *CSP-Venetian*, 1636–1639, 188.

21. Roe to Elizabeth, May 8, 1637, *CSPD, 1637*, 82.

22. Giovanni Giustinian to the Doge and Senate, 7 October 1639, November 11, 1639, *CSP-Venetian*, 578, 592.

23. Ashmolean Museum, *Thomas Howard, Earl of Arundel: Patronage and Collecting in the Seventeenth Century: the Ashmolean Museum* (Oxford: Ashmolean Museum, 1985), 19.

24. On the painting, see Ernest B. Gilman, *Recollecting the Arundel Circle: Discovering the Past, Recovering the Future* (New York: Peter Lang, 2002), chapter 1.

25. Gilman, *Arundel Circle*, 145–146.

26. Howarth, *Lord Arundel*, 169.

27. Boothby, *Madagascar*, 70, on posting the Declaration at the Exchange; the Earl of Arundel's Declaration, in Hervey, *Correspondence*, 506–508.

28. Boothby, *Madagascar*, 1.

29. The Earl of Arundel's Declaration, in Hervey, *Correspondence*, 506–508.

30. On possible reasons for the failure of scheme, see Gilman, *Arundel Circle, 25*; Boothby, 70, blamed Parliament. David Howarth, in the introduction to *Thomas Howard, Earl of Arundel*, 7, blamed Lady Arundel's aversion to the jungle. Augustine Bay, on the arid west coast of Madagascar, actually has no jungle, but Lady Arundel might not have realized this.

31. William Monson, "Advice how to plant the Island of St. Lawrence, the greatest Island in the World, and reckoned a Port of Africa," M. Oppenheim, ed., *The Naval Tracts of Sir William Monson in Six Books*, vol. 4, *Publications of the Navy Records Society* 45 (1913), 434–439.

32. Gerolamo Agostini to the Doge and Senate, January 16, 1643, *CSP Venetian*, 1642–1643, 230.

33. Carla Gardina Pestana, *The English Atlantic in an Age of Revolution, 1640–1661* (Cambridge, Mass.: Harvard University Press, 2004).

34. Boothby, *Madagascar*, 2, 18, 65.

35. Ibid., 2.

36. Archaeological evidence suggests that cattle were widespread on Madagascar by the twelfth century. R. E. Dewar, "Relationship between Human Ecological Pressure and the Vertebrate Extinctions," in Steven M. Goodman and Bruce D. Patterson, eds., *Natural Change and Human Impact in Madagascar* (Washington: Smithsonian Institution Press, 1997), 122.

37. William Hamond, *A Paradox. Prooving, That the Inhabitants of the Isle called Madagascar, or St. Lawrence…are the happiest People in the World* (London, 1640); Hamond, *Madagascar*; Boothby, *Madagascar*.

38. Waldegrave, *An Answer*, 5. Waldegrave believed that Boothby's elaborate praise would lead men to think that he was "besides his wits" (8). Paradise was a verb in usage at the time, but Waldegrave was creative in his invention of Canaanize.

39. Hamond, *Madagascar*, A3verso, 11.

40. Kent, *Early Kingdoms*, 89–90, 191.

41. Hamond, *Paradox* B1verso.

42. Ibid., A4verso.

43. Ibid., B2recto.

44. Hamond, *Madagascar*, A3recto.

45. Hamond, *Paradox*, A3recto–verso. This second pamphlet was an elaboration of the first, with two new features, including a dedication to John Bond, who had planned to lead 300 settlers to the colony in 1642.

46. Boothby, *Madagascar*, 2.

47. Huxley, *Endymion Porter*, 207.

48. Charges against Richard Boothby, G/40/11, fols. 1–36, IOR, BL.

49. Boothby, *Madagascar*, A4recto–verso.

50. Consultation held aboard the *Sun*, Augustine Bay, 12 May 1645; instructions for Thomas Page, and others, Add. 14,037, fols. 7verso, 8recto, BL. Records for the plantation at Augustine Bay are contained in a single folio volume in the British Library: the volume includes a record of consultations held concerning the colony and copies of letters sent by the colony's governor and other officers. Add. 14,037, "A Booke of Consultations belonging to the Plantation of Madagascar, als the Island of St. Lawrence," BL.

51. Hamond, *Madagascar*, A3recto–verso.

52. Boothby, *Madagascar*, 8. *Andriana* is a Malagasy word meaning lord, ruler, sovereign, king, or noble. The English represented it as Andria or occasionally Dian. Kent, *Early Kingdoms*, glossary, xvi.

53. Letters of Luis Mariano, Sahadia, 24 May 1617; Mozambique, 20 August 1617, in Grandidier, *Collection*, vol. 2, 237, 262–265.

54. Hamond, *Madagascar*, 14.

55. Boothby, *Madagascar*, 8.

56. Hamond, *Paradox*, B2recto.

57. Kent, *Early Kingdoms*, chapter 5.

58. Hamond, *Paradox*, B3recto.

59. Ibid., B2recto.

60. Hamond, *Madagascar*, 7.

61. Letter to England from John Smart, 18 August 1645, Add. 14,037, fol. 13verso, BL.

62. John Smart to Thomas Kynnaston, 15 December 1645, Add. 14,037, fol. 17recto-verso, BL. M. Goubard was probably David Goubard, who was employed by the Courten Associates and testified in 1641 about English losses to the Dutch. See J. D., *Compendious Narration*, 18–19.

63. Waldegrave, *An Answer*, 27.

64. Ibid., 6.

65. Yet Waldegrave's subsequent activities make him a suspicious source. He owed a large debt—possibly even his life—to the East India Company, which had rescued him from the Indies after he evacuated Madagascar with the rest of Smart's company. The East India Company actually rewarded Waldegrave with £5 for his book. Court of Committees, 1 June 1649, B/22, fol. 178verso, IOR, BL. Waldegrave overcame his aversion to Madagascar and returned there to take part in the Assada plantation. He appeared in a consultation aboard the *Lioness*, off the coast of Assada in 1650. E/3/22, fol. 15verso, IOR, BL.

66. Waldegrave refuted the comparison with the people of Virginia. Even the enemy the English encountered in Madagascar was different from the open enemy of Virginia. The English, Spanish, and Portuguese did well against such a clear enemy, but the people of the Bay were crafty: they would trap the English with promises and with "heathenish Rhetorique and circumstances," yet would try to kill or starve their European visitors. Waldegrave, *An Answer*, 24.

67. Waldegrave attacked the use of headrights. He thought men might be deceived: the voyage was so long to Madagascar and the expense of transporting goods so great that men who paid their own way would find promises to be empty. What worked for Virginia would not, he insisted, work for Madagascar. Waldegrave, *An Answer*, 24.

68. Boothby, *Madagascar*, Virginia attack (18), headrights (61), Trinidad (61–64).

69. Hamond, *Paradox*, B4verso.

70. See, for example, answer to a protest by Thomas Spencer (a Courten employee), 5 May 1646, I/3/20, fol. 17, IOR, BL.

71. See N. A. M. Rodger, "Guns and Sails in the First Phase of English Colonization, 1500–1650," in Nicholas Canny, ed., *The Origins of Empire* (Oxford: Oxford University Press, 1998), 79–98.

72. Waldegrave, *An Answer*, 16.

73. Ibid., 4.

74. The Dutch suffered one particularly catastrophic voyage in 1646. Following convention, they left a letter at Augustine Bay for subsequent travelers to find and read to learn of their plight. Their ship the *Delft* carried 190 sick people; 40–50 were well, and they buried 72. They had been unable to get refreshment from the people there,

despite promises, and with their depleted population limped on to Mozambique. E/3/20, fol. 56, IOR, BL.

75. Edward Terry's account of his voyage to India in 1616 points to some of the problems involved in transporting dogs safely. His own fleet started out with eight mastiffs to be shipped to the Mughal. One leapt overboard to try to attack a school of porpoises and drowned. Four died of mange. One died during a fight at sea with the Portuguese. Two were left alive to carry to the emperor, and each was transported in a "little Coach." Edward Terry, *A Voyage to East-India* (London, 1655), 149–150.

76. Copy of a general letter sent from Soldana Bay to England, January 27, 1645; Letter for England from Captain Smart, written at the Bay, 18 August 1645, Add. 14,037, fols. 4–5, 12verso, BL.

77. Steven R. Pendery, "St. Croix Island, Maine: Lost and Found," a paper presented at a conference on Lost Colonies, Philadelphia, March 2004.

78. James A. Williamson, *English Colonies in Guiana and on the Amazon, 1604–1668* (Oxford: Clarendon Press, 1923), 163–164.

79. On the importance of rivers for settlement, see Lauren Benton, "Lost in Atlantic Space: Colonizing and Intelligence in Riverine Regions, 1450–1650," a paper presented at a conference on Lost Colonies, Philadelphia, March 2004.

80. 18 August 1645, Add. 14,037, fol. 14recto, BL.

81. F. Ariey et. al, 162.

82. On modern malaria rates, see F. Ariey et al, 164.

83. Waldegrave, *An Answer,* 6.

84. Copy of a letter to England, 18 August 1645; Letter to England, 15 December 1645, Add. 14,037, fols. 13–14verso, 17verso, BL.

85. Copy of a letter to England, 18 August 1645, Add. 14,037, fol. 13recto, BL

86. Letter to Kynnaston, 15 May 1646, Add. 14,037, fol. 23verso, BL.

87. Smart to Kynnaston, 15 December 1645, Add. 14,037, fol. 17verso, BL.

88. Boothby, *Madagascar,* 1.

89. Letter to Thomas Kynnaston, Add. 14,037, fol. 16verso, BL. The ships arrived in late August or September.

90. To Company from Francis Breton, and others, Swally Marine, January 3, 1645/6, E/3/19, fol. 299, IOR, BL.

91. John Smart to Thomas Kynnaston, 15 December 1645, Add. 14,037, fol. 16verso, BL.

92. M. R. Jury, "The Climate of Madagascar," in Goodman and Benstead, *The Natural History of Madagascar,* 75–87, 75 (for Nosy Be); 78–79 (for southwest). On tapping baobabs, see Peter Tyson, *The Eighth Continent: Life, Death, and Discovery in the Lost World of Madagascar* (New York: William Morrow, 2000), 93.

93. Copy of a letter to England, 18 August 1645, Add. 14,037, fols. 13–14verso, BL.

94. Waldegrave, *An Answer,* 8.

95. Ibid., 11.

96. Consultation, 14 March 1645/6, Add. 14,037, fol. 21recto, BL.

97. Waldegrave, *An Answer,* 14.

98. Smart to Thomas Kynnaston, 15 May 1646, Add. 14,037, fol. 24recto, BL.

99. Boothby, *Madagascar*, 10.

100. John Smart to friends, Augustine Bay, 18 May 1646, Add. 14,037, fol. 26recto, BL.

101. Archaeological and documentary sources point to these political and social changes in regions such as Anosy in the southeast, where the French had a post at Fort Dauphin. Henry T. Wright and Jean-Aime Rakotoarisoa, "Cultural Transformations and Their Impacts on the Environments of Madagascar," in Goodman and Patterson, eds., *Natural Change and Human Impact in Madagascar*, 317.

102. H. T. Wright and J. A. Rakotoarisoa, "The Rise of Malagasy Societies: New Developments in the Archaeology of Madagascar," in Goodman and Benstead, *The Natural History of Madagascar*, 118.

103. F. Ariey, M. Randrianarivelojosia, L. J. Sahondra Harisoa, and L. Raharimalala, "Malaria," in Goodman and Benstead, *The Natural History of Madagascar*, 162. The fevers continue; the forests are rapidly disappearing.

104. John Smart to Thomas Kynnaston, 15 December 1645, Add. 14,037, fol. 17recto, BL. Unfortunately, Smart did not describe the disguise, saying it would be "to long to relate." East India Company items refer to this man as Massacory. E/3/20, fol. 43verso, IOR, BL.

105. Consultation on shore, 6 January 1645/6, Add. 14,037, fol. 30recto, BL. The English called the people they encountered on Madagascar "blacks," in distinction to the terminology they used to describe slaves from Africa in the Americas in this same period, which was usually "negro." John Smart was abroad when this incident occurred.

106. Letter to Mr. Thomas Kynnaston, 15 May 1646, Add. 14,037, fol. 23verso, BL.

107. Augustine Bay, To worthy friends Mr. Thomas Spencer, Mr. Ro. Hogg, Mr. Jno Dudson, Mr. Jeremy Weddell, 18 May 1646, Add. 14,037, fol. 26recto; John Duisson to "worthie Frende" at Augustine Bay, 20 August 1646, describes the letters "buried under a Rock nere to ye great Rock yt hath ye Kings coulors on it, at ye foote of the hill at ye landing place," I/3/20, fol. 42recto, IOR, BL. Some of the survivors were taken to Rajapur and then on to England, others went to Goa, and some ended up at the East India Company factory at Surat, where the factor, Francis Breton, employed and supported some. One widow remarried there. Francis Breton to East India Company, 25 January 1646/7, I/3/20, fol. 101recto, IOR, BL.

108. This was Fort Dauphin, which the French began building in 1644 after an earlier site nearby proved unhealthy. Brown, *Madagascar Rediscovered*, 49–50.

109. Consultation on board the *Sun*, St. Augustine Bay, 14 August 1645, Add. 14,037, fol. 10recto, BL.

110. Copy of a letter for England, 18 August 1645, Add. 14,037, fols. 12verso, 13recto, BL. Beads had long been an important trade item in the region. See W. G. N. van der Sleen, "Ancient Glass Beads with Special Reference to the Beads of East and Central Africa and the Indian Ocean," *The Journal of the Royal Anthopological Institute of Great Britain and Ireland* 88, no. 2 (July–Dec., 1958), 203–216. *Vakana* means "bead"

in standard Malagasy, or "vacca" in the west coast dialect. My thanks to Pier Larson for this information.

111. Smart to Thomas Kynnaston, 15 May 1646, Add. 14,037, fol. 24recto, BL.

112. Francis Breton to the East India Company, 30 March 1646, E/3/20, fol. 6verso, IOR, BL.

113. John Farren to Captain John Smart, April 8, 1646, E/3/20, fol. 9recto, IOR, BL.

114. Andrew Trumbull to the East India Company, Jettapore Road, 10 February 1645/6, I/3/19, fol. 332; Francis Breton to the East India Company, Swally Marine, 25 January 1646/7, I/3/20, fol. 100verso, IOR, BL.

115. John Brookehaven to the East India Company, 20 August 1646, E/3/20, fol. 43verso, IOR, BL. For the lingering bitterness of the Courten-East India Company rivalry, see Darell, *Strange News*. Darell, indeed, was such a loyal Courten supporter that he believed that the younger William Courten maintained rights not only to trade with "East-India, Mallabar, Acheen, and China," but also to trade with Barbados and any other islands in the West Indies (38).

116. John Duisson to "worthie Frende," Augustine Bay, 20 August 1636, I/3/20, fol. 42recto–verso, IOR, BL.

117. Francis Breton to East India Company, 31 March 1646, I/3/20, fol. 122verso, IOR, BL.

118. Smart to John Farren from Johanna, 23 June 1646, Add. 14,037, fol. 31verso, BL.

119. Smart to Thompson and William Hix, Johanna, 24 or 27 June, 1646, Add. 14,037, fol. 32recto, BL.

120. Francis Breton to the Company, Swally Marine, 25 January 1646/7, E/3/20, fol. 101recto, IOR, BL.

121. Smart to Mr. Wm. Courteen and Mr. Tho. Kynnaston, Add. 14,037, fol. 42recto, BL.

122. Court of Committees, 19 March 1646/47, B/22, fol. 44recto, IOR, BL.

123. Records for the Assada plantation appear in scattered references in the East India Company records, especially the Court Books, Despatch Books, and Original Correspondence, all located in the British Library.

124. Robert Hunt, *The Island of Assada, neere Madagascar, Impartially defined...Clearly demonstrating to the Adventurer or Planter, the right way for disposing his Adventure.* (London, 1650), 1.

125. Copy of letter to King of Assada, E/3/22, fols. 19recto–20verso, IOR, BL.

126. Hunt was correct at least in identifying general trends on Barbados, although he overstated the details. Richard S. Dunn found that land prices reached £5/acre by 1646, and that between 1646 and 1648 five plantations were sold for prices between "£1,800 to £4,500 per hundred acres." Dunn, *Sugar and Slaves: the Rise of the Planter Class in the English West Indies, 1624–1713* (New York: Norton, 1973), 66.

127. Hunt, *Assada*, 6. These proposed freedom dues were spectacular in comparison with freedom dues in the Atlantic and Caribbean colonies, where servants might be promised a hoe, a bushel of corn, or a new shirt, and all items were dependent

on court enforcement. Hilary McD. Beckles provides a useful table comparing freedom dues in *White Servitude and Black Slavery in Barbados, 1627–1715* (Knoxville: University of Tennessee Press, 1989), 142. See also Games, *Migration*, 89–90.

128. Hunt, *Assada*, 3

129. Hunt, *Assada*, 4; for the indifference of planters, see, for example, Richard Ligon, *A True and Exact History of the Island of Barbadoes* (London, 1673), 50.

130. Hunt, *Assada*, 4. In 1655, the estimated population of Barbados was 23,000 whites and 20,000 black slaves. Dunn, 87.

131. Chantal Radihalahy, "Mahilaka, an Eleventh-to-Fourteenth-Century Islamic Port: the First Impact of Urbanism on Madagascar," in Goodman and Patterson, eds., *Natural Change and Human Impact in Madagascar*, 342–363.

132. Instructions for Thomas Page and Jeremy Weddell (May 1645), Add. 14,037, fol. 8recto, BL.

133. See Philip J. Stern, "Politics and Ideology in the Early East India Company-State: The Case of St Helena, 1673–1709," *The Journal of Imperial and Commonwealth History* 35, no. 1 (March 2007), 1–23, for a lucid discussion of the state aspirations of the East India Company.

134. Journal of Captain Berblock, E/3/22, fol. 33recto, IOR, BL.

135. Hunt, *Assada*, 5.

136. Copy of letter to King of Assada, E/3/22, 19recto–20verso, IOR, BL.

137. Meeting for Assada, 28 January 1649/50, B/22, fol. 233recto, IOR, BL.

138. Copy of letter Hunt delivered to the King of Assada, E/3/22, fols. 19recto–20recto, IOR, BL.

139. Meeting of diverse committees for Assada, 16 September 1650, B/25, fol. 4verso, IOR, BL.

140. In 1635, for example, ninety-four percent of those bound for Barbados from London were men. E 157/20 1-e, TNA: PRO; see also Games, *Migration*, chapter 2.

141. List of persons on board the *Assada Merchant* "consigned last for the Plantation," E/3/22, fol. 37, IOR, BL.

142. Thomas Merry to the East India Company, 24 October 1650, Swally Marine, E/3/22, fol. 53recto, IOR, BL.

143. Court of Committees, 5 January 1649/50, B/22, fol. 226verso, IOR, BL.

144. See for example the journal of Mr. James Berblock, on the *Supply*, selections copied in East India Company correspondence, E/3/22, fols. 29recto–36, IOR, BL.

145. Journal of Charles Wilde, Sloane 3231, 26, BL. The East India Company seems here to have been following the advice of William Monson in his 1640 tract, in which he recommended that a few planters be placed on each outbound ship.

146. Journal of Charles Wilde, Sloane 3231, 21, BL.

147. The previous discussion is drawn from the journal of Mr. James Berblock, on the *Supply*, selections copied in East India Company correspondence, E/3/22, fols. 29recto–36, IOR, BL. On the abandonment of the plantation, see Thomas Merry's letter

to the East India Company, Swally Marine, 24 October 1650, E/3/22, fols. 47verso, 53recto, IOR, BL.

148. R. J. Barendse, *The Arabian Seas: The Indian Ocean World of the Seventeenth Century* (London: M.E. Sharpe, 2002), 93.

149. This hiring was an easier process than the negotiations surrounding the Augustine Bay survivors, since the Assada planters were already East India Company employees.

150. Arthur Porter (?) to Company from Surat, 10 January 1651/2, E/3/22, fol. 238verso, IOR, BL.

151. Captain Blackman's relation of his voyage to the East India Company, 14 January 1651/2, from Swally Marina, E/3/22, fols. 275recto–276 verso, IOR, BL.

152. J. T. Hardyman, "Outline of the Maritime History of St. Augustine's Bay (Madagascar)," *Studia, Revista semestral* 11 (January, 1963): 319–324.

153. Waldegrave, *An Answer,* 16.

CHAPTER 7

1. Patrick Copland, *Declaration how the monies were disposed* (London, 1622). The Virginia Company discussed Copland's donation at meetings in October and November of 1621 and gave him three shares (equal to 300 acres). *Records of the Virginia Company,* vol. 1, 538, 550–551, 559.

2. Peter Mancall, *Hakluyt's Promise: An Elizabethan's Obsession for an English America* (New Haven: Yale University Press, 2007), 139–140, 164; quotation from 140.

3. 10 October 1614, 12 October 1614, B/5, 243, 245, IOR, BL.

4. John Donne, *A Sermon upon the viii Verse…*(London, 1622).

5. See a helpful typescript book in the Reading Room of the Oriental and India Office Collections at the British Library, S. J. McNally, "The Chaplains of the East India Company" (1971, 1976).

6. Court of Committees, 13 December 1613, B/5, iii, IOR, BL.

7. John B. Pearson, *A Biographical Sketch of the Chaplains to the Levant Company, maintained at Constantinople, Aleppo and Smyrna, 1611–1706* (Cambridge: Deighton, Bell, and Co., 1883), 8; William Foster, ed., *The Travels of John Sanderson in the Levant, 1584–1602* (London: Hakluyt Society, 1931), 155.

8. *Records of the Virginia Company,* 22 February 1619/20, vol. 1, 314.

9. Patrick Copland, *Virginia's God be Thanked* (London, 1622), 30.

10. Court of Committees, 13 December 1613, B/5, iii–iv, IOR, BL [this section of the court book is a fragment of some earlier set of minutes, thus pagination is different]. For another reference to the need for a minister to combat the Jesuits at Surat, see 26 October 1614, B/5, 255, IOR, BL.

11. 26 October 1614, B/5, 255, IOR, BL.

12. John Sanford to Sir T. Edmondes, Madrid, 7 August 1611, Stowe 172, BL.

13. 29 November 1614, B/5, 292, IOR, BL.

14. March 14, 1613/14, 26 October 1614, B/5, 61, 255, IOR, BL. The Company also worried similarly in 1622 about Mr. Amy, who was believed to be too young for the East Indies and was ultimately not hired. January 9, 16, 1622, *CSPC-East Indies, 1622-1624*, vol. 4, 3, 6.

15. 24 March 1613/14, B/5, 78, IOR, BL. For "rehersall sermon" see 3 July 1622, *Records of the Virginia Company*, vol. 2, 74.

16. Pearson, 9.

17. 15 March 1608/9, B/3, fol. 114recto, IOR, BL. When John Covel was appointed by the Levant Company, his patron Elias Harvey told him that he was scheduled to preach, but was allowed to choose his own text. Elias Harvey to John Covel, 17 March 1669, Add. 22,910, fol. 29recto, BL.

18. 16 January 1622, *Records of the Virginia Company*, vol. 1, 575.

19. Pearson, 64-65. The sermon was John Luke, *A Sermon Preached before the Right Worshipfull Company of the Levant Merchants at St. Olavs Hart-street London Thursday Decemb. 15. 1664* (London, 1664). He preached from 1 Corinthians 15.29, "Else what shall they do which are baptized for the dead, if the dead rise not at all? why are they then baptized for the dead?"

20. Providence Committee, 20 February 1634/5, CO 124/2, 193-194, TNA: PRO.

21. November 21, 1621, *Records of the Virginia Company*, vol. 1, 544.

22. 22 March 1613/14, B/5, 76, IOR, BL.

23. Meetings, March-April, 1614, B/5, 68, 75, 85, 89, 96, 104, IOR, BL.

24. 12 January 1607/8, B/3, fol. 70verso, IOR, BL.

25. Pearson, 46, 50.

26. Patrick Copland to Sir Thos Smythe, March 4, 1618, on the *Royal James, CSPC-East Indies 1617-1621*, vol. 3, item 289, 135-136; Captain Pring described his disguise in a letter to the East India Company, March 18, 1618, aboard the *Royal James* at Swally, *CSPC-East Indies, 1617-1621*, vol. 3, 140, item 302.

27. Derek Massarella, *A World Elsewhere: Europe's Encounter with Japan in the Sixteenth and Seventeenth Centuries* (New Haven: Yale University Press, 1990), 240.

28. General Court for Providence, 19 June 1634, CO 124/2, 151, TNA: PRO.

29. Levant Company to William Bidulphe, June 1607, SP 105/110, fol. 10recto, TNA: PRO.

30. Pearson, 64.

31. Alan Macfarlane, *The Family Life of Ralph Josselin: A Seventeenth-Century Clergyman* (Cambridge: Cambridge University Press, 1970), 34.

32. John Walker to Leicester, 22 April 1582, Cotton Othe E. viii, fol. 145recto, BL.

33. Pearson, 52 (extracts from Levant Company minute books).

34. 26 February 1613/14, B/5, 41, IOR, BL.

35. 3 July 1622, *Records of the Virginia Company*, vol. 2, 89. The men were Samuel Seward, Mr. Launce, and Mr. Pemberton.

36. 11 September 1621, *Records of the Virginia Company*, vol. 3, 506.

37. Edmund Castell, *Lexicon Heptaglotton* (London, 1669); William Seamon, *Domini nostri Iesu Christi Testamentum Novum. Turcice redditum. Operâ Gu: Seaman* (Oxford, 1666); William Seaman, *Grammatica linguae Turcicae, in quinque partes distributa. Authore Gulielmo Seaman* (Oxford, 1670); Matthew Poole, *Synopsis criticorum aliorumque S. Scripturae interpretum. Volumen I. Complectens libros omnes à Genesi ad Jobum, divisum in duas partes* (London, 1669), vol. 1; (London, 1671), vol. 2. Pearson, 65.

38. Pearson, 66.

39. Michael McGiffert, ed., *God's Plot: The Paradoxes of Puritan Piety, Being the Autobiography and Journal of Thomas Shepard* (Amherst: University of Massachusetts Press, 1972), 46–62.

40. Hugh Peter, *A Dying Father's Last Legacy* (London, 1660), 97–100.

41. Based on a database of clergy I have constructed.

42. Pearson, 22.

43. Edmund Calamy, *The Nonconformist's Memorial*, three volumes (London, 1802), illustrates these patterns of migration in scores of individual biographies. For a similar study of the sufferings of conforming ministers, see David Lloyd, *Memoires of the lives, actions, sufferings & deaths of those noble, reverend and excellent personages...* (London, 1668).

44. Pearson, 10.

45. See Games, *Migration*, 61–64, on the need for and extent of deception.

46. John Oxenbridge, *A Seasonable Proposition* (London, 1670), 2, 6.

47. Wood to Gabriel Barber, 1634, Roger Wood's Letterbook, Fragment F, Bermuda Colonial Records, Bermuda Archives.

48. Elias Harvey to John Covel, London, 17 March 1669, Add. 22,901, fol. 29recto, BL.

49. Of the eight Smyrna chaplains whose educational affiliation is known, all went to Cambridge. Degrees are recorded for six of the Aleppo chaplains: all went to Oxford. Seven of the ten Istanbul chaplains attended Cambridge, and the other three attended Oxford.

50. Frederick Weis's compilation of the 1,676 clergy who served in New England pulpits through 1776 reveals 96 men (6 percent) with Cambridge degrees and 43 (2.5 percent) with Oxford degrees (the presence of Harvard meant that almost every minister who had been born in the colonies attended the Massachusetts college). These men were vastly outnumbered by the 946, or 57 percent, with Harvard degrees and 436 (26 percent) with Yale degrees. I analyzed the educational backgrounds of 114 clergy of the 1620s and 1620s. Frederick Lewis Weis, *The Colonial Clergy and the Colonial Churches of New England* (Lancaster, Mass.: Society of the Descendants of the Colonial Clergy, 1936), 16.

51. Pearson, 29. Burroughs did not take the job, but remained interested in work outside England and later preached in Rotterdam. *Alumni cantabrigienses* (Cambridge: Cambridge University Press, 1922–1954), vol. 1, pt. 1, 263.

52. *A description of the present state of Samos, Nicaria, Patmos, and Mount Athos. By Joseph Georgirenes, Arch-Bishop of Samos. Now living in London. Translated by one that knew the author in Constantinople. July 14. 1677* (London, 1678).

53. Quoted in Zachary Twells, *The Lives of Dr. Edward Pococke*...(London, 1816), 15.

54. Twells, *The Lives of Dr. Edward Pococke,* 1–85. Pocock was not alone in acquiring a job once he was already overseas. Edward Terry was offered a job as Thomas Roe's chaplain in India after Roe's chaplain, John Hall, died.

55. Calculations derived from men profiled in McNally, "The Chaplains of the East India Company," 5–128.

56. John Eliot, *The Holy Bible: containing the Old Testament and the New. Translated into the Indian language* (Cambridge, Mass., 1663).

57. See the reference in company records to plans to put him at school in England and then send him back to India to convert people there, 19 August 1614, B/5, 202, IOR, BL; for discussion of his baptism, 18 July 1615, B/5, 448, IOR, BL. For acquisition of the child, see also William Foster, ed., *The Voyage of Thomas Best to the East Indies 1612–1614* (London: Hakluyt Society, 1934), xx–xxi.

58. Copland, *Virginia's God be Thanked*, 29–30.

59. Oxenbridge, *Seasonable Proposition*, 6.

60. Whitaker to Crashaw, Jamestown, 9 August 1611, in Alexander Brown, *The Genesis of the United States*, two volumes (Boston: Houghton Mifflin, 1891), vol. 1, 499.

61. J. Frederick Fausz, "Opechancanough: Indian Resistance Leader," Gary Nash and David G. Sweet, eds., *Struggle and Survival in Colonial America* (Berkeley: University of California Press, 1982): 21–37.

62. John Sanderson to Richard Colthurst at Aleppo, 12 March 1600, in *Sanderson*, 198.

63. Journal of Richard Madox, Cotton Titus B viii, for detail about fish see fol. 186recto; glossary, fol. 191recto; Java, fol. 191verso, BL. Madox's journal was published by the Hakluyt Society. Elizabeth Story Donno, ed., *An Elizabethan in 1582, The Diary of Richard Madox* (London, 1976). It appears in manuscript in Cotton Titus B viii, Cotton Otho E viii, and Cotton Appendix xlvii, at the BL.

64. Samuel Johnson to John Dury, 21 December 1633, Sloane 1465, fol. 195verso, BL.

65. Patrick Copland to John Winthrop, 9 December 1639, Bermuda, *Collections of the Massachusetts Historical Society*, fifth series, vol. 1, 277–280.

66. John Sanford to Sir T. Edmondes, 6 March 1610/11, Stowe 171, fol. 370, BL.

67. Covel Journal, Add. 22,912, fol. 108recto, BL.

68. Thomas Smith, *An Account of the Greek Church* (London, 1680), A2recto.

69. Covel to George Davis (consul at Naples), 5 July 1678, Rome, Add. 22,910, fol. 164verso, BL.

70. Covel Journal, August 15, November 1, 1671, Add. 22,912, fol. 147recto, BL.

71. Ibid., Add. 22,912, fol. 227recto, BL.

72. Ibid., Add. 22,912, fol. 158verso, BL.

73. Add. 22,912, fol. 188verso, BL. The Ragusan ambassador represented the interests of merchants from Dubrovnik. Another Englishman, the scientist John Greaves, was

fascinated by the reported prevalence of witchcraft in Cairo, practiced by those he identified as "Arabians" and "Moors." Thomas Birch's notes on Greaves' letters, Add. 4,243, fol. 58recto–verso, BL.

74. August 10, 1675, Add. 22,912, fol. 237verso, BL.

75. Edward Terry, *A Voyage to East-India. Wherein Some things are taken notice of in our passage thither, but many more in our abode there, within that rich and most spacious Empire of the Great Mogul. Mix't with some Parallel Observations and inferences upon the storie, to profit as well as delight the Reader* (London, 1655), 270–274.

76. Twells, *The Lives of Dr. Edward Pococke,* 103.

77. Covel to George Davis (consul at Naples), 5 July 1678, Rome, Add. 22,910, fols. 164recto–165recto, BL.

78. Pearson, 16.

79. John Sanford to Sir T. Edmondes, 6 March 1610/11, Stowe 171, fol. 370, BL.

80. Covel Journal, October 13, 1670, Add. 22,912, fol. 16verso, BL.

81. Charles Robson, *Newes From Aleppo* (London, 1628), 9.

82. May 18–21, 1613, *Voyage of Thomas Best,* 57. Best beat Fenn, and Fenn drew a dagger on Best. Fenn was found guilty and could have been executed, but the ambassador asked for his life, and Best gave him Fenn.

83. John Walker to Leicester, 14 June 1582, Cotton Othe E. viii, fol. 148recto, BL.

84. The Narrative of The Rev. Patrick Copland, in *Voyage of Thomas Best,* 208.

85. *The Voyage of Thomas Best,* 112 (two sermons, 18 October 1612), 102 (the whale, 23 June 1612); 152 (drunk mariners, 22 February 1613), 116 (drinking with prostitutes, 10 November 1612).

86. *Voyage of Thomas Best,* 112, 114–115.

87. Covel Journal, November, 1670, Add. 22,912, fol. 35, BL.

88. East India Company Court Minutes, October 10, 1621, *CSPC-East Indies, 1617–1621,* vol. 3, item 1125, 467.

89. John Byrd to the East India Company, February 23, 1621, the *Clove, CSPC-East Indies, 1617–1621,* vol. 3, item 979, 415–416.

90. Robson, *Newes from Aleppo,* 1.

91. Terry, *A Voyage to East-India,* 218.

92. I looked at the *Book of Common Prayer* for 1611 and 1634.

93. Louis B. Wright, ed., *A Voyage to Virginia in 1609; Two Narratives: Strachey's "True Reportory" and Jourdain's Discovery of the Bermudas* (Charlottesville: University Press of Virginia, 1964).

94. Edward Maunde Thompson, ed., *The Diary of Richard Cocks* (London: Hakluyt Society, two volumes, 1883), 6 July 1621, vol. 2, 174.

95. Journal of John Luke, December 27, 1670, Add. 36,528, fol. 8verso, BL.

96. Journal of John Luke, 13 February 1671, Add. 36,528, fol. 27verso, BL.

97. Cotton Othe E viii, fol. 132recto–verso, BL.

98. Strachey, *True Reportory,* 53.

99. William Ford, *A Sermon Preached at Constantinople* (London, 1616), A2verso, 26, 50, 52, 60.

100. Strachey, "*True Reportory*," 80–81; John Smith, *Advertisements* (London, 1631), in Philip L. Barbour, ed., *The Complete Works of Captain John Smith, 1580–1631,* three volumes (Chapel Hill: University of North Carolina Press, 1986), vol. 3, 295.

101. Nathaniel Butler, *The Historye of the Bermudaes or Summer Islands* (London: Hakluyt Society, 1882), 154.

102. 4 October 1614, B/5, 239, IOR, BL.

103. August 19, 1616, William Foster, ed., *The Embassy of Sir Thomas Roe to the Court of the Great Mogul, 1615–1619* (London: Hakluyt Society, 1899), 245–246; 246n.

104. John Sanford to Sir T. Edmondes, Madrid, 30 March 1612, Stowe 172, fol. 226verso; same to same, Madrid, 5 November 1612, Stowe 173, fol. 188recto, BL; Terry, *Voyage to East-India*, 58.

105. Journal of John Luke, 10 December 1670, Add. 36,528, fol. 3recto, BL.

106. Fragment of Walker's journal, Cotton Otho E viii, fols. 163–164, BL.

107. *A Second Courante of Newes* (London, 1622), 2.

108. *Voyage of Thomas Best*, 5 January 1613, 142.

109. Fragment of Walker's journal, Cotton Otho E viii, fol. 162recto, BL.

110. Oxenbridge, *Seasonable*, 7.

111. Terry, *Voyage to East-India*, 156.

112. John Sanford to Sir T. Edmondes, Madrid, 7 August 1611, Stowe 172, fol. 154verso, BL.

113. Entries for 19 February 1638/9, 10 March 1638/9, Nathaniel Butler's Diary, Sloane 758, BL.

114. Lewis Hughes to Sir Nathaniel Rich, 12 February and 16 March, 1619/20, in Ives, ed., *Rich Papers*, 166.

115. Butler, *Historye*, 172.

116. Games, *Migration*, 154–156.

117. Journal of John Luke, 10 December 1670, Add. 36,528, fol. 3recto, BL.

118. Ibid., 25 December 1670, Add. 36,528, fol. 7verso, BL.

119. George Bishop, *New England Judged* (London, 1661), 19–20. The classic introduction to the Quakers remains Hugh Barbour, *The Quakers in Puritan England* (New Haven: Yale University Press, 1964); on the misfortunes of the Quakers in Massachusetts, see Carla Gardina Pestana, *Quakers and Baptists in Colonial Massachusetts* (Cambridge: Cambridge University Press, 1991).

120. "Father White's Briefe Relation," in Clayton Colman Hall, ed., *Narratives of Early Maryland, 1633–1684* (New York: Charles Scribner's Sons, 1910), 37.

121. Games, *Migration*, 150–151.

122. John Ball, *A Tryall of the New-Church Way in New-England and in Old* (London 1644), n.p. The manuscript was written in 1637.

123. For an extensive discussion of the circulation of radical ideas, the Presbyterian campaign against toleration, and the presence of New England religious radicals in

England, see John Donoghue, "Radical Republicanism in England, America, and the Imperial Atlantic, 1624–1661" (Ph.D. Dissertation, University of Pittsburgh, 2006), chapter 5.

124. I have explored some of these ideas in Games, *Migration*, chapter 5. Ministers in trade factories seem to have been less divisive politically. This is certainly the argument of Pearson, 9–10.

125. Patrick Copland to Adrian Jacobson, from the *Royal James* in Bantam Road, April 20, 1619, *CSPC-East Indies, 1617–1621*, vol. 3, 269.

126. Covel traveled abroad again, although he ultimately ended his long life (he died in 1722) at Christ's College, Cambridge.

CHAPTER 8

1. For a good overview, see David B. Quinn, *Ireland and America: Their Early Associations, 1500–1640* (Liverpool: Liverpool University Press, 1991). For the early ventures in South America, see Joyce Lorimer, *English and Irish Settlement on the River Amazon 1550–1646* (London: Hakluyt Society, 1989). Donald H. Akenson offers a tantalizing exploration of what an Irish empire might have looked like in *If the Irish Ran the World: Montserrat, 1630–1730* (Montreal and Buffalo: McGill-Queen's University Press, 1997).

2. James Scott Wheeler, *Cromwell in Ireland* (New York: St. Martin's, 1999), 225.

3. Letter to Captain Henry Ashton and the commissioners of Barbados, 27 March 1640, Hay Papers, GD34/922, NAS.

4. Games, *Migration*, 191–206.

5. On responses to this mobilization, see John Donoghue, "Radical Republicanism in England, America, and the Imperial Atlantic, 1624–1661" (Ph.D. Dissertation, University of Pittsburgh, 2006), chapters five and six.

6. On the prosperity of Munster, see Nicholas Canny, *Kingdom and Colony: Ireland in the Atlantic World, 1560–1800* (Baltimore: The Johns Hopkins University Press, 1988), 77.

7. In terms of the percentage of colonists who died, the 1641 rebellion obviously cannot compare with the destruction of the 1622 attack on the English population in Virginia, which killed one-third of the colonists. But the 1641 rebellion lasted for years, with guerrilla forces ("Tories") waging war against English armies well into the 1650s.

8. Nicholas Canny, *Making Ireland British, 1580–1650* (Oxford: Oxford University Press, 2001), 535, 550.

9. Estimates for the number of English dead range from 8,000 to 300,000 (which would far exceed the total number of English in Ireland at the time).

10. Karl S. Bottigheimer, *English Money and Irish Land: The 'Adventurers' in the Cromwellian Settlement of Ireland* (Oxford: Clarendon, 1971), 112–113.

11. Oliver Cromwell, *Letters from Ireland, Relating the several great successes* (London, 1649), 8–9.

12. Oliver Cromwell, *A Letter from the Lord Lieutenant of Ireland... Together with a relation of the Taking in of Wexford* (London, 1649), 6–7.

13. Ibid., 8. For other letters of this genre, see Oliver Cromwell, *A Letter from the Lord Lieutenant of Ireland... Relating the good Successes God hath lately given to the Parliaments Forces there* (London, 1649); and Oliver Cromwell, *A Letter from the Lord Lieutenant of Ireland, Concerning the Surrender of the Town of Ross* (London, 1649). Cromwell's letter about taking Enistery and other towns was similarly ordered to be sent to all London ministers to read publicly on the next Sunday in the city while worshippers gave thanks for God's mercy in the Irish victories. Oliver Cromwell, *A Letter from the Right Honorable The Lord Lieutenant of Ireland... Concerning the Taking in and Surrendring of Enistery* (London, 1649), A1verso.

14. *Propositions Approved of and Granted by the Deputy-General of Ireland to Colonel Richard Laurence, for the Raising in England and Transporting into Ireland... 25 February 1650/51* (London, 1650 [1651]), 1300–1303.

15. Letter to Parliament, 5 May 1652, MS Firth c. 5, fol. 16recto, Firth Papers, Bodleian.

16. MS Firth c. 5, fols. 17recto, 18recto, 19verso, Firth Papers, Bodleian.

17. Edmund Calamy, *The Nonconformist's Memorial; being an account of the Lives, Sufferings, and Printed Works of the Two Thousand Ministers Ejected from the Church of England*, ed. Samuel Palmer, three volumes (London, 1802), vol. 3, 196.

18. Richard Lawrence, *The Interest of England in the Irish Transplantation* (London, 1655), 19.

19. David Leslie to Lords and Commissioners of the High Court of Parliament or Committee of Estates, 27 March 1647, Thomas Birch, *A Collection of the State Papers of John Thurloe*, seven volumes (London, 1742), vol. 1, 89. One captain in command at Leismoir in Scotland, for example, surrendered, securing his own life but giving up 27 Irish soldiers for execution.

20. Canny, *Making Ireland British*, 555, 561.

21. Letter from certain ministers, 31 December 1650, *Collections of the Massachusetts Historical Society*, fourth series, vol. 2, 115.

22. Proclamation, 18 October 1661, J. H. Lefroy, *Memorials of the Discovery and Early Settlement of the Bermudas or Somers Islands 1511–1687* (London, 1879), vol. 2, 159–160.

23. Richard Bagwell, *Ireland Under the Stuarts and During the Interregnum*, three volumes (London: Longmans, Green, and Co., 1916), vol. 2, 317–319.

24. In October of 1653, anyone who had taken part in the rebellion in its first year (when most of the attacks on Protestants were concentrated), or who had been rebels, or who had any claims to land had to move west of the Shannon River. Bagwell, *Ireland Under the Stuarts*, vol. 2, 324.

25. Bagwell, *Ireland Under the Stuarts*, vol. 2, 323–324.

26. Canny, *Making Ireland British*, 230.

27. Aidan Clarke, *Prelude to Restoration in Ireland: The End of the Commonwealth, 1659–1660* (Cambridge: Cambridge University Press, 1999), 12–13.

28. Fleetwood to Thurloe, May 23, 1655, *Thurloe Papers*, vol. 3, 468. Fleetwood was appointed Lord Deputy in August of 1654. His opposition to the new government in England (the creation of Oliver Cromwell as Lord Protector) led to his replacement by Henry Cromwell in November of 1657.

29. Vincent Gookin, *The Great Case of Transplantation in Ireland Discussed* (London, 1655), 18–21.

30. The disruptions of war led to famine, and there are references to plague as early as 1651.

31. Gookin, *Great Case*, 16–17, 19, 21.

32. Richard Lawrence responded to Gookin in *The Interest of England in the Irish Transplantation State* (London, 1655). Gookin then wrote a second pamphlet, *The Author and Case of Transplanting, Vindicated Against the Unjust Aspersions of Colonel Richard Lawrence* (London, 1655).

33. Gookin, *Author and Case*, 51.

34. Ibid., 52.

35. The Nine Years' War from 1594 to 1603 witnessed similar attacks on New English colonists in the Munster colony. The English army was merciless in its reprisals on the Irish in Munster. Although the two populations were segregated after the war, the English remained dependent on Irish labor and thus a degree of cohabitation was essential. Quinn, *Elizabethans and the Irish*, 116–119.

36. Fleetwood to Thurloe, May 23, 1655, *Thurloe Papers*, vol. 3, 468.

37. Cromwell to Thurloe, 30 January 1655/6, *Thurloe Papers*, vol. 4, 483.

38. Carla Gardina Pestana, *The English Atlantic in an Age of Revolution, 1640–1661* (Cambridge, Mass.: Harvard University Press, 2004), 186–187.

39. Jane H. Ohlmeyer, "Early Modern Ireland and English Imperialism," in Kevin Kenny, ed., *Ireland and the British Empire* (Oxford: Oxford University Press, 2004), 55

40. Henry Cromwell to Thurloe, 18 September 1655, in *Thurloe Papers*, vol. 4, 40.

41. Canny, *Making Ireland British*, 455–456. Despite the wars and epidemics of the period, the Irish population may in fact have doubled over the course of the seventeenth century, from 1.4 million in 1600 to 2.8 million in 1712. See L. M. Cullen, "Population Growth and Diet, 1600–1850," J. M. Goldstrom and L. A. Clarkson, eds., *Irish Population, Economy, and Society: Essays in Honour of the Late K. H. Connell* (Oxford: Clarendon Press, 1981), 90.

42. Extracts from a copy of a letter from J. Leveret to Governor Endicot, London, 20 December 1656; copy of the Court's letter to Cromwell, Boston, 24 October 1656, both reproduced in Thomas Hutchinson, *The History of the Colony and Province of Massachusetts Bay*, ed. Lawrence Shaw Mayo (Cambridge, Mass.: Harvard University Press, 1936), vol. 1, 163–164; Hugh Peters to John Winthrop, Jr., 3 March 1654/5, Winthrop Papers, reel 5, Massachusetts Historical Society, Boston.

43. On recruitment from Nevis, see the correspondence between the Nevis governor Luke Stokes and John Thurloe in *Thurloe Papers*, vol. 5, 66–67, 77, 769; vol. 6, 110. See also S. A. G. Taylor, *The Western Design: An Account of Cromwell's Expedition to the Caribbean* (Kingston: The Institute of Jamaica and The Jamaica Historical Society, 1965), chapter 1.

44. Bagwell, *Ireland under the Stuarts,* vol. 2, 337.

45. Henry Cromwell to Secretary Thurloe, 29 August 1655, *Thurloe Papers*, vol. 3, 744. Note the contrast with Richard Hakluyt's earlier advocacy of using soldiers for colonies. Richard Hakluyt, "Discourse of Western Planting," in Peter C. Mancall, ed., *Envisioning America: English Plans for the Colonization of North America, 1580–1640* (Boston: Bedford Books, 1995), 53.

46. T. C. Barnard, *Cromwellian Ireland: English Government and Reform in Ireland 1649–1660* (New York: Oxford University Press, 1975, 2000), 9.

47. Barnard, *Cromwellian Ireland,* 56–57, quotation from 14.

48. Ibid., 56–58.

49. Fleetwood to Thurloe, from Athlone, 18 June 1655, *Thurloe Papers*, vol. 3, 558–559.

50. Fleetwood to Thurloe, June 20, 1655, *Thurloe Papers*, vol. 3, 566.

51. Brewster to Thurloe, Dublin, 22 October 1656, *Thurloe Papers* vol. 5, 508.

52. Henry Cromwell to Thurloe, 14 November 1655, 30 January 1655/6, *Thurloe Papers*, vol. 4, 198, 483. Henry repeated his January request for the aid of London merchants in a letter to Thurloe, 14 October 1656, *Thurloe Papers*, vol. 5, 494.

53. Council to Thurloe, April 20, 1657, *Thurloe Papers*, vol. 6, 209–210.

54. Barnard, *Cromwellian Ireland*, 44–45.

55. Letter from J. Leveret to Endicot, London, 20 December 1656, Hutchinson, *History*, vol. 1, 163.

56. Pestana, *English Atlantic*, chapter 2.

57. On these recruitment efforts, see Games, *Migration*, 136.

58. David Cressy, *Coming Over: Migration and Communication between England and New England in the Seventeenth Century* (Cambridge: Cambridge University Press, 1987), 192.

59. Quoted in Michael MacCarthy-Morrogh, *The Munster Plantation: English Migration to Southern Ireland, 1583–1641* (Oxford: Oxford University Press, 1986), 203.

60. St. John D. Seymour, *The Puritans in Ireland, 1647–1660* (Oxford: Clarendon Press, 1912), 6.

61. Series of instructions to the four commissioners sent to govern Ireland, October, 1650, in Seymour, *Puritans in Ireland*, 14–15.

62. I can find no record of Patient in James Savage, *A Genealogical Dictionary of the First Settlers of New England*, four volumes (Boston, 1860–1862, repr. 1965), but on his New England background see Seymour, *Puritans in Ireland*, 59.

63. Letter from Certain Ministers and Others of New England to Cromwell, Upon his Application to Persons here to settle in Ireland, *Collections of the Massachusetts Historical Society*, fourth series, vol. 2, 115–118.

64. Games, *Migration*, 46.

65. For Ludlow, see two dated but often informative studies: R. V. Coleman, *Roger Ludlow in Chancery* (Westport, Conn., 1934), and John M. Taylor, *Roger Ludlow, The Colonial Lawmaker* (New York, 1900). "Adam his Indian" is mentioned in "A true relation of a Conspiracy of Maantanemo [August, 1642]," *Collections of the Massachusetts Historical Society*, third series, vol. 3, 161. T. C. Barnard notes Ludlow's singular qualifications for Ireland in *Cromwellian Ireland*, 289, but remarks that his talents were not exploited properly there. See also Darrett Bruce Rutman, "A Militant New World 1607–1640" (Ph. D. Dissertation, University of Virginia, 1959; reprint New York: Arno Press, 1979), 567.

66. Coleman, *Roger Ludlow*, 16.

67. Commission printed in Taylor, *Roger Ludlow*, 148.

68. Edmund Ludlow fell out of favor when he opposed Cromwell becoming Lord Protector. For the meeting at Holyhead see C. H. Firth, ed., *The Memoirs of Edmund Ludlow* (Oxford: Clarendon Press, 1894), vol. 2, 104.

69. Richard S. Dunn, James Savage, and Laetitia Yeandle, eds. *The Journal of John Winthrop, 1630–1649* (Cambridge, Mass.: Harvard University Press, 1996), 477, 481.

70. Robert Pentland Mahaffy, ed., *Calendar of State Papers Relating to Ireland, 1647–1660* (London, 1903), 11, 16.

71. Wheeler, *Cromwell in Ireland*, 100.

72. Bagwell, *Ireland Under the Stuarts*, vol. 2, 215.

73. Patrick Francis Moran, *Historical Sketch of the Persecutions Suffered by the Catholics of Ireland Under the Rule of Cromwell and the Puritans* (Dublin, 1917), 110.

74. Wheeler, *Cromwell in Ireland*, 98.

75. Letters from Irish Commisioners to the Speaker, Dublin, 18 September 1651 and 8 October 1651, Firth, ed., *Memoirs*, vol. 1, appendix 4, 490–491, 493.

76. Bagwell, *Ireland under the Stuarts*, vol. 2, 280–281.

77. Stephen Saunders Webb, *The Governors-General: The English Army and the Definition of Empire, 1569–1681* (Chapel Hill: University of North Carolina Press, 1979), 40–41.

78. Letter from Cooke to Commissioners of Ireland, March 17, 1652, printed in Firth, ed., *Memoirs*, vol. 1, 303. The practice of burning Irish fields and property was commonplace. Food was sufficiently abundant to keep the English supplied, but the devastation of the English campaign caused great hardship for the surviving Irish.

79. Letter to the Speaker of Parliament, Dublin, 13 April 1652, MS Firth c. 5, fol. 15recto, Bodleian. Cooke left behind two children from an earlier marriage, a pregnant wife, and "a very small Estate" besides his salary in arrears. His brother Joseph in New England was named administrator of the estate there, along with Henry Dunster (Savage, vol. 1, 446).

80. See various petitions in the *Calendar of State Papers Relating to Ireland, 1647–1660*, 616–618, 835.

81. Henry Cromwell to Thurloe, 14 November 1655, *Thurloe Papers*, vol. 4, 198. John's widow Joan stayed in Europe, but John's son Simon claimed his father's property in

Ipswich for himself. *The Probate Records of Essex County, Massachusetts* (Salem: The Essex Institute, 1916), vol. 1, 277–278.

82. Stephen Paschall Sharples, ed. *Records of the Church of Christ at Cambridge in New England, 1632–1830* (Boston: E. Putnam, 1906), 5.

83. Savage, vol. 1, 20.

84. Ninety-eight men graduated in the College's first seventeen classes: thirty-three went to Europe, primarily England but also Ireland and the Netherlands (although some later returned to America), fifty-four stayed in North America, the fates of five are unknown (these men likely returned to England), three recent graduates were lost at sea bound for England in 1657, and three went to the island colonies. These statistics are based on an analysis of John Langdon Sibley, *Biographical Sketches of Graduates of Harvard University* (Cambridge, Mass: Charles William Sever, 1873), vol. 1. The impulse to return was particularly strong in the College's first ten graduating classes: of fifty-five graduates, twenty-four returned to England.

85. New Englanders were not peculiarly recalcitrant in this regard: it was difficult to recruit ministers for Ireland from England as well (Seymour, *Puritans in Ireland*, 61).

86. Copy of the Court's letter to Oliver Cromwell, 1651, in Hutchinson, *History*, vol. 1, appendix, 431–432.

87. Letter to Mr. Noxond in England, copied to "Mr Comfort Starr lately come out of New England," Dublin, 20 August 1653, MS Firth c. 5, fols. 118verso–119recto, Firth Papers, Bodleian. This minister might be Mr. George Moxon, who went to New England and served as pastor at Springfield. He returned to England in 1653 and preached at Astbury, Cheshire. Calamy, vol. 1, 325.

88. Comfort Starr was born in Ashford, Kent, the son of a physician. He returned to England some time after he graduated from Harvard in 1650. He preached at Carlisle until he was ejected in 1662 and then at Lewes, Sussex. Calamy, vol. 1, 378; Savage, vol. 4, 170; Sibley, vol. 1, 162.

89. Seymour, *Puritans in Ireland*, 103.

90. Hutchinson, *History*, vol. 1, 163. John Taylor, in *Roger Ludlow*, wrote that Cromwell also targeted William Hooke of New Haven and Samuel Desborough and William Leete of Guilford. Taylor, 150.

91. I'm not sure who William Courbett is—perhaps this is Thomas Cobbett.

92. Savage, vol. 2, 82. Dunster's flirtation with antipedobaptism would seem to have disqualified him, not least since Henry Cromwell worried about the Anabaptists in Ireland, but it did not.

93. Seymour, *Puritans in Ireland*, 224.

94. Mr. Ed. Wale to Dr. Harrison, Waterford, 14 December 1655, *Thurloe Papers*, vol. 4, 314.

95. Henry Cromwell to Thurloe, 17 December 1656, *Thurloe Papers*, vol. 5, 710.

96. Seymour, *Puritans in Ireland*, 52, 60.

97. Savage, vol. 1, 71.

98. Mather was appointed in August of 1655 to a committee to examine the ministers of Cork. He refused to displace episcopal ministers in Munster. Seymour, *Puritans in Ireland*, 91. One later biographer attributed to him the statement that he had been called "to preach the Gospel, and not to hinder others from doing it." Quoted in Robert H. Murray, *Dublin University and the New World* (London: The Society for the Promotion of Christian Knowledge, 1921), 20.

99. On the Irish witch trial, see Seymour, *Puritans in Ireland*, 140. In the 1650s, there were vigorous witch hunts in England, and witch trials on a smaller scale in Bermuda and in the New England colonies of Massachusetts and Connecticut. Pestana similarly looks at the punishment of Quakers and the presence of witchcraft accusations in her exploration of religious reformation in the English Atlantic. See Pestana, *English Atlantic*, 130–156.

100. Jane H. Ohlmeyer, introduction, in Ohlmeyer, ed., *Ireland from Independence to Occupation, 1641–1660* (Cambridge: Cambridge University Press, 1995), 22.

101. Éamonn an Dúna, "Mo lá leóin go deó go n-éagad," quoted and translated in Canny, *Making Ireland British*, 574.

102. "An Síogaí Rómánach," quoted and translated in Canny, *Making Ireland British*, 575.

103. Henry Cromwell to Thurloe, 28 April 1658, *Thurloe Papers*, vol. 7, 101.

104. Henry Cromwell to Lord Falconbridge, 28 April 1658, *Thurloe Papers*, vol. 7, 101. Italics added.

105. Michael J. Braddick, "The English Government, War, Trade, and Settlement, 1625–1688," in Nicholas Canny, ed., *The Origins of Empire* (Oxford: Oxford University Press, 1998), 287–289.

CONCLUSION

1. David Armitage, *The Ideological Origins of the British Empire* (Cambridge: Cambridge University Press, 2000), 29.

2. Michael J. Braddick, *State Formation in Early Modern England c. 1550–1700* (Cambridge: Cambridge University Press, 2000), 411–413; Elizabeth Mancke, "Empire and State," in David Armitage and Michael J. Braddick, eds., *The British Atlantic World, 1500–1800* (New York: Palgrave MacMillan, 2002), 182.

3. Fynes Moryson, *An Itinerary Written by Fynes Moryson gent. First in the Latine Tongue, and then translated by him into the English* (London, 1617), Part 3, 29.

4. Letter to the Duke of York from T. Bockman in Tangier, 10 November 1662, Sloane 2448, fols. 46–47, BL. These fears characterized the entirety of English occupation: see for example letters to Sir Richard Bulstrode in 1679 and 1680, Add. 47,899, fols. 268–269, 273–274, 334, BL. On the ban of "Moors" from the city, see 29 January 1662, anonymous journal, V.a.184, Folger.

5. See, for example, the journal of John Luke, who reported regularly on viewing the pier, and on the status of repairs during his time in Tangier between 1670 and 1673. Add. 36,528, BL.

6. The following paragraphs are drawn from Mr. James Wilson to (?), 5 October 1661, Add. 4191, fols. 11–14, BL. Routh cites another version of this proposal in Harl. 1595, BL, in which the author is anonymous. E. M. G. Routh, *Tangier, England's Lost Atlantic Outpost, 1661–1684* (London: J. Murray, 1912), 21. For another look at the English in the Mediterranean in this period, see the first part of Linda Colley, *Captives* (New York: Pantheon, 2002).

7. Wilson anticipated the recruitment schemes of the Jersey and Pennsylvania plantations in North America, which similarly relied on continental pietists to settle land.

8. Routh, *Tangier*, 272.

9. Ibid., 272–273.

10. Petition to Henry Norwood, n.d. but fall/winter 1668 or 1669, Sloane 3510, fols. 44–45, BL.

11. Sloane 3511, miscellaneous items relating to Tangier, order dated 19 October 1672, fol. 168, BL.

12. February 16, 1670, Journal of John Luke, Add. 36,528, fol. 29recto, BL.

13. On diplomatic volatility, see for example V.a.184, in which the narrator describes the need to lie to the governor of Gibraltar about the English reasons for being there: the English had to tell the governor they were chasing after Turks. They could not reveal that they had come from Tangier, because "the spaniards are very much vexed at the delivery of Tanger to the English."

14. John Smith, Account of a voyage to Smyrna, 1664–1665, Sloane 1700, fols. 13recto–17; Journal of Charles Wilde, Sloane 2439, fol. 5recto, BL.

15. Sixty-one were redeemed in September, and 106 in October. Miscellaneous papers relating to Tangier, Sloane 3511, fols. 154–167, BL.

INDEX

Cobbett, Thomas, 274
Cocks, Richard, 88, 96–97, 99, 105–6,
    108, 136
  cultural connections by, 114–15
  Dittis and, 111
colonies. *See also* specific colonies
  adaptability necessary to, 198
  Catholicism and, 250
  Cromwell, H., on, 284–86
  disease and, 200–202
  England committing to, 286
  evangelism and, 233–34
  export agriculture and, 142, 147
  fortification of, 152
  as geopolitical tool, 286–87
  governors of, 9
  internal conflicts in, 170
  leadership of, 147–48, 149
  Madagascar and, 190–91, 198
  migration to, 256–57, 285
  ministers of, 221–22, 233
  ministers promoting, 223
  plantation, 12, 124, 142, 147, 199, 292
  puritanism and, 230, 233
  regulation of, 292
  religion at, 238, 250–52
  religious disputes exported to, 222
  relocation to, 188
  starting populations of, 199
  trade factories v., 185
  travel and, 21
  utopian themes and, 191–92
commercial cultures, 84
Commonwealth, 12, 228
communion, 239, 248
Company of Royal Adventurers Trading
    to Africa. *See* Royal African
    Company
confession, traditions for, 220
confirmation, 241
Congregationalists, 229, 280
Connecticut, 165
Consular Service, 169
consuls, 147–48
  affairs managed by, 165–66
  salaries of, 169
  wives and, 172–73
conversion, 64–65, 68
  captivity and, 72–73

  consequences of, 73–74
  Covel accused of, 236–37
  inducements to, 73
  Inquisition and, 74
  Islam and, 68, 73, 243
  ministers and, 243
Cooke, George, 275, 276t, 277–79
Copland, Patrick, 3, 7, 10–11, 238, 246
  Atlantic ventures of, 4, 6
  Bermuda and, 4, 252
  changing view of, 252
  East India Company and, 3, 8, 14, 226,
    239–40, 252
  evangelism by, 4, 6, 233–34
  Japan and, 235
  Jesuits and, 224
  Pacific ventures of, 3
  school fundraising by, 219
  Somers Island Company and, 8
Coredalio, Theodoro, 163
de Coronado, Franscisco, 20
Correr, Anzolo, 186
Coryate, Thomas, 41, 42, 246
cosmopolitanism, 14
  adaptability and, 286
  clergy and, 252
  Covel defense of, 237
  duty constraining, 174
  emergence of, 9, 10, 290
  trade and, 9, 81
  xenophobia v., 290
Cotton, John, 275, 281
Council of Ireland, 271
Council of Trade, 292
Courten Association, 194, 199, 216
  Dutch model used by, 185
  East India Company and, 206–7
  organization of, 182
Courten, William, 181, 192
  Howard (Arundel) and, 186
  trade association organized by, 182
Covel, John, 46, 169–70, 226, 230, 235, 236,
    237, 238, 240, 252
Covenant of 1643, 228
Cromwell, Henry, 267, 268, 270, 271, 279,
    280, 282, 283, 296
  on colonial environments, 284–86
  Irish colonization critiqued by, 284–86
Cromwell, Oliver, 152, 252, 267